Managing
in the
Global Economy

Managing in the Global Economy

Richard M. Steers and Luciara Nardon

Routledge
Taylor & Francis Group

LONDON AND NEW YORK

First published 2006 by M.E. Sharpe

Published 2015 by Routledge
2 Park Square, Milton Park, Abingdon, Oxon OX14 4RN
711 Third Avenue, New York, NY 10017, USA

Routledge is an imprint of the Taylor & Francis Group, an informa business

Library of Congress Cataloging-in-Publication Data

Steers, Richard M.
  Managing in the global economy / by Richard M. Steers and Luciara Nardon.
    p. cm.
  Includes bibliographical references and index.
  ISBN 0-7656-1551-7 (pbk. : alk. paper)
  1. International business enterprises—Management. 2. International
trade—Cross-cultural studies. 3. Strategic planning. 4. International
economic relations. I. Nardon, Luciara, 1972- II. Title.
  HD62.4.S736 2006
  658'.049—dc22   2005007422

ISBN 13: 9780765615510 (pbk)

Brief Table of Contents

Detailed Table of Contents

Part II. Culture, Organization, and Strategy

Part III. Managing Global Operations

Preface

As with any academic pursuit, the study of international management is best thought of as a journey. We begin at various points along the road based on our expertise and prior experience, and then progress at our own pace toward our final destination. Along the way, friends and colleagues—and sometimes complete strangers—offer advice and point out interesting things to look for. We sometimes find ourselves in unfamiliar territory, and when we get lost we ask for help. But throughout the journey, experienced travelers carry a road map that provides useful information and keeps them on track toward their ultimate goal. Our hope and intent here is to provide such a map—a guidebook that that can be used by informed travelers in their international adventures.

Our interest in writing this book emerged from our classroom experience. In teaching courses on international management, our aim has always been to integrate an understanding of global economics and geopolitical challenges with a thorough understanding of how cultural differences influence management processes across borders. Global management is not just about understanding cultural differences; it also requires solid knowledge of economic forces and legal-political forces that can constrain managerial action, regardless of culture. In our view, effective global managers must understand all three of these forces—economic, legal-political, and cultural—as they relate to one another and to the practice of management.

In addition, we have always emphasized in our courses that effective managers must understand how their partners or adversaries on the other side of the table, or the other side of the world, behave. That is, when an American or Canadian manager negotiates with a Japanese or Chinese manager, it is important for each to understand how the other approaches the bargaining process. These approaches can be very different. Likewise, when a German or Italian manager is assigned to work with a team from Malaysia or Brazil, it is important that each party understands how the other approaches work-group processes. Again, these approaches can be very different. As a result, our approach to teaching, and our approach to writing this book, has been to develop parallel learning tracks, one focusing on international management issues and one focusing on cultural differences as they relate to these management issues. Both tracks will become evident as the reader progresses through the book.

Simply put, this book examines the challenges and prospects facing contemporary managers in the new global economy. We think of it as a primer on international management, with particular emphasis on developing global managers who are skilled in economics, strategy, and general management. Considerable attention is devoted throughout the book to developing an in-depth understanding of the role of cultural differences in managerial effectiveness. The book is divided into three parts: the emerging global economy; culture, organization, and strategy; and managing global operations. Management topics include organizing for international business, global business strategy, building strategic alliances, international negotiations, global staffing, managing a competitive workforce, total quality management (TQM) and employee involvement, and managing multicultural teams. We present a new model of culture and management that ties these topics together. Throughout, the book integrates current conceptual materials on global management with in-depth country analyses and real-world business examples, as well as ample opportunities to apply what has been learned. Our aim in writing this book has been to explore these interrelated topics in ways that readers can both understand and use in their future careers.

As with all writing projects, there are many people who helped make this book a reality, and we would like to acknowledge their assistance and support here. First and foremost, we owe a significant debt of gratitude to our students, in both the United States and the Netherlands, who taught us so much about managing in the global economy. It is often assumed that classroom education runs largely in one direction, from instructors to students. It is often forgotten that significant learning can also flow in the opposite direction—from students to instructors—if the quality and enthusiasm of the students is high. Indeed, we believe this reciprocal process of discovery is the defining characteristic of a learning community, and in this regard we have been very fortunate.

We also appreciate the people at M.E. Sharpe, especially Harry Briggs, Elizabeth Granda, and Angela Piliouras, both for their belief in this project and for their unceasing support and encouragement throughout the publication process. In an era of homogenized books and formulaic publishers, the people at M.E. Sharpe genuinely care about the creative process and publishing innovative books that can make a difference in the intellectual and professional lives of readers. Their approach to publishing has made our task both more enjoyable and more meaningful.

In addition, we note that publications do not emerge in a vacuum. They require an intellectual environment that is both challenging and supportive. They require colleagues who are both constructive in their criticism and sincere in their praise. We believe we have found such an environment in the Lundquist College of Business at the University of Oregon. In particular, we wish to thank our colleagues Alan Meyer, Peter Mills, Rick Mowday, Anne Parmigiani, Mike Russo, and Jim Terborg for their long-standing friendship and support. We also wish to acknowledge the help of our colleagues from other schools who took the time to review various parts of the manuscript and offer comments. These include Nancy Adler, McGill University (Canada), J. Stewart Black, University of Michigan (United States), Chris Earley, London Business School (United Kingdom) and National University of Singapore (Singapore), Rosalie Tung, Simon Fraser (Canada), and Oded Shenkar, The Ohio State University (United States).Without colleagues like these, the intellectual environment in management research and education would be poorer indeed.

Finally, we wish to offer a special thanks to our families—especially our spouses, Sheila Steers and Santiago Garcia Rodriguez—for their patience, support, and encouragement throughout the duration of this project. Families are important, and without the love and support of those around us this project would have been much longer and much less enjoyable. For this we are deeply and willingly indebted.

We close with a quote from Mahatma Gandhi that we believe captures the essence both of this book and of the increasingly important role of global managers: "We must be the change we wish to see in others." What this means to us is that global managers in the future must lead, not follow. They must develop sufficient management and cultural skills to show others how to help build more productive and more sustainable companies and countries. And, above all, they must develop and internalize a worldview that allows them to proceed from a position of knowledge, strength, and understanding to succeed in managing across borders.

Richard M. Steers
Luciara Nardon

PART I

THE EMERGING GLOBAL ECONOMY

1 Managing in the Global Economy: An Introduction

At the present time, there is a greater need for effective international and cross-cultural communication, collaboration, and cooperation, not only for the effective practice of management but also for the betterment of the human condition. Ample evidence shows that the cultures of the world are getting more and more interconnected and that the business world is becoming increasingly global. As economic borders come down, cultural barriers will most likely go up and present new challenges and opportunities for business. When cultures come in contact, they may converge in some aspects, but their idiosyncrasies will likely amplify.

—Robert House, GLOBE Research Project[1]

No one ever said being a manager was easy, but it seems to get more difficult with each passing year. As competitive pressures increase across most industries and services, so, too, do the pressures on managers to deliver results. Succeeding against the odds often catapults a manager into the higher echelons of the organization, with a concomitant increase in personal rewards. But failure to deliver often slows one's career advancement, if it doesn't stop it altogether. The stakes are very high for both managers and their companies.

Popular slogans may help explain this turn of events. Consider Intel's "faster-better-cheaper" or Ted Turner's "lead, follow, or get out of the way."[2] Anyway we look at it, competitive pressures are growing. Why? There are many reasons, but a principal cause lies in the world's unrelenting drive to build—and capitalize on—a more integrated and more productive global economy that leads to lower consumer prices and higher corporate profits. When consumers go shopping in any country, most want to buy products or services of the highest possible quality for the lowest possible price. Few people enter stores and ask to pay more so that workers who made the product or provided the service can receive a higher income. Likewise, few people offer to pay more for a product so local firms can remain in business instead of going bankrupt. In the final analysis, from a consumer's standpoint it is frequently all about money. The more companies satisfy consumer demands, the more likely they are to survive and prosper. Like it or not, this is the reality facing most contemporary organizations.

In this endeavor, the above observation by Robert House is germane. As he correctly notes, succeeding in today's demanding global economy requires a greater degree of international and cross-cultural communication, collaboration, and cooperation than ever before. As the various cultures of the world become more interconnected, economically and politically, companies must work harder to understand and interact in cross-cultural ways. In short, companies must increasingly think in *global* terms, as national and even regional companies are increasingly becoming a thing of the past. During the days of the American frontier in the mid- and late 1800s, there was a popular saying: Go west, young man. Today, the advice is very different: Go global. The future has shifted unequivocally, as have the opportunities, and smart companies and their managers respond accordingly.

The responsibility of managers in all of this is to make it happen—to maximize consumer benefit and the company's bottom line. At the same time, society asks—and often demands—that managers pay fair wages, provide safe and equitable working conditions for their employees, follow all pertinent laws and regulations in the countries where they do business, protect the environment, act in socially responsible ways, and abide by conventional ethical norms and professional standards. It is an understatement to point out that accomplishing these often conflicting goals is no easy task. In view of this, the question for today's managers is how they can best prepare themselves for this brave new world of international business.

IMPORTANCE OF GLOBAL BUSINESS

The world facing global managers today is complex, challenging, and constantly changing. This can be illustrated in several ways. For starters, consider the sheer size and power of the global economy. While the United States has a population approaching 300 million people and a gross domestic product (GDP) of over $10 trillion, these numbers almost pale in comparison to comparable statistics on a global scale (see Chapter 3). In point of fact, no one country controls the global economy, although a small consortium of countries comes close. In many industries today, chief competitors come from around the world, and each competitor has its own unique competitive strengths. For example, the global automobile industry today includes major competitors from Japan, Germany, South Korea, France, the United Kingdom, Sweden, and the United States. Soon, other major competitors, such as China and perhaps India, will enter this crowded global market. The situation is similar in other key industries, including home electronics, information technology (IT) services, telecommunications, medical equipment, software development, pharmaceuticals, and defense technologies. In each industry, the questions are the same: Who will succeed and who will fail? And what will determine success?

Not only do companies face an increasing number of highly skilled global competitors, but many of these competitors approach business in very different ways.

Exhibit 1.1

World's Largest Economies (GDP in $ billions)

Country	GDP	Country	GDP
1. United States	10,065	11. Brazil	502
2. Japan	4,141	12. India	477
3. Germany	1,846	13. South Korea	422
4. United Kingdom	1,424	14. Netherlands	380
5. France	1,309	15. Australia	368
6. China	1,159	16. Russia	310
7. Italy	1,088	17. Taiwan	282
8. Canada	694	18. Argentina	268
9. Mexico	617	19. Switzerland	247
10. Spain	581	20. Belgium	229

Source: Based on *The Economist Pocket World in Figures* (London: Profile Books, 2004), p. 24.

These differences can be seen in widely varying national laws, trade policies, business regulations, labor policies, and so forth. They can also be seen in the fundamental differences in the ways companies approach both partners and competitors. Sometimes countries have clearly formulated labor laws that are rigorously enforced and universally applied. Others have equally clear labor laws that are weakly enforced and only intermittently applied. Knowing the difference is important. Sometimes business is based on long-standing and seemingly inefficient personal friendships, instead of the "best practices" we read about in textbooks. Sometimes "benchmarking" means making products using traditional methods, instead of building products against the best competition available. And sometimes business partners have different ideas about what constitutes a legitimate sales commission. The challenge for companies and their managers is first to understand these differences—to clearly understand the local business landscape—and then to formulate appropriate responses that are consistent with the firm's strategies, business practices, and ethical standards.

In addition, while international trade has increased more than 600 percent in the past thirty years, some countries have benefited significantly more than others. Indeed, only seven countries account for nearly 60 percent of today's global exports: Japan, Canada, Germany, France, Italy, the United Kingdom, and the United States.[3] In other words, some countries are doing much better in the export game than others, and this success has direct consequences for national economic development and prosperity (see Exhibit 1.1). Exports stimulate the economies of producer nations and support their manufacturing and services base. At the same time, failure to export (or to be allowed to export) to foreign countries can lead to closed factories, unemployment, and economic stagnation. It is for reasons such as these that organizations such as the World Trade Organization (see Chapter 3) were established to break down tariff barriers and encourage more open trade around the world. This does not guarantee success for less developed countries, but it is at least meant to start leveling the playing field.

FACTORS INFLUENCING GLOBAL BUSINESS: AN ORGANIZING FRAMEWORK

Understanding the global business environment is a difficult challenge. A myriad of complex and often contradictory factors help determine who wins, who loses, and how the game is played. Moreover, many of these factors change—often abruptly and in unpredictable ways—over time. Global managers must continually be alert to possible changes in the environment, as well as challenges, and be prepared to take decisive action when appropriate. To understand this complex global business environment, we suggest dividing it conceptually into four parts, as follows (see Exhibit 1.2):

• *Economic environment.* The *economic environment* of global business consists of issues of supply and demand, the impact of global economics and foreign investment decisions made by companies, and the national trade policies and economic development strategies of various governments as they attempt to support their local businesses. An understanding of the emerging forces both for and against globalization is also helpful. Key to understanding the economic environment of global business is an awareness of the various theories of international trade and competitive advantage as they affect both national and corporate success.

• *Legal-political environment.* The *legal-political environment* of global business relates to how political or governmental actions affect international business, as well as how companies and managers make ethical decisions governing business practices. Central to this discussion is the issue of political risk, a key challenge to firms trying to succeed in the global marketplace. Also central is the legal environment of global business, consisting of both national laws and regulations and international laws and agreements as they relate to doing business globally. As we will see, some laws are aimed at facilitating international business transactions, while others are not.

• *Cultural environment.* As House notes above, as economic barriers to trade decrease, cultural barriers may increase and present new challenges and opportunities for global firms. As various cultures begin interacting more frequently, they may converge in some aspects, but their idiosyncrasies may become accentuated. This represents a significant managerial challenge. The *cultural environment* of global business focuses on how cultural differences across nations and regions can affect the ways in which national and international business is transacted. For example, what is it about a particular culture that either facilitates or inhibits entrepreneurship, trade, and success in global markets? How does culture influence the ways in which companies are organized, approach strategic decisions, and manage their workforce?

• *Global business environment.* Finally, as shown in Exhibit 1.2, the intersection of these three forces—economic, legal-political, and cultural—forms the arena in which companies compete—the *global business environment.* It represents the "eye of the hurricane" in international business. This is where global managers succeed or fail, and an understanding of this environment is crucial to success. It also represents the principal focus of this book. It creates an organizing framework for understanding how global business works and what managers can do to make it work better.

Exhibit 1.2 **Environment of Global Business**

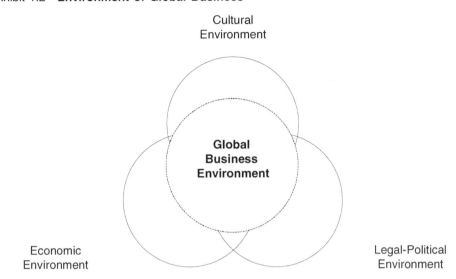

THE GLOBAL MANAGER

Over the years, various researchers have tried to capture the essence of good management in succinct theories or models. By far the most popular model comes from Henry Mintzberg.[4] He suggests that managerial work is largely characterized by ten traits: figurehead, leader, liaison, monitor, disseminator, spokesperson, entrepreneur, disturbance handler, resource allocator, and negotiator. These traits, in turn, can be organized into three clusters: interpersonal, informational, and decisional. That is, effective managers must master three key roles if they are to help their organizations meet the challenges of the twenty-first century:

   • *Interpersonal role.* The manager who masters the *interpersonal role* must ask and be able to answer the question, How can we build and lead effective groups and organizations?
   • *Informational role.* How can we collect, organize, and disseminate relevant information in a timely fashion? is the question a manager who has mastered the *informational role* must be able to answer.
   • *Decisional role.* Successful managers must master the *decisional role*; in other words, they must be able to respond to the question, How can we make creative strategic and tactical decisions on behalf of the organization and secure broad-based support for such actions?

   While Mintzberg's model focused on North American managers, it is possible to identify ways in which these various managerial roles apply internationally. It is also possible to show how cultural differences influence each of these roles (see Exhibit 1.3). If culture

Exhibit 1.3

Cultural Influences on Management

Managerial Roles	Differences Across Cultures
Interpersonal Role:	
Figurehead	Figureheads have considerable symbolic value in some cultures; in others, being described as a figurehead is not a compliment.
Leader	Individualistic cultures prefer highly visible take-charge leaders; collectivistic cultures prefer more consultative leaders.
Liaison	Some cultures prefer informal contacts based on long-standing personal relationships; others prefer to use official representatives.
Informational Role:	
Monitor	Culture often influences both the extent of information monitoring and which specific information sources receive greatest attention.
Disseminator	In some cultures, the context surrounding a message is more important than the message itself; in others, the reverse is true.
Spokesperson	Culture often influences who is respected and seen as a legitimate spokesperson for an organization.
Decisional Role:	
Entrepreneur	Some cultures are highly supportive of innovation and change; others prefer the status quo and resist change.
Disturbance handler	Some cultures resolve conflict quietly; others accept and at times encourage a more public approach to conflict resolution.
Resource allocator	Hierarchical cultures support differential resource allocations; egalitarian cultures prefer greater equality or equity in distributions.
Negotiator	Some cultures negotiate all items in a proposed contract simultaneously; others negotiate each item sequentially.

Source: Based on the work of Henry Mintzberg, *The Nature of Managerial Work* (New York: Harper and Row, 1973).

influences effective management, the case for studying global management as opposed to "national" management becomes irrefutable. In other words, in view of current global realities and international challenges facing contemporary organizations, knowledge of how to manage across borders represents a key asset in every successful manager's tool kit. This is true whether the manager is continually flying around the world on business, living overseas as an expatriate manager, or living in his or her home country dealing with international visitors and business partners. The only question is how best to gain this knowledge.

Two key points should be made here. First, the work of Mintzberg and others suggests that most managers share certain common responsibilities, such as figurehead, leader, liaison, monitor, and so forth. Second, we suggest further that culture plays a major role in determining how these various roles are played out in organizations. If these two assertions are correct, contemporary managers face a serious challenge in preparing themselves to become truly *global* managers. Specifically, the managers of tomorrow will need to invest time and energy in understanding the economic, political, legal, and cultural forces that differentiate one region of the world from another. They will also need to hone their intuitive, perceptual, and interpersonal skills so they can first sense and then respond appropriately to the subtleties of the various cultures they encounter.

THE ROAD AHEAD

This book will examine in three distinct parts the challenges facing global managers. Part I examines the nature and characteristics of today's emerging global economy in some detail. We begin with a look at the challenges and prospects associated with globalization. Based on this, we examine the global economy from both an economic and a political, legal, and ethical standpoint. We look at national trade policies as they relate to competitive advantage. And we consider the topic of economic integration and regional trading blocs, with a particular emphasis on the North American Free Trade Agreement (NAFTA) and the European Union. Each chapter throughout the book begins with a specific country application to set the stage for the discussion that follows.

Part II focuses on organizing for global competition. The theme here is culture, organization, and strategy. We begin with an in-depth look at culture and cultural differences as they relate to management and business practices around the world. We examine variations in organizational models for doing business globally, as well as the strategies that often drive organizational choices. We consider the challenges and prospects of building strategic alliances and working with alliance partners. Finally, we look in some depth at the topic of international negotiation.

Part III focuses on managing global operations. We begin here by looking at the basic staffing issues facing global firms. We move from here to consider strategies to develop and manage a global competitive workforce, with a particular emphasis on work motivation and leadership across cultures. Next, total quality management (TQM) is reviewed, including TQM and employee involvement strategies. The unique challenges of managing multicultural teams are then examined.

Throughout Parts II and III of this book, a dual learning platform is used. That is, for each chapter topic, we focus on both the managerial issues involved, as well as how the topic under study applies to one or two specific countries. For example, when we look at international negotiation, we focus largely, although not exclusively, on negotiation practices in Japan and Brazil. When we consider managing multicultural teams, we focus on France and Malaysia. By doing so, we hope to introduce both critical management techniques and critical cultural differences as they relate to these management practices.

Each chapter closes with two Global Manager's Workbook exercises that provide opportunities to apply what has been learned in the chapter. These exercises are original to this book and are based on real-life cases or events, although the names have often been changed to provide for anonymity. In these exercises, we have tried to present a fair and balanced look at the challenges facing global managers, present and future, as well as the kinds of skills they will need to succeed in the new emerging global economy. Finally, we end with a field project aimed at integrating what has been learned throughout the book (see appendix).

KEY TERMS

cultural environment
decisional role
economic environment
global business environment
informational role
interpersonal role
legal-political environment

GLOBAL MANAGER'S WORKBOOK 1.1:
ARE MANAGEMENT STYLES CONVERGING?

Robert House suggests at the beginning of this chapter that when cultures increasingly come in contact with one another, they may converge in some respects but their idiosyncrasies may also become accentuated. In this regard, several researchers have suggested that management styles around the world—especially in the industrialized world—are beginning to converge and that this convergence will likely increase over time as a result of increased globalization pressures. Other researchers suggest, equally strongly, that a convergence of management styles across various national cultures will never occur. Instead, management styles around the world will remain culturally distinct, requiring global managers to adapt to various local conditions if they are succeed. With these conflicting positions in mind, please answer the following questions.

1. Do you believe that management styles around the world will begin to converge in the future as a result of globalization pressures or that cultural differences will override globalization pressures and make such convergence very difficult, if not impossible? Why?
2. If you believe that management styles around the world will in fact converge in the future, describe what this convergence will look like. What will characterize this new management style?
3. If you believe that management styles around the world will not converge over time, what can global managers do to prepare themselves for a career that involves doing business in various countries that are characterized by highly diverse cultures?

GLOBAL MANAGER'S WORKBOOK 1.2:
SPECIAL ASSIGNMENT—ROMANIA

You have just received word that you will leave on Saturday morning for Romania, where you have been asked to serve as interim manager for a local McDonald's fast-food restaurant in Bucharest. McDonald's has been operating in Romania for several years and has a strong clientele. You will be gone for about six months; housing has been arranged for you. If you do a good job, it will look good on your résumé. If you do a poor job, your résumé and future career prospects may suffer. Your problem is this: While you have experience working in the fast-food industry, you know very little about Romania. With this in mind, consider the following questions.

1. As an interim McDonald's manager in Bucharest, what personal skills and abilities that you currently possess can you draw upon to succeed?
2. What skills and abilities will you need to learn quickly to survive?
3. How will you acquire these new skills on the run?
4. Upon your return, you have promised yourself that you will never again work in the fast-food industry. Even so, what do you think you will have learned from your experience in Romania that may help you in your future career?

NOTES

1. Robert House, "Introduction," in *Culture, Leadership, and Organizations: The GLOBE Study of 62 Societies,* by Robert House, Paul Hanges, Mansour Javidan, Peter Dorfman, and Vipin Gupta (Thousand Oaks, CA: Sage, 2004), p. 1.

2. Ken Auletta, *Media Man: Ted Turner's Improbable Empire* (New York: Norton, 2004).

3. "America Flies to War," *Economist,* October 9, 2004, p. 59.

4. Henry Mintzberg, *The Nature of Managerial Work* (New York: Harper and Row, 1973); Henry Mintzberg, *Structure in Fives: Designing Effective Organizations* (Englewood Cliffs, NJ: Prentice Hall, 1993).

2 | Challenges and Prospects of Globalization

OUTSOURCING TO INDIA

It was once said that the sun never set on the British Empire. No longer. Today the sun does set on the British Empire, but not on a host of global giants such as Microsoft, Citigroup, Unilever, Procter & Gamble, Volkswagen, Toyota, and Sony. What do these companies have in common? They all outsource to India. In fact, everyone seems to be outsourcing to India these days. Almost overnight, this country of 1 billion people has emerged from economic obscurity to become a major international business powerhouse, particularly in information technology (IT) services and back-office operations.[1] Many economists consider India to be a poster child for successful economic development and a role model for other aspiring nations. Consider the following examples:

- India is now the location of choice for developing new software applications and code-writing work in finance, digital appliances, and industrial plants. U.S. companies with major operations in India include Microsoft, General Electric, and American Express.
- Indian companies including Wipro, InfoSys, and Tata now manage countless IT networks and reengineering business processes for European and American companies.
- Thousands of young and well-educated Indians now work in customer service operations, processing insurance claims, loans, bookings, and credit card bills for customers in various Western countries.
- Intel and Texas Instruments are among many American and European Union high-tech firms that employ highly skilled Indian engineers to develop the next generation of microprocessors and multimedia chips.
- Many investment banks, brokerage houses, and accounting firms from the United States have opened offices in India to conduct and manage their financial research.

- Indian firms conduct critical research for such technology-driven companies as GE Medical, General Motors, Cummins Engine, and Ford Motor Company. More engineering hubs are planned.
- European and American firms have hired thousands of math experts from India to devise models for risk analysis, consumer behavior, and industrial processes.
- As research and development (R & D) costs in the pharmaceutical industry escalate, biotech and clinical testing companies are increasingly moving to India to develop and test competitive products for their markets back home.
- India excels in manufacturing, not just services. For example, the giant Tata Group manufactures steel, cars, and trucks, operates software services and telecom companies, provides electricity to Bombay, and runs a chain of luxury hotels.

However you look at it, India has achieved remarkable success in a short period of time. A number of very successful and often very wealthy entrepreneurs have emerged, while legions of young, well-educated, English-speaking professionals—men and women—have secured well-paying jobs by Indian standards in new companies from Bangalore to Bombay to Delhi. Recent business magazines have touted India's success with lead stories entitled "India's Shining Hopes," "The Rise of India," and "Innovative India." And recent economic data back up such claims.[2]

But India's gain in the global economy may be someone else's loss. Again, consider outsourcing. Outsourcing has been with us for a long time; it was historically called offshore production. What has changed in recent years is that while many people have long accepted that blue-collar production jobs will increasingly migrate to countries with lower labor costs (such as China, Mexico, and Vietnam), few expected this same trend would affect white-collar jobs. Fewer still thought it would affect their own particular jobs. Consider that the average annual salary for a software programmer in the United States is about $70,000, while the same job would pay about $10,000 in India. IT managers in the United States typically earn about $60,000 annually, while their Indian counterparts earn around $9,000. And accountants in the United States often start at around $50,000, while in India this figure is closer to $5,000.[3] No wonder so many white-collar professionals in some of the world's most developed nations are getting nervous.

Despite India's progress, it still has a long way to go. With 17 percent of the world's population, it accounts for less than 2 percent of global GDP and only 1 percent of global trade.[4] It remains a land of great contrasts, and vast numbers of people are not participating in the economic renaissance. Because of India's recent success in attracting so many professional jobs, wages are beginning to rise, jeopardizing one of the country's principal bases of competitiveness.[5] And some Indian companies are beginning to worry about a backlash from countries such as the United States, the United Kingdom, Germany, and France, which are losing tens of thousands of jobs to India annually.[6] Still, despite these challenges, most experts believe that India is definitely on the move.

CHALLENGES OF GLOBALIZATION

India provides just one example of the challenges and prospects facing both countries and their global firms and managers. Many other examples are available. Russia is trying to overcome rampant corruption in its business sector and open its economic system in order to build companies that can compete effectively in the global economy. Turkey is trying to join the European Union so its companies can gain greater access to world markets. And South Africa continues to try to shed the vestiges of its old apartheid system and build a new, stronger economy based on egalitarian principles. All these efforts face an uphill battle in view of the realities of today's global economy.

One of the best-known authorities on the corporate challenges of globalization is Japanese management consultant Keniche Ohmae. He has written several books on this subject that have received worldwide attention from both managers and academicians interested in international business. His two principal books are *Triad Power*, in which he introduced the notion of the *triad* (initially representing Japan, Europe, and the United States, but later broadened to include North America, Western Europe, and much of Asia) as the key to understanding global marketing, and *The Borderless World*, in which he further developed the addage "Think globally, act locally."[7] Both books are widely read today and are considered "must reading" by many successful global managers.

Ohmae's argument about the inevitability of globalization is simple. He asserts that, like it or not, countries around the world—including both developed and developing nations—are moving inextricably toward a true interconnected global economy. He characterizes these trends as follows:

1. Competition is increasing from all quarters, and modern corporations no longer have anyplace to hide. If they cannot compete globally, they run the risk of becoming extinct due to manufacturing inefficiencies or poor products and services.
2. People around the world increasingly prefer brands to national makes. That is, they want an iPod or a 325i not because they are American or German but because Apple and BMW make them. They represent the best technology and the best image; where they are made is secondary.
3. Customers are increasingly demanding more for less. They are putting increased pressure on both the price and the quality of products and services that various firms offer. This creates increased pressures for efficiency that many firms would prefer not to face.
4. Tariff barriers are declining around the world, and many governments are now encouraging rather than inhibiting global competition, believing that their home companies can—and must—succeed in this new global environment.
5. National boundaries are becoming less important as global companies increasingly operate in a borderless world. Witness the crumbling borders of the expanding twenty-five-nation European Union, where regional rules and

policies often trump national ones. Increasingly, companies are becoming nationality-less, held together by shared values, not shared passports. An increasing portion of international trade now bypasses national borders altogether (e.g., Internet sales).
6. With the demise of the cold war, there is less pressure to ignore unfair market advantages among friendly countries in order to support long-standing political alliances. For example, for many years the United States ignored Japan's closed markets because it wanted to retain the Japanese government as an ally against Russia and China. Today, these traditional political allies are increasingly seen not so much as friends as competitors.
7. Smart companies are going global in order to spread product development costs across multiple regional markets. They seek global products that can yield the economies of scale necessary to survive in highly competitive markets.

If these assertions are accurate, it is incumbent upon successful companies to view the world as one interrelated global market. Companies therefore require a worldview. Globalization provides a means by which firms can move their products into the international sector by using local talent. It is both a way of thinking and a way of acting. However, according to Ohmae, this by itself is insufficient for long-term success. Successful firms must not only seek the advantages of global manufacturing and sales; they must also temper this endeavor with some degree of localization of both products and services to ensure that regional customers are fully satisfied and will return to purchase more products in the future. Again, we are reminded of the widely cited dictum "Think globally, act locally."

To accomplish this, successful firms must take advantage of any commonalities that occur around the world (for example, sharing R & D costs for products). The role of corporate headquarters is to provide an overall corporate strategy that guides and controls worldwide business endeavors. Corporate headquarters also provides a mission and values for the entire firm. With this as a foundation, companies develop their global products. Beyond this, however, successful companies make a concerted effort to provide local or regional units with sufficient autonomy to tailor these globalized products to fit local tastes and to market them in a manner consistent with local cultures. Local managers take the lead in these efforts. In this way, a truly globalized company gets the best of both worlds: they achieve significant economies of scale by identifying and manufacturing global products that are then localized to meet the particular tastes of the local cultures. Ohmae's arguments are summarized in Exhibit 2.1.

STAGES IN GLOBALIZATION

In his research, Keniche Ohmae goes one step further to suggest that in a very general way successful global firms tend to pass through five relatively distinct phases in their development as global competitors. Each stage gets the company closer to its global customers. Moreover, at least ostensibly, each stage also saves the company

Exhibit 2.1

Think Globally, Act Locally

Strategic Focus	Management Implications
Think globally	• Develop a headquarters that is both secure and strategically oriented. • Headquarters provides the mission, values, control systems, and overall corporate objectives. • Source technology, talent, and resources globally. • Develop global product platforms; seek economies of scale.
Act locally	• Give local branch organizations considerable autonomy within the larger corporate framework. • Network with headquarters for administration and financial support, coordination, and overall control. • Tailor global products to fit each unique local market, where possible. • Produce, market, and service products locally.

Source: Based on Keniche Ohmae, *The Borderless World: Power and Strategy in the Interlinked Economy* (New York: Harper Business, 1999).

money as a result of increased economies of scale derived from their evolving success in the marketplace. The five *stages of globalization* are as follows:

1. *Creating export-oriented companies.* In stage one, companies interested in going international manufacture their products in their home country (e.g., the United States or Germany) and then export them through a foreign distributor who handles the distribution, marketing, and on-site servicing. Once the products leave the factory, they essentially become the distributor's responsibility. The manufacturer's job is to monitor compliance with quality control specifications and local customer satisfaction.

2. *Establishing overseas branches.* As the business grows, companies next consider establishing overseas branches to handle marketing, distribution, and customer service. In this way, they can follow their products more closely to the market and exert greater control over all aspects of the business. They may also save money by handling these operations within the firm instead of outsourcing them.

3. *Moving production overseas.* In stage three, business reaches a point where a company can justify opening a production facility for its products overseas nearer the emerging markets. Consider General Motors, clearly an American company that has established major manufacturing, sales, and distribution networks around the world. With increasing sales, overseas production becomes a money-saving mechanism that can reduce both labor and distribution costs. GM, for example, recently bought Korea's Daewoo Motors to secure less expensive manufacturing facilities that were near its targeted East and Southeast Asian car markets. Some Daewoo designs are now being manufactured in GM's Chinese production facilities.

4. *Achieving complete insiderization.* In stage four, companies begin to shift control over several support functions (e.g., customer service, financing, accounting, legal services) to autonomous local branches overseas. Ohmae calls this "com-

plete insiderization." Complete *insiderization* means that the firm is now beginning to "clone" itself around the world and establish minicompanies in its image to manage most of the local operations. For example, Coca-Cola routinely establishes local companies in various countries around the world to oversee the production and distribution of its products using its closely held American product formula. Ford-Europe is another example. Indeed, many Europeans think of Ford as a European company, not an American one. These companies are still American with an American outlook, but they have decentralized many of their basic business functions to local managers in various countries around the world. Ohmae suggests that this is where most modern multinational firms are in the chain of development.

5. *Achieving complete globalization.* In the final stage of development, companies begin viewing the world as one global marketplace, at which point we can say that they have achieved *complete globalization.* Managers do not think of themselves as American or Japanese or German. Rather, they think of themselves and their company as a truly global enterprise that transcends borders and competes everywhere. Such companies source people, raw materials, capital, and technology where they are best and cheapest. They manufacture where they can get the best price. They then sell to the world. Throughout, they take basic global products and localize them to suit each individual market. Examples of truly globalized firms include Sony, Honda, and Nike. Indeed, Sony refers to its global manufacturing philosophy as "global localization." Others refer to this simply as *glocalization.*[8]

Again, it is important to recognize that all companies do not follow this same five-stage trajectory. Some try and begin as truly global companies (e.g., Japan's Sony), while others wish to remain forever as national companies that do business internationally (e.g., Germany's Porsche). Others wish to change or evolve over time but find it difficult or impossible for a variety of reasons. The benefit of Ohmae's model is not to prescribe a correct path for development, but rather to identify the different challenges faced by companies depending on how they attempt to do business in the global environment.

THE GLOBALIZATION ENIGMA

In recent years, the term globalization has become a buzzword, a business strategy, and a political battle cry. It means different things to different people, and, to be frank, most speakers on the subject understand very little about the topic. As a result, it is sometimes difficult to discuss the causes—and consequences—of this important phenomenon rationally. An attempt is made in this chapter to explore the concept of globalization as it affects both international competition and the managerial responsibilities and challenges associated with it.

Some observers have argued that attempts to understand globalization in the real world often gets confused by well-intentioned but nonetheless biased observers. That is, genuine understanding of the issues can be difficult because of a tendency for some people to focus intensely on only one aspect of this complex issue and ignore or downplay others. For example, it has been suggested that sociologists often ignore economic and marketplace realities and focus instead on the negative social consequences of globalization. At the same time, it is argued that many economists ignore these social consequences and prefer instead to emphasize economic growth and trade statistics. Both approaches have limitations in developing a better understanding of globalization and its consequences. Our position on this issue is simple: To understand globalization and its impact on companies, employees, and society at large, it is first necessary to understand global economic principles, not from a theoretical standpoint but from an applied one (see Chapters 3 and 4). Based on this knowledge, an intelligent observer is free to move from facts to opinions in whichever direction he or she chooses. But an understanding of global economics must come first.

LOCAL POLITICS, GLOBAL BUSINESS

There is a popular saying among politicians that "all politics is local." That is, in the final analysis, people are self-centered and will vote on issues based on how the issues affect them personally, particularly when money is involved. As a result, it is often dangerous for politicians to take a stand, however worthy, that benefits people around the world at the expense of their local constituents. By contrast, the challenge for business managers is that, while all politics may be local, all business is global. Businesses must increasingly consider the global consequences of their plans and strategies, if for no other reason than the reality that global factors (e.g., governments, competitors, financial markets, access to raw materials, labor costs) frequently determine their relative success in the marketplace.

Globalization as a concept can be thought of much like we think about the Internet. It has no central driver and little oversight. No one is in charge—certainly not nation-states. Instead, the so-called market is in control. This can be both good and bad. On the one hand, markets tend to drive prices down and quality up. They tend to be impartial and reward competition. On the other hand, markets have no soul. Some win and some lose, and the market really doesn't care. As a result, globalization tends to foster strong competition, but with little concern for its social or political consequences. In this process, politics frequently plays a role, and for this reason global managers must have an awareness of legal and political processes from an international perspective in order to succeed (see Chapter 5).

FREE TRADE VERSUS MANAGED TRADE

For many people in business, globalization means *free trade*—a belief in the mutual benefits of competition (see Exhibit 2.2). In theory, free trade increases access to new markets, as well as to cheaper labor. This, in turn, leads to lower prices for consumers around the world and, simultaneously, to greater corporate profits. New job opportunities emerge for people in developing countries from companies drawn there by lower labor costs. Increasing technology transfer to these developing countries also helps support the development of national infrastructures that help them

Exhibit 2.2

Free Trade versus Managed Trade

Type of Trade	Characteristics
Free trade	Belief in free and open competition in the global marketplace; governments and international institutions (e.g., the World Trade Organization) intervene only to enforce basic laws of free competition (e.g., reduce trade barriers, provide protection against monopolies)
Managed trade	Belief in some government intervention in the marketplace to protect the interests of small or local enterprises (e.g., local coffee growers) against the economic or political power of large multinationals or to protect the cultural or technological integrity of a nation from external economic abuse (e.g., U.S. and EU subsidies to Boeing and Airbus to protect local high-tech jobs)

move up the economic hierarchy. Ultimately, as a result of free trade and competition, everyone benefits, according to advocates of this position.

For many politicians, environmentalists, and social activists, however, globalization means something very different. It is frequently seen as exploitation of workers in underdeveloped countries—a "race to the bottom" in which poorer nations compete against each other to see who can offer the lowest labor costs and the worst working conditions to secure at least some employment for their people. Powerful multinational firms that are responsible only to their stockholders increasingly ignore workers' rights and standard of living. Government oversight and concern for human rights are eclipsed by concern for profits and market dominance. Corporations, not people, become richer. In turn, this process often leads to a degradation of the environment. Concern is frequently expressed that environmental standards (regarding, e.g., air and water pollution, global warming, etc.) are often ignored by countries and companies interested in creating employment and economic development at almost any cost. Ultimately, there is concern about a loss of national boundaries, with a concomitant loss in local control and autonomy. The principle of local, and even national, democracy may be threatened in the surging tide of self-serving corporatism—or so say the opponents of globalization.

The irony here is that both sides to this debate generally agree on what is happening in the global economy. Like Keniche Ohmae, both sides recognize that, like it or not, we are moving increasingly toward one true interconnected global economy. But while both sides may agree about what is happening, they disagree—sometimes strenuously—about what to do. Many economists and business executives believe that with increased competition, companies, particularly those in competitive industries, must globalize (i.e., become true citizens of the world) in order to survive and prosper. Otherwise they will become obsolete and disappear. By contrast, opponents of free trade argue that completely open markets allow big and powerful firms (mostly from the United States, the European Union, and Japan) to perpetually dominate the weaker regions of the world. They argue instead for *fair trade*—more accurately referred to as *managed trade*. Advocates of managed trade believe that there is a proper role for national governments to play in ensuring that the small, the weak, and the underdeveloped are not disadvantaged or exploited in world trade. They argue, therefore, that it is sometimes necessary to curb the power of big business, the World Trade Organization (WTO), and the International Monetary Fund; erect national trade barriers to protect local economies and cultures; and seek international agreements to protect workers' rights and the environment. Advocates of managed trade argue that they are not antibusiness; rather, they believe—strongly—that other stakeholders in local economies need to have a strong voice and should not be swamped by the power of big business. There must be a humane balance of interests.

The challenge for business leaders is not to determine who is right and who is wrong. Both sides have merit. Rather, their challenge is to somehow navigate through this sea of conflict to achieve corporate objectives in ways that benefit the largest number of legitimate stakeholders (employees, stockholders, strategic partners, local governments, etc.) over the long term. Failing to achieve this objective increases the risk that some disgruntled stakeholder for whatever reason will attempt—possibly successfully—to derail the business enterprise. Intelligent companies and their managers are increasingly unwilling to assume this risk.

THE GLOBAL CORPORATE ELITE

A related concern in both international relations and international business is the relative economic and subsequent political power of a small number of global companies. One way to see this is to look at the world's forty largest global corporations and their nationalities in terms of market value (Exhibit 2.3). As can be seen, twenty-six of the forty largest global firms are American (fourteen out of the top twenty firms are American), six are British (including one joint venture with the Netherlands), four are Swiss, two are Japanese, and one each is Italian and French. This suggests that economic power is indeed highly concentrated in the hands of a small number of rich and powerful countries. This economic disparity presents both challenges and opportunities to both the haves and the have-nots, as we shall see in Chapter 5.

In this regard, consider the following challenge: As we move toward a technology-driven world, economic and subsequently political power will increasingly be determined by those companies and countries that control both the hardware and the software that make the world run. Currently, a small number of countries (e.g., Germany, Japan, France, England, Korea and the United States) control most of the cutting-edge hardware and virtually all of the important software. This doesn't leave much for other nations. These industrialized nations are obsessed with protecting intellectual property rights because they own so many of them. They are also obsessed with opening markets around the world because they believe they can compete successfully in so many arenas. What are other nations to think? What are other nations to do? How can they build their economies without risking becoming colonies of the industrialized nations? And how can other countries protect their cultures—the very DNA that determines who they are—from undue influence and possible domination from the industrialized world over the long term?

While most Westerners seem largely unconcerned about this trend, others throughout the world who populate the less developed nations are becoming increasingly

Exhibit 2.3

World's Largest Corporations (market value in $ millions)

Company (Nationality)	Market Value	Company (Nationality)	Market Value
1. General Electric (U.S.)	$341,755	21. Cisco Systems (U.S.)	$126,846
2. Exxon Mobil (U.S.)	301,496	22. Novartis (Swiss)	124,407
3. Microsoft (U.S.)	294,687	23. GlaxoSmithKline (UK)	120,446
4. Pfizer (U.S.)	249,290	24. Coca-Cola (U.S.)	108,899
5. Citigroup (U.S.)	240,888	25. Verizon Communications (U.S.)	108,735
6. Wal-Mart Stores (U.S.)	225,889	26. ChevronTexaco (U.S.)	104,330
7. BP (UK)	193,600	27. Altria Group (U.S.)	100,387
8. AIG (U.S.)	185,810	28. Merck (U.S.)	99,928
9. Bank of America (U.S.)	183,410	29. Wells Fargo (U.S.)	99,144
10. Royal Dutch/Shell (Dutch/UK)	175,502	30. Nestle (Swiss)	95,306
11. Johnson & Johnson (U.S.)	172,476	31. NTT DoCoMo (Japanese)	92,820
12. HSBC Holdings (UK)	171,135	32. Dell Computer (U.S.)	88,168
13. Vodafone (UK)	155,068	33. Roche Holding (Swiss)	87,440
14. Procter & Gamble (U.S.)	144,671	34. Royal Bank of Scotland (UK)	87,048
15. IBM (U.S.)	142,734	35. SBC Communications (U.S.)	85,413
16. Toyota Motor (Japanese)	142,104	36. PepsiCo (U.S.)	85,351
17. J.P. Morgan Chase (U.S.)	141,037	37. Home Depot (U.S.)	81,964
18. Intel (U.S.)	137,704	38. ENI (Italian)	81,754
19. Berkshire Hathaway (U.S.)	133,700	39. United Parcel Service (U.S.)	81,277
20. Total (French)	126,968	40. UBS (Swiss)	79,152

Source: "The Global Giants," *Wall Street Journal,* September 27, 2004, p. R10.

alarmed. Perhaps the challenge for Western countries—and Western companies—is to move into the global marketplace in synergistic ways that encourage and support both developing nations and aspiring companies. Given the right support, these fledgling companies in out-of-the way countries could develop into useful local partners for the major multinationals as the complex web of international business intensifies. On the other hand, without this support, these local companies could emerge as competitors or even spoilers who control access to needed resources and emerging markets.

GLOBALIZATION: A POINT OF VIEW

Globalization is not new. What is new is the magnitude of globalization and its impact on social welfare, environmental sustainability, and international trade. In 1975 (at the height of the cold war), 8 percent of all countries worldwide had democratic market-oriented governments, and foreign direct investment totaled $23 billion. By 1997, a little more than twenty years later, 28 percent of all countries had such governments, and foreign direct investment totaled $644 billion. Today, these figures continue to rise.

LEXUS AND THE OLIVE TREE

To provide a conceptual framework for better understanding globalization, as well how this trend affects various groups and societies, we turn to syndicated *New York Times* columnist Thomas Friedman and his book *The Lexus and the Olive Tree*.[9] (A similar though more controversial viewpoint on the trends and consequences of globalization can be found in Samuel P. Huntington's *The Clash of Civilizations and the Remaking of World Order*.[10]) In his book, Thomas Friedman uses metaphors to suggest a simple but elegant thesis on the meaning of globalization in today's contemporary society.

According to Friedman, *globalization* can be defined as the inexorable integration of markets, capital, nation-states, and technologies to a degree never seen before. This enables individuals, corporations, and nation-states to reach around the world farther, faster, deeper, and cheaper than ever before. The process is also creating a powerful backlash from those left behind by the new economic and political system. Friedman argues that globalization represents a major paradigm shift in international politics, economics, and business that is characterized by four trends:

- From the former cold war era, in which the world was divided into friends versus enemies, to a new era in which there are essentially no friends and all countries and companies are viewed as competitors.
- From traditional East-West conflicts between Russia and her Eastern Europe allies and the United States and her Western European allies to North-South conflicts between the industrialized North and the impoverished South.
- From first versus third world conflicts to fast- versus slow-world conflicts, in which some countries (located in all parts of the world) move swiftly to innovate and support new ventures, technologies, and markets, while others resist change and are often left behind.
- From concerns about communitarianism to a more narrow focus on individualism; that is, people in an increasing number of countries are becoming less willing to sacrifice for the common good and more interested in how actions benefit them individually.

According to Friedman, these changes lead logically to a fundamental conflict based not on politics, as was the case during the cold war, but on economics and financial power. Friedman characterizes these two sides by the terms the "Lexus" and the "olive tree." The *Lexus* (of Toyota fame) represents countries characterized by an emphasis on open markets, new technologies, a philosophy of faster-better-cheaper, achievement, strong competition, and high levels of capital investment and wealth accumulation (see Exhibit 2.4). Freeman uses the Lexus metaphor because this brand is often seen as having high status, technological sophistication, and upscale cost.

By contrast, the *olive tree* characterizes countries that stress cultural roots, family values, traditions, concern for friends and family, nationalism, and tribalism.

Exhibit 2.4

Lexus versus Olive Tree Philosophy

Lexus Philosophy	Olive Tree Philosophy
Belief that people control their own destiny; mastery over nature	Belief that God determines the future; live in harmony with nature
Forward-looking; progressive	Backward-looking; status quo
Belief in open markets; global competition	Belief in local markets; protectionist
Focus on innovation and new technologies	Focus on cultural roots and traditions
Faster-better-cheaper	Patience and forbearance
Democratic; egalitarian	Autocratic; tribalistic
Material progress important	Family and friends important
Internationalist orientation	Nationalist orientation

Source: Based on Thomas Freidman, *The Lexus and the Olive Tree* (New York: Anchor Books, 2000).

The essence of the olive tree philosophy is that you can be a rich person by your-self, you can be a smart person by yourself, but you cannot be a complete person by yourself. Cultural assimilation and community harmony are more important than individual achievement or success. According to Freeman, there is an emerg-ing conflict between individualistic "future-oriented" societies and the more col-lectivistic "tradition-bound" societies, and the realities of globalization favor the former over the latter.

Finally, Friedman identifies what he calls the *golden straightjacket* as a dysfunc-tional consequence of well-intentioned globalization efforts. When countries sup-port economic policies that engender confidence and support by the international investment community (e.g., balanced budgets, moderate tax rates, light govern-ment regulation, privatization), they frequently begin to lose political autonomy and control over their own affairs. (Witness the recent events in Argentina.) The national agenda is supplanted by a global agenda, with a commensurate loss of local control. Herein lies the contradiction inherent in globalization efforts: According to Fried-man, a country can develop economically or it can maintain local control over its development and destiny. In too many cases, it cannot do both.

GLOBALIZATION 3.0

Recently, Friedman has expanded his work on globalization to include what he calls *Globalization 3.0*.[11] By this he means that globalization as a world-changing phenomenon has passed through three phases. Phase one involved the globaliza-tion of countries and ran from roughly 1400 through World War I. In this phase, nations tried with varying degrees of success to define their relationships with other nations. The age of imperialism from the seventeenth to nineteenth centuries, when several of Europe's largest countries tried to divide up much of the rest of the world as colonies, provides a good example of this. Phase two involved the globalization of companies and ran from World War I through about 2000. This was the age of when many well-known multinational corporations were born and companies began seeing their markets in global terms. Phase three—the current phase—involves the globalization of individuals and began about 2000. This is when globalization is experienced on a personal level; it affects individuals. Friedman illustrates this phase with an example of an Indian entrepreneur who hires young people trained in Hindu temple art to make computer-assisted character designs for U.S. and European computer game companies. This is a global application of a traditional Hindu art form, and it indicates just how personal globalization can become.

Moreover, because of a decline in the cost of both transportation and telecommunications, combined with the proliferation of personal computers and the bandwidth and common software applications that connect them, global companies are now able to build what Friedman calls *global workflow platforms*. These platforms can divide up any service job and, with scanning and digitization, outsource each of its components to teams of skilled knowledge workers around the globe, based on which team can perform the function with the highest skill at the lowest cost. This is exactly what we saw in the example that opened the chapter. Friedman's advice to large and small countries around the world: Get on board the global train and find a place to add value; otherwise you risk being left behind completely.

A number of important social questions follow naturally from Friedman's thesis. To begin with, how much globalization is enough? Is there a point beyond which more globalization is a dangerous thing? Have we already passed that point? Second, rhetoric aside, who benefits and who loses from globalization? Companies? Governments? Large nations? Rich people? As Harvard University's president Larry Summers notes, "I'm all for a global economy, but we have to look out for people here."[12] What happens to people as globalization forces continue? And third, could we stop globalization if we wanted to, or is it some kind of force that generates its own power and energy and is essentially unstoppable? Questions such as these represent the future with which all aspiring business managers and entrepreneurs must grapple. The manner in which these issues are framed and dealt with will in large measure determine not only who succeeds and who fails but also what kind of world future generations live in. It is on this unrelenting and critical challenge and its implications for management that this book is focused.

In summary, globalization presents countries and companies with both challenges and opportunities. The manner in which they respond—or do not respond—will in large measure determine who wins and who loses. Those that succeed will need to have sufficient economic grounding, political and legal skills, and cultural awareness to decipher the complexities that characterize their surrounding environment. And tying this all together will be the management know-how to outsmart, outperform, or outlast the competition on a continuing basis.

KEY TERMS

complete globalization   golden straightjacket
fair trade   insiderization
free trade   Lexus (as a metaphor)
global workflow platforms   managed trade
globalization   olive tree (as a metaphor)
Globalization 3.0   stages of globalization
Glocalization   triad

GLOBAL MANAGER'S WORKBOOK 2.1:
GLOBALIZATION AND YOU

This exercise will require some preparation time prior to class. Please answer the following questions about how you personally fit into the global economy.

1. Locate the following personal items and determine where each was made or assembled. Then note why you think each particular item was made where it was.

   - The shirt or blouse you are currently wearing
   - The shoes you are currently wearing
   - The coat or jacket you last wore
   - The ballpoint pen or marker you have in your pocket or purse
   - Your backpack
   - Your wristwatch
   - Your computer
   - Your music player
   - Your television
   - Your alarm clock
   - The furniture where you live
   - The dishes you commonly use
   - The car you use most frequently (*Note:* This may require some research, since the cars sold in one country can be made in several locations. For example, Volkswagen makes cars for the U.S. market in both Germany and Mexico, Toyota in Japan and the United States, and Honda in Japan, the United States, and Canada. Your local auto dealer can help.)

2. What does the above list of items tell you about the nature of the economy where you live?

3. What in your opinion are your own home country's five most important industries (in manufacturing and/or services)? Why did you select these five industries?

4. In your opinion, what single product or service made or originating in your home country best exemplifies your country around the world? That is, what single product is your country best known for around the world? Why did you select this item?
5. Finally, how do you think globalization will change your own life over the coming years?

GLOBAL MANAGER'S WORKBOOK 2.2: MEETING THE GLOBALIZATION CHALLENGE

It was noted above that the phenomenon of globalization is not new. What is new is its magnitude, impact, and speed of global economic and political forces on companies, employees, governments, social welfare systems, environmental quality, and international trade. This is truly a revolution, and its consequences remain unclear. With this in mind, consider the following three questions.

1. Do you believe in free trade or managed trade? Why?
2. In your judgment, what are the five major challenges of globalization in the world today? How many of these challenges affect multinational companies?
3. Based on your assessment, what specifically can managers of multinational companies do to respond to these challenges?
4. Finally, what can responsible governments do to respond to these challenges?

NOTES

1. Manjeet Kripalani, "Ratan Tata: No One's Doubting Now," *Business Week*, July 26, 2004, pp. 50–52; Simon Long, "India's Shining Hopes: A Survey of India," *Economist*, February 21, 2004, pp. 3–20; Saritha Rai, "Microsoft Expands Software Development to India Site," *Register Guard*, November 16, 2004, p. B1.
2. Long, "India's Shining Hopes."
3. Ibid.; Kripalani, "Ratan Tata."
4. Long, "India's Shining Hopes."
5. Noam Scheiber, "As a Center for Outsourcing, India Could Be Losing Its Edge," *New York Times*, May 9, 2004, p. 3.
6. S. Srinivasan, "Indians Worry About Backlash," *Register-Guard*, April 14, 2004, p. D1.
7. Keniche Ohmae, *Triad Power: The Coming Shape of Global Competition* (New York: Free Press, 1985); Keniche Ohmae, *The Borderless World: Power and Strategy in the Interlinked Economy* (New York: Harper Business, 1999).
8. Arvind Phatak, *International Management: Concepts and Cases* (Cincinnati, OH: Southwestern, 1997).
9. Thomas Freidman, *The Lexus and the Olive Tree* (New York: Anchor Books, 2000).
10. Samuel P. Huntington, *The Clash of Civilizations and the Remaking of World Order* (New York: Simon and Schuster, 1996).
11. Thomas Friedman, "Globalization 3.0 Has Shrunk the World to Size Tiny," *Yale Global Online*, April 7, 2004, http://yaleglobal.yale.edu/.
12. Stephen Shepard, "Plain Talk from Larry Summers," *Business Week*, November 8, 2004, p. 74.

3 Economic Foundations of Global Business

SLOVAKIA'S EMERGING AUTOMOBILE INDUSTRY

A large number of the cars driving down the busy streets of Berlin, Paris, Copenhagen, and Rome may soon have something in common: They will be made in Slovakia. Germany's Volkswagen currently produces about 300,000 cars annually in Slovakia, while France's Peugeot-Citroen and Korea's Kia Motors will each open major new assembly plants shortly. All these cars being made in a country of 5.4 million people will soon make Slovakia the biggest producer of cars in the world on a per capita basis.[1]

Why Slovakia? The attraction is obvious: cheap labor, good infrastructure (e.g., roads, telecommunications), and a central location in the heart of an expanding European Union. Slovakia's unemployment rate is about 18 percent and the government values the new jobs. The cost of labor in Slovakia is about one-fifth that of Western Europe, even after its entry into an expanded European Union. Including wages and benefits, while the average German autoworker earns more than $40 per hour and the average French autoworker earns close to $30, the average Slovak autoworker earns less than $8.[2] In addition, the Slovak government has moved aggressively to curb welfare costs and revise its antiquated tax system to encourage more foreign direct investment. The government is now targeting the development of a service industry to balance its emerging strength in manufacturing.

Slovakia currently ranks behind Poland, Hungary, and the Czech Republic in both per capita GDP and average annual income. However, because of its aggressive development policies, this gap is rapidly shrinking. As a result, in addition to building cars for export to other European countries, Slovaks will soon be buying more cars for themselves as they begin to prosper with the emerging industry.

The long-term challenge for Slovakia will be its dependence on the car industry as a means of economic development. As the economy grows and wages rise, Slovakia will become less attractive to manufacturers. In the same way that car

27

manufacturers shifted production from Spain and Portugal to Eastern Europe, they may very well leave Slovakia as fast as they arrived. Global competition can be very unforgiving.

ECONOMIC ENVIRONMENT AND GLOBAL COMPETITION

The manufacture of automobiles in Slovakia illustrates a principal challenge of the new global economy. Like it or not, and despite various governments' best efforts, economics is all about who wins and who loses. In the area of international trade, this challenge is particularly acute because in the final analysis it determines who eats and who doesn't, who gets rich and who remains poor. Because of this, any effort to manage enterprises in the global economy requires an understanding of how the global economy works.

To accomplish this, we present a distilled version—a primer—on international economics and competitive advantage in a manner that highlights what global managers genuinely need to understand to succeed in a very competitive global environment. This chapter begins with the issue of country competitiveness and productivity, a key to economic success. Next, various theories of international economics are reviewed as they relate to competitive advantage. This is followed by a look at several of the key institutions facilitating global trade. Finally, a glossary of critical terms used to understand international trade is presented.

COUNTRY COMPETITIVENESS

One way to frame issues of international trade is to consider the concept of country competitiveness. Simply put, *country competitiveness* refers to the extent to which a country is capable of generating greater wealth than its competitors in global markets. This includes the extent to which a nation can create a supportive environment that both encourages and sustains domestic and international business prowess. An example of this can be seen above: the Slovak government took concrete steps to encourage foreign direct investment by various international automobile companies.

A second example of country competitiveness can be seen in a comparison of China and India. Both these countries have become fierce global competitors, but they compete based on different strengths, as shown in Exhibit 3.1. Perhaps as a result of these differences, China has emerged principally as a manufacturing powerhouse, while India has emerged largely although not exclusively as a services powerhouse. Even so, both remain developing countries and neither is yet considered among the world's most competitive nations as we shall see.

Governments and companies are keenly aware of which nations provide the most competitive business environments. This information is used by companies in making foreign direct investment decisions and in sizing up competing firms within an industry. Governments that are looking for countries that seek to impede international trade also make use of this information. Exhibit 3.2 presents a recent list of the

Exhibit 3.1

Competitive Advantage in China versus India

Competitive Forces	China versus India
Growth	For several years, China's GDP growth rate has risen by an average of 8 percent annually; India is just now beginning to catch up.
Infrastructure	China has better highways, deep water ports, power plants, and industrial parks than India.
Foreign direct investment	China attracts $50 billion in FDI annually, compared to only $4 billion for India.
Exports	China exports close to $300 billion in products annually, four times as much as India.
Language	The vast majority of educated Indians speak fluent English, providing a huge advantage in IT services and back-office operations.
Capital markets	Private firms in India have easier access to new venture funding; China prefers the state sector.
Legal systems	Contract law and copyright protection are more developed in India than in China; the Indian government is far more aggressive in protecting intellectual property rights than the Chinese government.
Form of government	China remains a highly autocratic communist state, while India has a long if quarrelsome tradition of democracy.
Demographics	53 percent of India's population is under twenty-five years of age, compared to 45 percent for China.

Sources: Manjeet Kripalani and Pete Engardio, "The Rise of India," *Business Week,* December 8, 2003, pp. 66–68; Simon Long, "India's Shining Hopes: A Survey of India," *The Economist,* February 21, 2004, pp. 3–20.

world's most competitive nations in rank order. This list varies somewhat from year to year but, not surprisingly, changes little over time.

In addition, Exhibit 3.3 presents country ratings on various economic indicators, including national population, total GDP, per capita GDP, and a ranking of business attractiveness (that is, the extent to which countries are seen as supporting business activities through their economic policies and political processes, with lower numbers being more attractive to business enterprise).

PRODUCTIVITY

At the core of the notion of country competitiveness is productivity. *Productivity* is the value of the output produced by a unit of labor or capital. It represents a principal determinant of a country's long-term per capita income and standard of living. In the example above, Slovak workers' lower wages should allow foreign

Exhibit 3.2

World's Most Competitive Nations (in rank order)

Highly Competitive	Moderately Competitive	Less Competitive
1. United States	17. Norway	36. Greece
2. Finland	18. Belgium	37. Slovakia
3. Luxembourg	19. New Zealand	38. Slovenia
4. Netherlands	20. Chile	39. South Africa
5. Singapore	21. Estonia	40. Philippines
6. Denmark	22. France	41. Mexico
7. Switzerland	23. Spain	42. India
8. Canada	24. Taiwan	43. Russia
9. Hong Kong	25. Israel	44. Colombia
10. Ireland	26. Malaysia	45. Poland
11. Sweden	27. South Korea	46. Turkey
12. Iceland	28. Hungary	47. Indonesia
13. Austria	29. Czech Republic	48. Venezuela
14. Australia	30. Japan	49. Argentina
15. Germany	31. China	
16. United Kingdom	32. Italy	
	33. Portugal	
	34. Thailand	
	35. Brazil	

Source: Based on *The World Competitiveness Yearbook 2004* (Lausanne, Switzerland: International Institute for Management Development, 2004), p. 23; and *The Economist Pocket World in Figures* (London: Profile Books, 2004), pp. 56–58.

companies such as Volkswagen, Peugeot-Citroen, and Kia to build cars there for less money than elsewhere in Europe, thereby increasing their productivity and motivation to invest in that country. The companies increase their profitability and return on investment and the local workers find new sources of employment. If other firms in other industries also begin investing in Slovakia and if local workers continue to enhance their skill levels, logic suggests that over time Slovakia would move up in the rankings in global competitiveness (from its current position at 37). Supporters of free trade argue that this represents a win-win outcome in terms of economic development.

However, at the center of any discussion on competitiveness is the question of how much competition is necessary or even desirable for economic well-being. Is there such a thing as too much competition? What are the social and environmental consequences of unrelenting pressures to win at any cost? And what happens to those people and those countries that for whatever reason are unable to compete? As noted in Chapter 2, this issue presents a particularly sensitive challenge to global managers, who must somehow find a balance between corporate profitability and corporate social responsibility.

Exhibit 3.3

Country Ratings of Economic Activity

Country	Population	Total GDP (US$ billions)	Per Capita GDP (US$)	Business Attractiveness
Algeria	30,800,000	$54.7	$1,776	—
Argentina	37,500,000	268.6	7,170	45
Australia	19,300,000	368.7	19,070	15
Austria	8,073,000	188.5	23,350	19
Belgium	10,264,000	229.6	22,370	13
Brazil	172,600,000	502.5	2,911	38
Canada	31,000,000	694.5	22,390	2
Chile	15,400,000	66.5	4,310	20
China	1,285,000,000	1,159.0	902	37
Colombia	42,800,000	82.4	1,925	44
Czech Republic	10,270,000	56.8	5,530	26
Denmark	5,330,000	161.5	30,290	7
Egypt	69,100,000	98.5	1,425	—
Finland	5,180,000	120.9	23,340	3
France	59,500,000	1,309.8	22,030	12
Germany	82,000,000	1,846.1	22,510	16
Greece	10,625,000	117.2	11,030	30
Hungary	10,544,000	55.3	5,240	27
India	1,025,100,000	477.3	466	39
Indonesia	214,800,000	145.3	676	—
Ireland	38,400,000	103.3	26,890	10
Israel	6,173,000	108.3	17,550	23
Italy	57,500,000	1,088.8	18,930	24
Japan	140,400,000	4,141.4	32,520	28
Luxembourg	367,000	15.4	41,950	—
Malaysia	22,600,000	88.0	3,890	31
Mexico	100,400,000	617.8	6,150	33
Netherlands	15,900,000	380.1	23,860	1
New Zealand	3,532,000	46.8	13,240	14
Norway	4,486,000	166.1	37,020	21
Pakistan	145,000,000	58.7	405	—
Peru	26,100,000	54.0	2,070	42
Philippines	77,100,000	71.4	926	35
Poland	38,600,000	176.3	4,570	29
Portugal	10,036,000	109.8	10,940	22
Russia	144,700,000	310.0	2,142	46
Saudi Arabia	21,000,000	186.5	8,870	41
Singapore	4,105,000	85.6	20,850	6
Slovakia	5,000,000	18.9	3,790	34
South Africa	43,800,000	113.3	2.586	36
South Korea	47,100,000	422.2	8,970	25
Spain	39,900,000	581.8	14,570	18
Sweden	8,834,000	209.8	23,750	11
Switzerland	7,171,000	247.1	34,460	8
Taiwan	22,300,000	282.3	12,660	17
Thailand	63,600,000	114.7	1,803	32
Turkey	67,600,000	147.7	2,140	—
United Arab Emirates	2,654,000	67.6	25,470	—
United Kingdom	59,500,000	1,424.1	23,920	4
United States	285,900,000	10,065.3	35,200	5
Venezuela	24,600,000	124.9	5,070	—

Source: The Economist Pocket World in Figures (London: Profile Books, 2004); *The World Competitiveness Yearbook* (Lausanne, Switzerland: International Institute for Management Development, 2004); Oded Shenkar and Yadong Luo, *International Business* (New York: Wiley, 2004); G. O'Driscoll, K. Holmes, and M. O'Grady, *Index of Economic Freedom* (Washington, DC, Heritage Foundation, 2004); and *World Book Encyclopedia* (Chicago: World Book, 2004).

Exhibit 3.4

Evolution of International Trade Theories

Theory	Author	Contribution
Competition Among Nations		
Mercantilism	European origins	Recommends accumulation of gold and silver; supports protectionism; defends colonization
Absolute advantage	Smith	Promotes the advantages of specialization and economies of scale
Comparative advantage	Ricardo	Promotes the advantages of relative competitive advantage; introduces the concept of opportunity cost
Relative factor endowments	Heckscher-Ohlin	Countries create competitive advantage by producing and exporting products that require resources they have in abundance
Product life cycle	Vernon	Recognizes that competitiveness can vary by the stage of a product's life cycle
Competition Among Firms and Industries		
New trade theory	Krugman, others	Argues that increasing returns from economies of scale promote trade, both between and within industries
National competitive advantage	Porter	Argues that competitiveness is based on factor endowments, demand conditions, supporting industries, and rivalries and business policy

COMPETITION BETWEEN NATIONS

Theories of international trade began to appear in the sixteenth century and have evolved considerably over time. The first wave of theories (frequently called the "classical" theories) emerged during the time of the rise of the European nation-states and focuses principally on how countries, as opposed to companies, successfully compete in the global marketplace (see Exhibit 3.4).

MERCANTILISM

The earliest formal theory of international trade is called *mercantilism* and dates from the sixteenth century. The mercantilist doctrine asserts that a country's national wealth is measured by its holdings of gold and silver and that the goal of any country is (or should be) to enlarge these holdings as much as possible. To achieve this, a country must maximize the difference between its exports and its imports by promoting the former and resisting the latter. If a nation's exports exceed its imports, the debtor countries must ultimately make up the deficit by paying the creditor nation in gold or silver, allowing the creditor nation to amass more wealth.

Mercantilism allowed the aristocracy of Europe to amass great fortunes; indeed, it helped create the class system of Europe that remains in various forms to this day. In addition, mercantilism allowed countries to pay for standing armies to maintain or expand their territories—a popular European pastime during the sixteenth through the eighteenth centuries. Mercantilism favored manufacturers and, to a lesser extent, their workers by protecting both sales and local jobs. This was accomplished through subsidies for home industries aimed at expanding the nation's exports and through import tariffs and quotas aimed at restricting the importation of foreign goods.

At the same time, mercantilism created significant tax burdens to support the generous industrial subsidies given to targeted industries. Since the aristocracies in most countries paid few if any taxes, this burden typically fell on the middle and lower classes. Moreover, government import restrictions served to raise prices on the local goods that were available, again a significant burden on those least able to pay. Finally, mercantilism fostered colonialism, as well as imperialism. A country that had colonies could access raw materials at reduced prices to feed its factories and then sell finished goods back to its colonies at vastly inflated prices. Indeed, this practice was one of the principal causes of the American Revolution, which led to the creation of the United States.

While mercantilism is often dismissed as an antiquated economic theory, it lives on today in the form of various protectionist practices that can be found throughout the world. Indeed, all nations employ some form of protectionist practices in their fundamental economic policies, despite frequent denials and political rhetoric to the contrary. Modern-day mercantilists are called *protectionists,* although they would not typically refer to themselves in this manner. They support various forms of import tariffs or quotas, as well as government subsidies that benefit local industries over foreign competition.

A clear example of this can be seen in ongoing conflicts between Boeing and Airbus over government subsidies to their commercial aircraft business.[3] Boeing receives large U.S. government contracts to fund technology research for its defense business; much of what is learned through this research is then transferred to the company's commercial aircraft division. Boeing also receives major tax breaks from several U.S. states, as well as from the Japanese government, for manufacturing parts of their planes in these locations. Meanwhile, Airbus receives large government-funded loans (called *launch aid*) from France, Germany, Spain, and the United Kingdom to develop new planes; many of these "soft" loans have never been repaid despite the profitability of the company. Both sides claim that their competitor is receiving unfair government subsidies, a violation of WTO guidelines. In point of fact, however, this conflict has less to do with the legitimacy of government subsidies —both companies are heavily subsidized—and more to do with winning in the highly competitive commercial aircraft industry.

THEORY OF ABSOLUTE ADVANTAGE

In 1776, Scottish economist Adam Smith, who is considered to be the father of free market economics, wrote a treatise entitled *An Inquiry into the Nature and Causes of the Wealth of Nations* (commonly referred to simply as *The Wealth of Nations*).[4] In his book, Smith attacked the intellectual basis of mercantilism and argued that it actually

Exhibit 3.5

Production Output in the Manufacture of Wine and Clocks

Products	Without International Trade			With International Trade		
	France	Switzerland	Total Hourly Production	France	Switzerland	Total Hourly Production
Wine (liters)	10	5	15	20	0	20
Clocks	2	5	7	0	10	10

weakens a nation because it robs individuals of their ability to trade freely and benefit from voluntary exchanges. Moreover, by avoiding imports at almost all cost, a country must spend its resources producing goods that it may not be best suited to make. The resulting inefficiencies reduce the wealth of the country as a whole, even though certain special interest groups (e.g., wealthy merchants) may benefit.

Instead, Adam Smith advocated free trade among nations as the best means of expanding wealth. This is referred to as the doctrine of *laissez-faire.* His *theory of absolute advantage* focused on the importance of gaining competitive advantage through specialization. That is, Smith argued that countries could expand their national wealth by specializing in the production and export of only those goods and services in which they were more competitive than their neighbors. At the same time, countries should import goods and services from other countries that were more productive in producing those particular goods and services.

An example from the time illustrates this point: Suppose that France can produce more wine than Switzerland on an hourly basis, but that Switzerland can produce more clocks. According to Adam Smith, each country would be better off using their limited resources to specialize in what they do best and then trade with the other nation for the other commodity. To be more precise, consider that because of its wine-making expertise France can produce ten liters of wine per hour, while Switzerland can produce only five liters, as shown in Exhibit 3.5. At the same time, Switzerland can produce five clocks per hour because of its clock-making experience, while France can only produce two. If there is no trade, both countries together can produce fifteen liters of wine and seven clocks. However, if they each specialized in what they can do best, together they can produce twenty liters of wine (all made in France) and ten clocks (all made in Switzerland). In this way, both countries achieve greater economies of scale and consumers in both countries receive maximum benefit. Obviously this is a simple example. Today we might compare manufacturing semiconductors and automobiles. Even so, the principle remains the same: specialization can lead to competitive advantage.

While the theory of absolute advantage is simple, it illustrates how the concept of economies of scale works. *Economies of scale* represent reductions in the unit cost of items due to an increase in the numbers of items produced. Thus, if France can increase wine production to the point where it reduces its per-liter cost, it would have a greater advantage in the marketplace, making it difficult for rivals to either enter or remain in this market. The same would apply to Switzerland and its clocks.

This theory also helps explain the advantages of economies of scope. *Economies of scope* represent declines in the average cost of items due to an increase in the number of related products sold. In our old example, France's wine-making expertise might give it a competitive advantage in making and selling wine-making equipment or other agricultural products, while Switzerland's clock-making expertise might give it an advantage in manufacturing other products that rely on gears or precision instruments. A more modern example of this can be seen at Hewlett-Packard, where the company uses its dominance of the computer printer industry to also make and sell various lines of related products and technologies (e.g., PCs, digital cameras, paper for both printers and photo processing, etc.), frequently using the same distribution channels. By doing so, HP gains a competitive advantage over its competitors. Not to be outdone, Dell Computer recently expanded its PC business to include printers for the same reason.

THEORY OF COMPARATIVE ADVANTAGE

According to David Ricardo, an early-nineteenth-century British economist, Adam Smith got it only half right. Ricardo asked a simple question: What if one nation (say France) was more productive in making both wine and clocks?[5] According to Adam Smith, there would be no trade, because France had an absolute advantage in both products. However, this was obviously not the case. Ricardo solved this dilemma with his *theory of comparative advantage*. The theory is simple: To achieve the greatest wealth, a country should produce and export only those goods and services for which it is *relatively* more productive than other countries and import those goods and services for which other countries are *relatively* more productive than it is.

Why? Because of opportunity cost. *Opportunity cost* is the cost associated with not pursuing alternative courses of action. In our example above, suppose that France could produce both wine and clocks more efficiently than Switzerland could. Specifically, suppose France could produce ten liters of wine and seven clocks, while Switzerland could produce only five of each. According to Ricardo, if France could produce wine more efficiently than it could make clocks (that is, if it could achieve a greater return on its investment from wine), it would be giving up an opportunity cost by using its limited resources to also make clocks. If it made only wine, its greater efficiency with this product would lead to even more national wealth. Thus, in our example, France should focus on wine and buy clocks from Switzerland, even though the Swiss were less productive in clock making. France would still be ahead. It is all about where you can get the greatest return on your investment.

THEORY OF RELATIVE FACTOR ENDOWMENTS

David Ricardo's theory of comparative advantage suggests that opportunity costs will (or at least should) determine what a country will produce most efficiently and most profitably. However, his theory ignores the fact that different countries often have different opportunity costs. This issue was examined by two Swedish economists, Eli Heckscher and Bertil Ohlin, in what is called the *theory of relative factor endowments*.

It is also referred to as the *Heckscher-Ohlin theorem,* or simply the H-O theorem.[6] This theory attempts to explain the relationship between a country's *factor endowments* (e.g., land, labor, capital) and its comparative advantage in international trade.

Specifically, H-O theory asserts that a country will have a comparative advantage in products and commodities in cases where production requires considerable resources that the country has in abundance. Such products would be exported, while the same country would import commodities that require substantial inputs of resources that are scarce in that country. In other words, countries can gain a competitive advantage in global trade by specializing in industries for which they have an abundance of input resources. As a result, differences in comparative advantage are based largely on differences in the structure of each country's economy. For example, Argentina has a comparative advantage in the export of both grains and beef because of its abundance of farm and grazing land, while Singapore has an advantage in the export of technology-based products because of its large numbers of highly skilled technical workers.

However, the Hecksher-Ohlin theorem is based on at least two limiting assumptions. First, it assumes that the same amounts of capital and labor are required to produce a product in any country. For example, it assumes that if it takes two units of labor and two units of capital to produce wine in France, it will also take two units of labor and two units of capital to produce it in Switzerland. This is obviously not always the case. Second, it assumes that available technology and skilled human capital are constant across nations, ignoring the fact that there are often different ways to make the same product (e.g., automation vs. manual labor). The more recent product life cycle model has attempted to resolve these contradictions.

PRODUCT LIFE CYCLE THEORY

In the 1960s, Raymond Vernon added to our understanding of international trade by pointing out that the comparative advantage that a nation or firm enjoys at one stage of a product's life cycle may disappear at another stage.[7] This is called the *product life cycle theory,* while the actual process by which this theory works is referred to as *dynamic competitive advantage.*

Vernon identified three stages in the product life cycle of a typical product: new product stage, maturing product stage, and standardized product stage. In the *new product stage,* a firm introduces a new, innovative product. Because the product is new, it typically requires intensive research and development, highly skilled labor, and production capabilities that are near the initial targeted markets, usually rich or developed countries such as those in the United States, Japan, or Western Europe. In this stage, there is little or no international trade. When a product enters the *mature product stage,* the second phase, demand for the product expands and the firm builds new factories both at home and abroad to serve the emerging international markets. Finally, in the *standardized product stage,* the market for the products stabilizes, the product becomes more of a commodity than a brand, and pressures to lower costs accelerate. For this reason, production shifts to developing countries that can produce at lower costs.

To see how this theory can be used to understand international trade and global business strategy, consider the example of photocopiers. In the 1960s, photocopiers were produced in the United States only by Xerox Corporation and sold exclusively to U.S. customers (new product stage). As demand began to grow, Xerox initiated several international joint ventures with local firms in other countries (e.g., Fuji-Xerox in Japan) to open new markets. Foreign competitors, such as the Japan's Canon and Ricoh, also began entering the market (maturing product stage). Today, photo-copiers have essentially become a commodity product; most people want a copier, not specifically a Xerox copier. They are produced in low-cost countries such as Thailand, Mexico, and China and then exported to the United States and Japan (standardized product stage). As a result, the American company Xerox initially had the upper hand in the copier market because it had proprietary technology and was first to market. However, as global markets began to open and became more competitive, Xerox was forced to alter its business plan in order to survive. It went from a position of comparative advantage to one of being a commodity producer of fairly standardized copiers.

Other examples of Vernon's product life cycle theory are easy to find. Take semiconductors. Initially, semiconductors were a very high-tech product that required highly advanced technological capabilities to manufacture. They were made exclusively in Japan and the United States. Then Germany and Korea caught up to meet the emerging global markets. Cost pressures on commodity chips soon led U.S., Japanese, Korean, and German companies to increasingly manufacture in China. Now China is developing its own chips.

COMPETITION AMONG FIRMS AND INDUSTRIES

It is important to understand that the early theories of international trade focused principally on building nations and industries, and paid less attention to individual companies. Indeed, companies were important in most of these theories only to the extent that they facilitated national economic development. The focus was squarely on nation building, and the fundamental question was which industries nations should emphasize in order to prosper. In short, such theories focused largely on *interindustry trade,* or trade among various industries in the global economy. As such, attempts were made to explain why France might specialize in wine and Switzerland in clocks. Or, for a more modern example, why has China specialized in developing its manufacturing sector while India has focused on its service sector? In large measure, these models fail to explain *intraindustry trade,* that is, trade among nations in the same industries. For example, they do not explain why Germany, Japan, and the United States all import *and* export automobiles. In recent years, attention has shifted more directly to examining how individual firms compete across borders within specific industries, such as automobiles, electronics, and aerospace.

This shift to firm-based theories of international trade began for two principal reasons. First, earlier theories had proven to have only limited explanatory power in terms of national economic development. They were too simplistic. Second, multi-national corporations (MNCs) grew in size, scope, and power, and existing theories of international trade were not prepared to deal with this growth. It was felt that new models were required that focused on how companies, not countries, compete in the global economy. Two recent intraindustry, or firm-based, theories of trade attempt to explain global competition within a specific market or industry: the so-called new trade theory posited by Paul Krugman and others and the theory of national competitive advantage suggested by Michael Porter.

NEW TRADE THEORY

In the past several years, a number of economists have begun to examine trade theory in light of recent changes in the global economy. The emerging model is referred to as the *new trade theory*.[8] The new trade theory makes a clear distinction between interindustry trade and intraindustry trade. While interindustry trade can often be explained by the Hecksher-Ohlin theorem or the product life cycle theory, discussed above, intraindustry trade results from specialization within an industry.

The new trade theory argues that countries do not necessarily specialize and engage in trade in order to capitalize on their differences. They also trade because they receive increasing returns on their investments, which make specialization in itself advantageous. A key concept here is economies of scale, or the reduction of the unitary cost of production due to increased production, as noted above. In some industries, such as the semiconductor industry, economies of scale are so large that the world market can accommodate only a few large-scale producers, such as Samsung, Hynix, and Micron Technologies. The cost of establishing a rival manufacturer is so great that it would be cheaper to import chips from existing suppliers than to try to compete.

The notion of economies of scale has two main implications here: First, it helps to explain the existence of trade between two countries with similar factor endowments. That is, even if several countries have similar factor endowments (e.g., accessible capital, a highly skilled workforce, technological expertise, and engineering prowess), one may choose to seek global competitive advantage by specializing in commercial aircraft, as in the case of France and the United States, while another may choose to pursue competitive advantage in optics and digital cameras or in consumer electronics, as in the case of Japan and Korea. In this way, each nation will generally seek competitive advantage in those arenas where they can achieve the greatest returns from larger economies of scale, making use of their particular factor endowments.

Second, the concept of economies of scale helps to explain intraindustry trade, that is, why countries simultaneously import and export products in the same industry. Economies of scale will lead firms to specialize in narrow product lines. Other firms, in other countries, will produce variations on these products—similar products that exhibit somewhat distinct characteristics. For example, American automobile manufacturers are noted for making quality pickup trucks and SUVs, while German manufacturers are noted for making performance luxury cars that are typically characterized by a higher degree of craftsmanship and engineering than their American counterparts. Thus, while American and German cars are essentially the same from a functional standpoint—that is, they both provide transportation—consumers frequently see and are willing to pay more in the marketplace for subtle yet important distinctions. As a result, both Germany and the United States manufacture and export cars to each other in the global automobile industry, but each seeks slightly different segments of the available market. Another example of this can be seen in the niche market for regional commuter jets, where Boeing and Airbus do not compete. Here, Canadian and Brazilian aircraft manufacturers such as Canadair and Embraer largely control the market.

THEORY OF NATIONAL COMPETITIVE ADVANTAGE

The second theory of trade that focuses largely on intraindustry competition is Michael Porter's *theory of national competitive advantage.*[9] This is also referred to as the "diamond framework" for assessing global competitive advantage (see Exhibit 3.6). Porter argues that success in international trade derives from the interaction of four key variables: factor endowments, demand conditions, related and supporting industries, and interfirm rivalries and business policies. These factors are found in both the general business environment and the specific corporate environment.

First, a country's *factor endowments* include those resources that are already available to entrepreneurs and firms. Traditionally, factor endowments are thought of as including land, labor, and capital, but Porter expands this definition to include educational and skill levels (a nation's *human capital*) and the quality of a nation's infrastructure (e.g., roads, telecommunications, power grids, airports, etc.). These factor endowments provide the foundation on which firms attempt to grow and compete, according to Porter.

A second critical factor in the strategic success of global firms is being surrounded by a strong market for the products they intend to produce and sell. This is referred to as *demand conditions.* When Japan first entered the consumer electronics market in the 1960s, it began by capitalizing on a strong local market for televisions, radios, and so forth. This allowed companies such as Matsushita, Hitachi, and Toshiba to build and refine their products to world-class status while still operating in their relatively protected home markets. Then, based on this experience—and the cash flow it generated—these companies expanded overseas with high-quality and consumer-tested products that went on to dominate global markets. But their success began with strong local demand for their products at home.

The third source of competitive advantage is the existence of strong *supporting industries.* Porter argues that being surrounded by companies in a firm's own industry can lead to more competitive products for that firm. This is caused by a ready access to cutting-edge technologies in the local environment and to suppliers who can quickly become partners in new ventures. This synergistic payoff is illustrated by the intensive intellectual and scientific environment of California's Silicon Valley, where talented people, leading research universities, specialized R & D laboratories, well-connected suppliers, and emerging technologies all come together to create a unique supportive environment for competitive enterprise.

Finally, Porter argues that strong *industrywide rivalries* force companies to improve their competitive position. In a highly competitive world, winners survive and

Exhibit 3.6   **Porter's Model of National Competitive Advantage**

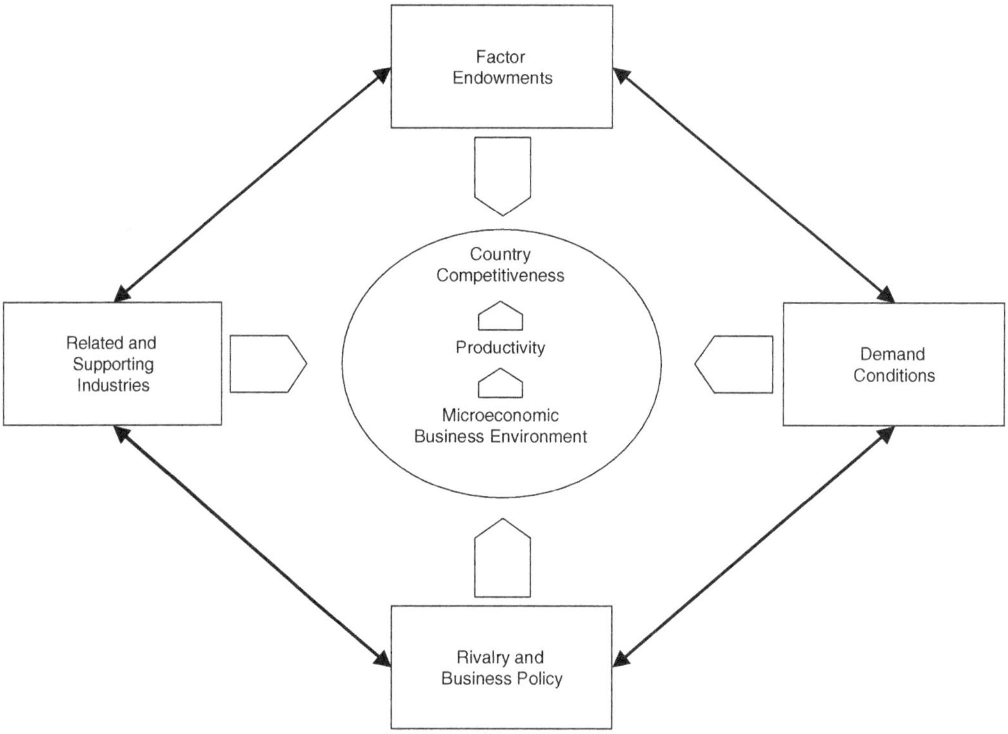

Source: Adapted from Michael E. Porter, "The Competitive Advantage of Nations," *Harvard Business Review,* March–April 1990, pp. 73–93.

prosper while losers and stragglers frequently disappear. Successful firms must create winning corporate strategies, restructure themselves to operate efficiently in pursuit of their strategies, and compete head-on against strong rivals. Indeed, many economists have argued that highly successful technology companies such as Intel, Apple Computer, and Hewlett-Packard might not have existed, let alone prospered, if it were not for the pressure cooker environment of Silicon Valley.

COMPETITIVE ADVANTAGE IN THE BRAZILIAN SHOE INDUSTRY

An example of how Porter's theory of national competitive advantage works can be seen in the case of the evolution of the Brazilian shoe industry in Vale dos Sinos. Brazil's shoe industry is one of the most important in the world, producing more than 600 million pairs of shoes and exporting more than $1.5 billion in annual sales, principally to the United States and Western Europe.[10] The industry is clustered in the Vale dos Sinos region of Brazil, where 85 percent of Brazil's leather shoes are produced. German immigrants colonized this region in the 1800s and brought with them the skills and technology to work with leather. By the 1870s, the development of a rail system linking this region to Porto Alegre, the state's capital, transformed the region into a commercial shoe-manufacturing center, attracting both workers and new companies.

Using Porter's model, the Vale dos Sinos region offered the industry certain factor endowments that included a highly skilled labor force that came initially from Germany but later from other regions of Brazil as the industry matured. Demand conditions included the region's well-established infrastructure, which linked the region with the state capital and from there to world markets. And the region provided a number of supporting industries, including major cattle producers, an extensive leather-processing industry, and several major producers of machinery used to produce shoes and other leather artifacts. In addition, the region offered a strong service industry in support of its exports, including banks, telecommunications, transportation, and international trade specialists.

While these three components—factor endowments, demand conditions, and supporting industries—were sufficient to guarantee a profitable global position for the Brazilian shoe industry through the 1980s and early 1990s, the lack of rivalry and sound business policy emerged in the mid-1990s as a principal reason for the industry's eventual decline. At this critical time, China entered the market as a low-cost shoe producer, capitalizing on its abundant supply of both cheap labor and cattle hides and bolstered by strong government incentives. Large Chinese companies soon captured a significant share of the market, becoming the largest exporters of shoes in the world. By contrast, Brazilian shoe manufacturers generally consisted of small independent manufacturers that did not have the capital, labor cost advantage, or economies of scale to compete effectively. They had also become complacent about their long-standing ready access to North American markets and were entrenched in more traditional but less efficient ways of doing business. Soon, many of these companies went out of business.

Following this setback, the Brazilian shoe industry launched a major transformation in the way it approached global business strategy. It moved to professionalize its management, invest in new laborsaving manufacturing technologies, improve product quality, and invest in new shoe designs. At the same time, it shifted its principal focus away from the cost-conscious North American market to the more style-conscious European market. This strategy allowed the Brazilians to capitalize on their quality image and charge upscale prices to cover their costs. As these companies entered the twenty-first century, Brazilian exports were again on the move.

INSTITUTIONAL INFLUENCES ON TRADE AND ECONOMIC DEVELOPMENT

As discussed above, global competition is influenced by a number of critical national and firm-level variables. However, any assessment of the conditions that facilitate or inhibit competition would be incomplete without recognizing the central role played by several international institutions, such as the World Bank, the International Monetary Fund, and the World Trade Organization. Collectively, these institutions help create, develop, and support infrastructure development, stable

Exhibit 3.7

Institutions Facilitating Trade and Economic Development

Institution	Purpose	Membership
World Bank	Makes hard loans to developing countries to build infrastructure	183 member nations
International Monetary Fund (IMF)	Makes emergency loans to stabilize local currencies with IMF conditionality	183 member nations
World Trade Organization	Promotes free trade by negotiating and enforcing multilateral trade agreements with member nations	144 member nations
Organization for Economic Cooperation and Development	Provides a multinational forum for discussing economic issues and developing strategies for global economic development	30 market-oriented democracies
G-7 and G-8	Provide a multinational forum for discussing global economic (and at times political) issues	United States, Canada, France, Italy, United Kingdom, Germany, and Japan (G-7), and Russia (G-8)
International Labor Organization	Promotes fair labor standards throughout the world; no legal enforcement authority	UN affiliate

currencies, and open trade policies—the proverbial "level playing field" that is necessary to develop and sustain global trade over the long term. These institutions develop and enforce the "rules of the game" for both countries and global companies. Without this infrastructure, legitimate trade across borders would be nearly impossible in today's hypercompetitive economy, as trust levels and guarantees would be threatened. Here we examine six of the more important international institutions in support of global trade (see Exhibit 3.7). Global managers need not be experts on these organizations. However, it is important that they understand on a fundamental level what these organizations do and how they affect international trade and economic development.

We begin with what might be called the "big three" of international trade: the World Bank, the International Monetary Fund, and the World Trade Organization. This is followed by a look at three other key institutional influences on international trade and economic development: the Organization for Economic Cooperation and Development, the G-7 or G-8, and the International Labor Organization. Together, these six international organizations yield considerable influence in determining not only the rules of the game, but who gets to play.

WORLD BANK

Established in 1945 as a result of the Bretton Woods (New Hampshire) conference on economic recovery, the initial goal of the *World Bank* was to help finance reconstruction of the war-torn European economies after the Second World War. By 1950, however, its mission had evolved to help build the economies of the world's developing nations. As its mission has expanded over time, so, too, have the number of organizations that now comprise the bank, known collectively as the World Bank Group.

The World Bank is owned and administered by 183 member countries. The bank gets its money from member contributions and loans by its members from world capital markets. By statute, the bank can make loans only to developing countries to help build their infrastructure. This includes public sector development projects (e.g., power plants, roads and highways, and railroads), agricultural improvements, education, population control, and urban development. The World Bank is not a charity or a vehicle for foreign aid. An important principle of the World Bank is its *hard-loan policy,* which requires the bank to make loans only when there is a reasonable expectation that the loan will be repaid in a timely fashion.

By contrast, and in response to criticism from developing countries about their inability to qualify for World Bank developmental loans, the *International Development Association* was established by the World Bank to provide soft loans to these countries. *Soft loans* frequently bear significant risk of not being repaid, and World Bank members underwrite any losses.

International Monetary Fund

The *International Monetary Fund* (IMF) was also established as a result of the Bretton Woods economic conference in 1945. Like the World Bank, it consists of 183 member countries that jointly oversee its operations. The principal purpose of the IMF is to ensure monetary and currency stability over time by making emergency loans to countries that are in trouble economically and whose currencies have fallen in value. When the value of a country's currency declines rapidly, international commerce across its borders can be severely threatened, as can future foreign direct investment in that country. This occurred in Korea in 1997, for example, when the value of the Korean won plummeted to half its value in just six weeks. As a result, financial markets were thrown into turmoil as international bankers wondered about their loans and investors around the world worried about their stocks and bonds.

In such cases, the IMF provides emergency loans to stabilize a country's currency in exchange for rigid compliance with stringent macroeconomic policies. Heavy borrowers from the IMF usually must agree to monetary and fiscal policies set down by the IMF (called *IMF conditionality*), which typically include IMF-mandated targets on domestic monetary supply, exchange rate policy, tax policy, banking reform, and government spending. Like the World Bank, the IMF is not a charity and pushes countries with troubled currencies hard—some say too hard—to initiate fundamental economic reforms aimed at restoring global confidence in the local currency and economy.

World Trade Organization

Established in 1995, the *World Trade Organization* (WTO) is the successor organization to GATT (or General Agreement on Tariffs and Trade) and was created to facilitate free trade and the reduction of trade barriers around the world. Membership includes 144 nations who agree to abide by WTO principles governing free trade and who further agree to be subject to WTO discipline in cases of noncompliance. The World Trade Organization is charged with achieving three principal goals to facilitate global trade. First, the WTO aims to promote trade by encouraging member nations to adopt nondiscriminatory trade policies. Second the WTO aims to reduce all remaining trade barriers through multilateral negotiations among member nations. Finally, the WTO aims to establish impartial procedures for resolving trade disputes when they arise among member states. All WTO rules, policies, and agreements governing global trade must be unanimously approved by member nations.

To accomplish this, the WTO works under a set of five principles that collectively shape its policies and actions. These principles are as follows:

- Members should not discriminate among their trading partners (all partners are granted *most-favored-nation status*), nor discriminate between their own and foreign products, services, or employees.
- Members should lower trade barriers through multilateral negotiations.
- Members agree not to arbitrarily raise trade barriers (including tariffs and nontariff barriers) against foreign companies, investors, and governments.
- The WTO discourages unfair trade practices, such as export subsidies and dumping products below cost to gain market share.
- The WTO gives less developed nations more time to adjust, greater flexibility, and special privileges.

Member nations that think they are being unfairly treated in international trade (e.g., when another country unilaterally raises its import tariff on a particular product) can appeal to the WTO, which will adjudicate the complaint and render a judgment. When the U.S. government unilaterally increased steel tariffs in 2002 to protect its local producers, several governments in Europe, Asia, and Latin America quickly appealed. Eventually, the WTO declared the increase illegal (see Chapter 4). WTO judgments carry the force of international law, although appeal processes can at times be long and drawn out. In the end, the WTO maintains considerable enforcement powers to facilitate compliance with trade barrier reduction directives agreed to by its members. Failure to comply with WTO directives can lead to trade sanctions or significant compensation to the aggrieved party.

ORGANIZATION FOR ECONOMIC COOPERATION AND DEVELOPMENT

The *Organization for Economic Cooperation and Development (OECD)* is a Paris-based intergovernmental organization consisting of thirty market-oriented democracies whose purpose is to promote economic growth. Members include twenty-three Western European countries and seven Pacific Rim countries (Australia, New Zealand, Japan, South Korea, Mexico, Canada, and the United States). The OECD provides its member states with a forum in which they can compare their experiences, discuss mutual problems, and seek solutions that can then be applied within their national contexts. It has been particularly active in efforts to reduce bribery and corruption in international trade (see Chapter 4).

G-7 AND G-8

The *G-7* is an association of the heads of state from the seven most powerful industrial economies in the world: Canada, France, Italy, United Kingdom, Germany, Japan, and the United States. Recently, Russia was invited to join in these meetings, at which time the group is called the *G-8*. The group meets annually to discuss economic conditions in the global economy.

INTERNATIONAL LABOR ORGANIZATION

A UN affiliate consisting of government, labor, and industry representatives, the *International Labor Organization* (ILO) was founded following World War I to promote fair labor standards in health and safety, working conditions, and freedom of association for workers throughout the world. The role of the ILO is not to promote or oppose free or managed trade per se. Rather, it is to represent and protect workers around the world as their governments increasingly move toward globalization. To achieve this objective, the ILO has identified three principle purposes:

- The formulation of minimum labor standards covering freedom of association, the right to organize, collective bargaining, abolition of forced labor, equality of opportunity, and nondiscrimination in the workplace.
- Technical assistance for vocational training and rehabilitation, employment policy, labor administration, labor law and industrial relations, working conditions, management development, cooperatives, social security, labor statistics, and occupational health and safety.
- Promotion of the development of independent employers' associations and workers' associations and the provision of training and advisory services to these organizations.

The ILO enjoys widespread support across Europe, particularly in Scandinavia, but is often ignored in many other parts of the world. It has no legal authority to enforce its conventions, and some of its proposals are seen in many countries as interference with basic labor market economics or with national sovereignty. Even the United States has refused to ratify most of the ILO conventions to protect workers' rights. Hence, the ILO seems to exist with varying degrees of effectiveness to represent the conscience of the world in its treatment of workers.

DEVELOPING GLOBAL ECONOMIC LITERACY

To be successful, it is essential that global managers understand how the global economy works, as well as the language used by economists and managers when discussing it. In other words, global mangers require some degree of "economic literacy" as it relates to international trade. To accomplish this, a layman's glossary is presented here, focusing on the more important concepts and terms relating to international trade, beyond those discussed above. These terms form the requisite vocabulary for managers involved in international business.

Balance of payments accounts. Records of a nation's aggregate payments to and receipts from other countries.

Bretton Woods Agreement. In 1944, forty-four countries met in Bretton Woods, New Hampshire, to design a new international monetary system following the collapse of the gold system, the Great Depression of the 1930s, and the Second World War. There was general agreement that fixed exchange rates were desirable in order to ensure long-term stability in international trade. The resulting agreement established two multinational institutions: the International Monetary Fund, to maintain order in the international monetary system, and the World Bank, to promote general economic development (described above).

Cartel. A group of businesses or nations that form an alliance to regulate production, pricing, and/or marketing of specific goods.

Commodity agreements. Agreements signed among groups of producers and consumers to guarantee stable prices for a commodity for a specific period of time.

Commodity cartel. A group of producing countries (e.g., OPEC nations, coffee- or rubber-producing countries) that collaborate to protect themselves from market fluctuations that routinely occur when such commodities are traded internationally.

Countertrade. A range of barterlike agreements by which goods and services are traded for other goods and services.

Economic exposure. The extent to which a firm's future international earning power is affected by changes in exchange rates.

Eurocurrency. Any currency banked outside of its country of origin. The *euro* prefix is a misnomer; eurocurrency can be created anywhere in the world. The prefix reflects the European origin of the market.

Eurodollar. U.S. dollars that are banked outside the United States. Eurodollars account for two-thirds of all eurocurrency.

Flight capital. Currency that is sent out of a politically unstable country for safekeeping in another country.

Foreign exchange market. The market for converting the currency of one country into that of another.

General Agreement on Tariffs and Trade (GATT). Established in 1947 following the Second World War, this agreement among 130 countries committed members to work toward the removal of barriers to the free flow of goods, services, and capital across borders. The most recent round of trade negotiations in 1993 (known as the Uruguay Round) further reduced trade barriers, extended GATT to cover services as well as manufacturing, provided extended protection of patents, trademarks, and copyrights, and established the World Trade Organization to police the international trading system.

Gross domestic product (GDP). The market value of a country's output attributable to factors of production located within the country's territory.

Gross national product (GNP). The market value of all the final goods and services that are produced by a national economy.

Invoicing currency. The currency in which an international transaction is invoiced or billed.

Most-favored-nation (MFN) status. A provision of any nation's trade policy that allows approved countries to export goods to the country under favorable tariff and tax conditions. In the case of the United States, MFN countries typically (but not always) support free trade principles, thereby allowing U.S. goods to be exported in exchange under favorable conditions. Signatories to the World Trade Organization automatically receive MFN designation among member nations.

Oligopoly. An industry controlled by a small number of firms, allowing significant control by these firms over the market.

Value-added tax (VAT). A tax (common in Europe) based on a percentage of the value added to a product at each stage of production and distribution.

In summary, this chapter has provided a primer on the global economy. An understanding of these fundamental economic principles as they relate to international trade is crucial for global managers to succeed. Management does not transpire in a vacuum. It requires the right economic landscape and the right institutional support. As such, knowledge of how the global economy works, and how multinational firms can adapt to and capitalize on this knowledge, becomes a critical asset in the global manager's tool kit.

KEY TERMS

balance of payments accounts	gross domestic product
Bretton Woods Agreement	gross national product
cartel	hard-loan policy
commodity agreements	Heckscher-Ohlin theorem
commodity cartel	human capital
countertrade	IMF conditionality
country competitiveness	industrywide rivalry
demand conditions	interindustry trade
dynamic competitive advantage	International Development Association
economic exposure	International Labor Organization
economies of scale	
economies of scope	International Monetary Fund
eurocurrency	intraindustry trade
eurodollar	invoicing currency
experience curve	laissez-faire
factor endowments	launch aid
flight capital	mature product stage
foreign exchange market	mercantilism
G-7	most-favored-nation status
G-8	new product stage
General Agreement on Tariffs and Trade (GATT)	new trade theory

(continued)

oligopoly
opportunity cost
Organization for Economic
  Cooperation and Development
  (OECD)
productivity
product life cycle theory
protectionist
relative factor endowments
soft loans

standardized product stage
supporting industries
theory of absolute advantage
theory of comparative advantage
theory of national competitive
  advantage
theory of relative factor endowments
value-added tax
World Bank
World Trade Organization

GLOBAL MANAGER'S WORKBOOK 3.1: HONDURAN TEXTILE TRADE

In 2004, Honduras was the third largest exporter of textiles to the United States. This industry accounted for most of Honduras's assembly jobs and was the backbone of its national economy. Honduras achieved this stature because of its abundance of skilled low-cost labor, its proximity to U.S. markets, and perhaps above all, its guaranteed U.S. market share. Indeed, for more than forty years, the U.S. government has allocated import quotas for textiles and other goods to various friendly countries, with each country receiving a certain share of the U.S. market. In this way, exporting countries had relatively predictable markets and could plan accordingly, while the United States was supplied with a steady and inexpensive supply of goods. Reasonable stability was assured on both sides. And since U.S. workers were priced out of this industry long ago, local politicians voiced few complaints.

This long-standing partnership changed dramatically in January 2005 when the U.S. government abolished country-by-country quotas on imported textiles.[11] Wholesalers and retailers would henceforth be free to buy their textiles from anywhere in the world at any price they could negotiate. As a result, Honduras now faces new and unanticipated competition from other leading textile exporters such as China, India, and Bangladesh. In this endeavor, Honduras's principal challenge will be labor cost. While the average textile worker in Honduras earns about $140 per month, a comparable worker makes $66 in China and only $19 in Bangladesh. For Honduras, this is no small problem, and its business and government leaders have mobilized to find suitable alternative markets or industries. The central question facing Honduras today is, What to do next? Maybe a more fundamental question is whether Honduras can survive free trade.

Based on what you have learned, please answer the following questions:

1. To what extent does Ricardo's theory of comparative advantage help explain the rise of the textile industry in Honduras?

2. To what extent does the Heckscher-Ohlin theorem help explain the rise of the textile industry in Honduras?
3. To what extent does Porter's theory of national competitive advantage help explain the rise of the textile industry in Honduras?
4. In your view, which of the above three theories of international trade provides the best explanation for the rise of the textile industry in Honduras? Why?
5. In your opinion, how will the termination of import quotas on textiles change the competitiveness of the Honduran textile industry? At this point, what do you think the Honduran government should do? What do you think Honduran business leaders should do?
6. Considering the various economic theories discussed in this chapter, which one do you think is most useful to managers in trying to understand how international trade actually works? Why?

GLOBAL MANAGER'S WORKBOOK 3.2: WORLD TRADE ORGANIZATION

The World Trade Organization was established to reduce trade barriers among nations. In view of the various competing political and economic interests of its member states, this is no easy task. Based on your research, consider the following questions:

1. Has the WTO been successful in achieving its mission to date? Why or why not?
2. Why is there so much criticism of the WTO? Is this criticism justified? Why or why not?
3. What are the principal advantages and disadvantages of using a global institution such as the WTO to facilitate international trade?
4. What recommendations would you offer to make the WTO more effective in achieving its objectives in the future?

NOTES

1. "Going East," *Economist,* March 4, 2004, p. 58; "Roads, Low Wages Help Slovakia Win New Auto Plants," *Wall Street Journal,* May 17, 2004, p. A18.

2. Stephen Power, "EU Auto Industry Faces Overhaul as Japanese Gain in Market Share," *Wall Street Journal,* October 14, 2004, p. A1.

3. "America Flies to War," *Economist,* October 9, 2004, p. 59.

4. Adam Smith, *An Inquiry into the Nature and Causes of the Wealth of Nations* (Oxford: Clarendon, 1776; repr., 1869).

5. David Ricardo, *On the Principles of Political Economy and Taxation* (1817; repr., New York: Dutton, 1948).

6. Bertil Ohlin, *Interregional and International Trade* (Boston: Harvard University Press, 1933).

7. Raymond Vernon, "International Investment and International Trade in the Product Life Cycle," *Quarterly Journal of Economics* (May 1966): 190–207.

8. Paul Krugman and Maurice Obstfeld, *International Economics: Theory and Policy* (Reading, MA: Addison-Wesley, 2000).

9. Michael Porter, *The Competitive Advantage of Nations* (New York: Free Press, 1990).

10. Fimec, "Press Kit 2003," http://www2.fenac.com.br/fimec; Rafael Vechio, "Autonomia Para a Competitividade: o Futuro da Indústria Coureira-Calçadista do Rio Grande do Sul" (Autonomy for Competitiveness: The Future of the Leather Shoe Industry in the Rio Grande do Sur), *Revista Electronica de Administracao,* July 2004, www.read.ea.ufrgs.br/read16/artigo/artigo9.PDF.

11. "The Looming Revolution," *Economist,* November 13, 2004, pp. 75–77.

4 National Trade Policy and Competitive Advantage

Shortly after Singapore won its independence from Great Britain in 1959 it faced a serious challenge. Now that it was on its own, how could it build a stable noncolonial economy and move toward increased economic prosperity for its 3 million citizens? Singapore was isolated in a generally underdeveloped region of the world (Southeast Asia), far from the burgeoning economic powerhouses of North America and Western Europe. Even Japan was thousands of miles away. The entire country encompassed only 239 square miles (618 sq km) and had no natural resources. On what basis would it compete?

To resolve this dilemma, a strong central government led by Prime Minister Lee Kuan Yew moved early to create a business-government partnership aimed at developing and coordinating the nation's most precious resource: its people. Lee created schools and universities and invested heavily in the development of the country's infrastructure, including a world-class airport, one of the largest and most technologically advanced deepwater ports in the world, and perhaps the best telecommunications systems in Asia. English was established as the principal national language. From former swamps Singapore built a clean, well-coordinated modern city-state based on technology and human capital. Good manners became a national obsession, and spitting on the sidewalk brought an immediate $500 fine. The penalty for possession of a controlled substance was death. And every university student, regardless of major, was required to take course work in human resources management. Singapore was determined to become a major player in the new global economy.

The government established several powerful agencies to guide economic development. The Economic Development Board was established to oversee the systematic planning for the entire economy. The board was given authority to control virtually every aspect of business and to offer incentives to attract competitive firms to help

51

build new industries, particularly in electronics. The National Computer Board was created to drive Singapore into the information age and exploit information technology as a targeted industry. The National Science and Technology Board was established to promote research and development in several technology sectors and to coordinate the efforts of several other government agencies (e.g., the Institute for Microelectronics and the Institute of Manufacturing Technology) in providing financial incentives for development.

With an increasingly educated population, Singapore targeted industrial development focusing on emerging technologies. Initially, it became a manufacturing center of choice for many multinational corporations, such as Hewlett-Packard, because of its cheap but highly skilled workforce. Since land was scarce, companies built high-rise factories instead of the typical factory sprawl found in many other developing countries. As it began to prosper and labor costs rose, Singapore moved increasingly into higher value-added economic endeavors.

One example of Singapore's recent success can be seen in its virtual monopoly over the hard disk drive (or HDD) industry.[1] Singapore identified HDDs as a potential market in the early 1980s, and through its continued determination, skilled labor force, and business-friendly policies it now controls more than 70 percent of the global market. Demand for HDDs is primarily driven by their technical and operating characteristics, allowing manufacturers to locate far from their consumer base. Companies go where they can achieve optimal manufacturing conditions for these high-tech devices, including skilled workers, reasonable costs, and excellent transportation and communications. Singapore provided just such a location. In the early 1990s, for example Seagate Technology moved its HDD manufacturing facilities to Singapore and is now Singapore's largest industrial employer.

Today, Singapore's workforce is rated as the best in the world based on factors such as relative productivity, worker attitude, technical skills, and legal frameworks, while Singapore itself is consistently rated as one of the world's most competitive nations. For Singapore, national planning worked. For other countries, however, it may not. As noted sociologists Ronald Inglehart and Wayne Baker point out, a review of Protestant, Orthodox, Islamic, and Confucian traditions "gives rise to cultural zones with distinctive value systems that persist after controlling for the effects of economic development. Economic development tends to push societies in a common direction, but rather than converging, they seem to move on parallel trajectories shaped by their cultural heritage."[2] In other words, each nation must find a strategy for economic development and international trade that is consistent with and supported by its own unique culture.

RATIONALE FOR NATIONAL TRADE INTERVENTION

In this chapter, we build on the example of Singapore and examine the issue of government intervention in international trade. We begin with a look at why governments create trade policies in the first place, as well as how they attempt to implement them. Next, we look at the specific issue of industrial policy as a strategy for

Exhibit 4.1

Countries Supporting Unfair Trade Advantages

Country	% in Agreement*	Country	% in Agreement*
United States	61	Taiwan	16
France	34	Singapore	13
Japan	34	Belgium	9
China	32	Australia	8
Germany	27	Canada	8
Italy	24	Netherlands	8
South Korea	23	Sweden	8
United Kingdom	23	Austria	7
Spain	17	Switzerland	6
Malaysia	16		

Source: Based on data discussed in Oded Shenkar and Yadong Lou, *International Business* (New York: Wiley, 2004), pp. 180–82.

*Percentage of global managers surveyed who rated each country as giving its own firms unfair advantages in international trade.

economic development, using Japan as an example. Common barriers to international trade are then discussed. Finally, the twin issues of international trade promotion and controlling unfair trade practices are examined. Throughout, the basic question to be addressed is how governments affect international trade and national competitive advantage through their policies and practices.

A central question that lies at the heart of debate over international trade and economic development concerns the appropriate role of government. That is, should governments take an active roll in facilitating local exports and perhaps restricting foreign imports, or should they limit their involvement to efforts to keep local markets open? This debate was mentioned in Chapter 2 with respect to the issue of free trade versus managed trade. However, around this central question are several other issues that relate to governments' role in trade. For example, should national governments protect so-called infant industries during their start-up phase so they have a chance to survive and grow into major global competitors? Should governments move actively against the products of foreign countries when they believe those products are being unfairly traded (e.g., sold for less than they cost to manufacture)? These questions are the province of national trade policies as they relate squarely to competitive advantage.

Consider: While the U.S. government continues to argue vigorously in favor of free trade and open markets, it, like most other nations, repeatedly acts to protect its local industries when they are under attack and cannot compete for whatever reason, fair or unfair. Indeed, a recent survey found that the U.S. government ranked higher that any other industrialized nation in the world in providing "unfair" support to its multinational companies in international trade (see Exhibit 4.1). Such support in-

Exhibit 4.2

Reasons for National Trade Intervention

Reasons	Purpose	Example
National defense	Control critical resources (e.g., food, infrastructure, military hardware) in case of national crisis	Japanese import tariffs on rice and other agricultural commodities to protect local food supply and local farmers
Infant industries	Provide sufficient time for emerging local industries to become sufficiently strong to compete globally	Korean tariffs and nontariff barriers on importing semiconductors until local industries could develop products and achieve sufficient economies of scale to compete in global markets
Local employment	Protect local industries from significant job losses and subsequent economic downturn	U.S. tariffs on imported steel to protect local steel producers and their employees
Strategic industries	Prevent loss of key strategic industries or technologies that could affect future economic growth and prosperity	U.S. and EU government subsidies to Boeing and Airbus to prevent the loss of key technologies required for the future

cluded applying diplomatic or political pressure, erecting various tariff or nontariff barriers, linking foreign aid or defense agreements to purchases, predatory pricing, and creating regulations that favor local industries. Thus, instead of discussing free trade versus managed trade—who is right and who is wrong—perhaps it is more accurate to discuss degrees of managed trade, since every nation in practice follows this approach. Hence, the question here is how and where—not whether—government intervention is appropriate in facilitating international trade.

At least four principal arguments can be advanced in support of some degree of government intervention in cross-border trade (see Exhibit 4.2). These arguments are based on national defense, protection of new and emerging industries, protection of employment, and protection of strategic technologies.

NATIONAL DEFENSE

The national defense argument for government intervention in support of international trade is based on the notion that in times of adversity nations must be able to defend themselves against hostile adversaries. To do this, they must be self-sufficient in critical raw materials, machinery, and technologies. Otherwise, they may not be able to access what they need for an adequate defense during times of national threat. As a result, many argue that nations should enact laws and policies that restrict foreign dominance over these critical industries. Indeed, most countries use the national defense argument in some form in their trade policies.

Two examples serve to illustrate this argument. First, after the oil crisis of the

1970s, the U.S. government moved to create a strategic oil reserve—literally storing massive amounts of crude oil in underground caves—to prevent another shortage in times of crisis. This reserve still exists. Second, many industrialized nations (including the United States) require that most of their naval vessels be built in local shipyards, despite the fact that construction costs are often far higher than could be found elsewhere. It is argued that because in times of war it may be difficult to secure the required ships from other (possibly adversarial) nations, countries are justified in restricting trade in this sensitive and critical area. These two examples illustrate the quandary many nations face in achieving a workable balance between self-defense and restricted markets.

Infant Industries

The infant industries argument for intervention in international trade is based on the practices associated with industrial policy (see Strategies for Economic Development below). Basically, the argument is that for a nation to develop economically it must build future-oriented industries (e.g., home electronics, semiconductors, automobiles) that can compete on a global level and generate foreign exchange. But this is often difficult for *late industrializers* (i.e., those nations that began industrializing later than others—for example, Korea and Taiwan compared to Japan) since global markets already exist with many strong competitors. As a result, emerging companies and industries cannot grow or develop. To remedy this situation—and get their country into the global marketplace—nations will often protect young *infant industries* from foreign competition while they develop.

An example of this can be seen in Japan's goal in the 1970s of becoming a major player in the lucrative metal-fabrication industry. To accomplish this, Japan eliminated all tariffs on the import of raw ores and ore concentrates necessary for metal production and fabrication. At the same time, it imposed sizable tariffs on the importation of fabricated metals. With inexpensive raw materials and little competition, Japan's metal-fabrication industry grew and developed into a major global competitor. As the industry matured, Japan reduced the protective tariffs and began to open its markets. It felt it was then in a position to compete.

Local Employment

As firms in many high-wage countries begin to lose business to lower-priced competition from abroad, governments frequently move to enact some form of tariff, quota, or other barrier to protect local firms and communities from significant job losses. This is the employment security argument for government intervention in international trade, and it is frequently practiced throughout the world, especially in more industrialized nations. An example can be seen in the U.S. steel industry: President Bush imposed significant import tariffs on steel in 2002 to protect less competitive U.S. steel mills. It was claimed at the time that local mills needed time to reorganize and become more efficient to compete globally. Foreign competitors and the World Trade Organization both disagreed and called the action protectionist and illegal under WTO accords. In 2003, the WTO declared this tariff to be illegal under WTO rules. However, it took threats of retaliation by both the European Union and Japan to convince President Bush to back down.

Another example of the employment security rationale for protection can be found across much of Europe, where local (and inefficient) farmers are often protected by import restrictions so they can continue their rural agrarian lifestyle. These governments have decided that it is in their national interest to retain and protect their traditional agricultural industries for both political and employment reasons. The imposition of more efficient farms could lead to massive unemployment in rural communities and the possible migration of unemployed farmers to unprepared cities in search of work.

STRATEGIC INDUSTRIES

Finally, national governments sometimes intervene in markets to protect strategic industries. Indeed, beginning in the early 1980s, a new theory of international trade began to appear, known as the *strategic trade theory*. This theory suggests that there are certain times when national governments must intervene in trade and create and nurture a particular critical industry to protect themselves from being seriously injured by the effects of monopolistic behavior from abroad. This theory is designed to apply only in markets that are incapable of supporting more than a handful of competitors on a worldwide basis.

The most common example used to illustrate this is Airbus, the massive EU-sponsored aircraft consortium.[3] The argument goes like this: If U.S.-based Boeing was allowed to achieve a complete monopoly in the commercial aircraft market, it could require any price for its product, and other countries would be forced to pay. Because of the massive barriers to entry into this industry (in technology and capital), other companies—and other countries—could not afford to compete. To protect their local economies from such restraint of trade—so the theory goes—industrialized nations should band together to create a viable competitor (in this case, Airbus). Such initiatives often require huge government subsidies. As a result of this action, the global marketplace for commercial airlines would remain competitive, prices would not escalate unduly, technology would remain at home, and the economies of the European Union would be better off. Needless to say, this approach to protecting local markets has its critics (including Boeing).

STRATEGIES FOR NATIONAL ECONOMIC DEVELOPMENT

There are many national strategies for economic development. Communism and socialism represent a state-controlled approach to development in which state bureaucrats determine what should be produced and how. As noted in Chapter 2, others believe in some form of a *free market* or unguided market, where consumers and the open marketplace presumably determine through consumer purchasing power which products and services will be made available at what prices. A third approach that has proved to be popular with particular developing countries is the use of government-directed *industrial policy* to shape development in ways the government thinks are best for the nation as a whole. Industrial policy is sometimes referred to as a *guided market* approach in contrast to the free or unguided market approach most often associated with the United States. It doesn't necessarily reject the concept of free markets; instead, it believes that such markets—especially in their early stages— require close cooperation between government and industry and government-led national planning to ensure that the national interest, as opposed to that of individual corporations, is best served.

The typical application of industrial policy by a country occurs when a partnership is created between the government and industry to facilitate the long-term economic development of the nation. The government plays an assertive role in guiding and supporting *targeted industrial development.* During this phase, the government works closely with selected companies to identify new (targeted) products or industries and then support company efforts to exploit these markets by providing them with key technologies, research funding, and financial support in the early stages of product development. Historically, such policies have been supported by highly protected home markets that effectively eliminated foreign competition—especially during the infant industries phase when a product or industry is in its early stages of development. This system is heavily dependent on close and mutually supportive business-government relations.

Two basic forms of industrial policy can be identified. The first is *export promotion,* in which national governments support local industries with capital and technology and then push them to take advantage of this support to mass-produce products for global export. Japan, then Korea, and now China used this policy in consumer electronics and in automobiles. By capitalizing on high-quality, low-cost labor, companies were able to produce products in large quantities at competitive prices and undersell the competition in foreign markets. By contrast, other countries (e.g., Australia, Argentina, India, and Brazil) have used *import substitution* as a development strategy, in which governments erect high import barriers that allow local manufacturers to build their businesses as a substitute for imported goods. Oftentimes, multinational corporations will then enter such countries and build local factories (and hire local workers) to avoid the import barriers. This, too, encourages local growth. Frequently, countries combine these two policies of actively supporting exports while protecting local industries from imports. Japan and Korea provide good examples of how this works, as illustrated in the next section.

By contrast, most U.S. businesses reject the notion of government-sponsored industrial policy as representing government intervention in restraint of trade and open competition. Instead of seeing government as a close ally, many U.S. firms see the government as an active opponent. The ideal role of government in the United States is often described as being a referee, keeping the playing field level and ensuring that all companies compete fairly. Ideal governments should create and enforce rules that stimulate competition. Instead of a government-led industrial policy, many U.S. businesses argue that the open marketplace and the investment community (led by Wall Street) should determine who innovates and prospers and who does not. Government should refrain from interference except to enforce mutually agreed upon rules governing commerce, such as antitrust legislation, employment law, or laws outlawing corporate corruption. In actual practice in the United States, however, both government and corporate actions often support somewhat more controlled markets with a high degree of government intervention aimed at supporting local enterprises in agriculture, services, and manufacturing. What companies say and what they do are often two very different things.

INDUSTRIAL POLICY AND ECONOMIC DEVELOPMENT: THE CASE OF JAPAN

Singapore's decision to go after the global market for hard disk drives, discussed above, provides a good illustration of industrial policy in action. The government determined that HDDs represented a logical step in its planned efforts to build economic wealth for its nation through a partnership between business and government. Incentives were provided to businesses, and the government required accountability. But Singapore's drive for economic success was actually based on what their leaders had learned from Japan. Beginning in the 1950s and continuing through the 1980s, Japan developed the preeminent model of industrial policy that would later influence many aspiring nations. Japan's efforts were based on the creation of a close, mutually reinforcing business-government partnership and made use of both export-promotion and import-substitution policies to achieve their economic and developmental goals.

From the beginning, the Japanese government used government-guided market intervention to select targeted industries or market sectors where they believed they could build competitive strength. They then supported targeted companies that were willing to enter these markets with government-funded technology and investment capital. New labor laws guaranteed an ample supply of highly skilled, low-cost, and largely trouble-free workers. Lastly, protective tariff barriers were erected to limit foreign competition within the country until the local firms had achieved the technological and manufacturing prowess, as well as the economies of scale, to compete effectively in world markets. Using this strategy, Japan first captured the global market for radios and televisions, then automobiles, and then semiconductors. The model worked so long as Japan's chief economic partners in North America and Western Europe did not object.

For several decades, Japan's industrial policy was formulated by the powerful *Ministry of International Trade and Industry (MITI)*. It is no coincidence that several of Japan's recent prime ministers have come from this powerful government agency. MITI's principal areas of responsibility included formulating nationwide economic policies and selecting specific firms to carry out these policies by entering specific emerging markets.[4] For instance, NEC received government support, encouragement, and financing in the late 1970s to develop a competitive edge in the semiconductor market. At the same time, Toshiba and Matsushita received help with technology acquisition and government financing to enter the home electronics industry. However, despite such intense planning, problems sometimes arose for other Japanese companies that were not selected by MITI for targeted growth and development. For example, Sony in electronics and Honda in automobiles had to build markets principally in North America because MITI initially blocked their development at home. Once these companies were firmly established in North America, they returned to Japan to begin successful marketing campaigns. Thus, while MITI could impede companies from entering nonapproved local markets, it could not completely control the drive of some of Japan's more highly motivated entrepreneurs.

In the past several years, following global trends toward more open markets and increased resistance from their economic partners, Japan has moved in the direction of less direct government influence over industrial development and corporate planning. MITI has evolved into a new government agency called the *Ministry of Economy, Trade, and Industry (METI).* The new agency still encourages targeted economic and industrial development but takes a more hands-off approach than its predecessor did. Also supporting Japanese business enterprise is the *Keidanren,* an association of executives from Japan's major firms. The *Keidanren* works closely with both METI and the government to formulate and implement policies that support both corporate and government economic interests for Japan. It is the chief spokesman for large industry and represents a powerful force in developing Japan's industrial policies.

Following Japan's lead, and before increased political pressures against such "closed market" practices emerged from North America and Western Europe, a number of developing countries in East and Southeast Asia adopted similar industrial policy strategies for their own economic development. The first four success stories that captured world attention (beginning in the early 1980s) became known as the *four tigers:* South Korea, Taiwan, Singapore, and Hong Kong. More "tigers" would follow, first within and then beyond Asia.

Today, WTO regulations prohibit many of the practices that characterized the original industrial policy model because they represent restraints on trade and violations of WTO agreements. Still, governments are still free within limits to help local enterprises grow and develop. What has changed as a result of the creation of the WTO, along with other institutional and political pressures, is that many of the newer government-led development strategies are more limited in scope and subtler in design.

BARRIERS TO INTERNATIONAL TRADE

Governments have many ways to encourage and protect local trade. One approach involves erecting trade barriers to protect local industries, often by ignoring or manipulating WTO guidelines. Efforts to erect trade barriers occur for many reasons and can be found throughout the export-import cycle. They can be classified into three general categories: (1) tariff or financial barriers imposed by exporting, importing, or third (or transit) countries; (2) nontariff barriers imposed by exporting countries; and (3) nontariff barriers imposed by importing countries. These barriers are summarized in Exhibit 4.3.

Exhibit 4.3

Tariff and Nontariff Barriers in International Trade

Barriers	Explanation
Tariff Barriers:	
Export tariff	Tax imposed by home country on goods as they leave a country
Transit tariff	Tax imposed by a third country on goods as they pass through one country on their way to another
Import tariff	Tax imposed by host country on goods as they enter a country; most common form is an ad valorem tax calculated as a percentage of the market value of the goods
Nontariff Barriers by Exporting Countries:	
Sanctions	Specific restraints against commerce with another country to force that country to change its behavior or foreign policy
Embargo	A comprehensive sanction to block all or most commerce with a particular country
Export controls and dual-use products	Restrictions on exports of sensitive goods or services to another (usually hostile) country; this is a particular concern when it involves dual-use products—products or technologies that can have both a civilian and a military application
Voluntary export restraints	Voluntary limits placed on the export of goods or services by a country or company to head off imposition of higher tariffs or import quotas from the receiving country
Nontariff Barriers by Importing Countries:	
Quotas	A numerical limit on the quantity of goods or services that can be imported into a country within a specified period of time
Government regulatory controls	Regulations on imported goods (e.g., product testing standards) that are not applied equally to local products
Restricted access to distribution networks	Structural impediments to access to local distribution channels as a result of cartel-like behavior by local businesses
Local purchase requirements	Requirements specifying that products must be either locally made or purchased through local vendors
Currency controls	Requirement that importers pay more for currency exchanges than local vendors pay
Investment controls	Government controls on foreign ownership of local businesses or industries (e.g., indigenization laws)

TARIFF BARRIERS

A *tariff* is a tax on goods or products that are traded internationally. Some tariffs are levied on goods as they leave a country (*export tariffs*) or as they pass from one country through another country to their ultimate destination (*transit tariffs*). However, most tariffs are collected on imported goods as they enter a country for ultimate sale or distribution (*import tariffs*). Countries levy import tariffs either to protect their local industries from foreign competition or to raise capital to further their economic development goals. In the United States, import tariffs are popular as a means of protecting politically powerful farming interests, especially for products such as fruits and vegetables. However, the United States also imposes import tariffs on major commodities and products that threaten politically powerful industries, such as steel (discussed earlier).

The most common form of import tariff is an *ad valorem tariff,* a tax that is assessed as a percentage of the market value of the imported goods (typically based on the product's estimated sales price within the country). Thus, in the United States, for example, imported cherries are taxed at 6.4 percent of their market value, pineapples at 2.1 percent, and leather gloves at 5.5 percent.

NONTARIFF BARRIERS BY EXPORTING COUNTRIES

Any government regulation, policy, or procedure other than a tariff or tax that constrains international trade is referred to as a *nontariff barrier* (NTB). The wide variety of nontariff barriers demonstrates the creativity of some governments in impeding trade when it meets national objectives. Exporting countries and importing countries can impose such barriers. Principal nontariff barriers by exporting countries—that is, limitations or proscriptions by a home country on goods or services that are intended to be exported to another country—include the following (see Exhibit 4.3):

A country may impose *sanctions*—restraints against commerce with another country—to force that country to change its behavior or foreign policy. Alternatively, a country (or group of countries) may impose an embargo against another country. An *embargo* is a comprehensive sanction against all (or most) commerce with a given country. For example, the United States has long embargoed all goods except medicine and some foods to Cuba because successive American governments sought to undermine the Cuban government and its policies. In both cases, home companies and their employees often face criminal charges should they violate these government restrictions.

Another exporting country constraint on international trade is export controls. *Export controls* are restrictions placed by one country on the export of sensitive goods or services to another (usually hostile) country. The United States and most EU countries routinely place export controls on nuclear materials and technology to third world nations as a means of restraining the development of nuclear weapons. This effort becomes problematic at times when it concerns *dual-use products,* products or technologies that can have both civilian and military applications. For example, some countries are willing to export sensitive nuclear technology to other nations so long as they believe it will be used exclusively in the construction of power generators and not for nuclear weapons. Other examples include machining equipment that can be used to produce either automobiles or cruise missiles and chemicals that can be used to manufacture either agricultural pesticides or poison gas. Judgments need to be made by the government of the exporting firms as to the desirability of such exports.

A good example of the lack of effective export controls can be seen in the 2004 revelation that Pakistan, a Western ally and nuclear power, had been exporting nuclear weapons technology for several years to nations that many in the global community considered to be unstable "rogue states" (e.g., North Korea and Libya). When news of Pakistan's sensitive exports became public, the Pakistani government disclaimed any knowledge of them and instead blamed the nation's chief nuclear scientist, who was officially described as working alone. Many global leaders were dismayed at Pakistan's willingness to export sensitive military technology in a world trying to limit nuclear proliferation.

A *voluntary export restraint* (VER) exists when a country acts voluntarily and preemptively to restrict its own exports to certain countries in order to head off the imposition of higher tariffs or import limitations. Often, these decisions are quietly negotiated between representatives of the two countries involved. An example of this can be seen in the Japanese automobile industry's continued practice of restricting exports of Japanese cars to European markets. Without this self-restraint, several EU governments had suggested that it might be necessary to impose import restrictions in order to protect their local automobile manufacturers. Indeed, when these voluntary limitations were loosened a bit in 1999 and Japan began to increase its market share in EU countries, governments again began to make noise.

NONTARIFF BARRIERS BY IMPORTING COUNTRIES

Finally, importing countries often impose (or try to impose) various nontariff barriers to protect their local industries and markets. Examples of typical nontariff barriers by importing countries include the following (see Exhibit 4.3):

A *quota* is a numeric limit on the quantity of a good that can be imported into a country during a specified period of time. Quotas are designed to protect local industries (e.g., agriculture, automobiles) from being flooded with lower-cost foreign imports. However, recent WTO agreements have made it more difficult for member countries to impose quotas, because they represent a restraint of trade. Instead, many countries are moving to a *tariff rate quota* (TRQ). This barrier imposes a low tariff rate on particular imported goods up to a certain quantity; after this limit has been reached, the tariff escalates dramatically, in effect limiting imports to the lower quantity.

Government regulatory controls are a gold mine for governments interested in protecting local industries. Government regulatory controls are policies and procedures implemented by national or local governments to regulate the manufacture or sale of goods and services. At times, such controls are intentionally designed to restrict access to or the competitiveness of imported products. Take the example of product and testing standards. A common form of NTB is a requirement that foreign goods meet a country's product or testing standards before they can be imported for sale or distribution. In theory, such testing is designed to protect local consumers from potentially harmful products, but in practice, such methods are often designed to restrain trade. Foreign firms often complain that such procedures discriminate against their products in favor of local products. In China, for example, imported agricultural chemicals must meet exacting testing standards that can cost as much as $5 million per product just for testing; these same standards are not applied to local Chinese manufacturers. Meanwhile, Taiwan uses very expensive purity testing standards for the importation of fruit juices (a local industry), but does not apply these same standards to its local firms. And the U.S. government has long prohibited the importation of pharmaceuticals from countries such as Canada, claiming that they cannot ensure product quality. Meanwhile, U.S. pharmaceutical companies reap windfall profits and U.S. consumers pay the highest prices in the industrialized world for medicines.

At times, foreign companies lose business because of *restricted access to distribution channels.* In such cases, normal distribution channels may be limited to established firms or firms that are associated with local stores, thereby making it difficult for foreign companies to get their imported products on the shelves for sale. For example, in Japan, most consumers buy their food and other products through neighborhood mom-and-pop stores that belong to interrelated networks of stores and distributors. These stores receive goods only from their network suppliers, making it difficult for outside companies (notably foreign companies) to get shelf space. Similarly, major Japanese *keiretsu* networks tend to buy largely from member firms, again making it difficult to break into such markets (see Chapter 9).

Many local and national governments require tax revenues to be spent as much as possible on locally produced goods and services. This is called a *local purchase requirement.* For example, the U.S. government specifies that government employees must travel on U.S.-owned airlines if at all possible. The U.S. Postal Service has a similar policy for awarding airmail contracts. In a like manner, Brazil gives preference to Brazilian firms in government contracts so long as the local company's bid is no more than 12 percent higher than foreign bids. In Belarus the limit is 20 percent. The idea here is that tax revenues should be spent to reinforce the local (and national) economy and sustain local jobs. Most countries have some form of such public-sector procurement procedures.

Some developing countries raise barriers to international trade through *currency controls.* Local exporters are allowed to exchange foreign currency at favorable rates to make their products competitive in world markets, while foreign importers are required to purchase local currency through a central bank at less favorable exchange rates, thereby raising the local prices for their products. Tourists are often required to pay higher exchange rates as a means of extracting as much foreign exchange as possible from the free-spending vacationers.

Many countries, including the United States and most industrialized nations, place some form of control on foreign investments and ownership. *Investment controls* are particularly common in such strategic areas as airlines, broadcasting, public utilities, defense contracting, and financial services. Such policies are designed to make it difficult for foreign firms (and possibly foreign governments) to control industries that governments deem are vital for national defense and economic stability. A popular type of investment control can be seen in various *indigenization laws* around the world. These laws require foreign companies that operate within a particular country to have a majority ownership by citizens of the host country. Such laws are aimed at protecting the local economy from becoming too dependent on the whims of foreign governments or multinational corporations.

INTERNATIONAL TRADE PROMOTION

In addition to policies aimed at inhibiting trade, governments also have at their disposal three principal means of encouraging or facilitating international trade: government subsidies, foreign trade zones, and export-financing programs. These programs are typically aimed at job creation or improving economically depressed areas by attracting new industries.

GOVERNMENT SUBSIDIES

Nations frequently play a role in trade promotion by offering *government subsidies* of varying types to local businesses that are actively involved in exporting. Frequently, these subsidies support government objectives or goals with respect to economic development, as was seen in the example of industrial policy above.

Subsidies usually take one of two forms. Some subsidies aim to help reduce the manufacturing or other related costs of products destined for export. In this way, the products are better positioned to compete in the global arena. These types of subsidies can be found in many products, ranging from agriculture to airplanes. For example, as noted earlier, competitors allege that Boeing receives funding from the U.S. government for aerospace and military research and applies the results to their commercial aircraft division. However, such subsidies are getting harder to defend under increasingly rigorous WTO rules.

Other subsidies take the form of tax incentives to companies that build a factory or other business in certain areas and create jobs, thereby supporting the local economy. By using such subsidies—usually from tax revenues—local and national governments hope to get the edge over other regions in job creation and economic development.

FOREIGN TRADE ZONES

A *foreign trade zone* (FTZ) is a geographical region where imported or exported goods receive preferential tariff treatment. (This should not be confused with a free trade area, which is discussed in Chapter 6.) Foreign trade zones are usually created to facilitate economic development and job creation. Most often, these zones allow companies to import components into the zone, process them further (e.g., assemble DVDs or computers), and then export the processed goods abroad without paying customs duties on the value of the imported components. Foreign trade zones can be small warehouses or factories or large cities. China has used several major FTZs to stimulate development, including the massive Shenzhen zone near Hong Kong. The *maquiladora* program, discussed in Chapter 6, is another good example. Both aim at job creation and sometimes technology transfer within specific regions.

EXPORT FINANCING PROGRAMS

In highly competitive industries, companies are always looking for any competitive edge possible. If two companies (e.g., Boeing and Airbus, which compete in the arena of military hardware) have equally good products and equally good after-sale service, then purchase decisions are often made based on the availability of financing—especially for very expensive products. As a result, many governments run government-owned agencies that are charged with assisting local firms in arranging *export financing*. In the United States, the Export-Import Bank of the United States, known simply as the *Eximbank*, fills this role. This bank provides direct loans and loan guarantees for about 2,000 transactions per year at a total annual value of about $12 billion. At the same time, a separate U.S. government agency, the *Overseas Private Investment Corporation (OPIC)*, provides political risk insurance to protect companies. Should a foreign government confiscate a shipment of goods by a U.S. firm, OPIC will reimburse the firm for its losses, as would be the case with any other insurance company. Most major industrialized nations have similar agencies.

COMBATING UNFAIR TRADE PRACTICES

When nations believe that unfair trade practices exist, their most likely official response would be to file a complaint with the World Trade Organization (see Chapter 3). Since the job of the WTO is to facilitate international trade and root out unfair trade practices, this agency is designed to be a company's and a country's first line of defense. However, many countries go beyond the WTO and try to police international trade themselves when they do not feel the WTO is acting fast enough (or favorably enough).

In the United States, for example, when an American firm believes it has been unfairly treated in international transactions, its first recourse is to file a complaint with the *International Trade Administration (ITA)*, a division of the U.S. Department of Commerce. The ITA determines whether the complaint has any merit. If so, it transfers the confirmed case of unfair trading to the *International Trade Commission (ITC)*, an independent U.S. governmental agency. If a majority of the six ITC commissioners determine that a U.S. producer has suffered material injury, it will impose duties on the offending imports to counteract the unfair trade practice. The most common forms of complaints brought before the ITA and the ITC involve allegations of unfair government subsidies that distort trade and unfair pricing policies (such as dumping; see section on anti dumping regulations below).

COUNTERVAILING DUTIES

A *countervailing duty* (CVD) is an ad valorem tariff on a good that is imposed by the importing government to counter the impact of foreign subsidies. It is usually calculated to roughly offset any advantage the exporter obtains from the subsidy. As a result, trade is driven by the competitive strengths of individual products instead of the subsidies provided by the government. For example, if a Danish subsidy to pork farmers allows Danish meats to capture a major share of the Canadian market through lower prices, the Canadian government will likely impose a countervailing duty to neutralize the competitive advantage of the Danish meat subsidy.

ANTIDUMPING REGULATIONS

In international markets, *dumping* occurs when a firm sells its product in a foreign market either (1) at a price below what it charges in its home market or (2) at a price below its cost of manufacture. Dumping is usually done to capture market share and drive out local competition. Most countries have *antidumping regulations* that outlaw such behavior, and countries often impose—or threaten to impose—countervailing duties on these products. A good example of this can be seen in the case of the Super 301 provision of the U.S. trade laws, discussed below.

SUPER 301

A method of controlling unfair trade practices that is unique to the United States is called *Super 301,* named for Section 301 of the 1974 Trade Act. Super 301 requires the U.S. trade representative, a member of the executive branch of the U.S. government, to identify publicly those countries that are engaging in flagrant unfair trade practices. The trade representative is then required by law to negotiate the elimination of these practices or, if that negotiation is unsuccessful, to impose appropriate retaliatory restrictions on the recalcitrant offenders, including tariffs or import quotas. In recent years, just the threat of being publicly identified as a violator of Super 301 has caused many companies to think twice about using unfair trade practices. The fact that the same government is prosecutor, judge, and jury probably serves to reinforce this reluctance.

In summary, governments often go to great lengths to influence international trade. At times, this involvement can be helpful both for global companies and for the global economy in general. At other times, however, persistent or one-sided government interference can become a serious impediment to trade. In such cases, managers and their companies are faced with a serious challenge in terms of making the best out of a bad situation. How they respond to this challenge will largely determine whether they, their companies, and the global economy survive and prosper over the long term.

KEY TERMS

ad valorem tariff
antidumping regulations
countervailing duty
currency controls
dual-use products
dumping
embargo
Eximbank
export controls
export financing
export promotion
export tariffs
foreign trade zone
four tigers
free market
government regulatory controls
guided market
import substitution
import tariffs
indigenization laws
industrial policy
infant industries
International Trade Administration
  (ITA)

International Trade Commission
  (ITC)
investment controls
Keidanren
late industrializers
local purchase requirement
Ministry of Economy, Trade, and
  Industry (METI)
Ministry of International Trade and
  Industry (MITI)
nontariff barriers
Overseas Private Investment
  Corporation (OPIC)
quota
restricted access to distribution
  channels
sanctions
strategic trade theory
Super 301
targeted industrial development
tariff
tariff rate quota
transit tariff
voluntary export restraint

GLOBAL MANAGER'S WORKBOOK 4.1: CULTURE AND INDUSTRIAL POLICY

It was shown above that industrial policy represents a unique approach to economic development. It is based on the creation of a close business-government relationship and government-led industrial targeting. Companies that cooperate with the government receive technology, capital, and protected markets in exchange. Indeed, partnership is at the core of industrial policy. With this in mind, consider the following questions:

1. Is the success of an industrial policy tied to the characteristics of particular cultures? That is, are some cultures more readily accepting or supportive of a strong government-led industrial policy than others?

2. If so, what are the defining characteristics of a culture that is best suited to use some form of national industrial policy for economic development?

3. In cultures and countries where strong government-led industrial policies may not work, what is the alternative that will bring about sound long-term economic development?

GLOBAL MANAGER'S WORKBOOK 4.2: CELTIC TIGER

Everyone is familiar with the Asian tigers, such as Korea, Taiwan, and Singapore, but few have ever heard about Europe's Celtic tiger, Ireland. In just fifteen years, Ireland has gone from Europe's worst economic performer to its best. Ireland's tiger-like performance in recent years has resulted in a per capita GDP that is 136 percent of the EU average; fifteen years ago it was 69 percent. Meanwhile, unemployment now stands at 4 percent, compared to 17 percent in 1987.[5]

What is perhaps most striking about Ireland's recent success story is how long it was in coming. The Irish economy remained sluggish (and worse) ever since it gained its independence from Britain in 1922. Only in the past fifteen years has Ireland's economy been on the move. Today it is a destination of choice of many multinational corporations from around the world, particularly the United States.

Why the change? Analysts credited the turnaround to several factors, including Ireland's improved fiscal and monetary policies, significant tax cuts, and economic development subsidies from the European Union. Indeed, Ireland's admission to the European Union opened significant markets to it. EU membership also made it more attractive for multinationals desiring to gain entry into lucrative European markets. Ireland also had a plentiful supply of skilled English-speaking workers, high standards of public education, and low corporate tax rates. This attracted countless IT, pharmaceutical, and health-care companies to invest in the region. The resulting investment and the jobs that followed launched an economic boom that continues today.

Ireland's economic development strategies have become a template for the European Union's new entrants from Eastern Europe and the Baltic region. If Ireland can do it, so can they, so the logic goes. However, from Ireland's standpoint, this imitation represents more of a threat than a compliment. That is, as more EU members mimic Ireland's strategy, Ireland's competitive position may suffer. Wages in the east are lower than those in Ireland, and future EU developmental aid is likely to flow east, not west. At the same time costs and wages are beginning to increase across Ireland as more and more global firms compete for the limited supply of skilled workers. So the question facing Ireland today is, What to do now? They cannot afford the luxury of resting on their laurels.

From what you have learned, consider the following questions:

1. Fifteen years ago, Ireland was widely considered to be an economic failure, a mismanaged country with little future. Irish citizens had emigrated by the tens of thousands in search of a better life. Why do you think it took Ireland so long (from 1922 to around 1987) to get its act together and begin building a vibrant economy?

2. Do you think the development policies used by Ireland can be applied successfully in Eastern Europe and the Baltic region among the European Union's new member states? Why or why not?

3. Ireland's recent economic success may be threatened by new EU entrants from Eastern Europe and the Baltic. What in your judgment should Ireland do today to meet the economic threat?

NOTES

1. Oded Shenkar and Yadong Luo, *International Business* (New York: Wiley, 2004).

2. Ronald Inglehart and Wayne E. Baker, "Modernization, Cultural Change, and the Persistence of Traditional Values," *American Sociological Review* 65, no. 1 (2000): 20.

3. Carol Matlack, "Mega Plane," *Business Week,* November 19, 2003, pp. 51–56.

4. Chalmers Johnson, *MITI and the Japanese Miracle* (Stanford, CA: Stanford University Press, 1982).

5. "Tiger, Tiger, Burning Bright," *Economist,* October 14, 2004, p. 42.

5 | Legal and Political Foundations of Global Business

SEEKING POLITICAL FAVORS IN NIGERIA

People often say that Nigeria possesses two attributes in abundance: oil and corruption. According to international trade experts, Nigeria is one of the most corrupt nations in the world. The prestigious *Economist* rates it second from the top on its list of the world's most corrupt countries.[1] If this is the case, how do global companies gain access to Nigeria's vast oil reserves to help supply an insatiable world demand for petroleum? Through bribery, of course. Companies that refuse to play—and pay—by the local rules risk being shut out of this lucrative market. But what happens if a company is bound by its home country laws not to engage in this form of bribery?

This is precisely the situation that confronted Halliburton when it sought a lucrative contract to develop a natural gas project in Nigeria. In 2004, both the French and U.S. governments simultaneously launched investigations into whether an oil consortium led by Halliburton paid $180 million in bribes and other illegal kickbacks to secure the contract.[2] If the allegations proved to be true, Halliburton and its officers would be guilty of violating the U.S. Foreign Corrupt Practices Act, a law that forbids U.S. companies or their employees from making any kind of illegal payments to secure business (see the section on laws and conventions on bribery and corruption below). Severe penalties, including sizable fines and jail time, await those convicted of violating this act.

Halliburton's CEO initially refused to comment on the allegations other than to say that this and similar allegations of violating U.S. trade sanctions with Iran were the result of "personal bias" against the company. He asserted that Halliburton won its contracts because of "what we know, not who we know."[3] Later, the company acknowledged "payments may have been made to Nigerian officials."[4]

The case of Halliburton in Nigeria illustrates a fundamental dilemma in international business. If a company follows its home laws but these laws do not bind its competitors from other countries, how does it compete in an environment characterized by corruption? How does it level the playing field? And how does it define and then implement appropriate ethical standards in a multicultural world? Such questions get to the heart of the legal, political, and ethical challenges facing global business today.

Legal, political, and ethical challenges to global business can be found in many arenas. To understand some of these challenges, it is useful to distinguish between challenges to business that emerge from the actions or inactions of a *host country,* a country where a global firm is trying to conduct business, and those that emerge from the actions of a *home country,* a country where a global firm is headquartered. For example, U.S.-based Intel manufactures semiconductors in China and Costa Rica, among other places. Its home country is therefore the United States, while China and Costa Rica are host countries to its global operations. To succeed, Intel must meet government requirements and local customs in all three countries. Multiply this simple example by the number of countries where many multinationals actually operate— Procter & Gamble, for example, operates in 144 different countries—and it is easy to see how complex legal, political, and social issues can become.

In this chapter, we examine four interrelated issues facing managers and companies as they attempt to conduct business in the global economy: (1) the legal environment of global business; (2) the so-called darker side of global business—political corruption, bribery, and the underground economy; (3) political risk; and (4) social responsibility as it relates to economic development, social development, and environmental quality and sustainability. We begin with an overview of several legal issues as they relate to global business.

LEGAL ENVIRONMENT OF GLOBAL BUSINESS

Local politics, laws, and ethical standards all play a crucial role in global business. Even the best corporate strategies or marketing plans can be sidetracked by unexpected legal or political impediments that serve to increase the costs or risks associated with doing business in a foreign country. It is therefore important for those involved in global enterprise of any sort—even if they never leave their home country—to understand the legal, political, and ethical environment of global business. As a former Citibank CEO observed, "We must never lose sight of the fact that we are guests in foreign countries and must conduct ourselves accordingly. Local governments can pass any kind of legislation and, whether we like it or not, we must conform to it."[5]

The *legal environment* of global business incorporates a number of relatively predictable constraints on doing business in various countries that are the result of legitimate (and sometimes illegitimate) actions of governments, including legislative action and government policies and regulations. These actions determine how business is conducted and, as such, are critical for the successful conduct of commerce across borders. The legal environment can be distinguished from the issue of political risk (see section below on political risk in foreign investments) in that it can largely be anticipated or understood in advance by firms who do their homework prior to foreign involvement. By contrast, political risk often represents threats to business operations that are less predictable or more difficult to anticipate in advance, as we shall see.

LEGAL SYSTEMS AROUND THE WORLD

Legal systems can vary significantly across national boundaries, and Westerners are often surprised to learn that the laws they learned or practiced at home may have no standing abroad. Why? Because legal systems in various countries developed over long periods of time and have been heavily influenced by historical, cultural, political, and religious traditions. For global managers, it is therefore important to understand the legal system of the country where contracts are being negotiated or disputes are being resolved. For example, in the United States, it is relatively easy to lay off employees without notice or compensation during difficult economic times. By contrast, in Belgium, as in most of the European Union, the law requires that workers being laid off receive at least three months' notice and three months' severance pay. Failure to adhere to this law invites serious penalties.

Some countries based their legal systems on long-standing *religious laws.* This is particularly true in Middle Eastern countries, where laws are often based on the precepts of Islam. Islamic law (*sharia* in Arabic) is derived from religious and legal interpretations of the Koran. For example, the Koran forbids charging interest on loans. As a result, businesses in Iran, for example, frequently charge up-front fees for loans instead of interest, while savings accounts receive a portion of the bank's profits instead of interest.[6]

Other nations have built their legal system on *common law,* the cumulative wisdom of judges on individual cases through the ages. Common law is in reality a compilation of case law over time. The legal systems of the United Kingdom and the United States have their roots in common law. An example of this can be seen in conflicts involving defective products and corporate liability. Due to the differing traditions in case law between the United States and the United Kingdom, American consumers have far greater leeway in suing manufacturers for defective products than do their British counterparts.

Statutory laws, laws passed through legislative action and meant to reflect popular sentiment, frequently supplement long-standing common law. For example, the United States prides itself on being an open society. To support this, the U.S. Congress passed the Freedom of Information Act, requiring federal, state, and local governments to make most governmental documents covering business-government contracts available to the public unless they involve issues of national security. The United Kingdom also prides itself on being an open society but tends to be more protective of the inner workings of government. As a result, the British government has greater leeway in keeping business-government transactions secret through their Official Secrets Act.

Finally, there are *civil laws* (or code laws), a codification of written statutes that identify what is permissible and what is not. Civil laws are frequently enacted by government agencies. An example of this can be seen in the nineteenth-century Napoleonic Code, which continues to serve as the basis for most laws in France today. All these types of laws and legal systems can affect the practice of global business and, therefore, it is important for global mangers to seek qualified help from legal experts from any country where they do business.

BASIC PRECEPTS OF INTERNATIONAL LAW

At the same time, it is important to recognize that certain international laws and legal principles transcend national boundaries and cultures. For example, all nations have a right to protect themselves from external threat and to exercise certain controls over their citizens, wherever they are living. Moreover, international legal principles require all nations to support the laws and court decisions of foreign nations, even when one of their own companies (or an employee of that company) believes it is being unfairly treated in these foreign courts. Finally, these internationally accepted legal doctrines allow countries to treat "aliens" (i.e., noncitizens) differently than they treat their own people. These principles are summarized in Exhibit 5.1. While most of these principles are aimed at protecting a nation's security or the rights of its citizens, there are times when the application of these principles can affect the behavior of multinational firms or their employees. As a result, experienced global managers must make an effort to understand both the legal system within a country and the legal principles that transcend national borders.

THE DARKER SIDE OF GLOBAL BUSINESS

While it is important for global managers to understand the legal systems in the countries where they do business, it is also important to recognize that many countries have both legal and nonlegal systems operating simultaneously. That is, existing legal systems in many countries are inadequate to safeguard such fundamental issues as property rights, personal safety, and the legitimate costs of doing business. While managers from more highly developed countries often view this problem in terms of right or wrong (legal or illegal), people in many developing countries often view it in terms of what is necessary. In countries where the government's reach is limited—or worse, corrupt—individuals and firms must often find alternative means in order to survive.

POLITICAL CORRUPTION

A major problem here involves political corruption. *Political corruption* refers to the degree to which governments are honest and evenhanded in the conduct of their affairs. Corruption and bribery obviously make it much more difficult to conduct business in a foreign country, not just because of the unethical nature of such activity and the unjustified increases in operating costs incurred, but also because of the resulting uncertainty surrounding future government actions and the actions

Exhibit 5.1

Basic Principles of International Law

Legal Principle	Definition
Act of state doctrine	All acts of other governments within their own borders are considered to be valid by the courts of other nations, even if these laws are illegal or inappropriate under the laws of other nations.
Appropriate forum for dispute resolution	A nation's courts are free to dismiss cases brought before them by foreigners at their discretion. This is done, in part, to avoid *forum shopping*, where plaintiffs seek a favorable location to bring their grievances against individuals, companies, or governments of another country.
Doctrine of comity	Local courts in one nation are obliged to enforce the laws and judgments of other governments so long as there is due process in these judgments and they do not violate existing treaty agreements.
Nationality principle	Every nation has legal jurisdiction over its own citizens regardless of where they are living.
Principle of sovereignty	In times of peace, each nation has a sovereign right to its existence, legal equality, jurisdiction over its territory, ownership of property, and diplomatic relations with other nations. National courts cannot be used to rectify injustices or impose penalties on another nation unless that nation agrees.
Protective principle	Every nation has jurisdiction over actions or behaviors that adversely affect its national security, even if the actions occurred outside that country.
Rights of aliens	There is no presumed equality between the citizens of a nation and aliens residing in that country. Governments are free to impose restrictions on the behavior of aliens that do not apply to their own citizens.
Territoriality principle	Every nation has a right to jurisdiction within its legal boundaries. It can make and enforce laws as it sees fit without outside interference so long as it does not violate international treaties or conventions to which it has agreed.

of competitors. Several organizations have tried in recent years to classify countries based on the degree to which political corruption represents a major problem in international business. One such effort is the Political Corruption Index, shown in Exhibit 5.2. According to this index, corruption is more likely to be found in Russia, Venezuela, and the Philippines (with scores of around 2.5 on a scale of 10.0) than in Finland, Denmark, and New Zealand (with scores around 9.5). As with any index, however, rankings of political corruption can be imprecise and are meant only to highlight the need for further investigation before making investment decisions.

When people think of corruption, they usually think of government officials illegally receiving bribes in exchange for undeserved favors. Such practices can obviously be found throughout the world, including in the most highly developed and wealthiest economies. However, there are also other shady activities that include routine business transactions between people that ignore or bypass local laws and

Exhibit 5.2

Country Ratings of Political Corruption, Risk, and Stability

Country	Political Corruption	Political Risk	Economic Freedom	Human Development	Judicial Fairness
Argentina	2.8	0.89	27	84.4	0.83
Australia	8.6	9.58	7	93.9	8.26
Austria	7.8	8.23	15	92.6	8.54
Azerbaijan	1.4	2.45	47	64.1	1.54
Belgium	7.1	7.21	16	93.9	4.99
Brazil	4.0	7.20	38	75.7	4.00
Canada	9.0	8.95	13	94.0	8.56
Chile	7.5	8.82	8	83.1	5.80
China	3.5	6.23	42	—	5.15
Colombia	3.6	4.27	33	77.2	2.51
Czech Rep.	3.7	7.56	22	84.9	4.89
Denmark	9.5	9.38	10	92.6	9.14
Finland	9.7	9.71	12	93.0	8.91
France	6.3	7.70	30	92.8	4.89
Germany	7.3	8.60	17	92.5	7.88
Greece	4.2	8.03	32	88.5	5.59
Hungary	4.9	7.85	23	83.5	4.74
India	2.7	5.92	43	—	5.17
Indonesia	—	2.52	40	—	1.74
Ireland	7.1	9.17	3	92.5	7.61
Israel	7.3	5.05	29	89.6	7.95
Italy	5.2	6.58	20	91.3	3.83
Japan	7.1	6.40	25	93.3	6.45
Luxembourg	9.0	9.63	4	92.5	7.26
Malaysia	4.9	7.55	39	78.2	5.86
Mexico	3.6	6.87	34	79.6	3.09
Netherlands	9.0	8.91	5	93.5	7.91
New Zealand	9.5	8.56	2	91.7	8.32
Nigeria	1.2	1.34	48	44.2	1.34
Norway	8.5	8.97	26	94.2	8.56
Philippines	2.6	4.25	37	75.4	2.89
Poland	4.0	3.65	31	83.3	2.57
Portugal	6.3	5.69	18	88.0	2.83
Russia	2.7	4.81	46	78.1	2.42
Singapore	9.3	8.63	1	88.5	8.50
Slovakia	3.7	4.09	35	—	2.96
South Africa	4.8	7.12	36	83.5	5.78
South Korea	4.5	5.64	28	88.2	4.80
Spain	7.1	9.00	19	91.3	4.87
Sweden	9.3	9.15	14	94.1	8.36
Switzerland	8.5	9.42	11	92.8	8.32
Taiwan	5.6	4.61	21	—	5.31
Thailand	3.2	7.27	24	76.2	4.89
Turkey	3.2	3.75	41	74.2	3.75
United Kingdom	8.7	9.04	9	92.8	7.31
United States	7.7	9.25	6	93.9	7.73
Venezuela	2.5	0.68	44	77.0	1.68

Sources: The Economist Pocket World in Figures (London: Profile Books, 2004); *The World Competitiveness Yearbook 2004* (Lausanne, Switzerland: International Institute for Management Development, 2004); Oded Shenkar and Yadong Luo, *International Business* (New York: Wiley, 2004); G. O'Driscoll, K. Holmes, and M. O'Grady, *Index of Economic Freedom* (Washington, DC: Heritage Foundation, 2002).

Note: Higher scores indicate less corruption and risk and greater human development and fairness; economic freedom is a ranking from high (1) to low (48).

regulations. Such transactions are usually referred to collectively as the underground economy.

THE UNDERGROUND ECONOMY

The *underground economy* involves business transactions that are essentially off-the-books or unrecorded. No public records are kept, no taxes are paid, and applicable laws are frequently ignored. Underground economic activities vary widely from paying under the table for a nanny or someone to mow the lawn to purchasing supplies for one's business outside of governmental regulations or oversight. Underground economies exist everywhere but are more prevalent in certain countries. According to *The Economist,* the underground economy in the United States accounts for less than 10 percent of the total GDP.[7] By contrast, in Brazil it is estimated that 40 million people out of a total population of 170 million are employed in the underground economy. Such differences have very clear implications for the conduct of business.

The underground economy is usually characterized by the manufacture or sale of products and services that are lawful but commercialized without the necessary licenses and without paying taxes. In many countries, a sizable underground economy is a sign that the legal system is not working well. The regulatory requirements may be excessively difficult to meet, making it difficult for small firms to comply, or the judicial system may be so weak that illegal activities may not be prosecuted or penalized.

The underground economy is a major challenge for companies operating abroad. Firms abiding by the law, complying with all regulations, and paying appropriate taxes usually end up with higher costs and a less competitive position than their underground competitors. Sometimes the "legal" price is twice as much as the price paid in the underground economy.[8] Countries with a sizable underground economy are usually countries with a low per capita income and price-sensitive consumers. This poses a challenge to global managers, who must be highly efficient in order to keep costs down and very creative in order to position the product competitively.

The underground economy often sells more than unregulated local products. Oftentimes, piracy, counterfeiting, and smuggling are involved. *Piracy* involves the overt theft of someone else's property rights for resale and personal gain. This can be seen in the widespread theft of intellectual property rights (such as software, CDs, DVDs) in such countries as Vietnam, China, Indonesia, Ukraine, and Russia.[9] *Counterfeiting* is an attempt to pass off illegally copied products as originals, particularly expensive brand-name clothes and shoes. Finally, *smuggling* refers to the illegal trade of goods that circumvents local custom duties, quotas, and other import or export constraints. Smuggling is most likely to occur when neighboring countries have significant differences in availability and prices of particular goods. In any case, such actions serve to diminish the possible return on foreign direct investment and are a good reason that some countries are publicly identified as centers of illegal trade.

LAWS AND CONVENTIONS ON BRIBERY AND CORRUPTION

Back in 1977, in response to growing political and business corruption around the world and several major corporate scandals involving U.S. firms, the U.S. Congress passed the *Foreign Corrupt Practices Act* (FCPA). This act was amended in 1988. The FCPA makes it illegal for American companies, their employees, or their agents to pay a bribe in any form to any foreign government official to help secure or retain business. Specifically, the act prohibits the following:

1. Any payment to a foreign official, foreign political party, or candidate for a foreign political office for the purpose of influencing any act or decision to obtain, retain, or assist in obtaining business for a company.
2. The maintenance of "off-book" accounts or slush funds.
3. Intentionally making false statements on company books, records, and supporting documents, such as payments for services or payments on expense accounts.
4. Engaging in overbilling, underbilling, or similar practices for the purpose of effecting transactions or improper payments that will not be accurately reflected in the company's books.
5. Making any payment that, in whole or in part, is used for purposes other than those designated by the documents supporting or authorizing them.

Following the passage of this law, American companies initially complained that the law placed them at a competitive disadvantage compared to other nations in securing business in countries widely known for corruption. Over time, however, first the World Bank and then the IMF began looking for a global solution to corruption. Finally, in 1994, the United States recommended that the Organization for Economic Cooperation and Development (OECD) collectively agree on standards for defining and outlawing bribery of foreign officials in international trade. While it was acknowledged that such proscriptions would not eliminate corruption, it was widely believed that having a general agreement on national policies would help mitigate the problem. In 1999, the OECD, an international body representing the world's richest nations, adopted the Combating Bribery of Foreign Officials in International Business Act. This agreement is commonly referred to as the *OECD convention on bribery.*

Modeled on the FCPA, this convention forbids the use of bribery or payoffs to secure trade. It also makes it illegal to deduct bribes and other side payments on corporate tax returns, a practice that was previously acceptable in many countries, including Germany, France, Greece, and Luxembourg. Today, however, only the thirty-five most industrialized nations have ratified the OECD convention, and enforcement by even these signatories is sometimes weak, making worldwide efforts to stem the problem of bribery and corruption an uphill battle and a competitive challenge for many global companies (see Exhibit 5.3).

An example of how global companies approach the issue of bribery and corruption can be seen in the case of Shell Energy. Shell maintains operations in 130 coun-

Exhibit 5.3

Signatories to the OECD Convention on Bribery

Argentina	Denmark	Japan	Slovakia
Australia	Finland	Korea	Slovenia
Austria	France	Luxembourg	Spain
Belgium	Germany	Mexico	Sweden
Brazil	Greece	Netherlands	Switzerland
Bulgaria	Hungary	New Zealand	Turkey
Canada	Iceland	Norway	United Kingdom
Chile	Ireland	Poland	United States
Czech Republic	Italy	Portugal	

tries and has often been confronted with demands for "facilitation payments" by local government officials. In response, the company developed a statement of general business principles that forbids such payments. Random internal and external audits are used to verify compliance with company directives, and company policy calls for the immediate termination of any employee who engages in such practices. Some believe this policy places Shell at a competitive disadvantage. Indeed, at least one major competitor acknowledges that it makes facilitation payments to safeguard its competitive position.[10] Even so, Shell continues its no-bribe policy. It reasons that is may lose some business opportunities in the short run but that over the long haul a strong antibribery policy is good business.

In the final analysis, managers should remember two things about bribery and corruption. First, bribery and corruption can be found throughout the political and business environment; they are not the exclusive purview of poor countries. Second, managers often have a choice in how they respond to corruption. In some cases, governments can help to minimize such practices. When this is not the case, companies can choose to not reinforce such behavior and hold their ground or do business elsewhere. While this may at times lead to short-term losses, it typically leads to long-term gains. The bottom line for managers and their companies is understanding what they stand for and not sacrificing principle for short-term promises.

POLITICAL RISK IN FOREIGN INVESTMENTS

In addition to the legal environment of global business and related issues of bribery and corruption, a third challenge for global companies is the extent to which their overseas operations are safe and secure. This issue is generally referred to as *political risk* and includes a number of factors within the host country that can threaten the viability of the firm's foreign investment and operations. Most political risks involve the possibility that political decisions, events, or conditions in a country or geographic region will change in unanticipated ways that adversely affect a company's profits, operations, or objectives, or some combination of them. When trouble occurs, investors and employees may lose money, profits, facilities, or even their lives.

Exhibit 5.4

Types of Political Risks

Political Risks	Explanation	Example
Ownership risks	Threats to a firm's property or assets in a foreign country	Intellectual property rights theft, expropriation, confiscation
Operating risks	Threats to a firm's ongoing operations or the safety of its employees	Unexpected changes in local laws, sabotage, bribery, armed insurrection, war, kidnapping, threats, terrorism
Transfer risks	Threats to a firm's ability to repatriate its investments or profits out of the country	Changes in foreign exchange controls

MACRO- VERSUS MICROPOLITICAL RISKS

Managers frequently differentiate between *macropolitical risks,* which affect all businesses operating in a host country, and *micropolitical risks,* which affect only certain firms or industries. When Cuban leader Fidel Castro unexpectedly outlawed using U.S. currency in his country in late 2004, everyone was caught off guard (a macropolitical risk). Cuban citizens, as well as all local businesses, were required to turn in their currency at a government-mandated 10 percent discount, leading to significant and unexpected losses.[11] Also in 2004, the U.S. government announced that only companies from countries that had supported its invasion of Iraq would be eligible to compete for lucrative reconstruction contracts (a micropolitical risk for companies from ineligible countries). In both cases, political risks can have a devastating impact on firms.

TYPES OF POLITICAL RISK

So what are the different types of political risks? Political risks can be categorized into three principal types: ownership risks, operating risks, and transfer risks (see Exhibit 5.4). All three of these forms are pervasive throughout the business world, and each represents a very real challenge to global managers.

• *Ownership risks. Ownership risks* are threats to a firm's property or the ownership of a firm's assets. Such threats can include *expropriation,* the forced transfer of ownership by a host government to a local firm or governmental agency with payment of some compensation, and *confiscation,* the forced transfer of ownership to a local entity without compensation. However, a far more common form of ownership risk is the theft of intellectual property rights, as discussed below.

• *Operating risks. Operating risks* are threats to a firm's ongoing operations or the safety of its employees. Such risks can result from unexpected changes in local laws, sabotage, bribery, armed insurrection, war, kidnapping, threats, and acts of terrorism.

• *Transfer risks.* A third type of political risk involves transfer risks. *Transfer risks* are threats to a firm's ability to transfer funds in and out of a country. This includes laws limiting the amount of foreign currency that a multinational corporation (MNC) can repatriate to its home country or its ability to use local currency to purchase certain items for import. This is often done through *exchange controls,* which are designed to force MNCs to keep their operating revenues and profits in the host country, as well as to purchase as much local content as possible for their manufacturing or service operations, thereby supporting the local economy.

Clearly one of the most challenging risks today involves the theft of intellectual properties. *Intellectual properties rights* include copyrights, patents, and branding of products—all of which provide value to the company and hence represent a loss when they are stolen. While intellectual property rights violations can be found in many countries, most experts believe that some of the worst violations can be found in China. These violations involve both counterfeiting and piracy of such products as software, music, and movies. Moreover, it is estimated that 70 percent of the 11 million motorcycles sold each year in China are knockoffs of original Japanese designs. Chinese companies also make look-alike products ranging from phony Perrier bottled water to phony Kellogg's breakfast cereal. Even the Chinese government values such losses to companies at close to $20 billion annually. It is estimated that many companies doing business in China routinely lose about 20 percent of their sales to such piracy.[12]

Despite being a signatory of the World Trade Organization, which bans such theft, the Chinese government has been slow to take action to stop these practices. Instead, it makes periodic and high-profile busts aimed largely at public relations, while claiming an inability or a lack of resources to take serious corrective action. As a result, many global companies have proceeded cautiously when entering such markets, where government support for ownership rights is honored more in words than in deeds.

POLITICAL RISK ASSESSMENT

Political risk is a major factor in corporate decisions concerning where to locate new overseas facilities. Each year, the *World Competitiveness Yearbook* publishes a list of countries based on their estimated level of political risk.[13] These ratings are shown in Exhibit 5.2, along with other indicators of political risk, corruption, and stability. Granted that wide variations often exist within a single country in terms of how this risk applies to individual companies, such evaluations nonetheless suggest caution for global companies.

Consider Argentina and Venezuela. Their political risk scores as shown in Exhibit 5.2 are 0.68 and 0.89 out of a possible 10.0. This ranks them forty-eighth and forty-ninth out of forty-nine countries, and alerts businesses around the world to be cautious in locating new plants there or signing contracts with local companies. By contrast, Finland and Luxembourg scored 9.71 and 9.63 (again out of a possible 10.0), ranking first and second on this same list. As a result, these two countries seem to be ideal locations for secure investments. Again, it is important to remember

Exhibit 5.5

Political Threats to Global Operations

Potential economic losses to global companies	Loss as a result of	
	Actions under the control of foreign governments	Actions outside the control of foreign governments
Involuntary loss of control over a foreign-controlled affiliate without adequate compensation	• Expropriation • Forced divestiture • Confiscation • Cancellation or unfair recalling of performance bonds • War	• Terrorism • Strikes • Extortion • Revolution
Reduction in the benefits expected from a foreign-controlled affiliate	• Restriction of access to financial, labor, or materials markets • Controls on prices, outputs, or activities • Currency or remittance restrictions • Value-added or export-performance requirements	• Nationalistic buyers or suppliers • Threats or disruptions to operations by hostile groups • Externally induced financial constraints • Externally imposed limits on imports or exports

Source: Adapted from J. de la Torre and D. Neckar, "Forecasting Political Risk for International Operations," in *Global Strategic Management,* ed. H. Vernon-Wortzel and L. Wortzel (New York: Wiley, 1990), p. 195.

that ratings of political risk are not always precise or reliable. Rather, their value lies in providing a cautionary note for managers considering business opportunities in various locations.

MANAGING POLITICAL RISK

What does all this mean for the global manager? Threats to business operations can come in many forms and in varying intensities. In some countries, entire local communities may boycott a foreign company's products over concern about foreign domination of local markets. Elsewhere, companies may face the forced divestiture of parts of their business by local governments. At times, governments may threaten outright confiscation or expropriation of an entire business for either economic or political reasons or may act to restrict a company's access to local markets. Terrorism, strikes, and wars represent very real threats, as do the frequently illegal but nonetheless pervasive actions by hostile local groups to curb business activities. Exhibit 5.5 summarizes such threats and highlights the fact that managers can be exposed to political risks not only because of government actions or inactions, but also because of events or circumstances outside government control. Such are the challenges of doing business internationally.

While political risk represents an ongoing threat to international business, compa-

Exhibit 5.6

Strategies for Reducing Political Risk

	Direct Approaches	Indirect Approaches
Reactive approaches	• Maintain redundant operations in multiple host countries • Hire host country employees and, especially, managers • Use home country government pressure on local host country	• Secure risk insurance • Do contingency planning
Proactive approaches	• Establish equity joint ventures with host country firms • Use local licensing agreements • Build collaborative relationships with locals • Promote host country goals	• Lobby home and host governments for support • Be a good local corporate citizen

nies are not without remedies. In fact, global firms can be both proactive and reactive in their efforts to minimize such threats, as shown in Exhibit 5.6. Reactive approaches include both direct and indirect strategies. Direct reactive strategies include establishing redundant or overlapping operations in more than one country so production can be moved out of a host country should trouble arise and hiring local host country managers who are both familiar with local laws and customs and well connected locally. Indirect reactive strategies include buying risk insurance (through such organizations as the Overseas Private Investment Corporation) and doing contingency planning in anticipation of possible local problems.

At the same time, there are several proactive strategies that can be initiated to minimize political risk. Direct proactive approaches include establishing an overseas firm as an equity joint venture or creating international licensing agreements (see Chapter 11) to share the risk with local companies or entrepreneurs, building collaborative relationships with influential local citizens (e.g., placing a well-respected local on the firm's board of directors), and promoting host country goals (e.g., creating local employment, helping build infrastructure, etc.). Indirect proactive strategies include lobbying efforts in both the home and host countries to secure added support for the venture and working hard to become a respected local corporate citizen (e.g., donating to local charities, helping build schools, etc.). The bottom line here in terms of protecting the firm's interests is the development of a mutually beneficial relationship between the company and its local host. As a general rule, the more respected and valued an enterprise is to the local government and local population, the less likely it will experience problems with local officials.

RISK AND OPPORTUNITY IN AZERBAIJAN

To illustrate the various political risks facing global companies, consider the case of British Petroleum PLC. When a consortium of several international oil companies led by BP was formed to extract oil in Azerbaijan near the Caspian Sea, it had no problem locating the oil.[14] The problem was how to get it to market once it was extracted. This problem was not just technical; it was also political. That is, every possible route for an oil pipeline carried considerable political, economic, or environmental risk, or a combination thereof, in this highly volatile region of the world. With a $3 billion up-front investment in pipeline construction alone, BP and its partners could not afford to make a mistake.

As BP considered its options for building a pipeline, none were particularly attractive. One option was to tap into an existing pipeline that went west to the Black Sea. Unfortunately, this pipeline passed through Russia's breakaway republic of Chechnya; the safety of neither the pipeline nor its employees could be assured. A second existing pipeline route to the west traveled through the rough mountainous terrain of Georgia, where security was difficult. Local residents routinely tapped into an existing pipeline in the area to siphon off oil to heat their homes. Moreover, some Russian politicians indicated their displeasure with this route, claiming that it threatened the energy security of their country. A less charitable interpretation was that they did not wish to lose their monopoly over the transport of Caspian Sea oil and the lucrative transit fees that this generated.

Turkish officials also opposed these two routes, but for different reasons. Turkey feared traffic jams and possible collisions of oil tankers going through the narrow Strait of Bosporus (which separates the continents of Europe and Asia at Istanbul) on their way to western markets. They suggested that BP build a new pipeline that would run from Azerbaijan to southern Turkey. Although this route would be expensive to build, Turkish officials argued that it was much safer since most of the pipeline traveled through Turkey itself. They failed to note that this route would also give Turkey considerable political and economic control over the pipeline.

Other pipeline alternatives involved going south or southeast. One alternative was to run a pipeline from Baku, Azerbaijan, south to Tehran and then south across Iran to the Persian Gulf. This would have been the cheapest route for the pipeline, but it would have traveled across a country that was often hostile toward the West. Moreover, the U.S. government exerted diplomatic pressure to discourage companies from doing business with Iran.

Alternatively, the pipeline could have been built from Baku across Turkmenistan and then southeast through Afghanistan and into Pakistan, ultimately ending in Karachi. A major problem with this route was that the proposed pipeline would also have run directly through Afghanistan, which itself has experienced almost continuous civil war since the 1970s and is presently occupied by a coalition of Western forces intent on eliminating the Al Qaeda terrorist network. Moreover, Pakistan recently experienced an increase in political turmoil caused by conflicts relating to both Afghanistan and India.

Finally, BP and its partners could have entered a joint venture with China to ship the oil to the east. Working with Japanese and Korean partners, China proposed financing and constructing a new pipeline that would carry oil along vast stretches of Kazakhstan and China and ultimately serve the rich oil markets in East Asia. In exchange, China wanted sizable transit fees from BP to use this route. Moreover, Xinjiang Province in western China was experiencing a small but tense rebellion by native Uighur separatists, who resented being exploited by the majority Han Chinese population in the area. How safe would BP's oil be?

Although none of BP's options looked very attractive, it had to find a way to get the oil to market. After long deliberations, BP finally decided to build its pipeline westward from Azerbaijan, across a relatively safe corner of Georgia, and down to the Mediterranean port city of Ceyhan in Turkey. The oil would then be transported across the Mediterranean Sea to world markets. While clearly not a perfect solution, BP concluded that this route minimized the dangers of terrorism and theft, avoided politically sensitive nations, minimized environmental threats, and presented a relatively cost-efficient and shorter pipeline across a relatively friendly territory. The new pipeline opened in 2005.

SOCIAL RESPONSIBILITY IN GLOBAL BUSINESS

Finally, what responsibilities do global companies have to the local communities where they do business? What are their responsibilities to help with local economic development? What are their responsibilities with respect to protecting the environment? What are their responsibilities to help facilitate social justice? This general area is usually referred to as corporate social responsibility and can be addressed in several ways. We begin with a look at how global companies can often impact local economic development for good or ill.

ECONOMIC DEVELOPMENT

One way to assess how countries have developed their economies over time, either on their own or as a result of foreign direct investment by multinationals, is to examine their level of economic freedom. *Economic freedom* is a measure of the extent to which national governments interfere or refrain from interfering in economic relations between individuals. In other words, how free local citizens are to engage in legitimate economic activities, including trade, owning property, and working in careers of their own choosing? Governments that consume larger percentages of their country's economic output, engage in price controls, limit property rights, promote unfair taxation policies, and sanction corruption in trade, banking, and other commercial activities tend to score low on this index.

Exhibit 5.2 provides a list of countries with their Economic Freedom Index rankings. Top-ranking countries in terms of economic freedom include Singapore, New Zealand, Ireland, the Netherlands, Luxembourg, and the United States. By contrast, people in China, Russia, India, and Venezuela rank far lower in terms of economic freedom according to this index. The question for both social critics and managers is the extent to which global firms have a responsibility to work to improve this situation.

Multinational corporations have been routinely criticized for ignoring their economic development responsibilities and exerting monopolistic powers in developing countries to such an extent that many smaller nations lose their political sovereignty. Companies dictate the terms of building factories in developing nations and governments can either agree or lose the jobs and economic development that such factories create. This assertion is consistent with Friedman's globalization thesis, discussed in Chapter 2. The basic argument is that because of the growing power of both multinational corporations and such global institutions as the World Trade Organization and the World Bank, whose officials are not popularly elected, national sovereignty to pursue a chosen destiny may at times be lost to the impersonality of globalization forces. Indeed, national cultures may themselves be threatened as foreign companies bring in their wealth, their power, and their customs. This threat is exacerbated by the belief in some circles that globalization is synonymous with Americanization. That is, some critics of globalization see a sinister plot by the United States, usually in concert with Western Europe, Japan, or both, to capture the world economy for their own selfish interests. The rest of the world thus becomes a colony to serve the financial interests of the privileged few.

Others take the opposite view—that an American-led coalition of willing economic partners is intentionally or unintentionally striving to use their economic wealth and democratic principles to motivate underdeveloped nations to join the twenty-first century. They suggest that when large companies enter an underdeveloped nation, they infuse capital and technology into the local economy and help build infrastructure that can be used by local entrepreneurs for development. They also nudge these countries toward greater levels of democracy in the process. In time, as the local economy grows in economic strength and power, the companies that began it all often find themselves forced to move elsewhere in order to compete.

Korea is often cited as an example of this development. Many Western companies, such as Nike and Reebok, entered Korea in the 1970s and 1980s to capitalize on the country's highly skilled but cheap labor. Tens of thousands of jobs were created and employee skill levels increased further. As the economy grew, however, these same companies were forced to move elsewhere in the 1990s since they could no longer produce their goods at world competitive prices. Korea had priced itself out of the market as a low-cost producer.

Who is right in this argument depends largely on one's unique life experiences and political point of view. What is indisputable, however, is that global firms entering less developed countries carry with them considerable wealth and power—and considerable social responsibility.

SOCIAL JUSTICE

As with economic development, questions are often raised concerning the most suitable role, if any, for global companies in helping achieve *social justice,* particularly in developing nations. That is, what is the responsibility of global firms in helping to develop social infrastructure, fairness, and improved quality of life in those places where they have operations? To answer this question, we must first look at how we measure social development. In fact, there are several ways to measure this, including assessing what has been called human development and judicial fairness.

One way to assess a country's level of social development is to consider where it is on measures of *human development.* This is often measured using the Human Development Index (HDI), a measure developed by the United Nations to assess quality of life across countries. The Human Development Index is based on three measures: life expectancy, literacy rates, and whether average per capita income is sufficient to meet basic needs for living (including adequate food, shelter, and health care). Country ratings for the HDI are shown in Exhibit 5.2. As can be seen, Norway, Sweden, Canada, Australia, Belgium, and the United States rank at the top of the list in terms of the most favorable quality of life, while Turkey, Thailand, and the Philippines rank much lower on the list. What does this mean? It means that people in countries such as Norway live longer, have a higher literacy rate, and have better access to food, shelter, and health care than people in, for example, the Philippines. Does this index change over time? Yes. As countries develop their economies and social structures, they progress up the list toward a better living environment for their people. Indeed, such is the goal of most honest governments.

A second way to estimate a country's level of social development is to look at its degree of *judicial fairness.* This measure represents an estimate of the degree to which a national judicial system is fair and impartial. Exhibit 5.2 lists country ratings for forty-six countries. As can be seen, according to these data Denmark, Finland, Canada, Norway, and Austria rank at the top in terms of judicial fairness, while Argentina, Venezuela, Indonesia, and Russia rank much lower on the list. Several major democracies, such as the United States, the United Kingdom, Japan, and France can be found toward the upper middle of this index.

While measures such as these are sometimes criticized for being too superficial and at times condescending, they nonetheless offer a useful way to gain a general understanding of the state of affairs in particular countries. The problem for global managers is to what extent they bear a responsibility for improving the conditions that go into creating these measures. This issue again places global companies on a collision course with advocates of national sovereignty. Firms that become actively involved in the social development of countries are often accused of political interference in national affairs, while those that refrain from such involvement are often accused of being indifferent to a nation's plight. There is clearly no winner here. As a result, even the most socially responsible global companies walk a fine line in their efforts to help improve local living conditions.

ENVIRONMENTAL QUALITY AND SUSTAINABILITY

Finally, research suggests that in many industries it may actually pay to be "green." That is, companies that are good environmental stewards also tend to be more profitable than their competitors, especially in more dynamic industries.[15] Such findings add substance to the assertion that socially responsible managers frequently find ways to support sustainability and environmental quality as part of their corporate strategies, not in spite of them, and that integrating environmental and sustainability perspectives into business practices can lead to improved overall corporate performance.

KEY TERMS

act of state doctrine
civil laws
common law
confiscation
counterfeiting
doctrine of comity
economic freedom
exchange controls
expropriation
Foreign Corrupt Practices Act
forum shopping
home country
host country
human development
intellectual properties rights
judicial fairness
legal environment
macropolitical risks
micropolitical risks

nationality principle
OECD convention on bribery
operating risks
ownership risks
piracy
political corruption
political risk
principle of sovereignty
protective principle
religious laws
rights of aliens
sharia
smuggling
social justice
statutory laws
territoriality principle
transfer risks
underground economy

GLOBAL MANAGER'S WORKBOOK 5.1: LEVELING THE PLAYING FIELD

The example of Halliburton in Nigeria highlights a common challenge faced by many global firms. Both the U.S. Foreign Corrupt Practices Act and the OECD Convention on Bribery forbid companies from paying bribes to foreign officials or governments to secure business. However, the FCPA applies only to U.S. companies, while OECD guidelines apply only to OECD member states. Meanwhile, many other nations around the world have not signed the OECD convention and are therefore not bound by its requirements.

1. Do you think U.S. and other OECD member companies should be required to abide by laws and conventions against bribery while some of their principal competitors who are not from OECD member countries do not?
2. If so, how can ethical companies compete in a global environment characterized by bribery and corruption?
3. What can the U.S. government or the OECD do to level the playing field and reduce corruption in global markets?

GLOBAL MANAGER'S WORKBOOK 5.2:
MANUFACTURING IN UNDERDEVELOPED COUNTRIES

Based on what you have learned, as well as your own beliefs and values, what are the pros and cons of manufacturing in underdeveloped countries? More specifically, is the issue of manufacturing in developing countries (such as Mexico, Vietnam, or Nigeria) an issue of corporate profitability or social responsibility? Consider the following issues.

1. In your view, are workers in underdeveloped countries who are employed by large multinational companies routinely being exploited? Why or why not?
2. If your answer to question 1 is yes, who is exploiting them? Companies? Governments? Families? Customers?
3. If your answer to question 1 is yes, what specific (and realistic) actions would you recommend to help alleviate this exploitation?
4. In general, what responsibilities do multinationals have to local communities when establishing or running factories in developing countries? How can they meet these obligations and still remain competitive in the global economy?
5. What obligations do multinationals have to their home country workers (e.g., U.S., German, or Japanese employees) when considering shifting production offshore (e.g., to Latin America, Asia, or Africa)? How can firms achieve a balance between these competing responsibilities?
6. If you were in charge of a large multinational firm, under what conditions would you build or operate a manufacturing facility in an underdeveloped country?

NOTES

1. *The Economist Pocket World in Figures* (London: Profile Books, 2004).

2. Russell Gold, "SEC Investigates Halliburton Unit Over Payments," *Wall Street Journal*, June 14, 2004, p. A3; Russell Gold and Charles Fleming, "In Halliburton's Nigeria Project, a Search for Bribes to a Dictator," *Wall Street Journal*, September 29, 2004, p. A1.

3. "Halliburton: A Scandal-Hit Firm Fights Back," *Economist*, February 19, 2004, p. A1.

4. Russell Gold, "Halliburton Concedes Possibility of Payments to Nigerian Officials," *Wall Street Journal*, November 8, 2004, p. A5.

5. Cited in Susan Schneider and Jean-Louis Barsoux, *Managing Across Cultures*, 2d ed. (London: Prentice-Hall, 2003), p. 310.

6. Virginia Postrel, "Economics and Islam," *New York Times*, August 12, 2004, p. 1.

7. "Blinded by the Dark," *Economist*, April 2, 1998, p. 15.

8. Bryan Husted, "Wealth, Culture and Corruption," *Journal of International Business Studies* 30, no. 2 (1999): 339–59.

9. The *Economist Pocket World in Figures.*

10. "Doing Well by Doing Good," *Economist*, April 22, 2000, p. 65.

11. "U.S. Dollar Out of Circulation in Cuba," *Register-Guard*, November 9, 2004, p. A2.

12. D. Chow, A *Primer on Foreign Investment Enterprises and Protection of Intellectual Property in China* (The Hague: Kluwer, 2002).

13. *World Competitiveness Yearbook 2004* (Lausanne, Switzerland: International Institute for Management Development, 2004).

14. Brushan Bahee, "Caspian Sea Crude Nears Delivery," *Wall Street Journal*, October 22, 2004, p. A12.

15. Michael Russo and Paul Fouts, "A Resource-based Perspective on Corporate Environmental Performance and Profitability," *Academy of Management Journal* 40, no. 3 (1997): 534–59.

6 Economic Integration and Regional Trading Blocs

POLAND JOINS THE EUROPEAN UNION

In May 2004, Poland and nine other predominantly Eastern European and Baltic countries joined fifteen current EU members to create an expanded and more powerful European Union.[1] Poland is by far the largest of the European Union's new members, with a population of 39 million and a gross domestic product of $230 billion. This accounts for more than half of the newcomers' total population and almost half of their total GDP. Poland became an instant leader in the larger European economic and political community. But exactly how Poland will play out this role remains to be seen.

Economic observers suggest that there are in fact two Polands. The first is a country consisting of scrappy young entrepreneurs—hardworking, well educated, and eager for foreign contracts and business opportunities. Indeed, more than 1.5 million new small and medium-sized businesses have begun operation in the past decade. Many of these are eager to meet the challenges of a new Europe. The other Poland, however, is a dysfunctional bureaucratic political system grafted onto a communist-era welfare state that seems to work hard to impede business and economic development. It supports nonproductive farmers and ignores the plight of its industrial and services sectors. Companies must file tax returns monthly, and decision making in government bureaucracies can be excruciatingly slow. Indeed, aspiring entrepreneurs can wait up to a year just to get permission to establish a new company. The roads and infrastructure in Poland are among the worst in Europe, and unemployment affects more than 20 percent of the workforce, while Poland's deficit as a percentage of GDP is the largest in Europe.

Membership in the European Union offers both opportunities and threats for a country like Poland. It could follow the example of Spain and Ireland, which made wise use of the European Union's developmental support. These countries restructured their state finances, deregulated their economies, and encouraged new busi-

90

ness development. Today, Spain and Ireland have solid economies. Alternatively, Poland could follow the example of Greece, which wasted billions of euros in EU subsidies on inefficient and corruption-plagued state-run companies and is still considered an economic basket case by many of its neighbors.

Many are hoping Poland will capitalize on the opportunities created by EU membership. Poland's labor costs are one-sixth those of neighboring Germany, and its average industrial productivity rate is rising at almost 4 percent per year, twice the EU average. Indeed, many economists hope that increased competition from low-cost and increasingly productive Polish factories and services will pressure Western European companies to restructure and become more efficient. The question seems to be whether Poland can reinvent its government in such a way that supports rather than impedes the nation's future economic and political progress.

RATIONALE FOR REGIONAL ECONOMIC INTEGRATION

As the global economy becomes more and more competitive, nations—and entire economic regions—have intensified their search for effective means to compete and prosper. An increasingly popular strategy involves regional economic integration. *Regional economic integration* occurs when two or more countries within a geographic region create a formal agreement to cooperate in ways that facilitate economic development and regional prosperity. These *regional trading blocs*, as they are called, typically agree to cooperate for two principal reasons: (1) to increase free trade within their collective national boundaries; and (2) to strengthen their region's ability to compete more effectively in global markets.

There are currently more than one hundred regional trading blocs around the world, although many have had little genuine impact on trade due to political conflicts and national self-interest. Key regional trading blocs are shown in Exhibit 6.1. While these trading blocs generally serve to stimulate trade among member states, there is also a tendency for this trade to come at the expense of trade with other nations that are not members.

Regional trading blocs generally serve to promote regionalism (that is, a feeling of "us" against "them"). This can have both positive and negative consequences. Such blocs can promote efficiency in the global economy to the extent that they promote *trade creation*; that is, the shifting of production from high-cost producers to low-cost producers within the bloc. For example, as ironic as it may sound, Germany was able to capture the European market for the manufacture of spaghetti away from Italy, not because it made better spaghetti but because it became the low-cost producer of the product. Germany used its highly efficient factories to capture the market from Italy's numerous small and inefficient family producers.

Efficiency can be impeded, however, by *trade diversion*, where production is shifted from low-cost external (nonmember) producers to higher cost internal (member) producers. A good example of this can be seen in the transfer of television tube and flat panel display manufacturing for American-bound televisions from Asia to Mexico, even though the Asian manufacturers were cheaper. Why was this done? NAFTA's rules of origin require that products entering the U.S. market duty-free must contain

Exhibit 6.1

Major Regional Trade Associations

Regional Trade Associations	Member States
Andean Community	Bolivia, Colombia, Ecuador, Peru, Venezuela
Asia-Pacific Economic Cooperation (APEC)	Australia, Brunei, Canada, Chile, China, Hong Kong, Indonesia, Japan, Malaysia, Mexico, New Zealand, Papua New Guinea, Peru, Philippines, Russia, Singapore, South Korea, Taiwan, Thailand, United States, Vietnam
Association of Southeast Asian Nations (ASEAN)	Brunei, Cambodia, Indonesia, Laos, Malaysia, Myanmar, Philippines, Singapore, Thailand, Vietnam
Central American Common Market	Costa Rica, El Salvador, Guatemala, Honduras, Nicaragua, Panama
Caribbean Community	Antigua and Barbuda, Bahamas, Barbados, Belize, Dominica, Grenada, Guyana, Jamaica, Montserrat, St. Kitts-Nevis, St. Lucia, St. Vincent and the Grenadines, Suriname, Trinidad-Tobago
Economic Community of West African States	Benin, Burkina Faso, Cape Verde, Gambia, Ghana, Guinea, Guinea-Bissau, Ivory Coast, Liberia, Mali, Mauritania, Niger, Nigeria, Senegal, Sierra Leone, Togo
European Union (EU)	Austria, Belgium, Cypress, Czech Republic, Denmark, Estonia, Finland, France, Germany, Greece, Hungary, Ireland, Italy, Latvia, Lithuania, Luxembourg, Malta, Netherlands, Poland, Portugal, Slovakia, Slovenia, Spain, Sweden, United Kingdom
Gulf Cooperation Council	Bahrain, Kuwait, Oman, Qatar, Saudi Arabia, United Arab Emirates
Latin American Integration Association	Argentina, Bolivia, Brazil, Chile, Colombia, Cuba, Ecuador, Mexico, Paraguay, Peru, Uruguay, Venezuela
Southern Common Market (Mercosur)	Argentina, Brazil, Paraguay, Uruguay
North American Free Trade Agreement (NAFTA)	Canada, Mexico, United States
Southeast Asian Association for Regional Cooperation	Bangladesh, Bhutan, India, Maldives, Nepal, Pakistan, Sri Lanka
Southern African Customs Union	Botswana, Lesotho, Namibia, South Africa, Swaziland

critical components that are manufactured in NAFTA countries, including Mexico.[2] As a result, much of the global production of television tubes and flat panel displays was shifted from a lower-cost external producer to a higher-cost internal provider to avoid import duties.

DEGREES OF REGIONAL ECONOMIC INTEGRATION

Economic integration can take several forms depending on the extent of integration desired by the members of the regional trading bloc. The forms range from a

Exhibit 6.2

Types of Regional Economic Integration

Form of Organization	Degree of Economic Integration
Free trade area	Elimination of internal trade barriers (e.g., tariffs, quotas) between various member states
Customs union	Elimination of internal trade barriers, plus a common policy on external trade with nonmembers
Common market	Elimination of internal trade barriers, a common policy on external trade, and the free movement of factors of production (e.g., labor, capital) across member states
Economic union	Harmonization of members' economic policies, including monetary policy, fiscal policy, social welfare policy; creation of one integrated economy
Political union	Substantial political as well and economic union among member states; creation of some form of international government

free trade area that reduces trade barriers between its members (e.g., elimination of import quotas and tariffs) to a full political union where countries join together politically as well as economically for common cause. Indeed, some trading associations, such as the *Asia-Pacific Economic Cooperation* (or APEC), are not really regional trading blocs at all in a technical sense, but rather loosely coupled cooperative ventures created by the countries of a particular region (the Asia-Pacific region in the case of APEC) to promote multilateral economic cooperation in trade and investment.

There are essentially five types of regional trading blocs: free trade area, customs union, common market, economic union, and political union (see Exhibit 6.2). As countries move from the relative independence of a free trade area to the much more highly integrated economic or political union, they increasingly lose political and economic autonomy and sovereignty as power is shifted to the central coordinating body of the bloc.

FREE TRADE AREA

A *free trade area* represents an agreement between two or more countries to eliminate internal trade barriers. (As noted in Chapter 4, a free trade area should not be confused with a foreign trade zone, where a country sets aside a specific geographical region—such as Shenzhen in China—and provides preferential tariff treatment within this zone for both imported and exported goods.) In a free trade area, goods and services can flow freely between the signatory countries duty-free. Free trade areas help expand markets for companies doing business within the area and sometimes make competing against those outside the area easier because of the economies of scale achieved through group membership.

A good example of a free trade area is that established by the *North American Free Trade Agreement (NAFTA)*, an agreement among Canada, Mexico, and the

United States to eliminate all trade barriers on the flow of goods across national borders. NAFTA is discussed in detail below to illustrate how a free trade area works (see section on NAFTA and the Maquiladora Program). The *Association of Southeast Asian Nations (ASEAN)* is another example of a free trade area. Although originally established in 1967 to promote peace, stability, and economic growth in the region, ASEAN has been slow to eliminate tariff barriers between its members.

CUSTOMS UNION

A *customs union* is an agreement among several nations not only to open a free trade area among their countries but also to develop a common policy on trade as it relates to nonmembers. It thus increases the "us versus them" feeling between nations as members of the customs union work to solidify the advantages they enjoy through membership.

An example of a customs union can be seen in the *Andean Community* (also called the Andean Pact), consisting of five nations in the northwest corner of South America. This venture, initially created in 1969 but considerably strengthened in 1990, was established to harmonize tariffs and foreign investment policies, and to develop a common external tariff for nonmembers. Mercosur (see section on Degrees of Regional Economic Integration below) is another example of a customs union, although it has long-term plans to evolve into a common market.

COMMON MARKET

A common market goes one step further than a customs union, in terms of both solidarity and loss of national autonomy. A *common market* combines the advantages of a free trade area and a customs union with a further agreement to eliminate barriers to the movement of the factors of production (such as labor, capital, technology) across members' borders. The predecessor of the current European Union was created as a common market, and it was envisioned that workers, capital, and technologies would easily cross member borders in ways that would enhance collective productivity and competitiveness to the benefit of all. While this occurred to a degree, it was not initially wholly successful. In particular, local politics and language barriers served to limit the effectiveness of many aspects of this agreement as member states continued to raise hurdles to the free movement of people and products across borders.

One of the best examples of an emerging common market is *Mercosur* (a Spanish acronym for "southern common market"), created in 1991 as a result of the *Treaty of Asunción*. Mercosur represents a coalition of South American nations including Argentina, Brazil, Paraguay, and Uruguay. Bolivia and Chile are currently associate members. The creation of Mercosur has led to a significant reduction in tariffs, resulting in rapidly increasing trade among members. It has also created an antidumping agreement to protect itself from nonmembers. As a result of the 1995 Ouro Preto Protocol, Mercosur now negotiates trade treaties with other nonmember nations and trading blocs on behalf of its members. Plans call for a directly elected Mercosur-wide parliament by 2006, not unlike the European Parliament. It is intended that this parliament will assume legislative decision-making authority on trade issues that affect Mercosur's members, replacing to some extent the various national legislatures.

ECONOMIC UNION

An *economic union* continues the move toward greater economic integration and less national autonomy by coordinating members' economic policies, such as monetary policy, fiscal policy, taxation, and social welfare policy, in order to blend economies into a single and hopefully more competitive economic entity. The most prominent example of an economic union is the current *European Union* (see section below on The European Union). The European Union created a central bank to manage fiscal policies, a new currency (the *euro*), a commission to oversee and implement a myriad of rules and policies governing members' behavior both toward their fellow member states and toward outsiders, and a court system to remedy member grievances. Throughout, the goal of the European Union has been to create a stronger, more competitive entity that is capable of fostering greater economic development and prosperity in an increasingly complex global economy.

POLITICAL UNION

Finally, at least in theory, members of a trading bloc can add a political dimension to their existing economic dimension and form a *political union*. The former Union of Soviet Socialist Republics (USSR) was supposed to be a political union of independent states, although it quickly degenerated into a centralized dictatorship.

A more recent example of a political union in the making can be seen in the ongoing efforts by some EU members to increasingly subordinate national political interests and decision making to the will of a multistate political organization. The creation of the European Parliament was the first step in such a union. This was followed by efforts to achieve a common multinational policy on taxation, foreign affairs, and defense. Recently, efforts have accelerated to implement a European constitution that takes precedence over the actions of individual national parliaments. In exchange for national subordination to the common good, member states would gain increased efficiencies in the conduct of political affairs (e.g., income taxes could be centrally collected and distributed) and increased bargaining power in the international arena. In the case of the European Union, this saga continues as a grand social and political experiment.

Based on this overview of variations in regional trading blocs, it is instructive to look at two examples of such efforts in some detail. Here, NAFTA and the European Union are examined and compared as illustrations of both a fairly straightforward economic arrangement and a highly complex economic and political one.

NAFTA AND THE *MAQUILADORA* PROGRAM

One of the most attractive manufacturing areas in the world today is Mexico. This is due in part to Mexico's close proximity to large North American markets and in part to recent efforts by Canada, Mexico, and the United States to forge closer economic ties, especially in the area of manufacturing. These ties were formalized through the creation of NAFTA, the North American Free Trade Agreement.

Contemporary trade relations among Canada, Mexico, and the United States evolved through three relatively distinct phases. Phase one, begun in 1965, was the creation of the *maquiladora* program in Mexico—a program to allow for the off-shore (or out-of-country) manufacture of goods in Mexico for reexport to the U.S. market. Phase two, begun in 1994, was the creation of a two-way free trade area with the establishment of NAFTA and encompassing Canada, Mexico, and the United States. Phase three involves the efforts by many governments in both North and South America to establish a *Free Trade Area of the Americas (FTAA)* incorporating all of North, Central, and South America.

MAQUILADORA PROGRAM

The *maquiladora* program was launched in 1965 prior to NAFTA as a means of creating employment and capitalizing on Mexico's low-cost but highly skilled labor to produce manufactured goods that could be sold competitively in global markets, principally the United States. (The program gets its name from the Spanish verb *maquilar*, which means to measure or take payment for grinding corn.) Subsequent to its creation, the program has undergone several changes to broaden its operating mandate in Mexico and provide at least minimum environmental and human rights guarantees.

Under the *maquiladora* program, international companies ship component parts duty-free to manufacturing facilities in Mexico, where they are assembled into finished products and delivered to the United States for sale. U.S. import duties are assessed only on the value added by Mexican workers. What makes this program different from many other U.S.-based manufacturing operations in Mexico is that, in exchange for relief from incoming tariffs by the Mexican government, the products produced in Mexico may not be sold in Mexico. They must be shipped to the United States.

As a result of this agreement, the fundamental investment strategy for companies interested in doing business in Mexico now focuses on whether to enter as a joint venture or a *maquiladora*. Entry strategies are closely linked to whether the firms wish to market their finished products in Mexico (requiring a joint venture) or solely manufacture products in Mexico for export to the United States (suggesting a *maquiladora*). Some of the key differences between a *maquiladora* and a joint venture in Mexico are shown in Exhibit 6.3.

The *maquiladora* program has been successful in providing manufacturing jobs for low-skilled Mexican workers, while producing high-quality, low-price products for U.S. markets. For example, Ford Motor Company currently manufactures 250,000 engines in Mexico for shipment to the United States, while General Motors assembles

Exhibit 6.3

Laws Governing *Maquiladoras* and Joint Ventures in Mexico

Legal Requirements	*Maquiladoras*	Mexican Joint Ventures
Equity ownership	100 percent foreign ownership permitted	Foreign firms may own no more than 49 percent of stock
Importation of equipment	Duty-free importation	Import permits and duties required
Importation of raw materials	Duty-free importation	Import permits and duties required
Currency exchange controls	Fixed assets may be purchased; no exchange controls for products in dollars; operating expenses sold in Mexico; for exported products, must be paid	No exchange controls for products sold in pesos in Mexico; for exported products, must purchase and sell foreign currencies through Mexican bank
Labor laws	Subject to federal labor laws	Subject to federal labor laws
Immigration requirements	Work permits easy for technical personnel only	Work permits difficult for all personnel
Taxes	Limited income taxes	Subject to normal income and value-added taxes

3 million car radios for shipment north. Currently, almost 90 percent of all *maquiladora* plants are along the U.S.-Mexican border, although some manufacturing facilities can now be found throughout Mexico.

Social critics of the *maquiladora* program argue that it exploits workers by hiring principally young (average age twenty-four), female (almost 70 percent) employees and then placing them in sweatshop-style working conditions. The work is repetitious, few career options exist, supervision is often autocratic, and wages are low. On top of this, worker complaints or efforts to unionize are frequently dealt with through immediate dismissals or physical threats. Some union organizers have even died under suspicious circumstances.

Supporters of the *maquiladoras* counter that the wages and working conditions in these factories, while clearly not up to U.S. standards, are significantly better than those offered by local Mexican competitors. It is also argued that these programs provide employment (especially for women) that would otherwise be unavailable. And worker skill levels are often enhanced as a result of work experience in the *maquiladoras*. Obviously, the desirability of the *maquiladora* program depends on one's point of view and whose values are applied. Hence the question: Are these programs a means of facilitating economic development for an underdeveloped nation or a tool to exploit defenseless workers under inhumane working conditions?

CREATION OF NAFTA

In 1988, Canada and the United States signed a treaty establishing a free trade area between the two countries.[3] The treaty took effect in 1989 and was designed to eventually eliminate all tariffs on bilateral trade. This was followed in 1991 by discussions aimed at including Mexico in the agreement. As a result of these negotiations, the North American Free Trade Agreement (NAFTA) was concluded in 1992 and formally went into effect in 1994. The agreement includes the following provisions:

- Eventual abolition of tariffs on 99 percent of all goods traded among the three countries.
- Removal of most trade barriers on the cross-border flow of services, allowing financial institutions, for example, unrestricted access to all markets.
- Protection of intellectual property rights.
- Removal of most restrictions on foreign direct investment among the three member countries, although special protection is provided for Mexican energy and railways, U.S. airlines and radio communications, and Canadian culture.
- Application of national environmental standards provided they have a scientific basis.
- Establishment of two commissions with the power to impose fines and remove trade privileges when environmental standards or legislation involving health and safety, minimum wage, or child labor are ignored.

The fundamental difference between NAFTA and the *maquiladora* program is that, while the *maquiladora* program is essentially a production agreement between the United States and Mexico governing the manufacture of parts and products for export to the United States, NAFTA is a free trade agreement aimed at eliminating tariff barriers and facilitating two-way trade among three countries, including Canada.

NAFTA AND THE TRUCKING INDUSTRY

If NAFTA is to succeed in creating a genuine regional trading bloc (like the European Union), the three countries that are parties to the agreement must collaborate openly and honestly. Unfortunately, all three countries have reasons to want to implement only specific aspects of the agreement while holding back on others. Consider the case of trucking in the United States.[4] Several years into NAFTA, the U.S. government continued to forbid Mexican truckers from coming more than twenty miles inside U.S. borders, despite the fact that open access to all U.S. roads and highways was guaranteed under NAFTA.

Under former President Clinton, it was argued that Mexican trucks were unsafe and that Mexican truckers were frequently overworked and underpaid, all of which contributed to unsafe conditions on U.S. highways. As a result, Mexican truckers heading north had to remain near the border and transfer their freight to American trucks and American drivers for passage farther inside the United States. This position received strong support from the Teamster's Union, which represents U.S. truck drivers and is concerned about both job security and highway safety. An influx of low-paid Mexican truckers into U.S. markets would seriously jeopardize the political and economic power of the Teamster's Union. It could also reduce the number of U.S. truck drivers. Mexico retaliated to the U.S. prohibition by refusing to allow American truckers more than twenty miles inside Mexico.

Mexico currently has more than 400,000 freight trucks. The average age of these trucks is twenty years old, compared to an average of five years for American trucks. Industry experts believe that it would require an annual investment of $1 billion over the next ten years to bring Mexico's fleet in line with America's. Even so, while a case can be made that U.S. safety standards in the trucking industry are higher than those in Mexico, the U.S. prohibition is nonetheless a violation of the free trade agreement. Mexico appealed the U.S. practice to a dispute resolution panel that ruled in 2001 that the United States had indeed violated the agreement with its ban. Failure to comply with this ruling could cost the United States up to $2 billion in fines.

The resolution panel also ruled that the United States had the authority to set its own safety standards, but that any vehicles meeting these standards must be allowed into the United States regardless of their country of origin. However, the volume of commercial traffic makes it impractical for overworked U.S. border inspectors to check every vehicle. The U.S. Department of Transportation recently noted that there are already shortfalls in U.S. inspections of Mexican trucks that are allowed to operate within the twenty-mile buffer zones. Moreover, in 2002, more than one-third of the Mexican trucks inspected were declared unsafe and denied entry.

The panel's findings seemed only to complicate the issue further in a politically divided Washington, D.C. Should the United States open its borders to possibly unsafe Mexican trucks to comply with NAFTA while simultaneously alienating the politically powerful Teamster's Union and possibly increasing the accident rates on U.S. highways? Or should it continue to ban Mexican trucks and violate NAFTA, thereby alienating Mexico and running the risk of incurring $2 billion in fines but supporting the Teamster's Union? Or is there a third course of action that might prove acceptable to all (or most all) sides to the dispute? Disputes such as this illustrate how difficult it can be to implement a free trade agreement between nations that on paper appears to be so logical.

EVALUATION OF NAFTA

The success or failure of NAFTA in economic terms can be measured in several ways. Trade and investment between member countries have increased dramatically. For example, in 1990, U.S. business with Canada and Mexico accounted for one-quarter of its trade. By 2003, however, this trade accounted for more than one-third of all U.S. trade. Meanwhile, U.S. foreign direct investment in Mexico has more than tripled since 1994, totaling $58 billion today.[5] In the process, considerable technology transfer has occurred from the United States to Mexico, and many Mexican workers are now better trained than in the past.

Also, as noted above, NAFTA led many U.S., Canadian, Asian, and European companies to move their manufacturing operations to Mexico to take advantage of both relatively cheap labor and close proximity to U.S. markets. To understand Mexico's wage competitiveness, note that in 2003 the average U.S. industrial worker earned $18.24 per hour, the average German worker earned $28.28, the average Japanese worker earned $19.37, and the average Korean worker earned $7.22. Adding fringe benefits to these wages increases them by roughly a third. At the same time, the average Mexican industrial worker earned just $1.75 per hour, with very few fringe benefits. In view of this highly competitive wage level, it is not surprising that many labor-intensive jobs have shifted to Mexico. For example, more than 500,000 Mexican workers now make parts or assemble vehicles for all of the world's major automobile firms. Volkswagen assembles both the Jetta and the Beetle in Mexico for the North American market, while DaimlerChrysler produces 250,000 cars and trucks annually for export back to the United States, including the PT Cruiser. Meanwhile General Electric encouraged many of its suppliers to move to Mexico to cut labor costs and reduce the risk of being dropped as a GE supplier. GE has embraced globalization of its production, reducing its U.S. workforce by 50 percent while doubling its foreign workforce. It currently employs 30,000 workers in Mexico, and conducts seminars for suppliers on how to do business in Mexico.

Despite the economic success of NAFTA, U.S. labor leaders worry that this agreement has resulted in significant job losses for U.S. workers. However, it is difficult to determine the accuracy of this assertion. Estimates of the impact of NAFTA on U.S. jobs range from the creation of 170,000 new jobs (due largely to increased Mexican demand for U.S. goods and services) to a loss of 490,000 jobs. Business leaders contend that while the United States may experience job losses in the manufacturing sector, a much larger number of higher-skill jobs have been created in the United States as a result of NAFTA, although this point has been argued.

And what about the future of NAFTA? In the decade since its founding, NAFTA has achieved some significant successes in terms of job creation in Mexico (and job creation in the United States and Canada, if you believe its advocates). It has also reduced the costs of thousands of industrial and consumer products in all three countries. Any way you measure it, trade among the three countries has increased.[6] At the same time, however, problems have emerged that were not anticipated back in 1994. In recent years, China and to a lesser extent countries in Southeast Asia have captured hundreds of thousands of manufacturing jobs that used to reside in Mexico, and many *maquiladoras* have shut down. China in particular offers manufacturers both lower labor costs and better infrastructure.[7] At the same time, the social and environmental problems in Mexico and indeed in the United States along the Mexican border have multiplied. A lack of adequate housing, clean water, sewers, and paved streets all plague the towns and cities in the *maquiladora* region.

BEYOND NAFTA

In recent years, and in spite of its problems, increased attention has focused on the possibility of expanding NAFTA to include all of Latin America. The resulting free trade area would be called the Free Trade Area of the Americas (FTAA) or *Área de Libre Comercio de las Américas* (ALCA) in Spanish.[8] Such a zone, if ultimately approved and implemented, would encompass thirty-four countries with a total population of 800 million and a combined economic output of $11 trillion. This proposal is consistent with the U.S. government's probusiness, proglobalization stance, but it is being resisted by several U.S. labor unions and politicians, who fear significant job losses. It is also being resisted by many Mexican politicians, who fear having to compete with other Latin American countries for manufacturing sites and ready access to U.S. markets. Mexico is working hard to solidify its relations with the United States and secure its current preferential treatment, which it achieved under NAFTA.

Initial plans called for implementing a final agreement on FTAA in 2005, but political posturing and substantial disagreements over economic policy have slowed this process. Disagreements between Brazil and the United States are at the heart of the slow pace of FTAA's implementation.[9] The Brazilian government has long sought to play a dominant role in trade in South America and has pushed hard for an integrated and powerful Mercosur (that does not include the United States). A U.S.-led FTAA represents a challenge to Brazil's leadership position. As a result, Brazil has proposed a free trade agreement between the so-called *G-20*, a Brazilian-inspired group of developing countries around the world that was created in 2003. It has also proposed what some call "FTAA lite," a program under which FTAA members would agree to some common product and trade standards and would cut tariffs on selected goods, but would not pursue across-the-board free trade. While the U.S. government officially endorses a strong and well-integrated FTAA, it has acquiesced to Brazil's proposal, largely because of its own unwillingness to negotiate open markets in agriculture (including such products as sugar and oranges) out of deference to U.S. agribusiness. The United States has also sought to weaken antidumping laws, another major concern of the Brazilians.[10]

While FTAA negotiations stall, several bilateral and multilateral agreements are currently being negotiated among the various countries of North, Central, and South America. The United States recently signed several bilateral agreements with nations (e.g., Chile) willing to exclude certain agricultural products from the agreements, while several Latin American nations, as well as Mercosur, have been negotiating with the European Union for closer trade ties. With such a profusion of separate agreements and little overall agreement among FTAA signatories, the future of a fully integrated free trade area covering the entire region is clearly in doubt.

THE EUROPEAN UNION

Clearly one of the largest and most successful efforts at regional economic integration is the twenty-five-nation European Union. The development of the European Union has evolved over several decades but initially resulted from two key political forces that emerged in the late 1940s. First, the devastation of two world wars in Western Europe created a strong, broad-based desire for long-term peace and political stability in the region. European political leaders began in the 1950s to explore ways to prevent future destructive conflicts. Second, both political and business leaders in the region realized shortly after World War II that their continent was in danger of becoming politically and economically subordinate to the United States. Only by joining together would Europe be sufficiently strong to become a competitive political and economic force in global affairs. Both of these factors proved to be strong motivators for the frequently contentious European leaders to come together for mutual defense and prosperity.

But accomplishing a comprehensive agreement on anything was no easy task in view of the highly divergent cultures that characterize Europe.[11] Consider just a few examples. Several European countries, such as the Netherlands and the United Kingdom, stress individualism, while others, such as Greece and Portugal, stress collectivism. Some cultures, such as those of Scandinavia, emphasize egalitarianism, while others, such as Belgium and France, prefer greater hierarchy in society and organizations. European countries can also be distinguished in terms of their tolerance for ambiguity, with Sweden and Denmark tending to prefer clear rules and policies and Greece and Portugal preferring fewer rules and policies. And countries can be distinguished in terms of the degree to which they stress materialism and assertiveness in everyday behavior, such as Italy, Germany, Austria, and the United Kingdom, or quality of life and the welfare of others, such as the Scandinavian countries. Obviously these are generalities, but they nonetheless provide a starting point for understanding the magnitude of the differences across European countries. There is obviously no "European" culture. Instead, each country manifests unique cultural differences that affect how it views problems and seeks solutions. As a result, the challenge for European leaders in trying to create a united Europe was to find a mechanism to build an integrated network of nations based on a foundation of heterogeneity. This was, and still is, a major challenge.

With this cultural diversity as a backdrop, European leaders began their methodical steps toward building economic and eventually political integration. The first postwar effort in this direction occurred in 1951, when six European nations (West Germany, France, Belgium, Italy, Luxembourg, and the Netherlands) formed the European Coal and Steel Community to remove barriers to intercountry shipments of coal, iron, steel, and scrap metal, all essential ingredients in reconstruction.

This was followed in 1957 with the *Treaty of Rome*, which formally established the *European Economic Community (EEC)*. (A summary of this and other key EU treaties is shown in Exhibit 6.4.) The Treaty of Rome established a common market and called for the elimination of internal trade barriers and the creation of a common external tariff. Member states were required to abolish all obstacles to the free movement of factors of production, goods, and services among members. This treaty also called for *harmonization* of member states' laws (i.e., the elimination of conflicting regulations) and a joint policy governing agriculture and transportation. A *Common Agricultural Policy (CAP)* was officially established in 1962 to stabilize food production in Europe and ensure a decent standard of living for farmers. In 1979, the *European Monetary System (EMS)* was established in an attempt to minimize exchange rate fluctuations between the currencies of member states and provide a greater degree of stability in trading.

In 1992, in recognition of Europe's progress toward a more integrated regional economy, the European Economic Community officially became the European Union as part of the Maastricht Treaty. Membership in the community grew to fifteen nations by 1996, including Great Britain, Ireland, Denmark, Greece, Spain, Portugal, Austria, Finland, and Sweden, in addition to the original six. The resulting community had a population of 380 million and a GDP slightly greater than that of the United States. In May 2004, membership again expanded to include ten new Baltic, Eastern European, and Mediterranean nations, including Cyprus, the Czech Repub-

Exhibit 6.4

Principal Treaties Governing the European Union

Treaty	Date	Provisions
Treaty of Rome	1957	Established the European Economic Community as a common market Established principle of harmonization
Common Agricultural Policy	1962	Stabilized food production in Europe Guaranteed decent standard of living for farmers
European Monetary System	1979	Minimized currency fluctuations between the currencies of member states
Single European Act	1987	Established a single market within the EU by 1992
Maastricht Treaty	1993	Established the European Union Created the Economic and Monetary Union Established the euro as a common EU currency Established the European Central Bank Established the principle of subsidiarity Called for establishment of a common defense policy
Treaty of Amsterdam	1997	Focused on reducing chronic unemployment Strengthened the role of the European Parliament Established a two-track system for future economic and political integration
Treaty of Copenhagen	2002	Expanded the European Union to include ten Baltic, Mediterranean, and Eastern European nations effective 2004
Treaty of Nice	2003	Reduced the number of topics where unanimity was required for Council of the European Union approval to reduce possible political gridlock Adjusted new EU voting procedures and introduced "qualified majority" in EU-wide voting Expanded areas where parliament shares in decision making with Council of the European Union

lic, Estonia, Hungary, Latvia, Lithuania, Malta, Poland, Slovakia, and Slovenia. With twenty-five members, the European Union has become one of the largest and most complex regional trading blocs in the world, with 455 million people and a per capita GDP of close to $19,000.

NAFTA VERSUS THE EUROPEAN UNION

The European Union differs from NAFTA in three important respects (see Exhibit 6.5). First, NAFTA was created as a free trade area, while the predecessor of the European Union, the European Economic Community, was created as a common market. This fact alone tells us something about the political underpinnings of these two organizations, as well as the long-term intentions and aspirations of the governments behind them. That is, from the outset, the parties to NAFTA were determined to retain a high degree of national economic and political autonomy. They wanted to get close to each other, but not too close. They therefore chose the weakest form of

Exhibit 6.5

Comparison of NAFTA and the European Union

Characteristics	NAFTA	European Union
Form of partnership	Free trade area	Economic Union
Number of members	Three nations	Twenty-five nations
Degree of integration	Economic alliance only	Economic and political alliance
Power distribution	Partnership of unequals	Partnership of relative equals
Economic distribution	Partnership of unequals	Partnership of relative unequals

	NAFTA	All twenty-five members	Fifteen original members	Ten new members
Total population	414,900,000	454,900,000	380,800,000	74,100,000
Total land mass (square miles)	8,224,511	1,589,000	1,294,000	295,000
Per capita GDP	$27,026	$18,905	$20,588	$10,256
Richest member	$34,940 (United States)	$43,090 (Luxembourg)		
Poorest member	$5,860 (Mexico)	$3,540 (Slovakia)		
Unemployment rate	(See note)	9.0%	8.0%	14.3%

Source: Wall Street Journal, March 30, 2004, p. C1; *The Economist Pocket World in Figures* (London: Profile Books, 2004).

Note: Unemployment rates for Canada and the United States are 9.3 percent and 5.6 percent, respectively. An accurate unemployment rate for Mexico is unavailable but likely exceeds 15 percent.

alliance, a free trade area, as opposed to a more integrated common market. By contrast, European nations sought greater economic integration from the outset, as evidenced by their ultimate evolution into an economic union. In the minds of their leaders, they were rebuilding Europe as much as their individual nations.

Second, NAFTA was created exclusively an economic trading bloc; no political role was envisioned as increasingly became the case in Europe. NAFTA members wanted nothing to do with formulating a political alliance beyond those already formed by their individual governments. By contrast, EU members saw closer and more formal political ties as a necessary and positive condition for sustained economic growth and development in the future.

Finally, to secure U.S. congressional approval of the NAFTA treaty, Mexico agreed to stipulations in amendments to the treaty concerning protection of both the environment and workers' rights and working conditions. While critics argue that these stipulations are both weak and largely unenforceable, they nonetheless legally recognize the importance of these two issues to member states. While the European Union also has policies governing both labor and environmental issues (indeed, much stronger policies than those found in NAFTA), these policies were the result of political processes established by the European Union, not the result of negotiated amendments to secure the treaty. In the case of the European Union, there is widespread consensus among member states that workers' rights and environmental con-

Exhibit 6.6

Organization of the European Union

Administrative Unit	Membership	Principal Responsibilities
European Council	Heads of state of member nations, plus the president of the European Commission	Supreme political unit; meets four times a year to identify key issues facing the European Union and establish general goals and policies
European Commission	1 commissioner for each member state for five-year terms; headquartered in Brussels	Principal administrative unit; proposes and later implements policies and laws approved by Council of the European Union; commissioners represent EU interests, not national interests
Council of the European Union	1 representative per member state; representatives vary based on topic under discussion	Principal negotiating and decision-making unit; approves all laws and policies proposed by the European Commission; councilors represent national interests
European Parliament	732 representatives elected by popular vote by member states; meets in Strasbourg	Principal deliberative body; advises European Commission on policies and laws; increasingly shares decision-making authority with the Council of the European Union
European Court of Justice	1 justice appointed by each member state	Principal judicial unit; supreme court of appeals by European Commission or member states for adjudicating disputes and enforcing treaty obligations; justices represent EU interests, not national interests

cerns represented a social good. In the case of NAFTA, there is widespread mistrust among American politicians concerning Mexico's commitment to the enforcement of the environmental and workers' rights provisions of the treaty. At the same time, there is considerable mistrust among Mexican politicians about whether the United States views the treaty as a partnership of equals or a legal recognition of Mexico's subservience to U.S. economic goals.

POLITICAL STRUCTURE OF THE EUROPEAN UNION

The economic as well as political policies of the European Union developed through an evolving and somewhat convoluted political process that led to the creation of five principal organizations: the European Council, the Council of the European Union, the European Parliament, the European Commission, and the European Court of Justice (see Exhibit 6.6). Together, they form the backbone of a highly complex economic and political entity and one of the most powerful economic forces in today's global economy.[12]

European Council

The *European Council* consists of the heads of state of the member nations, plus the president of the European Commission. It is the supreme political unit of the European Union and normally meets four times a year to discuss major policy issues and determine policy directions for the entire European Union. The foreign ministers of member nations usually accompany heads of state to these meetings. Some member states have recently proposed that the European Council should become the government of Europe, perhaps with one of its members officially representing Europe on the world stage as some form of president. However, there is currently no agreement regarding who this person should be or how he or she should be selected. One option would be to have the council elect a member to this leadership role, while another option would be to appoint the president of the European Commission. Current debates over a possible European Union constitution are aimed at settling this issue.

European Commission

Many people believe that the most powerful part in the EU infrastructure is the European Commission. The *European Commission* is the administrative branch of the European Union and is responsible for proposing and subsequently implementing legislation governing EU affairs. It is also responsible for monitoring compliance with EU legislation by member nations. The commission is headquartered in Brussels, Belgium, with a staff of more than 10,000 bureaucrats. (When newspaper articles say, "Brussels decided that . . . ," they are referring to actions taken by this commission.)

The European Commission is administered by a group of commissioners, with one commissioner appointed by each member state to serve renewable five-year terms. Each commissioner is responsible for a specific portfolio (e.g., agriculture policy or competition policy) and is supposed to act for the good of the entire union and not advocate a particular national interest. A president and six vice presidents are selected from among these commissioners to serve renewable two-year terms.

A major responsibility of the European Commission is to propose legislation; no other EU entity is authorized to do this. Legislation is initiated through a proposal from the commission to the Council of the European Union and then to the European Parliament. The Council of the European Union cannot act without a specific commission proposal on the table. This procedure was designed to limit national infighting among the ministers by removing authority to propose legislation from nationally elected political representatives and assigning it to a (hopefully) more independent commission.

The European Commission is also charged with overseeing the implementation of all EU laws, although as a practical matter much of this responsibility is delegated to member states for implementation. When the commission detects noncompliance with an EU provision by a member state, it formally requests compliance. If compliance is not forthcoming, the commission then refers the case to the European Court of Justice for resolution.

Council of the European Union

The *Council of the European Union*, formerly known as the Council of Ministers, represents the interest of individual member states. This council is the principal negotiating and decision-making body of the union and is overseen by key representatives of the various member states. The council consists of one representative from the government of each member state. However, the particular representatives selected by each member often vary depending on which topics are being discussed at a given meeting. For example, if agricultural policy is under discussion, member states are likely to send their agriculture ministers to the meeting, while defense ministers would represent member states if the topic under discussion were EU defense policy. The Council of the European Union is the ultimate controlling authority within the EU structure, since it must approve all draft legislation from the European Commission before it becomes law.

European Parliament

The *European Parliament* consists of 732 members directly elected by the populations of the member states. In theory, the parliament represents the citizens of the European Union. It is the principal deliberative body and a source of social pressure throughout the European Union. The parliament meets in Strasbourg, France, and was initially intended to be a consultative, not legislative, body. It debated legislation proposed by the commission and forwarded its opinions to the Council of the European Union. It was empowered to suggest amendments to proposed legislation, although the council was not required to accept such proposals.

In recent years, however, the powers of the European Parliament have been increased significantly. First, it was given authority to vote on the appointment of commissioners and to veto some laws (e.g., the EU budget and single-market legislation). The *principle of codecision* emerged in 1992 with the Maastricht Treaty, whereby the parliament would share decision-making authority with the Council of the European Union on such issues as health care, education, and consumer protection. The Treaty of Amsterdam expanded this authority to include twenty-three additional areas for codecision, while the Treaty of Nice added another seven. If the Council of the European Union and the European Parliament cannot agree on a common policy, the parliament can veto any council action.

There is a growing debate among member nations concerning the appropriate level of power that the European Parliament should have. Some nations believe that the parliament should have increased authority to help offset the growing influence of the EU bureaucrats in Brussels who lack democratic accountability. Others believe, equally strongly, that a stronger European Parliament would mean weaker national legislatures—a move that would lead to lost national sovereignty. The debate continues.

European Court of Justice

The *European Court of Justice* is composed of one justice from each member nation and is the supreme appeals court for all laws governing the European Union. It is the principal judicial unit of the European Union. (The European Court of Justice should not be confused with the United Nations–affiliated *International Court of Justice,*

which meets in The Hague, Netherlands, and focuses on settling disagreements between countries regarding peace and human rights.) The European Commission or
any member state can appeal to the European Court of Justice to force another state
to meet its treaty obligations. At the same time, nations, companies, or institutions
can bring the European Commission or Council of the European Union to the court
for failure to act according to EU treaties. Judges, like members of the European
Commission, are required to act in the best interests of the entire European Union
and not represent their national interests.

In summary, to many outsiders—and to many insiders, too—the operation of the
European Union and its five principal institutions is difficult to understand. This
difficulty arises from a desire among EU leaders not to over-centralize power while
at the same time providing for progress in achieving EU goals. This represents a
delicate balance, both of diplomacy and of management. This complexity of the
operations of the European Union can be seen in the following summary of how the
EU legislative process works:

Step 1: The European Council establishes general goals and operating principles
governing the European Union.
Step 2: The European Commission proposes specific policies and laws to achieve
these goals and principles.
Step 3: The European Parliament advises the commission on these policies and
laws.
Step 4: The Council of the European Union approves or rejects the proposed policies and laws.
Step 5: The European Commission implements the approved policies and laws.
Step 6: The European Court of Justice adjudicates any policies and laws in case
of disputes.

Looking at this complicated process, one is tempted to conclude that, while the ancient Egyptians and Chinese may have invented bureaucracy, the Europeans developed it into an art form.

ECONOMIC STRUCTURE OF THE EUROPEAN UNION

Two events occurred in the late 1980s that had a profound impact on the future
development of the European Union. The first was the collapse of communism in
Russia and Eastern Europe. This event not only served to significantly reduce long-
standing political and military tensions in the region, but also created genuine opportunities for major expansion and consolidation of the European Union. The second
event was much quieter but nonetheless equally important. It was the adoption of the
Single European Act in 1987.

Single European Act (1987)

The *Single European Act* committed EU members to work together toward the establishment of a single market across member states by the end of 1992 (see Exhibit 6.4).

This act resulted from growing frustration among member states that the region was not living up to its promise or expectations. Trade barriers remained across much of Europe, and harmonization of many laws and policies remained elusive as member states resisted changes that adversely affected their own citizens. Major government subsidies to national firms also caused considerable friction. Business leaders from across Europe responded to the apparent political paralysis by leading a campaign to create a level playing field for all companies across Europe. In 1987, the parliaments of the various member states ratified the act.

To create a single market by 1992, the Single European Act included the following specific provisions:

- Removal of all frontier controls between EU countries, allowing people to move freely across national borders.
- Application of the principle of "mutual recognition" to product standards; that is, any product standards of a member state must be accepted by other states so long as they meet basic health and safety concerns.
- Open procurement procedures on all public projects to contractors and suppliers from across the European Union.
- Elimination of all barriers to competition among retail banking and insurance.
- Removal of all restrictions on foreign exchange transactions between member states.
- Elimination of all restrictions on *cabotage*, the right of foreign truckers to pick up and deliver goods across borders.

In addition to a reduction in the number of regulations and trade barriers of European firms, significant economies of scale were also anticipated as a result of this act. These measures were intended to increase the competitive pressures on countries and companies alike and make EU members more competitive in the global marketplace. All provisions of the act were to take effect by 1992. Still, despite significant progress, the goal of a single market was far from being achieved due to deep and enduring cultural and language barriers. Nationalistic feelings ran high, and distrust across nations remains an obstacle to long-term success.

Maastricht Treaty (1993)

In December 1991, European members met in Maastricht in the Netherlands to take up the issue of currency reform. When the resulting *Maastricht Treaty* (also called the Treaty on European Union) was ratified and implemented in November 1993, it surprised even some European leaders with its sweeping changes (see Exhibit 6.4). At Maastricht, EU members agreed to the main elements of what some considered to be a future Europe-wide government. Included in the Maastricht Treaty was the creation of the *Economic and Monetary Union (EMU)* and a distinctly new European currency, the *euro*.

The Maastricht Treaty also established a new independent *European Central Bank (ECB)*, located in Frankfurt, Germany, and similar in function to the U.S. Federal Reserve Bank. The ECB has a clear mandate to manage monetary policy and ensure price stability. Trading in the new euro-denominated assets began in January 1999, creating the world's second largest currency after the dollar. Notes and coins denominated in euros entered circulation in 2002.

The impact of the new monetary policy remains to be seen. On the positive side, the new euro has reduced the constant currency conversions that slowed business transactions across Europe, thereby saving an estimated $12 billion in annual exchange costs. It also provided much of the European Union with one stable currency, avoiding currency fluctuations that were previously common in intercountry transactions. It allowed for clearer cost and price comparisons across countries, since all prices are now quoted in the same currency. This, in turn, should further enhance competitive pressures. However, on the negative side, Great Britain, Sweden, and Denmark refused to embrace the new euro and instead decided to retain their own national currencies for fear of losing national identity and control over their own monetary policies. As a result, multiple currencies still exist in the European Union.

In addition to a new monetary policy, the Maastricht Treaty also changed the political landscape in Europe. It established the foundation, if not the reality, for: (1) a common foreign and defense policy; (2) a common citizenship; and (3) a European Parliament with more power and control over the affairs of citizens in all European countries. In particular, the European Parliament can now veto new national laws. However, at the insistence of Great Britain and Denmark, the *principle of subsidiarity* was included in the treaty, requiring that EU interference in national matters occur only in areas of common concern (e.g., regional defense) and that most policies be established at the national level.

Treaty of Amsterdam (1997)

The *Treaty of Amsterdam* took European integration one step further (see Exhibit 6.4). It obligated member states to work together on three key challenges: (1) attacking the European Union's chronic high levels of unemployment, particularly among young people; (2) strengthening the role of the European Parliament by expanding the number of areas that require the codecision procedure; and (3) establishing a two-track system in which groups of member states can voluntarily proceed with economic and political integration more quickly than the European Union as a whole, if they wish.

Treaty of Copenhagen (2002)

The *Treaty of Copenhagen* opened the way for a major expansion of the European Union by adding ten new members from the Baltic and Mediterranean regions and Eastern Europe effective 2004. It also opened the possibility of admitting other Eastern European countries, such as Bulgaria and Romania, as well as Turkey, in the future. Originally agreed to by EU leaders in 2000, the treaty was held up until late 2002 by Ireland, which feared a loss of both power and economic support as the European Union's limited resources were spread among the new—and largely impoverished—nations.

Because all major EU decisions must be unanimously approved by all fifteen nations, any single one can hold up or veto any new initiative as Ireland did.

Treaty of Nice (2003)

Finally, the *Treaty of Nice* was negotiated to streamline EU operating procedures in view of the 2004 expansion to twenty-five members. Both new and old members had expressed concerns that the union was designed for fifteen members and that new procedures had to be formulated to make a smooth transition to a larger group. To reduce the possibility of political gridlock as the number of members increased, this treaty reduced the number of areas where unanimity was required for council approval. At the same time, the treaty expanded the number of areas where the European Parliament had legislative authority.

A unique aspect of the Treaty of Nice involves how voting is done in the Council of the European Union. Like the Maastricht Treaty, the Treaty of Nice expanded the areas where the Council of the European Union could make decisions by a *qualified majority* (defined as 71 percent of the votes cast) instead of by unanimity. However, since the number of votes allocated to each member state for determining a qualified majority was not based squarely on population, larger members became concerned that they might lose power to smaller members as EU membership expanded. Because of this, treaty negotiators changed the definition of a qualified majority. According to the new agreement, a qualified majority on future votes can be attained only if two (double majority) and sometimes three (triple majority) conditions are met. First, a proposal must receive between 71 percent and 74 percent of the total votes cast. (This range in percentage points allows for new EU members that might be admitted in the future.) This gives power to the larger member states, since voting is based on population. Second, a majority of member states must vote for the proposal. This gives power to the smaller member states, since each member essentially gets one vote. Finally, any member can ask to verify that the qualified majority represents at least 62 percent of the total population of the entire union. If this condition is not met, the decision cannot be adopted. If you are looking for evidence of the complexities of EU operations and legislative processes, this is a prime example.

EUROPEAN UNION AND THE WORKPLACE

The European Union has also worked to standardize labor relations policies as they affect the workplaces of their member states. This is largely accomplished through the European Community Charter of Fundamental Social Rights, or simply the social charter as it is typically called. The *social charter* provides a framework for EU legislation on employee relations at all levels. Its twelve principal provisions include:

1. *Free movement of labor.* All workers have a right to free movement within the union.
2. *Compensation.* All employees are to be paid fairly within EU guidelines. Wage levels must ensure an adequate standard of living. This is often inter-

preted throughout Europe as a de facto minimum wage. Moreover, wages for part-time workers must be proportional to those of full-time workers in the same jobs.

3. *Working conditions.* All employees are guaranteed a written employment contract, specified rest periods, paid leaves for cause, paid vacations, paid sick leave, a specified number of paid national holidays, and severance pay in case of layoffs or bankruptcies.

4. *Social security.* All workers are entitled to social security benefits, regardless of their status. Persons outside the labor market (e.g., retired persons, people with long-term illnesses) must receive sufficient resources and social assistance to maintain their standard of living.

5. *Collective bargaining.* Both employers and employees have a right of free association (e.g. joining a trade union or employer's confederation) to protect their social and economic interests. However, they cannot be compelled to join such associations. Workers are guaranteed the right to negotiate collective bargaining agreements in good faith, and both management and labor have a right to take collective action (e.g., strikes and lockouts) in case of disputes within the bounds of national labor laws.

6. *Vocational training.* Workers are guaranteed access to vocational training with no discrimination based on nationality.

7. *Equal opportunity.* No employer can discriminate against an employee based on age or gender in determining employment, remuneration, working conditions, social protection, educational training, and career development.

8. *Worker participation.* Employers must share pertinent financial information on company performance and consult with all employees prior to making major decisions that may affect present or future employment or working conditions (see Chapter 15). National labor laws govern the manner in which this provision is implemented.

9. *Health and safety.* All workers are entitled to safe and secure working conditions. Again, implementation of this provision is subject to national labor laws.

10. *Child labor.* The minimum employment age must not be lower than the school-leaving age, and neither of these can be lower than fifteen years of age. The duration of work is limited, and night work is prohibited for those under eighteen. After leaving school, young people are entitled to receive initial vocational training of a reasonable duration.

11. *Retirement.* All retired people are guaranteed a decent standard of living. Typically this is accomplished through a combination of company-sponsored and state-sponsored support programs.

12. *People with disabilities.* All people with disabilities are entitled to concrete measures aimed at improving their social and professional integration. These measures focus on vocational training, ergonomics, accessibility, mobility, means of transport, and housing.

These twelve principles establish a minimum set of policies governing employee relations in the workplace. As noted above, the implementation of these policies is largely determined by the various member states, which are free to raise but not lower these standards. In many EU countries, these policies are actually significantly higher than EU standards due to the political realities on the ground, such as strong labor unions, limited numbers of skilled workers, and so forth. Overall, however, EU guidelines provide a minimum guarantee to all workers in an effort to ensure humane working conditions regardless of job classification.

OTHER BENEFITS OF EU MEMBERSHIP

In addition to the economic, political, and workplace benefits resulting from EU membership, member states also benefit in a myriad of other ways from the European Union's ability to launch new initiatives with greater economies of scale than would be possible for individual member states. In particular, member states can pool their resources for investments in projects that require major capital outlays but have common benefits for all. In this way, their combined economic power puts them on a par with the United States for major investments and projects. As a result, the European Union has formed a number of agencies designed to pool resources for the members' mutual benefit.

Among these is the *European Space Agency,* which was created to facilitate space exploration and compete with the United States, Russia, Japan, and China in the emerging markets of satellite technology and global telecommunications. In addition, *Eureka* (European Research Cooperation Agency) funds projects in the fields of energy, medical technology, biotechnology, communications, information technology, transportation, materials science, robotics, production automation, lasers, and the environment. The principal goal of Eureka is to foster research and development on products and production technologies that will increase the competitiveness of Europe. A third agency is *Erasmus*, an EU-wide student exchange program that allows students to study at various universities throughout Europe and use those credits toward graduation at their home universities. In view of the European Union's goal of furthering European integration, providing easy access for students to study outside their national borders represents a sound investment. To date, more than 1 million university students have participated in the EU-wide exchange program.

FUTURE OF THE EUROPEAN UNION

The European Union has made significant progress in becoming a major political and economic force in the global economy. As it moves forward, however, it faces a number of challenges. First and foremost, issues of national sovereignty must be resolved. As with any complex international alliance, a delicate balance must be achieved—and maintained—between the interests of the alliance as a whole and the political and economic interests of the various member nations. The European Union must also be able to support a stable monetary system over the long term, including a stable euro, as well as genuine long-term political cooperation among its members.

Another challenge facing the European Union is that the economies of its new members are far weaker than those of more established ones, leading to considerable concern about the potential dilution of their collective economies. As a result, the European Union has established a series of *convergence criteria* for new members. These criteria require that a country's inflation rate, long-term interest rate, currency exchange rate, deficit-to-GDP ratio, and outstanding debt must be within specified limits and not dissimilar from those of current EU members. These limits are designed to ensure the financial and economic stability of new members, as well as the long-term stability and viability of the entire union.

Finally, the European Union must cope with an expanding list of nations that are seeking membership.[13] Romania and Bulgaria are expected to gain admittance to the European Union in 2007, if all goes according to the plans made in Copenhagen. At that same meeting, it was agreed that the European Council would begin to address whether to open negotiations with Turkey over possible EU membership. Turkey has been pressing hard for membership, but this poses serious questions for the European Union.[14] Critical issues here include whether a predominantly Muslim country can find a home in the European Union. Is Turkey really "European"? Will Turkey enforce the European Union's vigorous human rights standards? What rights will Turkey's long-subjugated Kurdish minority have under EU membership? Will admitting Turkey to the European Union increase the flow of biased Turkish immigrants to Western Europe where the jobs are? How far to the east should the boundaries of the European Union be? Finally, what kind of precedent would admitting Turkey have on future applications to join the European Union? Can any country that meets certain political and economic criteria apply for membership? Local observers suggest that it might take ten to fifteen years before Turkey would be fully accepted into the European Union, if at all. Only time will tell.

In the meantime, expanding the European Union presents both threats and opportunities. On the one hand, EU expansion will provide considerable market opportunities and market power in the global economy, as well as increased political stability and security for the European community as a whole. On the other hand, expansion will also dilute the sovereignty and influence of current EU member states, as well as their economic security and stability—a particular concern of Great Britain. Overall, then, the current twenty-five-member European Union exists in a state of contradiction, moving forward while at the same time anxious about the future. Still, the European Union remains today one of the world's most daring—and most successful—efforts at building political and economic community.

KEY TERMS

Andean Community	cabotage
Asia-Pacific Economic Cooperation (APEC)	Common Agricultural Policy (CAP)
	common market
Association of Southeast Asian Nations (ASEAN)	convergence criteria
	Council of the European Union

(continued)

customs union	Maastricht Treaty
Economic and Monetary Union (EMU)	*maquiladora*
economic union	Mercosur
Erasmus	North American Free Trade
Eureka	Agreement (NAFTA)
euro	political union
European Central Bank (ECB)	principle of codecision
European Commission	principle of subsidiarity
European Council	qualified majority
European Court of Justice	regional economic integration
European Economic Community	regional trading blocs
European Monetary System (EMS)	Single European Act
European Parliament	social charter
European Space Agency	trade creation
European Union	trade diversion
free trade area	Treaty of Amsterdam
Free Trade Area of the Americas (FTAA)	Treaty of Asunción
G-20	Treaty of Copenhagen
harmonization	Treaty of Nice
International Court of Justice	Treaty of Rome

GLOBAL MANAGER'S WORKBOOK 6.1: FUTURE OF NAFTA

NAFTA is different from the European Union in that it is exclusively a free trade agreement with a limited intent to facilitate trade among its three members. Using what you have learned above, consider the following questions:

1. What are the advantages and disadvantages of belonging to a free trade area such as NAFTA compared to an economic union such as the European Union?
2. Should NAFTA's three members consider moving toward a more integrated form of economic cooperation, such as an economic union? Why or why not?
3. If NAFTA did move to an economic union, what would the impact on each of its three members be? Who would benefit most?
4. Should NAFTA expand its borders to include other countries in Central and South America? What are the challenges in making this expansion happen?

GLOBAL MANAGER'S WORKBOOK 6.2: FUTURE OF THE EUROPEAN UNION

The discussion in this chapter demonstrates the evolving nature of the European Union. What began in the 1950s as a handful of nations has grown into a twenty-five-nation economic and political powerhouse. The central question now facing the European Union is, Where to go from here? A key part of this question focuses on whether or not to expand the boundaries of the European Union further by adding new members. A number of countries have expressed interest in becoming members, and the European Union's leadership seems willing to talk. Based on what you have learned, answer the following questions:

1. In the future, what criteria should be used to evaluate new countries for possible EU membership? In your answer, please include consideration of economic, geographic, and cultural issues.
2. One particular country currently seeking EU membership is Turkey. What are the challenges associated with incorporating Turkey into the European Union?
3. Several of the most recent members of the European Union are former members of the former Soviet Union's Warsaw Pact (e.g., Poland, Hungary). Other Eastern European countries from this pact are now seeking membership (e.g., Romania, Bulgaria). Ultimately, the question facing the European Union is whether to allow Russia itself to join. While Russia has not applied for membership, it raises an interesting question about the ultimate size, shape, and character of the European Union. What in your judgment are the advantages and disadvantages of asking Russia to join the European Union?
4. Finally, what does it mean to be European? Will this meaning change significantly if the European Union continues to grow and develop following its current path?

NOTES

1. David Fairlamb, "Poland and the EU," *Business Week*, May 10, 2004, pp. 54–56; Katherine Schmidt, "European Workers' Losing Battle," *Business Week*, August 9, 2004, p. 41.
2. "Alphabet Spaghetti," *Economist*, October 31, 1998, p. 19.
3. Peter Garber, *The Mexico-U.S. Free Trade Agreement* (Cambridge, MA: MIT Press, 1993).
4. Randi Bjornstad, "Ruling May Affect Trucks from Mexico," *Register-Guard*, February 13, 2001, B1.
5. "Free Trade on Trial," *Economist*, January 3, 2004, p. 13.
6. Finlay Lewis, "NAFTA Gets Mixed Reviews After 10 Years," *San Diego Union-Tribune*, January 2, 2004, p. 1; David Bacon, "NAFTA's Legacy: Profits and Poverty," *San Francisco Chronicle*, January 14, 2004, p. 2.
7. Geri Smith, "How China Opened My Eyes," *Business Week*, November 8, 2004, p. 66.
8. Ibid.
9. Geraldo Samor, "Gaps Between Brazil, U.S. Threaten Trade Talks," *Wall Street Journal*, November 16, 2004, p. A22.
10. "Looking South, North, or Both?" *Economist*, February 5, 2004, p. 35.
11. Richard Hill, *We Europeans* (Brussels: Europublications, 1997).
12. Gideon Rachman, "A Divided Union," *Economist*, September 25, 2004, pp. 3–5.
13. Ibid.
14. John Carreyrou, "EU Extends a Hand to Turkey," *Wall Street Journal*, October 7, 2004, p. A18.

PART II

CULTURE, ORGANIZATION, AND STRATEGY

7 Cultural Foundations of Global Business

Cultural differences can often be illustrated through humor, although at times this can be a risky proposition. Consider the following story about two cows:[1]

- *German company.* You have two cows. You engineer them so they are all blond, drink lots of beer, give excellent-quality milk, and can run fifty miles an hour. Then you lose your competitive edge because your cows demand thirteen weeks of annual vacation.
- *Japanese company:* You have two cows. You redesign them so they are one-tenth the size of ordinary cows but can produce twenty times the milk. They learn to travel on unbelievably crowded trains. Most were at the top of their class at cow school.
- *French company.* You have two cows. You go on strike because you want three cows. You go to lunch and drink some wine. Life is good.
- *Russian company.* You have two cows. You drink some vodka. You count them again and now you have five cows. You drink some more vodka. You count them again and now you have forty-two cows. The mafia shows up and takes however many cows you actually had.
- *Brazilian company.* You have two cows, but you don't know where they are. Walking along the beach one day, you meet a beautiful woman. You break for lunch. Life is good.
- *American company (New York).* You have two cows. You sell one, lease it back to yourself, and do an initial public offering (IPO) on the second one. You force the two cows to produce the milk of four cows. You are surprised when one cow drops dead. You spin an announcement to Wall Street analysts that you have downsized and are reducing expenses. Your stock goes up.
- *American company (California).* You have millions of cows. Most are illegals.

Is this story funny? Many would argue that it is because such stories present realistic if exaggerated caricatures of the various cultures involved, and that we can learn a great deal about cultures from humor so long as we do not take things too seriously. Indeed, if cultures were not significantly different, such humor would not be so pervasive. Others would argue that this type of humor represents the worst in cultural stereotyping and should be avoided. Either way, it must be recognized that cultures can, in fact, be very different and that many of these differences can be systematically observed and compared, with or without humor. If these comparisons are done with sufficient accuracy, valuable lessons can be learned that can help the global managaer. However, for this to happen in earnest it is necessary to have more structured ways of comparison than simple humor. Such an understanding of culture and cultural differences is essential for managers working across national boundaries. With this in mind, we focus in this chapter on how cultural differences can affect both interpersonal behavior and business success in the global economy. We begin with a look at what is meant by culture.

UNDERSTANDING CULTURAL DIFFERENCES

There are many ways to understand the role of culture in organized settings. One way is to visit foreign lands and talk with local people about their customs and social norms. Another way is to study the works of noted anthropologists and other social scientists. A third way is to consider the observations of people whose opinions we respect. Consider the following three observations:

• More than seven hundred years ago, Chinese scholar Wang Ying-lin compiled a book of ancient wisdom called the *Trimetric Classic* (or Three Character Classic) in which he observed that all people are basically the same; it is only their habits that are different.[2]

• More than three hundred years ago, French mathematician and philosopher Blaise Pascal observed, "There are truths on this side of the Pyrenees that are falsehoods on the other."[3] In other words, things that are believed to be true in one country are sometimes thought to be false in another. Pascal was not referring to two countries widely separated by vast stretches of geography, like China and Mexico. He was referring to France and Spain, separated only by the Pyrenees Mountains. (For those who think this is just a quote from ancient times, Delaney points out that Microsoft *Encarta* comes in sixteen different languages, and that many of the entries in this encyclopedia differ based on where the software is sold. Apparently, "facts" can still differ based on culture.)[4]

• Much more recently, INSEAD professor Andre Laurent observed that managers who readily accept that the cuisine, literature, music, and art of various countries can differ significantly often have difficulty recognizing that management in those countries can also differ.[5]

Wang, Pascal, and Laurent, each from a very different time in history, all understood what has too frequently eluded contemporary managers: National culture can make a difference in determining how we think and how we behave. This is equally true in our personal lives and our work lives. Unfortunately, too many managers have ignored even the most rudimentary cross-national differences while working overseas and, as a result, have missed significant opportunities for themselves and their companies. Today, it is difficult to conceive of successfully engaging in international business without first understanding the cultural characteristics of the region where the business is conducted. Countries such as India, Germany, Thailand, and Mexico approach many business activities in fundamentally different ways, and a failure to understand these differences unnecessarily penalizes the uninformed. As a result, smart managers learn as much as they can about cultural differences before launching any business initiatives overseas.

DEFINITION OF CULTURE

Culture is both simple and difficult to understand. It is simple because definitions abound that are easily understood by any reader. At the same time, however, culture can be difficult to comprehend because of its subtleties and complexities. As anthropologist Edward Hall observed, "I have come to the conclusion that the analysis of culture could be likened to the task of identifying mushrooms. Because of the nature of the mushrooms, no two experts describe them in precisely the same way, which creates a problem for the rest of us when we are trying to decide whether the specimen in our hands is edible."[6] Similarly, the ancient Chinese philosopher Lao Tzu once observed that "water is the last thing a fish notices," using water as a metaphor for culture. That is, most people are so strongly immersed in their own culture that they often fail to see how it affects their patterns of thinking or their behavior; they are too close to it. (If you don't believe this, try writing down ten adjectives that best describe your own national culture. Then ask a friend from another country to write down ten adjectives that describe your culture. Compare the two lists.)

Finding a suitable working definition of culture can be difficult. Fons Trompenaars, for example, defines culture as the way in which a group of people solves problems and reconciles dilemmas.[7] Clifford Geertz defines culture as the means by which people communicate, perpetuate, and develop their knowledge about attitudes toward life; culture is the fabric of meaning in terms of which people interpret their experience and guide their action.[8] For our purposes, we will take a simple approach and define *culture* as the collection of beliefs, values, behaviors, customs, and attitudes that distinguish the people of one society from those of another.[9] Or, as Hofstede suggests, culture is the collective programming of the mind that distinguishes the members of one human group from those of another.[10] It is the glue that ties a group or society together and signifies what it stands for. In both the personal and the business world, culture determines the rules that govern how people and organizations operate.

Researchers often differentiate between *objective culture,* consisting of a country or region's external or physical manifestations of culture (e.g., architecture, music, food, dress, and so forth), and *subjective culture,* consisting of the ways in which people categorize their inner experiences, form beliefs and values, and establish roles and expected patterns of behavior. This distinction becomes important as we attempt to understand how societies develop and enforce normative patterns of behavior both inside and outside the workplace.

CHARACTERISTICS OF CULTURE

Using a definition of culture like this leads to the identification of at least six characteristics that further our understanding of this enigmatic phenomenon:

• *Learned behavior.* Culture reflects learned behavior that is transmitted from one member to another. People are not born with a culture; they acquire it from their family, friends, and associates. In collectivistic cultures such as China, Korea, and Thailand, family members are taught from an early age to protect and defend their family at all costs and not to bring shame on it. The family unit is what protects, nurtures, and sometimes constrains people throughout their lives, as well as looking after them in their old age. To violate a family trust threatens the very existence of the family and hence oneself. But such beliefs are learned, not inherited.

• *Shared values.* Culture is shared by all or most of the members of a society and indeed sometimes defines the membership of a society. People who share a culture are members of a society, while those who do not are often seen as outsiders or aliens. Thus, cultures create us-versus-them situations in which individuals must sometimes choose between following the will of the group and risking being castigated or expelled. For example, many cultures around the world routinely expel members who marry outside their race, culture, or religion. For people in these cultures, such marriages can threaten the established culture with a perceived dilution or dissipation of what the culture stands for.

• *Mutually reinforcing influences.* The various elements that comprise culture are interrelated and mutually reinforcing. In Japan, for example, a group-oriented, hierarchical culture stresses harmony and loyalty. As a result, Japanese companies have historically supported lifetime employment for their employees and use a subtle communication style for many interactions. Rewards are often based more on seniority than on personal achievement. By contrast, the United States tends to be a highly individualistic culture that celebrates personal achievement. As such, most U.S. companies seek employees who are competitive in nature and use pay-for-performance reward systems to retain only the most successful competitors. This practice is sometimes referred to as "refining the gene pool."

• *Evolution over time.* Because culture is learned, it is also adaptive and evolves over time in response to a myriad of external forces that can affect society. Following the Second World War, for example, Germany was divided into eastern and western sectors. East Germany was converted into an authoritarian communist state, while West Germany supported democracy, individualism, and capitalism. Contacts across borders were highly restricted, particularly after the Berlin Wall was erected in the early 1960s. Over time, despite a common heritage dating back centuries, this absolute division created major cultural differences be-

Exhibit 7.1 **Cultural Overlaps and the Risk of Stereotyping**

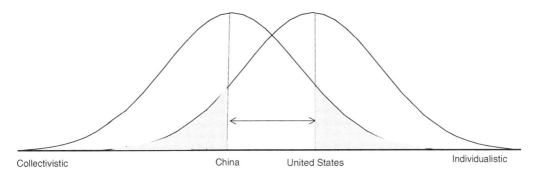

Collectivistic   China   United States   Individualistic

tween *Ossies* (East Germans) and *Wessies* (West Germans). Following reunification almost fifty years later, both sides realized that they had grown apart culturally as well as economically. This schism still adversely affects Germany today through differences in work ethics, entrepreneurial drive, economic prosperity, and political beliefs.

• *Impact on attitudes and behaviors.* Culture and personal values help determine societal norms governing appropriate and inappropriate behavior. The resulting social norms influence in no small way the attitudes people form and the behaviors they initiate. As a result, the role of culture in determining organized behavior in work situations cannot be underestimated.

• *Heterogeneous.* Finally, a cautionary note is in order here. Cultures are not monolithic. In fact, significant individual differences can be found in all cultures around the world. For example, while people often describe the United States as a highly individualistic culture and China as a highly collectivistic culture, there are in fact many collectivistic Americans and many individualistic Chinese (see Exhibit 7.1). In fact, many cultures overlap considerably with those of their neighbors, having more in common than not. These differences—and similarities—must be clearly recognized when one is trying to make comparisons across cultures or nations. While we often generalize about various cultures in order to facilitate an understanding of cultural trends, it would be highly inaccurate to conclude that all members of any culture behave in the same way.

INSIDE CHINA: A STUDY IN CULTURE

There are many ways to study culture. In this chapter, we examine four popular models. However, as a prelude to this, we first examine the culture (or, more accurately, cultures) of China. China has one of the oldest and richest cultures in the world, and more people speak Mandarin Chinese as their first language than any other language in the world by far—including English (see Exhibit 7.2). It thus provides a good starting point for our introduction to culture.

From the standpoint of international economics, China today is one of the most

Exhibit 7.2

Top Ten World Languages

Language	Number of People Who Use as First Language
Mandarin Chinese	885,000,000
Spanish	332,000,000
English	322,000,000
Bengali	189,000,000
Hindi	182,000,000
Portuguese	170,000,000
Russian	170,000,000
Japanese	125,000,000
German	98,000,000
Wu Chinese (Shanghainese)	77,000,000

Source: Based on *Language Magazine,* April 2000, vol. 10, no. 3, pp. 3–4.

vibrant and dynamic overseas locations for manufacturing.[11] While offshore production occurs literally around the world, China is rapidly becoming the location of choice for many global firms due to its inexhaustible supply of highly skilled workers, good infrastructure, and low labor costs. Add to this the decision by the Chinese government to facilitate foreign direct investment and its recent membership in the World Trade Organization and you get a recipe for manufacturing success. Perhaps this is why so many products we buy today bear the label "Made in China." Because of this, it is important to understand how business is done in the world's most populous nation. And to do this, it is important to understand the cultural foundations of this historic nation.

In many societies—notably those in East and Southeast Asia—the predominant business model is organized around the family. In China, for example, while very large state-run or formerly state-run enterprises exist, small and medium-sized family-controlled firms conduct most of the business. This is especially true in southeastern China around Hong Kong and the Guangzhou region. Family-based organization and management is consistent with the Confucian values found in many of these same societies that emphasize the importance of the family as the basic building block of a society.[12] In view of this, it is important to understand how families and extended social relationships can affect how business and management are done.

Confucius and the Five Cardinal Virtues

Contrary to popular Western belief, *Confucianism* is a philosophy, not a religion. *Confucius* was a senior civil servant in China in the sixth century B.C.E. The name "Confucius" is actually a Latin form of the title *Kongfuzi,* which means "Great Master Kong." Confucius's actual name was Kong Qui. He was a moral philosopher, best known for his thoughts on correct moral character and personal responsibility. Although he never published his thoughts or philosophy, his disciples

Exhibit 7.3

Confucian Principles and Business Practices

Cardinal Virtue	Role in Business Practice
Filial piety	Employees are expected to show unquestioned respect for superiors, while superiors are obliged to look after their subordinates.
Absolute loyalty	Employees are expected to show absolute loyalty to their employer and follow his or her directives without question.
Seniority	Employees expect to work their way up the organization by following those ahead of them and not by jumping ahead.
Subservience	Sex-role differentiations favor men over women in allocating power and authority in many situations.
Mutual trust and obligation	Trust is an inviolate principle among coworkers and partners, and harmonious relations must be maintained at all costs to avoid losing face.

collected them and subsequently published them in a classic book called the *Analects.*

Known for his wisdom and insight, Confucius promulgated a code of ethical behavior that was meant to guide interpersonal relationships in everyday life. This code was summed up in the so-called *five cardinal virtues.* While these principles suggest a way of living in the broader society, they also have implications for business practices, as noted in Exhibit 7.3. The five cardinal virtues adapted to the workplace can be summarized as follows:

• First and foremost, *filial piety* requires a son to show love, respect, and absolute obedience to his father at all times. This principle is inviolate. From this principle we can see the origin of the *familism* that permeates many Asian societies to this day. One's family is vitally important because it defines who people are and where they belong in the larger society. The family looks after its own, a factor that often leads to the nepotism that is frequently seen in Asian companies. As a part of this familism, we see, too, the special emphasis that is placed by the family on education and continual self-improvement as a means of aiding in the development of one's self, family, and community. Each individual has an obligation to maximize his or her contribution to the family.

• There must be absolute loyalty to one's superiors in all things. Here can be seen the origins of the strong commitment felt by so many Asian employees toward the company and its leader. The president of the company traditionally embodies the essence of the company itself, and as such is to be respected and followed without question.

• Social order is to be arranged according to strict seniority, with the young showing respect and obedience to the old and the old assuming responsibility for the well-being and future of the young.

• In traditional China, women were subservient to their husbands in all things. Their role was primarily that of homemaker, and it was rare to see women in business. While sex-role stereotyping still exits today, in recent years it has diminished in magnitude, and Chinese women are now much more likely to be treated as equals, especially in the more prosperous urbanized areas of the country such as Shanghai and Beijing. It is very common now to see women running both large and small businesses and, indeed, observers suggest that women in China now have more equality than women in most other Asian countries.

• Finally, mutual trust between friends and colleagues must be preserved at all times. This is seen as the key to all human relationships and a major determinant of the humanity and solidarity of the culture. Even today, maintaining mutually supportive relationships among work associates is a never-ending pursuit for employees at all levels in the organization. Business activity is based more on personal relationships and contacts than on written contracts. Reciprocity and exchange represent an important part of this process.

Confucius and his followers saw the universe—and hence society—as a hierarchical system ruled by an educated aristocratic elite. Concepts such as democracy and equality were disdained, while learning and education were highly prized. Confucian society stressed the virtues of self-discipline, hard work, diligence, and frugality.[13] Hence, the fundamental nature of human relationships was not interactions among equals but rather interactions among unequals. That is, correct interpersonal behavior was determined by one's age, gender, and position in society, and a breach in this social etiquette carried with it severe penalties.

These five cardinal virtues are reinforced by two additional characteristics of societies: rank and group harmony. First, consider the importance of rank. Confucian principles were designed to recognize hierarchy and differences between class members. As a result, the behavioral requirements of individuals differed according to who was involved in the relationship. Among equals, certain patterns of prescribed behavior existed. You can see this today when two strangers discover upon meeting for the first time that they both attended the same high school or college. An instant bond emerges and there is a sense of immediate camaraderie. On the other hand, for people from outside this common background or clan, there is frequently hostility or distrust. Foreign observers note that some people can be very blunt and impolite when talking with total strangers, yet very hospitable and generous when dealing with friends or acquaintances. It is a question of belonging.

In addition, within one's broad circle of acquaintances, there is a clear responsibility for maintaining group harmony. Again, this principle stresses harmony between unequals. That is, it links persons of unequal rank in power, prestige, or position. Since strong personal relationships outside the family tend to occur only between persons of equal rank, age, or prestige, harmony is the means of defining all other necessarily more formal relationships. It is everyone's responsibility to continually maintain this harmony among one's acquaintances and family members, and considerable effort is invested in doing so, including gift giving.

SUN TZU AND THE ART OF WAR

Perhaps somewhat surprisingly, the basic tenets of Confucianism have a good deal in common with those of a famous Chinese warlord from about the same period named

Exhibit 7.4 **Foundations of Traditional Chinese Social Relationships**

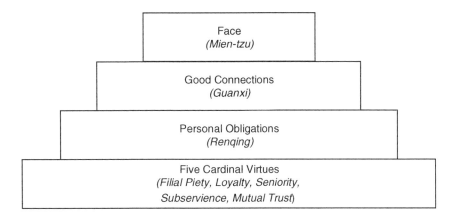

Sun Tzu (fourth century B.C.E.). Sun Tzu was a military general known for his battle-field prowess and continual victories. He is reputed to be the author of *The Art of War,* a classic book on the art of warfare that some Westerners believe provides significant insights into corporate strategy in competitive markets.[14]

Sun Tzu suggested three basic principles of (military) strategic leadership. First, it is important for leaders to have moral influence over their followers, controlling their hearts, not just their bodies. Second, leaders must be well rounded, instead of merely having technical knowledge. And finally, leaders must understand that everyone—both friends and enemies—has strengths and weaknesses, and it is paramount to know when and where one has a competitive advantage. He is reputed to have said that when you know your enemy (i.e., competitors) as well as you know yourself, you will always win.[15]

Both Sun Tzu and Confucius believed in order and hierarchy, self-control, a sense of moral justice, a holistic approach to organized life, and behavior directed toward a common good. It is surprising that a famous philosopher and a distinguished military leader shared much the same philosophy about life. Perhaps this is a testament to the strength of the underlying moral philosophy that governs China, then and now.

GUANXI AND SOCIAL EXCHANGE

Based on this background on early Chinese philosophy, it is possible to delve a bit further into the Chinese social patterns that are at the heart of successful business relations. In general, three concepts—*guanxi* (good connections), *mien-tzu* (face), and *renqing* (personal obligations)—supplement the five cardinal virtues to help explain traditional patterns of Chinese social behavior (see Exhibit 7.4).

Good Connections (Guanxi)

First, consider good connections, better known as *guanxi. Guanxi* can be defined as a strong personal relationship between two people with implications of a continual exchange of favors. Others define it simply as good connections or tight social networks based on trust, common background, and experience. Two people have *guanxi* when they can assume that each is conscientiously committed to the other regardless of what happens. This bond is based on the exchange of favors (i.e., social capital), not necessarily friendship or sympathy, and it does not have to involve friends. It is more utilitarian than emotional. It also tends to favor the weaker of the two parties in ongoing exchanges, an outgrowth of the Confucian doctrine of looking after those less fortunate than oneself. Failure to meet one's obligations under this equity arrangement causes severe loss of face and creates the appearance of being untrustworthy.

La (or "pulling") *guanxi* is the most commonly used strategy for building *guanxi*. Pulling *guanxi* is the process by which an individual may take the initiative and try to build an exchange relationship with another person—perhaps by offering favors or compliments in the hope that this effort will eventually be reciprocated. Accepting such favors carries reciprocal obligations on the part of the recipient. As such, building—and sometimes avoiding building—*guanxi* is an ongoing social challenge.

Face (Mien-tzu)

The second factor in determining social relationships in China (and elsewhere in Asia) is *face*. A central tenet of Confucianism is to maintain long-term social harmony.[16] This is based both on the maintenance of correct relationships between individuals and on the protection of one's face (*mien-tzu;* dignity, self-respect, prestige). All social interactions must be conducted so no party loses face. Face can be classified into two types: *lian* and *mianzi. Lian* is associated with personal behavior, while *mianzi* is something valuable that can be achieved. Under this system, a Chinese may be criticized for having no *lian* and will be seen as being unsuccessful if he has no *mianzi.* Normally, people of higher rank possess greater *mianzi.* Together *lian* and *mianzi* determine who has face, who gains it, and who loses it. As a result, face represents a key component in the exercise of *guanxi.* If a person has little *mianzi,* he or she has limited social capital with which to cultivate social connections.

Simply put, face represents the confidence society has in one's moral character. It represents one's self-image or reputation. The loss of face makes it impossible for an individual to function properly in the community. This occurs when an individual, either through his own actions or the actions of people close to him, fails to meet essential requirements placed upon him by virtue of his social position. Hence, if an individual cannot keep a commitment—however small—he loses face. Similarly, a person loses face when he or she is not treated in accordance with his or her station or position in society. Thus, a senior manager will lose face if it becomes known that a junior colleague is earning a higher salary or was promoted ahead of him or her.

Personal Obligations (Renqing)

The third important factor in determining social relationships is *personal obligations.* Personal obligations, or *renqing,* accrue to individuals as a result of past *guanxi* relationships. That is, they involve unpaid debts or favors that are owed to others as a result of past favors in a continuing exchange relationship between friends and colleagues. In addition to various social expressions (such as offering congratulations or condolences and making gifts on appropriate occasions), *renqing* often include a display of human empathy and personal sentiments. They focus on social emotions—emotions played out in public—rather than personal emotions, which are frequently hidden from view. If one fails to follow the rule of equity in the exchange of *renqing,* one loses face, hurts the feelings of others, and looks inconsiderate. This applies even to one's closest friends. As a result, some have translated *renqing* as "humanized obligations" instead of "personal obligations," which implies that a continued exchange of favors with a sentimental touch is involved.

CHINESE FAMILY BUSINESS AND THE GONG-SI

In view of China's strong cultural traditions, it is not surprising that its companies, both large and small, reflect this heritage. Chinese companies are generally called *gong-si* (pronounced "gong-suh"). While the term *gong-si* originally referred to private, typically family-owned enterprises, recent Chinese corporate law now uses this term to refer to all companies, regardless of whether they are large or small, family-owned or state-owned. To clarify this difference, smaller family-run enterprises are now often called *jia zu gong-si.*

Found throughout China, Taiwan, and elsewhere in the world where overseas Chinese congregate, the *Chinese family business* tends to be a small entrepreneurial venture owned by family members and typically employing members of the extended family as well as others whom the family feels it can trust.[17] These firms are particularly prevalent in southern China and among overseas Chinese. As a rule, Chinese family firms are considerably smaller and exhibit greater independence than their Japanese or Korean counterparts.

The dominant management style of the *gong-si* is patrimonialism, which includes paternalism, hierarchy, mutual obligation, responsibility, familism, personalism, and connections.[18] As a result, typical Chinese family businesses are often characterized by power and influence being closely related to ownership, autocratic leadership, and a personalistic style of management designed in part to pay honor to the founder or leader.

Following from Confucian thought, the family is the most fundamental revenue and expenditure unit. Within a family, each member contributes his or her income to a common family fund. Each member then has a right to a portion of these funds, while the remainder belongs to the family as a whole. The interests of the entire family take precedence over individual members and others outside the family. As a result, business owners tend to regard the business as the private property of the core family (not an individual) and are therefore reluctant to share ownership with outsiders or to borrow from individuals or organizations unrelated to the family in some way. Top management positions are often filled with family members, sometimes despite a lack of managerial competence. Company size tends to be small. More than 90 percent of these firms employ fewer than fifty people, including family members, and focus their energies on a small area of business—production, sales, or service.[19]

Gong-si companies have little formal structure, few standard operating procedures, and little specialization.[20] While they lack formal structure and procedures, personal relationships are likely to take precedence over more objectively defined concerns such as organizational efficiency. Who one knows is often more important than what one knows, and employee loyalty is often preferred over actual performance. Decisions are frequently based either on intuition or on long-standing business relationships. According to Chinese business expert Ming-Jer Chen, if these family firms have a competitive advantage it lies in their small size, flexibility, network of connections, and negotiation skills.[21]

A NEW GENERATION OF CHINESE MANAGERS

As noted above, cultures can sometimes evolve over time in response to external stimuli. China provides a good example of this type of evolution. Perhaps one reason Chinese culture has endured for so many millennia is that it is at once both strong and flexible. Its roots are very deep, yet it is sufficiently flexible to adapt to shifting political sands (from empire to nationalism to communism to quasi-capitalism). As China has begun to prosper in response to its newfound economic freedoms, and as more young Chinese are exposed to Western thought (e.g., capitalism, democracy, individualism), a clear evolution in management thought can be seen from older managers to younger ones.[22] Many young Chinese managers, with greater educational opportunities and more overseas experience, are beginning to develop their own framework for business management that differs significantly from that of their parents. This new approach can perhaps best be described as a blend of old and new, East and West. The trend in Chinese management philosophy is changing rapidly toward a greater emphasis on competitiveness, innovation, and individual responsibility, as shown in Exhibit 7.5.

Clearly there are variations around this trend, so caution is in order against overgeneralization. Even so, these changes are real and widespread. How they will influence future successes or failures of Chinese businessmen and women remains to be seen. What is clear, however, is that these changes pose a significant challenge for all partners doing business in the region, regardless of their home country.

THE CULTURE THEORY JUNGLE

Using China as an example, we turn now to look at some of the principal theories of culture as they relate to global business. Understanding cultural differences has been an important area of study for many years—many decades, in fact. At present, there are more than a dozen models of cultural differences, each claiming to offer the best way to understand and measure culture. This presents global managers with a genuine challenge: How do they make sense out of this "culture theory jungle"? How do they identify a model that best facilitates their own particular needs in managing or doing business across national boundaries? To understand this dilemma, as well as possible ways to resolve it, we examine four models developed by Edward Hall, Geert Hofstede, Fons Trompenaars, and Robert House and his GLOBE associates.

Exhibit 7.5

Evolution of Chinese Management Philosophy

Older Generation	Younger Generation
Emphasis on *guanxi,* personal obligations, and face	Emphasis on *guanxi,* personal obligations, and face
Belief in doing things in the traditional way; resistance to change	Belief in change and innovation; seeks quick return on investments
Belief in being content with what one has	Belief in achievement and new opportunities
Emphasis on ethical behavior	Emphasis on strategic behavior
Focus on experience	Focus on education
Holistic approach to work; emphasis on balance between work and nonwork	Emphasis on work over nonwork
Paternalistic; managers must serve as father figures for workers	Professional; managers must hire and reward competent workers
Belief that people must conform for the greater common good	Belief that people must maximize their individual talents
Belief that top managers are responsible for solving problems	Belief that employees at all levels are responsible for solving problems.
Belief that younger managers are too mercenary, selfish, and short-sighted	Belief that older managers are too traditional, slow, and backward-looking

Each model has a distinct focus, although there is some overlap in places. Taken together, they help us understand how we can make some sense out of this intractable topic.

HALL'S CULTURAL DIMENSIONS

Edward T. Hall, a noted cultural anthropologist, has written extensively on how cultures differ across national boundaries.[23] In his later career, he worked closely with his wife, Mildred Reed Hall, also a noted anthropologist.[24] Using ethnographic methods, Hall's work focuses principally on how cultures vary in interpersonal communication, but also includes work on personal space and time. These three cultural dimensions are summarized in Exhibit 7.6. Many of the terms we use today in the field of cross-cultural management are derived from this work.

The first of Hall's three dimensions relates to interpersonal communication patterns, specifically how much context surrounds the messages. Hall distinguishes between low- and high-context cultures. In *low-context cultures*, such as Germany, Scandinavia, and the United States, the context surrounding the message is far less important than the message itself. The context provides the listener with little information relating to the intended message. As a result, speakers must rely more heavily

Exhibit 7.6

Hall's Cultural Dimensions

Cultural Dimensions	Scale Anchors	
Context: Extent to which the context of a message is as important as the message itself	*Low-context:* Direct and frank communication; message itself conveys its meaning. Examples: Germany, United States, Scandinavia	*High-context:* Much of the meaning in communication conveyed indirectly through the context surrounding a message. Examples: Japan, China
Space: Extent to which people are comfortable sharing physical space with others	*Center of power:* Territorial; need for clearly delineated personal space between themselves and others. Examples: United States, Japan	*Center of community:* Communal; comfortable sharing personal space with others. Examples: Latin America, Arab states
Time: Extent to which people approach one task at a time or multiple tasks simultaneously	*Monochronic:* Sequential attention to individual goals; separation of work and personal life; precise concept of time. Examples: Germany, United States, Scandinavia	*Polychronic:* Simultaneous attention to multiple goals; integration of work and personal life; relative concept of time. Examples: France, Spain, Mexico, Brazil, Arab states

Source: Based on Edward T. Hall, *The Silent Language* (New York: Anchor Books, 1981); Edward T. Hall and Mildred R. Hall, *Understanding Cultural Differences* (Yarmouth, ME: Intercultural Press, 1990). Country examples come from Hall (1981).

on providing greater message clarity, as well as other guarantees such as written documents and information-rich advertising. Language precision is critical, while assumed understandings, innuendos, and body language frequently count for little.

By contrast, in *high-context cultures* such as Japan and China, the context in which the message is conveyed (that is, the social cues surrounding the message) is often as important as the message itself. Indeed, the way something is said is often more important in communicating a message than the actual words that are used. Here, communication is based on long-term interpersonal relationships, mutual trust, and personal reputations. People know the people they are talking with, and reading someone's face becomes an important—and necessary—art. As a result, less needs to be said or written down. These subtleties in communication patterns often go unnoticed by many Westerners, who are looking or listening very carefully to every word that is spoken—only to miss the real message. Examples of high- and low-context cultures are shown in Exhibit 7.7.

Hall's second dimension focuses on how people view their personal space. In some cultures, including those of North America, northern Europe, and much of Asia, people tend to remain relatively far apart when talking with each other (even among good friends) so as not to invade anyone's personal space. In other cultures, such as those in Latin America and many Arab countries, people tend to stand much closer together when talking or doing business, frequently touching one another. Hall distinguishes between these two patterns of behavior by referring to the first as focusing on *centers of power* ("This is *my* space!") and the second as focusing on

Exhibit 7.7 **High- and Low-Context Cultures**

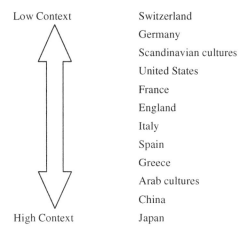

Low Context	Switzerland
	Germany
	Scandinavian cultures
	United States
	France
	England
	Italy
	Spain
	Greece
	Arab cultures
	China
High Context	Japan

centers of community ("This is *our* space!"). Violating someone else's personal space is considered extremely impolite in some cultures, while being aloof or standoffish is seen as equally impolite in others.

Another example of the use of personal space can be seen in the way office architecture is used in office layouts. Some countries use open layouts (i.e., all employees, including managers, sit in the same large room as one community), while other countries stress closed office architecture (i.e., most managers have their own private offices away from their subordinates—and from each other). Consider the impact of such structural differences on communications and corporate culture. In open architecture arrangements, most communication—including what the boss says—quickly becomes common knowledge, whereas this communication in a closed office layout often remains confidential, even if there is no need for confidentiality. As a result, if it is true that "information is power" in organizations, open office architecture serves to reduce the power of many managers. Is this good or bad? Consider: Under which system—open or closed—is employee trust most likely to be fostered? And which would you prefer?

Finally, Hall suggests that cultures can often be distinguished by the manner in which they use time in work-related activities. Some cultures, like those of Germany, Scandinavia, and the United States, are decidedly *monochronic.* This means that they tend to stress a high degree of scheduling in their lives, concentration of effort on one activity at a time, and elaborate codes of behavior built around promptness in meeting obligations and appointments. Put simply, they tend to be a bit linear in their thinking and behavior, always focusing on the ultimate goal. By contrast, *polychronic* cultures tend to emphasize building and maintaining human relationships and social interaction over establishing and maintaining arbitrary schedules and appointments. Such individuals tend to engage in multiple activities simultaneously, with frequent interruptions. Outsiders often describe them as being chaotic, unfocused, or disorganized. They see themselves as working hard but handling many competing tasks simultaneously. Examples of polychronic cultures include southern Europe (France, Spain, Portugal, and Italy), as well as most Latin American and Arab countries.

How can this model help us understand the example of Chinese culture discussed above? When Hall's model is applied to China, we see a culture characterized by high-context communication with subtle messages, extensive use of body language and gestures, and implied meanings associated with spoken messages. In addition, we see a society that is moderately polychronic (i.e., approaching multiple tasks simultaneously) with a moderate focus on centers of community (i.e., a balance between preserving personal space and communal space). Such information can make a real difference to global managers in helping them understand the environment they are entering and take steps to respond accordingly. According to Hall, successful managers understand these three aspects of culture, both individually and collectively, and incorporate this knowledge into their management style when dealing with employees or business representatives from other countries. Failure to understand these differences, however, will likely increase the possibility of misunderstandings, hurt feelings, and even failure in business transactions.

HOFSTEDE'S CULTURAL DIMENSIONS

Geert Hofstede is a widely respected Dutch management researcher who has dedicated his life to studying managerial differences around the world.[25] Based on a major study of employees working for a large multinational corporation (IBM), he began developing a model that has become the most widely used approach to studying cultural differences as they relate to business organization and management. (It should be noted that Hofstede's original model has gone through several iterations; the most recent version of this model is presented here.) Hofstede's model, first published in his classic book, *Culture's Consequence: International Differences in Work Related Values,* is based on the assumption that different cultures can be distinguished based on differences in what they value.[26] That is, some cultures place a high value on equality among individuals, while others place a high value on hierarchies. Likewise, some people value certainty in everyday life and have a difficult time with unanticipated events, while others have a greater tolerance for ambiguity and seem to relish change. Taken together, Hofstede argues, these value dimensions allow us to gain considerable insight into organized behavior.

Initially, Hofstede asserted that cultures could be distinguished along four dimensions. He later added a fifth dimension based on his subsequent research with Michael Bond. The final five dimensions are illustrated in Exhibit 7.8. We briefly examine each of these five dimensions here.

Hofstede's first dimension, *power distance,* refers to the beliefs that people have about the appropriateness of either large or small differences in power and authority among the members of a group or society. Some cultures, particularly those in several Asian, Arab, and Latin American countries, stress high power distance, believing that it is natural or beneficial for some members of a group or society to exert considerable control over their subordinates. Subordinates are expected to do what

Exhibit 7.8

Hofstede's Cultural Dimensions

Cultural Dimensions	Scale	Anchors
Power distance: Beliefs about the appropriate distribution of power in society	*Low power distance:* Belief that effective leaders need not have substantial amounts of power compared to their subordinates. Examples: Denmark, Ireland, Norway, Israel, Sweden	*High power distance:* Belief that people in positions of authority should have considerable power compared to their subordinates. Examples: Malaysia, Mexico, Saudi Arabia
Uncertainty avoidance: Extent to which people feel threatened by uncertain or unknown situations	*Low uncertainty avoidance:* Tolerance for ambiguity; little need for rules to constrain uncertainty. Examples: Singapore, Denmark, Sweden, United Kingdom	*High uncertainty avoidance:* Intolerance for ambiguity; need for many rules to constrain uncertainty. Examples: Greece, Portugal, Uruguay, Japan, France, Spain
Individualism-collectivism: Relative importance of individual versus group interests in society	*Collectivism:* Precedence of group interests over individual interests. Examples: Japan, Korea, Indonesia, Pakistan, Latin America	*Individualism:* Precedence of individual interests over group interests. Examples: United States, Australia, Netherlands, Italy, Scandinavia
Masculinity-femininity: Assertiveness versus passivity; material possessions versus quality of life	*Masculinity:* Most value placed on material possessions, money, and the pursuit of personal goals. Examples: Japan, Austria, Italy, Switzerland, Mexico	*Femininity:* Most value placed on personal relationships, quality of life, and the welfare of others. Examples: Sweden, Norway, Netherlands, Costa Rica
Long-term orientation: Long-term versus short-term outlook on work, life, and relationships	*Short-term orientation:* Past and present orientation; most value placed on traditions and social obligations. Examples: Pakistan, Nigeria, Philippines, Russia	*Long-term orientation:* Future orientation; most value placed on dedication, hard work, and thrift. Examples: China, Korea, Japan, Brazil

Source: Based on Geert Hofstede, *Culture's Consequence: International Differences in Work Related Values,* rev. ed. (Thousand Oaks, CA: Sage, 2001). Hofstede's fifth dimension, long-term orientation, is also referred to as Confucian dynamism. Country examples are taken from his book.

they are told with few questions. However, this control does not necessarily have to be abusive; rather, it could be benevolent: a strong master exerts control to look after the welfare of the entire group. Other cultures, particularly those in Scandinavia, prefer a low power distance, believing in a more egalitarian or participative approach to social or organizational structure. They expect subordinates to be consulted on key issues that affect them and will accept strong leaders to the extent that they support democratic principles. According to Hofstede, the United States is somewhere toward but not at the low end of the power distance scale, suggesting that while Americans may admire John Wayne and other take-charge leaders, they do not necessarily support highly autocratic ones.

Hofstede's second dimension focuses on the extent to which people are comfortable with uncertainty or ambiguity in the workplace; this is referred to as *uncertainty avoidance.* In some cultures, such as those of Scandinavia and the United States, people are generally comfortable not knowing everything and can deal effectively with this lack of knowledge. They have an aversion to highly structured organizations and excessive rules. They sometimes feel that standardization and too much order stifles creativity. In Hofstede's model, such cultures are described as having low uncertainty avoidance. By contrast, in other cultures, such as Japan, France, and many Latin American countries, people feel a stronger need for certainty, clarity, and predictability. They seek written rules and strong social norms to guide behavior. Working in formal, highly structured organizations with clear job descriptions and clearly defined roles and norms provides order, comfort, and a sense of security. According to Hofstede, these cultures have high uncertainty avoidance.

The dimension that has received the most attention among managers is Hofstede's third dimension: the degree to which a society stresses *individualism* or *collectivism.* Many Western countries are clearly individualistic in nature. People are taught that they are responsible for themselves and that in a sense the world revolves around them. Their job is to become independent and reap the rewards of their individual endeavors. Individual achievement is admired, and people are taught not to become too dependent on organizations or groups. By contrast, collectivistic cultures, such as several from East and Southeast Asia, stress group interests over those of the individual. Collectivistic cultures stress personal relationships, achieving harmony as an overriding societal objective, and the central role of the family in both personal and business affairs. One's identity is difficult to separate from that of one's group. Group decision making is preferred, and groups protect their members in exchange for unquestioned loyalty. This is not to say that individuals are not important; they are. Instead, collectivistic cultures tend to believe that people can attain their full potential only as a member of a strong group.

Perhaps Hofstede's most controversial dimension is his fourth, referred to as *masculinity-femininity.* Hofstede's research led him to conclude that some cultures tend to exhibit aggressiveness in pursuing their goals and place a high value on achievement, decisiveness, and assertiveness. Hofstede referred to these cultures as "masculine." (Subsequent researchers have referred to this as "aggressive goal behavior" in the recognition that many women obviously share a strong achievement orientation, decisiveness, and assertiveness.) Hofstede identifies Japan, Austria, and Italy as strongly masculine countries, while Germany and the United States are described as moderately aggressive cultures. By contrast, "feminine" cultures tend to stress communal goals and quality of life over individual achievement. In fact, assertiveness is often ridiculed in such cultures, and people often tend to undersell themselves. Quality of life is often emphasized over careers. Hofstede identifies the Netherlands and the Scandinavian countries as examples of "feminine" cultures. This is not to say that goals are unimportant to these cultures. Rather, achieving such goals is not viewed as the overall purpose of life. Goals are seen as means, not ends, to a good life.

Finally, in his later work, Hofstede added *long-term orientation* as a fifth dimension in recognition of a certain uniqueness characterizing East Asian cultures. This dimension was originally referred to as "Confucian dynamism." Long-term orientation as a cultural characteristic focuses on the extent to which cultures emphasize working for today compared to working for tomorrow. In some cultures (e.g., Korea, Japan, and Taiwan) people tend to have a long-term orientation that values hard work, personal sacrifice for future benefits, dedication to a cause, and personal thrift. The emphasis is on sacrifice so that future generations can prosper. This outlook is thought to have been a primary ingredient in the success stories of countries such as Korea, Singapore, and Taiwan that engaged in late industrialization (see Chapter 4). By contrast, other cultures tend to focus more on the past or present, emphasizing respect for traditions and fulfillment of one's social obligations over achievement or investments. Indeed, some cultures (and their religions) suggest that since no one can see into the future, attempts to change it border on being immoral. It is better to focus on today and let tomorrow happen as it will. These cultures exhibit what Hofstede calls a *short-term orientation*. He identifies Pakistan, Russia, and several countries in both northern and southern Africa as examples of cultures with a short-term orientation.

When Hofstede's model is applied to our example of China, it points to a culture that is characterized by a high power distance (high power centralization) and moderately high uncertainty avoidance, which leads to considerable rules and laws aimed at reducing unanticipated events. In addition, Hofstede's model suggests a highly collectivistic society with moderate masculinity (i.e., assertiveness) and a long-term or future orientation. One might contrast this with several Western cultures that tend to stress greater individualism and lower power distance between people in a society. Again, while not explaining the whole of Chinese society, this model nonetheless highlights certain aspects of this culture in ways that can be of use to global managers.

TROMPENAARS'S CULTURAL DIMENSIONS

Fons Trompenaars—also a Dutch management researcher—presents a somewhat different model of culture based on his study of managers (initially from Royal Dutch/ Shell) over ten years.[27] Trompenaars's model is based on the earlier work of Harvard sociologists Talcott Parsons and Edward Shils and focuses on variations in both values and relationships across cultures.[28] The model consists of seven dimensions (see Exhibit 7.9). The first five focus on relationships among people, while the last two deal with time orientation and relationship with nature.

Trompenaars's first dimension focuses on whether cultures believe that fairness is achieved by applying the same rules to everyone or by taking into consideration the particulars of each situation. Cultures characterized by *universalism* believe that everyone should be treated equally based on prespecified and universally applied laws and policies. That is, there is a "correct" way to treat people, and this way applies to everyone. In the United States, for example, hiring practices and performance evaluations are typically based on strict company policies that comply with federal laws. In theory, if not always in practice, nepotism is illegal and everyone is treated equally. By contrast, cultures characterized by *particularism* believe that

Exhibit 7.9

Trompenaars's Cultural Dimensions

Cultural Dimensions	Scale Anchors	
Universalism-particularism: Are rules or relationships more important?	*Universalism:* Reliance on formal rules and policies that are applied equally to everyone. Examples: Austria, Germany, Switzerland, United States	*Particularism:* Rules must be tempered by the nature of the situation and the people involved. Examples: China, Venezuela, Indonesia, Korea
Individualism-collectivism: Do people derive their identity from within themselves or their group?	*Individualism:* Focus on individual achievement and independence. Examples: United States, Nigeria, Mexico, Argentina	*Collectivism:* Focus on group achievement and welfare. Examples: Singapore, Thailand, Japan
Specific versus diffuse: Are an individual's various roles compartmentalized or integrated?	*Specific:* Clear separation of a person's various roles. Examples: Sweden, Germany, Canada, United Kingdom, United States	*Diffuse:* Clear integration of a person's various roles. Examples: China, Venezuela, Mexico, Japan, Spain
Neutral versus affective: Are people free to express their emotions or are they restrained?	*Neutral:* Refrain from showing emotions; hide feelings. Examples: Japan, Singapore, United Kingdom	*Affective:* Emotional expressions acceptable or encouraged. Examples: Mexico, Brazil, Italy
Achievement versus ascription: How are people accorded respect and social status?	*Achievement:* Respect for earned accomplishments. Examples: Austria, United States, Switzerland	*Ascription:* Respect for ascribed or inherited status. Examples: Egypt, Indonesia, Korea, Hungary
Time perspective: Do people focus on the past or the future?	*Past/present-oriented:* Emphasis on past events and glory. Examples: France, Spain, Portugal, Arab countries	*Future-oriented:* Emphasis on planning and future possibilities. Examples: China, Japan, Korea, Sweden, United States
Relationship with the environment: Do people control the environment or does it control them?	*Inner-directed:* Focus on controlling the environment. Examples: Australia, United States, United Kingdom	*Outer-directed:* Focus on living in harmony with nature. Examples: China, India, Sweden, Egypt, Korea

Source: Based on the work of Fons Trompenaars and Charles Hampden-Turner, *Riding the Waves of Culture: Understanding Cultural Diversity in Global Business,* rev. ed. (London: McGraw-Hill, 1998). Country examples are from this book.

rules and policies are only guidelines. Each situation must be considered on its own merits and it is necessary to incorporate possible extenuating circumstances or personal relationships that may be involved. In other words, there is no "correct" way of dealing with everyone. Thus, while members of particularistic cultures value the rule of law, they believe that its application must be flexible and tempered with considerations for the people and the circumstances involved. As a result, the consideration of family and friends will often take precedence over the law. An example of particularism can be seen in the common practice in such countries as Venezuela, Indonesia, and the Philippines to hire one's friends and family members, often regardless of their level of qualifications.

The second dimension here mirrors Hofstede's earlier work that differentiates between *individualism,* where people think of themselves primarily as individuals, and *collectivism,* where people think of themselves primarily as members of a group. The only difference between these two sets of dimensions can be found in their application. For example, while Hofstede lists Mexico and Argentina as relatively collectivist, Trompenaars lists them as individualistic. Whether this resulted from different measurement techniques or from changes in the cultures in the ten years between the two studies has not been explained.

Trompenaars's third dimension focuses on the extent to which an individual's various roles in life should be kept separate or integrated. In *specific cultures,* life is largely compartmentalized and the various roles each individual fills are often played out in isolation from one another. For example, an individual can simultaneously be a corporate vice president, a church member, a food bank volunteer, and a parent. These roles frequently require different behaviors, dress, titles, and levels of formality. As a vice president, the individual may have to be well dressed, formal, and authoritative, but as a volunteer this same individual may have to be casually dressed, informal, and participative. Enacting these different roles is often easy because the roles are separate and distinct and seldom overlap. By contrast, in *diffuse cultures,* the boundaries between one's various roles become blurred and often overlap. Relationships are more carefully chosen and more deeply seated, and people tend to get to know others better across a variety of different roles. Throughout much of Asia, for instance, one's supervisor often serves many roles, including boss, confidant, father figure, and patron.

The fourth dimension in Trompenaars's model focuses on emotion. Some cultures expect their members to be stoic and to suppress any outward emotional displays as being inappropriate. People are cautious in revealing their basic thoughts and beliefs, and control over one's emotions is admired. Physical contact and expressive gestures are to be avoided. Trompenaars refers to these as *neutral cultures.* A prime example of a neutral culture is Japan. By contrast, other cultures such as Brazil and Italy not only accept but often encourage outward displays of emotion. In this case, feelings and opinions are freely expressed and emotional expression is often uninhibited. Animated expressions and gesturing are common, as is touching. Such cultures are referred to as *affective cultures.*

The fifth dimension focuses on how status and rewards are allocated in cultures. In *achievement cultures,* status and rewards are based on an individual or group's accomplishments, while in *ascription cultures* such recognition is based largely on things such as seniority, inheritance, class, or gender. Achievement cultures use titles only when they are relevant, and their leaders typically earn respect through superior performance. By contrast, people in ascription cultures use titles routinely as a means of reinforcing a hierarchy and typically select their leaders based on age or background.

In addition to these five dimensions focusing on interpersonal relations,

Trompenaars adds two more dimensions. The first of these is *time perspective.* To succeed in business, managers must have a shared understanding about what time means. However, when this concept is taken across cultures, considerable differences can often be found. For example, some cultures tend to be rather precise about time (one o'clock means one o'clock), while others take a more flexible approach (one o'clock may, in fact, mean one thirty or possibly two o'clock). While Americans are often heard saying, "Time is money," implying a sense of urgency in the use of time, Mexicans are often heard to say *"mañana,"* implying no such urgency. It is not that one group is right and the other is wrong; rather, cultural differences often drive what is acceptable behavior. Nowhere is this truer than with respect to time.

As conceptualized by Trompenaars, the time dimension considers how various cultures deal with past, present, and future time. For example, some cultures, such as Spain, Israel, and most Arab countries, tend to have a *past or present orientation.* There is an emphasis on past events and former glories, and history is often seen as providing a context for understanding the present and the future. Such cultures often believe in a preordained future—the will of God or the way of nature—and long-term planning is seen as having little value. Stability and continuity are revered, and elders are respected for their wisdom. Other countries, such as those in East Asia, northern Europe, and North America, tend to have more of a *future focus.* They place a greater emphasis on planning and on exploring future possibilities. They believe that cultures make their own history. Leaders are respected more for what they have accomplished than for their seniority. Knowledge is more important than wisdom and hard work brings its own rewards.

The final dimension focuses on people's *relationship with the environment.* The fundamental issue for this dimension is whether people believe they control their environment or their environment controls them. Some cultures, referred to as *inner-directed cultures,* tend to believe that they control their own destinies. Such societies are more likely to try to change their surroundings and pursue their own goals. Americans are often cited as good examples of an inner-directed society, although Australia and the United Kingdom are also good examples. By contrast, *outer-directed cultures* tend to believe that it is important to adjust their lives to external realities, since they do not control most of life's outcomes. As a result, they tend to strive for stability and living in harmony with nature. Many East Asian, Southeast Asian, and Arab cultures are cited as examples of outer-directed cultures.

When we apply Trompenaars's model to China, the following portrait emerges. Chinese culture is described as particularistic; that is, rules and laws do not apply universally but rather depend on the situation (e.g., connections). China is also outer-directed, trying to live in harmony with nature. It is moderately collectivistic (more individualistic than in Hofstede's prediction) and is neutral on affective response (i.e., people tend not to show their emotions in public). The Chinese are seen as having a moderately long-term focus (again, less than in Hofstede's view) and a mid-range position between achieved and ascribed status (i.e., how people gain status in a society). Finally, China is seen as being highly diffuse, with people's multiple roles intersecting and overlapping, in contrast to the more separated roles typically found in the West. The picture that emerges is not dissimilar to that of Hofstede; however, the different starting point in the analysis leads to somewhat different conclusions. Even so, a lot can be learned at least on a general level from using this model about people living and working in mainstream China.

GLOBE's Cultural Dimensions

Finally, in one of the most comprehensive efforts to identify cultural dimensions, Robert House led an international team of researchers that focused on understanding the influence of cultural differences on leadership in organizations.[29] Their investigation was called the GLOBE study, for Global Leadership and Organizational Behavior Effectiveness. In their research, the GLOBE researchers identified nine cultural dimensions as summarized in Exhibit 7.10. While several of these dimensions have been identified previously (e.g., individualism-collectivism, power orientation, uncertainty avoidance), others are unique (e.g., gender egalitarianism, performance orientation). Moreover, the GLOBE researchers concluded from their analyses that it was possible to divide the individualism-collectivism dimension into two subdimensions, one focusing on institutional (or societywide) individualism and one focusing on in-group individualism, consisting of family, friends, and organizations.

Based on this assessment, the GLOBE researchers collected data in sixty-two countries and compared the results as they relate to leadership behavior. Systematic differences were found across the cultures. For example, participatory leadership styles that were often accepted in the individualistic West were suspect in the more collectivistic East. Asian managers placed a heavy emphasis on paternalistic leadership and group maintenance activities. The GLOBE study also found that charismatic leaders could be found in most cultures, although they were highly assertive in some cultures (e.g., Britain's Tony Blair) and passive in others (e.g., India's Mahatma Gandhi). A leader who listened carefully to his or her subordinates was more valued in the United States than in China. Furthermore, Malaysian leaders were expected to behave in a manner that was humble, dignified, and modest, while American leaders seldom behaved in this manner. Indians preferred leaders who were assertive, morally principled, ideological, bold, and proactive, while family and tribal norms supported highly autocratic leaders in many Arab countries.[30]

To continue our example from above, when the GLOBE researchers look at Chinese culture, a rather complex picture emerges. Mainstream Chinese culture is described as high in power distance and in collectivism (both like Hofstede) and high in uncertainty avoidance (stronger than Hofstede's observation). The Chinese are also seen as being high in *assertiveness orientation* (much like Hofstede's masculinity dimension) and moderately high in *future orientation* (again much like Hofstede's observation). In addition, the GLOBE researchers observe that Chinese culture has a moderately high *performance orientation*, relatively low *gender egalitarianism*, and low *humane orientation*.

As with the other models, a number of useful generalizations can be found using this model. These can then be compared to observations from other cultures to better

Exhibit 7.10

GLOBE's Cultural Dimensions

Cultural Dimensions	Description
Power distance	Degree to which people expect power to be distributed equally
Uncertainty avoidance	Extent to which people rely on norms, rules, and procedures to reduce unpredictability of future events
Humane orientation	Extent to which people reward fairness, altruism, and generosity
Institutional collectivism	Extent to which society encourages collective distribution of resources and collective action
In-group collectivism	Extent to which individuals express pride, loyalty, and cohesiveness in their organizations and families
Assertiveness	Degree to which people are assertive, confrontational, and aggressive in relationships with others
Gender egalitarianism	Degree to which gender differences are minimized
Future orientation	Extent to which people engage in future-oriented behaviors such as planning, investing, and delayed gratification
Performance orientation	Degree to which high performance is encouraged and rewarded

Source: Based on Robert House, Paul Hanges, Mansour Javidan, Peter Dorfman, and Vipin Gupta, *Culture, Leadership, and Organizations: The GLOBE Study of 62 Societies* (Thousand Oaks, CA: Sage, 2004). Note that the GLOBE model does not use scale anchors; instead, scores are measured on a numeric continuum ranging from low to high.

understand the managerial implications. Clearly one of the principal contributions of the GLOBE project is to systematically study not just cultural dimensions but how variations in such dimensions affect leadership effectiveness. With this knowledge, global managers are better prepared for the realities of doing business in a turbulent world of business.

COMPARING MODELS OF NATIONAL CULTURES

The four culture models reviewed here attempt to accomplish two things. First, each model offers a well-reasoned set of dimensions along which various cultures can be compared. They offer us a form of shorthand for cultural analysis. We can break down assessments of various cultures into power distance, uncertainty avoidance, and so forth, allowing us to organize our thoughts and focus our attention on what otherwise would be a monumental task. Second, three of the models offer numeric scores for rating various cultures. For example, we can use Hofstede to say that Germany is a 35 while France is a 68 in the power distance dimension, suggesting that Germany is more egalitarian than France. Regardless of whether

Exhibit 7.11

Applying Various Culture Models to China

Culture Model	Description of Chinese Culture
Hall	Moderately polychronic High-context communication Moderate center of community (i.e., communal)
Hofstede	High power distance Moderately high uncertainty avoidance High collectivism Moderate masculinity High long-term orientation
Trompenaars	Particularistic orientation Outer-directed; live in harmony with nature Moderate collectivism Neutral (low emotion) Moderate long-term focus Balance of achieved and ascribed status Highly diffuse (highly integrated roles)
GLOBE	High power distance High uncertainty avoidance High in-group collectivism High institutional collectivism High assertiveness Moderate future orientation Moderately high performance orientation Moderately low gender egalitarianism Low humane orientation

these ratings are highly precise or only generally indicative of these countries, they force managers to confront cultural differences and consider the managerial implications.

As a result of these differences in focus and orientation, each model provides a different, although sometimes overlapping, portrait of a single culture. Exhibit 7.11 summarizes what these four models say about Chinese culture. Which of these models would be most helpful to a manager being sent to China for the first time? Which is best suited to lead a manager out of the culture theory jungle? In summary, despite the limitations of the various models, they can nonetheless be useful for managers. They provide a heuristic for identifying focal points for cross-cultural comparisons, thereby allowing managers to be better prepared for overseas assignments. In the next chapter, we turn our attention to how managers might make better use of models such as these to assess cultural differences in the world of business.

KEY TERMS

achievement cultures	individualism
affective cultures	inner-directed cultures
ascription cultures	long-term orientation
assertiveness orientation	low-context cultures
centers of community	masculinity
centers of power	monochronic
Chinese family business	neutral cultures
collectivism	objective culture
Confucianism	outer-directed cultures
Confucius	particularism
culture	past or present orientation
diffuse cultures	performance orientation
egalitarian cultures	personal obligations
face	polychronic
familism	power distance
femininity	relationship with the environment
filial piety	short-term orientation
five cardinal virtues	specific cultures
future orientation	subjective culture
gender egalitarianism	Sun Tzu
gong-si	time perspective
guanxi	uncertainty avoidance
high-context cultures	universalism
humane orientation	

GLOBAL MANAGER'S WORKBOOK 7.1: PROMONTORY POINT

What is the significance of Promontory Point, Utah, in U.S. history? And what, if anything, does it say about U.S. culture, past or present? Consider the following true story. In 1862, in the middle of the American Civil War, the U.S. Congress passed the Pacific Railroad Act authorizing the construction of a transcontinental railroad across the United States from Chicago, Illinois, to Sacramento, California.[31] The new railroad would help unify the country politically and economically, facilitate the agricultural and ultimately industrial development of the vast open territories of the American Midwest, and help populate the vast, wide-open spaces (with mostly white settlers). Building a two-thousand-mile-long railroad was a huge but magnificent challenge and reflected a young America's self-confidence, optimism, and self-image, as well as its concept of its own manifest destiny.

To complete this massive undertaking, Congress selected two railroads, the Union

Pacific in the East and the Central Pacific in the West, and agreed to pay each company in cash and adjacent land for each mile of track they laid until the two lines met. The fact that much of this land already belonged to Native American tribes by treaty was largely ignored. In setting up the competition between the two railroads, Congress hoped to establish a horse race that ensured that the entire transcontinental line was completed as rapidly as possible.

Building the railroad was no easy task. Not only would the companies have to cross one of the world's largest prairies, but they would also have to build countless tunnels and bridges across one of the world's most formidable mountain ranges, the Rocky Mountains. To complete the work, the Central Pacific imported thousands of Chinese laborers, while the Union Pacific hired thousands of mostly Irish immigrants. They were typically assigned the most difficult, and sometimes the most dangerous, jobs. (After the completion of the railroad, most of the Irish became U.S. citizens; most of the Chinese were deported.) Since each company was paid by the mile, an all-out single-minded effort would be required to cover as much land as possible as quickly as possible to maximize each company's income and profit.

As the two railroads approached each other in the Utah Territory, instead of meeting they began making plans to build past each other in parallel lines, the Central Pacific heading east and the Union Pacific heading west. Since they were paid for each mile of rail they constructed, the companies reasoned, why link up? After all, while the legislation paid the railroads until the two lines met, it did not actually require them to meet. Finally, a frustrated and embarrassed Congress intervened and passed a second law mandating that the two lines meet at Promontory Point, Utah. The companies complied. On May 10, 1869, the two lines were joined at the stipulated site and the transcontinental railroad—the first of its kind on any continent—was at last completed.

1. Based on what you have learned, identify what you believe are the principal cultural traits that best characterized the United States during the mid-1800s, when the transcontinental railroad was under construction.
2. From your reading of history, how was U.S. culture of the mid-1800s different, if at all, from the prevailing cultures of Western Europe (e.g., England, France, Germany) at this same time? How was it different from the prevailing cultures of East Asia (e.g., Japan, China) at this same time?
3. In your judgment, what if anything has changed in the prevailing cultural traits of the United States today compared to the mid-1800s?
4. Use one of the four culture models discussed above to describe what you consider to be the culture in the United States today.

GLOBAL MANAGER'S WORKBOOK 7.2: DINING OUT IN LOUGANG

When journalist Peter Hessler was invited for lunch in the rural Chinese village of Luogang in Guangdong Province, he was in for a surprise.[32] After he was seated at a table in the Highest Ranking Wild Flavor Restaurant, the waitress asked him bluntly,

"Do you want a big rat or a small rat?" Unsure of what to do, Hessler asked the waitress what the difference was and was informed that the big rats eat grass while the small rats eat fruit. Both tasted good, he was assured.

As he contemplated his choice, Hessler looked at the people sitting at the next table. A young boy was gnawing on a rat drumstick, but he couldn't tell whether it was from a big rat or a small one. After asking himself how he got into this predicament, he finally made a decision: a small rat. He chose an item from the menu called simmered mountain rat with black beans. He selected this over other possibilities, including mountain rat soup, steamed mountain rat, simmered mountain rat, roasted mountain rat, mountain rat curry, and spicy and salty mountain rat.

The Chinese say that people in Guangdong will eat anything. Besides rat, people at the Highest Ranking Wild Flavor Restaurant can order turtledove, fox, cat, python, and an assortment of strange-looking local animals whose names don't translate into English. Selecting a menu item involves considerations beyond flavor and texture. You order cat not just because you enjoy the taste but also because cats are believed to impart a lively *jingshen* (spirit). You order a snake because it makes you stronger. And you order the private parts of a deer to make you more virile. Why would you eat a rat? Because it will keep you from going bald and make your white hair turn black.

After a few minutes, the waitress asked Hessler to come back to the kitchen and select his rat. In the back of the kitchen, he saw several cages stacked on top of one another. Each cage contained about thirty rats. "How about this one?" the waitress asked. "Fine," Hessler replied. The waitress then put on a white glove (presumably for hygiene purposes) and grabbed the chosen rat. "Are you sure this is the one?" she asked. The rat gazed at Hessler with its little beady eyes. He nodded his approval. Then the waitress grabbed the rat by its tail and flipped her wrist, thereby launching the rat through the air until it landed on its head on the concrete floor with a soft thud. There was little blood. Hessler was told that he could return to his table; lunch would arrive shortly.

Waiting for his meal to come, Hessler had an opportunity to speak with the owner of the restaurant. The first thing he noticed was the owner's full head of thick black hair. The owner said that local people have been eating rat for more than a thousand years. However, his customers insist on eating rats from the mountains because they are clean; they won't eat city rats, he insisted. He assured Hessler that the government hygiene department came by regularly to inspect his rats and had never found anything wrong. Before walking away, the owner smiled and said that you can't find food like this in America.

When lunch was finally served, Hessler tried to think of this as a new experience. He tried the beans first, and they tasted fine. Then he polked around at the rat meat. It was clearly well done and attractively garnished with onions, leeks, and ginger. Nestled in a light sauce were skinny rat thighs, short strips of rat flank, and delicate tiny rat ribs. He hesitantly took his first bite and found the meat to be lean and white without a hint of gaminess. It didn't taste like anything he had had before. It tasted like rat. Fortunately, he had lots of beer to wash it down with.

QUESTIONS FOR DISCUSSION

1. What would you do if you were faced with the situation that Peter Hessler experienced at the Lougang restaurant, especially if an important Chinese client had invited you to the restaurant?
2. Have you ever had a similar experience in another culture where you were pressured to eat or do something that was acceptable—or even required—in the local culture but which you found uncomfortable? What did you do?
3. Are there aspects of your own home culture that foreign visitors might find offensive or uncomfortable for some reason? What might you do to put your foreign guests at ease in this situation?

NOTES

1. Daria Snezko (MBA student), personal communication, April 23, 2004.
2. Wang Ying-lin, *Trimetric Classic,* trans. H. Giles (Shanghai: Kelly and Walsh, 1910). Some writers have attributed this observation to Confucius.
3. Nancy Adler, *International Dimensions of Organizational Behavior* (Cincinnati, OH: Southwestern, 1997), p. 3.
4. Kevin Delaney, "Microsoft's Encarta Has Different Facts for Different Folks," *Wall Street Journal,* June 25, 1999, p. A1.
5. Andre Laurent, "The Cultural Diversity of Western Conceptions of Management," *International Studies of Management and Organization* 13, no. 1–2 (Spring–Summer 1983): 75–96.
6. Edward T. Hall, *An Anthropology of Everyday Life: An Autobiography* (New York: Anchor Books, 1992), p. 210.
7. Fons Trompenaars and Charles Hampden-Turner, *Riding the Waves of Culture: Understanding Cultural Diversity in Global Business,* rev. ed. (London: McGraw-Hill, 1998).
8. Clifford Geertz, *The Interpretation of Cultures* (New York: Basic Books, 1973).
9. Clyde Kluckholn, *Culture and Behavior* (New York: Free Press, 1954).
10. Geert Hofstede, *Cultures and Organizations: Software of the Mind* (New York: McGraw-Hill, 1991).
11. Sameena Ahmad, "Behind the Mask: A Survey of Business in China," *Economist,* March 20, 2004, pp. 3–19.
12. Ming-Jer Chen, *Inside Chinese Business: A Guide for Managers Worldwide* (Boston: Harvard Business School Press, 2001).
13. Wenzhong Hu and Cornelius Grove, *Encountering the Chinese* (Yarmouth, ME: Intercultural, 1999).
14. Samuel Griffith, *Sun Tzu: The Art of War* (New York: Oxford University Press, 1971).
15. John Cullen and K. Praveen Parboteeah, *Multinational Management: A Strategic Approach* (Cincinnati, OH: Southwestern College Publishing, 2005), p. 27.
16. Christopher Earley, *Face, Harmony, and Social Structure* (New York: Oxford University Press, 1997).
17. Gordon Redding, *The Spirit of Chinese Capitalism* (Berlin: de Gruyter, 1990).
18. John Child, *Management in China During the Age of Reform* (Cambridge: Cambridge University Press, 1994).
19. Redding, *The Spirit of Chinese Capitalism.*
20. Ahmad, "Behind the Mask."
21. Chen, *Inside Chinese Business.*

22. Ahmad, "Behind the Mask."

23. Edward T. Hall, *The Silent Language* (New York: Anchor Books, 1959); Edward T. Hall, *The Dance of Life* (New York: Anchor Books, 1983).

24. Edward T. Hall and Mildred Hall, *Hidden Differences: Doing Business with the Japanese* (New York: Doubleday, 1987); Edward T. Hall and Mildred Hall, *Understanding Cultural Differences: Germans, French, and Americans* (Yarmouth, ME: Intercultural, 1990).

25. Hofstede, *Cultures and Organizations*; Geert Hofstede, *Culture's Consequence: International Differences in Work Related Values,* rev. ed. (Thousand Oaks, CA: Sage, 2001).

26. Hofstede, *Culture's Consequence.*

27. Trompenaars and Hampden-Turner, *Riding the Waves of Culture.*

28. Talcott Parsons and E. Shils, *Towards a General Theory of Action* (Cambridge, MA: Harvard University Press, 1951).

29. Robert House, Paul Hanges, Mansour Javidan, Peter Dorfman, and Vipin Gupta, *Culture, Leadership, and Organizations: The GLOBE Study of 62 Societies* (Thousand Oaks, CA: Sage, 2004).

30. Ibid.

31. Stephen Ambrose, *Nothing Like It in the World: The Men Who Built the Transcontinental Railroad: 1863–1869* (New York: Simon and Schuster, 2001); Mary Ann Fraser, *Ten Mile Day: The Building of the Transcontinental Railroad* (New York: Henry Holt, 1996).

32. Peter Hessler, "A Rat in My Soup," *New Yorker,* July 24, 2000, p. 38.

8 | Assessing Cultural Differences

MADE IN USA

The U.S. economy is second to none in size and strength around the world. U.S. companies are envied, emulated, respected, feared, and, at times, disliked. At the same time, U.S. managers are widely respected, admired, recruited, and, at times, criticized. Foreign observers have noted that while U.S. managers may make excellent teachers in the world of business, they often make poor students. That is, they are not always keen observers of events around them and, as a result, often pay a price for their lack of global sophistication and cross-cultural understanding. Why is this? To answer this question, consider how the world views typical U.S. managers.

Experts from many countries have tried to describe the typical American manager over the years.[1] While acknowledging that the United States probably has greater diversity than many other countries, these writers have nonetheless tried to characterize Americans using a small number of adjectives. The most common adjectives include the following:

- *Individualistic.* Perhaps no other country in the world stresses individual rights and responsibilities more than the United States does. Here, a "man's home is his castle" and success is determined by personal effort. It is important to be independent and stay out of other people's business.
- *Materialistic.* In U.S. society, which is focused on achievement, material possessions often represent symbols of success, and conspicuous consumption can become a lifestyle. This belief often leads to a short-term focus that requires considerable energy to achieve immediate results.
- *Informal.* Americans tend to be "laid back" and to spend their time "hanging out." They are often uncomfortable with formality and are quick to remove their coats, use first names, and discuss personal details with new acquaintances.

149

- *Linear.* Americans tend to be single-minded in the pursuit of their objectives and often rush headlong toward their goals with a determination that can border on obsession. They do things "24/7" and are never far from their cell phones, laptops, and PDAs. Work frequently takes precedence over family and friends.
- *Impatient.* Americans seem to be in a perpetual hurry; they want things done now. Time is seen as a measurable—and sometimes marketable—commodity that should be used wisely in the pursuit of one's objectives, whether business or pleasure.
- *Risk-oriented.* Americans tend to be optimistic and opportunistic, and are often comfortable taking risks in order to achieve desired objectives.
- *Superficial.* Americans often ignore the details or conflicting positions underlying complex issues and prefer to focus on the "big picture." They enjoy small talk but have little patience with cultural niceties or ceremonial observances. They sometimes have difficulty building deep or lasting relationships.
- *Blunt.* Americans tend to "put their cards on the table" from the start and are suspicious of anyone who does not reciprocate. Understanding nuances or subtleties in conversations is not their strong suit.
- *Naïve.* Americans are often described as being overly trusting and friendly toward people they hardly know. They come across to many foreigners as naïve and uninformed in matters of global importance. They are admired for their technical competence but not their sophistication.
- *Generous.* On a per capita basis, Americans give more money to charities than anyone else on the planet. Some say this is because they have more money to give away or because of U.S. tax policy, but there is more to it than this. There is a fundamental belief that people have a moral responsibility to support social causes, political causes, local causes, and sometimes perfect strangers to an extent seldom seen elsewhere.
- *Jingoistic.* Many Americans seem convinced that the United States is the greatest country in the world. There is no reason to discuss this; anyone who disagrees is simply wrong.

Do all Americans fit this description? Of course not. For starters, the United States is a very heterogeneous society consisting of many strong cultures. Most of its citizens, or their ancestors, migrated to the United States from various regions of the world in search of a better life and brought their cultures with them. It is therefore important to recognize that when people try to describe a "typical" American, they are often focusing on Anglo-Americans or, more accurately, European Americans. Other American cultures, including Asian Americans, African Americans, Native Americans, and so forth, can have very different cultural characteristics. And even among the European American community, stark cultural differences can be found. Indeed, the individualistic nature of the United States encourages and supports cultural diversity. Despite all of this, if so many observers from so many different backgrounds come to the same conclusions about the "typical" American, such observations are difficult to ignore.

Even so, a critical question is not so much how the typical American (or anyone else) is described, but rather against which standards he or she is judged. That is, what are the characteristics of different cultures, and how do these differences affect interpersonal assessments and relations? For example, people from more collectivistic cultures, such as China, often see Americans as highly individualistic, while many Americans see the Chinese as highly collectivistic. The point is not that one orientation is superior to the other. Rather, the point is that if both Americans and Chinese can better understand each other—if they can genuinely get inside each other's heads and learn what motivates each other—they are far more likely to succeed in forming partnerships or doing business together than if they remain mired in their own cultural crosscurrents.

NAVIGATING THE CULTURE THEORY JUNGLE

As is evident from Chapter 7, many different models of cultural differences can be identified. Indeed, only four such models were reviewed; there are many, many more. Unfortunately, these models frequently focus on different aspects of societal beliefs, norms, or values, and, as a result, convergence across the models is limited. From a managerial standpoint, questions are logically raised concerning which model best suits the needs of organizations and their managers. This lack of agreement concerning which cultural variables are most important presents managers with a dilemma in terms of managerial action. For example, is it more important for managers to compare cultures based on achievement versus ascription, as Trompenaars suggests, or on masculinity versus femininity, as Hofstede suggests? Is personal space a key variable in cross-cultural assessment, as Hall suggests, or is humane orientation more important, as House and his GLOBE associates suggest? Managers need a clear set of relevant and readily understood dimensions that can collectively identify and illustrate the critical variables in their world.

The challenge is simply put: What can managers do to escape from this culture theory jungle, this web of competing models? One strategy is to review the various competing models and select the one that best suits a manager's needs. Many managers and management researchers have done this. An alternative approach is to carefully select only those dimensions from the various models that meet the particular analytic needs of the manager. For example, if the issue facing a manager concerns an upcoming negotiation between Americans and Japanese, the individualism-collectivism dimension will likely become salient. However, if this same manager is facing a negotiation between Americans and Canadians, this dimension is probably far less relevant. If a manager is planning to build a facility in the Gulf region, with its strong Islamic traditions, the time dimension offered in several of these models is probably relevant. Meanwhile, the power dimension is likely to be important in most global business situations, since managers must understand whether the country to which they are traveling is egalitarian or hierarchical in its beliefs.

A third approach, the approach advocated here, is to integrate and adapt the various cultural models based on their utility for better understanding business and man-

Exhibit 8.1

Common Themes Across Four Culture Models

Culture Models	Hall	Hofstede	Trompenaars	GLOBE
Common Themes:				
Relationship with the environment*		X	X	X
Social organization†	X	X	X	X
Power distribution‡		X	X	X
Rule orientation§		X	X	X
Time orientation¦	X	X	X	X
Other Themes:				
Physical space	X			
Emotional displays			X	
Role integration			X	

*A common theme is the superordinate goal of a society to either control or accommodate its natural and social environment. Hofstede differentiates between masculinity and femininity, Trompenaars distinguishes between inner-directed and outer-directed goal behavior, and GLOBE incorporates the three interrelated issues of assertiveness, fairness, and performance orientation.

†A common theme is whether societies are organized based on individuals or groups. The GLOBE study subdivides this dimension into institutional and in-group levels. Hall's concept of content and context is also strongly influenced by individualism-collectivism.

‡The GLOBE study includes both general power distribution and the more specific issue of gender egalitarianism, while Trompenaars focuses only indirectly on power, emphasizing how status and respect are achieved.

§Trompenaars and GLOBE focus largely on rule making as a means of reducing uncertainty, while Hofstede focuses on the degree of tolerance for uncertainty as a prelude to rule making.

¦Hall focuses on the use of time in work behavior, while the other researchers focus on short- versus long-term time orientation.

agement in cross-cultural settings. Our approach is to examine previous models in light of management realities and challenges and then select and adapt those dimensions that can best help us address critical management issues. It is impossible for managers to study all aspects of culture. They need a heuristic or shorthand to help them gain conceptual entry into cultural differences in a reasonably efficient manner. This requires integrating the various models into a new approach for the study of management. We present such a model in this chapter.

A good starting point for accomplishing this is to conduct a comparative review of the various culture models. Exhibit 8.1 summarizes the common themes that are found across the four models reviewed in Chapter 7. Five relatively common, if interrelated, themes or orientations, emerge: relationship with the environment, social organization, power distribution, rule orientation, and time orientation.[2] Although their emphasis often differs, Hofstede, Trompenaars, and the GLOBE study all suggest cultural dimensions that incorporate these five themes.[3] In the case of the GLOBE study, multiple factors can often be subsumed under one general dimension. For example, GLOBE's power distance and gender equalization can be incorporated under our conceptualization of power distribution, while assertiveness, performance orientation, and humane orientation (which is defined by fairness and altruism), can be included under our conceptualization of relationship with the environment. GLOBE also differentiates between two types of individualism-collectivism, or social organization. Finally, two of Hall's dimensions (communication context and time orientation) also fit into our overall classification.[4]

At first glance, these five themes seem to replicate Hofstede's original dimensions. However, closer analysis suggests that the other models have served to amplify, clarify, and, in some cases, reposition dimensions so they are more relevant for the contemporary workplace. Indeed, we believe the commonality across these models reinforces their utility (and possibly validity) as critical evaluative components in better understanding global management and the world of international business. Each model has added something of value to this endeavor. This is not to imply that other themes or dimensions are unimportant—only that the need for parsimony suggests that these five dimensions be emphasized for purposes of analysis and assessment. As a result, we will adopt these five dimensions for purposes of analysis throughout the remainder of this book. To highlight their centrality across the various models, we refer to these as the *"big five" culture dimensions*. As noted below, however, clear definitions of each of these dimensions are required.

REFRAMING CULTURE: A "BIG FIVE" APPROACH

From the standpoint of understanding organized behavior in cross-cultural settings, a useful model of culture should identify the principal normative beliefs concerning appropriate behaviors that collectively influence how people approach work, organization, and management. Taken together, the "big five" cultural dimensions accomplish this in large measure. Specifically, they focus on five fundamental questions about culture as they relate to social interaction and business practices in the global economy:

1. How do people view their relationship with their natural and social environment? Is their goal to control or master their surroundings or to live in harmony with them?
2. What is the fundamental building block of a society: individuals or groups? How does a society organize for collective action?
3. How are power and authority distributed in a society? Is this distribution based on concepts of hierarchy or egalitarianism? What are societal beliefs concerning equality or privilege?
4. How much importance does a society place on rules, laws, policies, and formal procedures to regulate behavior compared to other factors such as personal relationships or the unique circumstances of various situations?
5. How do people in a society organize their time to carry out their work and nonwork activities? Do people approach work in a linear or a nonlinear fashion?

The approach taken in this book assumes that a global manager is an investigator or student of cultural differences, not just a passive observer who accepts the opinions or assessments of others. As such an investigator, he or she learns about cultural

---

Exhibit 8.2

The "Big Five" Cultural Dimensions

Cultural Dimensions	Focus of Dimensions	Scale Anchors
Relationship with the environment	*Relationship with the natural and social environment:* Extent to which people seek to change and control or live in harmony with their natural and social surroundings	Mastery versus harmony
Social organization	*Role of individuals and groups:* Extent to which social relationships emphasize individual rights and responsibilities or group goals and collective action	Individualism versus collectivism
Power distribution	*Power distribution in society:* Extent to which power in a society is distributed hierarchically or in a more egalitarian or participative fashion	Hierarchical versus egalitarian
Rule orientation	*Relative importance of rules:* Extent to which behavior is regulated by rules, laws, and formal procedures or by other factors such as unique circumstances and relationships	Rule-based versus relationship-based
Time orientation	*Time perception and tasks:* Extent to which people organize their time based on sequential attention to single tasks or simultaneous attention to multiple tasks	Monochronic versus polychronic

differences from multiple (and sometimes conflicting) sources and draws conclusions that fit his or her particular situation. Successful managers are thus intelligent consumers of the available information about various cultures and are cautious in interpreting such data.

Because managers must survive and succeed in normative environments—that is, business environments that are largely governed by local social norms and customs—emphasis is placed here on selecting cultural traits that relate to social norms and personal belief structures. Personal values and social norms establish the rules and expectations that largely determine attitudes and behaviors and therefore influence cross-cultural interactions. As a result, they represent a critical influence on how business is conducted and how people are managed in the global economy.

Taken together, the "big five" cultural dimensions help build a broad-based portrait of how management and business practices in one culture differ from those in another. Specific definitions guiding our approach to applying these dimensions are summarized in Exhibit 8.2. Since this model builds on the theory and research discussed in Chapter 7, only a summary of the five dimensions is presented here. See Chapter 7 for more details.

In reviewing these dimensions, it is important to remember that a country's placement within any of these dimensions is relative. For example, on the power distribution dimension, while all cultures use hierarchies in various forms, some cultures make greater use of them than others and therefore would rank higher on power dimension than would other cultures. Dimensions are thus discussed in a comparative manner, not an absolute one.

RELATIONSHIP WITH THE ENVIRONMENT: MASTERY VERSUS HARMONY

Most societies have a reasonably widely shared view with respect to their relationship to their surroundings. This relationship often represents an underlying motive structure for the society. That is, on a fundamental level, some societies seek to control their natural and social environment, while others seek to live in relative harmony with it. Schwartz refers to this as the distinction between a *mastery-oriented culture* and a *harmony-oriented culture.*[5] This distinction coincides with Hofstede's masculinity-femininity dimension, as well as with both Trompenaars's relationship with the environment dimension. Indeed, we adopt Schwartz's term for our purposes here. This dimension also incorporates several of the attributes from the GLOBE study, including assertiveness, a sense of fairness, and performance orientation, as noted above.[6]

Questions relating to the relationship with the environment dimension include the following (see Exhibit 8.3): Does a society emphasize competition in the pursuit of personal or group goals or striving for social progress, quality of life, and the welfare of others? Is a society assertive, proactive, and "masculine" (to use Hofstede's term) or passive, reactive, and "feminine"? Does a society tend to emphasize extrinsic rewards based on job performance or intrinsic rewards based on seniority or on one's position in the organization? Is there an emphasis on material possessions as symbols of achievement or on economy, harmony, and societal sustainability? Finally, do people tend to engage in conspicuous consumption or do they tend to be more modest and unpretentious?

An understanding of a culture's views on its relationship with the environment often helps managers determine how to structure work plans and incentive plans and may even influence leadership style (see Chapter 14). For example, most employees in a mastery-oriented culture will respond to challenges and personal incentives; they will strive for success. As such, they will likely be more responsive to decisive, autocratic leadership. Employees in more harmony-oriented cultures will more likely focus their attention on building or maintaining group welfare, personal relationships, and environmental sustainability. As such, they will likely be more responsive to participative leadership and more skeptical of proposed change. Managers who understand this are in a position to tailor their leadership style to fit the situation.

SOCIAL ORGANIZATION: INDIVIDUALISM VERSUS COLLECTIVISM

The *social organization* dimension focuses on the fundamental issue of whether society and interpersonal relationships are organized based on individuals or groups as their principal building blocks. That is, is a society largely *individualistic* or *collectivistic*? This dimension has been widely identified in previous models of culture as representing a key variable in understanding what differentiates one society from another (see Exhibit 8.4). Basic questions surrounding this dimension include the

Exhibit 8.3

Relationship with the Environment Dimension

Mastery	Harmony
Focus on changing or controlling one's natural and social environment	Focus on living in harmony with nature and adjusting to one's natural and social environment
Achievement valued over relationships	Relationships valued over achievement
Emphasis on competition in the pursuit of personal or group goals	Emphasis on social progress, quality of life, and the welfare of others
Emphasis on material possessions as symbols of achievement	Emphasis on economy, harmony, and modesty
Emphasis on assertive, proactive, "masculine" approach	Emphasis on passive, reactive, "feminine" approach
Tendency toward the experimental; receptivity toward change	Tendency toward the cautious; skepticism toward change
Preference for performance-based extrinsic rewards	Preference for seniority-based intrinsic rewards

Exhibit 8.4

Social Organization Dimension

Individualism	Collectivism
Person-centered approach valued; primary loyalty to oneself	Group-centered approach valued; primary loyalty to the group
Preference for preserving individual rights over social harmony	Preference for preserving social harmony over individual rights
Belief that people achieve self-identity through individual accomplishment	Belief that people achieve self-identity through group membership
Focus on accomplishing individual goals	Focus on accomplishing group goals
Sanctions reinforce independence and personal responsibility	Sanctions reinforce conformity to group norms
Contract-based agreements	Relationship-based agreements
Tendency toward low-context (direct, frank) communication	Tendency toward high-context (subtle, indirect) communication
Tendency toward individual decision making	Tendency toward group or participative decision making

following: Do people achieve self-identity through their own efforts or through group membership? Are individual goals or group goals more important? Do group sanctions reinforce personal responsibility or conformity to group norms? Is individual or group decision making preferred? Is business done based primarily on written contracts or on personal relationships? Is communication characterized primarily by low context (where the message contains all or most all of the intended message) or by high context (where the context surrounding the message also carries significant information)?

An understanding of this dimension is critical for managers to succeed overseas. For example, a global manager who initiates performance-based incentive systems that reward individual performance will likely have a difficult time succeeding in highly collectivistic cultures. Group-based rewards and incentives will likely be more successful in such circumstances. Likewise, overemphasizing participatory decision making in a highly individualistic culture may also be problematic. Again, the challenge for global managers is to develop administrative practices that support, not contradict, local customs and social norms.

POWER DISTRIBUTION: HIERARCHICAL VERSUS EGALITARIAN

As with relationship with the environment and social organization, power distribution has already been identified in several previous models as an important dimension for understanding cultures in general and business cultures in particular. *Power distribution* refers to the social norms governing whether power and influence in a society should be distributed in a *hierarchical* or *egalitarian* fashion (see Exhibit 8.5). Questions pertaining to power distribution include the following: Should authority ultimately reside in institutions such as dictatorships or absolute monarchies or in the people themselves? Should organizations be structured vertically (e.g., tall organization structures) or horizontally (e.g., flat organization structures or even networked structures)? Is decision making largely autocratic or participatory? Are leaders chosen because they are the most qualified for a job or because they already have standing in the community? Are leaders elected or appointed? Are people willing or reluctant to question authority?

A good example of how power distribution works can be found in Finland, a country that stresses egalitarianism with a passion. Many Finnish laws are based on the principle of equity, not equality. For example, traffic fines vary based on personal income; the more you make, the more you can afford to pay. Police departments maintain direct computer access to internal revenue files to calculate the fines on the spot. Hence, when Jaako Rytsola, a young Finnish entrepreneur, was stopped driving his BMW at forty-three miles per hour in a twenty-five-mile-per-hour zone, his speeding ticket cost him $71,400. And when twenty-seven-year-old millionaire Jussi Salonoja was caught doing forty miles per hour in a twenty-five-mile-per-hour zone, he was fined $216,900. A government minister noted that this was a "Nordic tradition." They have both progressive taxation and progressive punishment.[7]

RULE ORIENTATION: RULE-BASED VERSUS RELATIONSHIP-BASED

Perhaps the most intractable dimension used in the four culture models discussed above involves the issue of rules as a means of reducing uncertainty in society. Un-

Exhibit 8.5

Power Distribution Dimension

Hierarchical	Egalitarian
Belief that power should be distributed hierarchically	Belief that power should be distributed relatively equally
Belief in ascribed or inherited power with ultimate authority residing in institutions	Belief in shared or elected power with ultimate authority residing in the people
Emphasis on organizing vertically	Emphasis on organizing horizontally
Preference for autocratic or centralized decision making	Preference for participatory or decentralized decision making
Emphasis on who is in charge	Emphasis on who is best qualified
Respect for authority; reluctance to question authority	Suspicious of authority; willingness to question authority

fortunately, there is little agreement across the models. For example, Hofstede focuses principally on the degree to which societies can tolerate varying amounts of uncertainty and when they feel a need for rules and regulations, while Trompenaars and the GLOBE associates assume that all societies experience uncertainty and focus on how or when societies attempt to reduce it through the rules and regulations (see Chapter 7 for a discussion).[8] Hofstede and the GLOBE associates call this uncertainty avoidance, while Trompenaars follows Parsons and calls it universalism-particularism. In all cases, however, the use of rules to control behavior is central. Recent work by John Hooker provides a straightforward way to resolve this confusion.[9] He suggests the term *rule orientation* to describe the extent to which societies use either rules (e.g., laws, policies, social norms) or influential people (e.g., parents, supervisors) as a principal means of controlling for human unpredictability in society. Cultures are divided into rule-based and relationship-based, as discussed below. This definition is compatible with GLOBE's definition as the extent to which people "seek orderliness, consistency, structure, formalized procedures, and laws to stabilize as much of their daily lives as possible."[10] We will adopt this approach for our purposes here.

In *rule-based cultures*, there is a tendency to promulgate a multitude of laws, rules, regulations, bureaucratic procedures, and strict social norms in an attempt to control as many unanticipated events or behaviors as possible. People tend to conform to officially sanctioned constraints because of a moral belief in the virtue of the rule of law and will often obey directives even if they know violations will not be detected. Waiting for a red light in the absence of any traffic is a good example of this behavior. Rules and laws are universally applied (at least in theory), with few exceptions for extenuating circumstances or personal connections. There is a strong belief in the use of formal contracts and rigorous record keeping in business dealings. Things are done "by the book," and infractions often bring immediate sanctions or consequences. Finally, decisions tend to be made based on objective criteria to the extent possible. All this is aimed at creating a society with no surprises. Germany, the Netherlands, the Scandinavian countries, the United States, and Canada are often identified as rule-based cultures.

By contrast, *relationship-based cultures* tend to use influential people more than abstract or objective rules and regulations as a means of social control.[11] This personal control can come from parents, peers, superiors, supervisors, government officials, and so forth—anyone with influence over the individual. In this sense, relationship-based cultures tend to be particularistic, and individual circumstances often influence the manner in which formal rules are applied. In addition, greater emphasis is placed on developing mutually beneficial interpersonal relationships and trust as a substitute for strict rules and procedures. There is generally less record keeping, and things tend to be done on an informal basis. There is also greater tolerance for noncompliance with bureaucratic rules in the belief that formal rules cannot cover all contingencies and that some flexibility is often required. Finally, decisions tend to be made based on a combination of objective and subjective criteria and with less formality.

This is not to say that relationship-based cultures do not value laws and official procedures; they do. Rather, laws and procedures are often followed only to the extent that one's social network embraces them and sees either the virtue or the necessity of following them, not because of some innate belief in their moral correctness, as is the case with rule-based cultures. Where predictability of behavior is important, it is motivated largely through contacts, not contracts, and interpersonal trust and mutual support between partners are critical. Russia, Greece, Venezuela, Italy, Portugal, Japan, and Spain are often cited as examples of relationship-based cultures. These differences are summarized in Exhibit 8.6.

TIME ORIENTATION: MONOCHRONIC VERSUS POLYCHRONIC

Finally, understanding differences in *time orientation* is important whether a manager is working overseas, negotiating a contract, or trying to build or maintain a strategic alliance or a multicultural team. Understanding how people use their time on work-related activities is critical to managerial action. Each of the four culture models discussed above includes a time dimension, although it is often measured differently. Hall discusses time as it relates to organizing work activities, observing that some cultures tend to approach work activities in a linear or single-minded fashion while others approach multiple tasks simultaneously. Hofstede and the GLOBE group focus on time more in terms of whether people tend to be past-oriented or future-oriented. And Trompenaars's approach is a blend of these two, suggesting that one's time orientation (past, present, or future) influences the degree to which people approach tasks sequentially or simultaneously.[12]

While all of these approaches add value to the study of cultural differences, from a managerial standpoint Hall's approach of differentiating between *monochronic* and *polychronic* cultures seems most useful. That is, global manag-

Exhibit 8.6

Rule Orientation Dimension

Rule-based	Relationship-based
Individual behavior largely regulated by rules, laws, formal policies, standard operating procedures, and social norms that are widely supported by societal members	While rules and laws are important, individual behavior often regulated by unique circumstances or influential people, such as parents, peers, or superiors
Universalistic: Laws and rules designed to be applied uniformly to everyone	Particularistic: Individual circumstances often require modifications in rule enforcement
Emphasis on legal contracts and meticulous record keeping	Emphasis on interpersonal relationships and trust; less emphasis on record keeping
Rules and procedures spelled out clearly and published widely	Rules and procedures often ambiguous or not believed or accepted
Rules internalized and followed without question	Rules sometimes ignored or followed only when strictly enforced
Emphasis on doing things formally, by the book	Emphasis on doing things through informal networks
Low tolerance for rule breaking	Tolerance for rule breaking
Decisions based largely on objective criteria (e.g., rules, policies)	Decisions often based on subjective criteria (e.g., hunches, personal connections)

ers need information about how employees in various countries approach work—how they use their time to pursue their work responsibilities. We therefore focus on Hall's approach here (see Exhibit 8.7). The central point in understanding time orientation is whether people approach their work one task at a time in a somewhat linear fashion or attempt to perform multiple tasks simultaneously. Do people have a precise concept of time and tend to be very punctual, or do they have a relative concept and tend to be late? Do they need a steady flow of information to do their job, or does their culture already provide them with this information? Are people more committed to their jobs or to family and friends? Do they separate work and family life or see them as an integrated whole? Do they take a linear or nonlinear approach to planning? And, finally, are they focused and impatient or unfocused and patient?

Again, in using these dimensions it is important to remember that all members of a particular country will not necessarily share the same basic cultural traits. Cultural dimensions attempt to identify trends, and every culture has outliers who manifest different traits. Moreover, some countries may have meaningful cultural differences between the various regions of the country. Switzerland, for example, has three distinct cultural subgroups (Italian, German, and French), and many believe that the United States has cultural subgroups depending on both ethnicity and geographic region. Even so, identifying general cultural tendencies can be a useful tool for gain-

Exhibit 8.7

Time Orientation Dimension

Monochronic	Polychronic
Sequential attention to individual tasks	Simultaneous attention to multiple tasks
Linear, single-minded approach to work, planning, and implementation	Nonlinear, interactive approach to work, planning, and implementation
Precise concept of time; punctual	Relative concept of time; often late
Approach is job-centered; commitment to the job and often to the organization	Approach is people-centered; commitment to people and human relationships
Separation of work and personal life	Integration of work and personal life
Approach is focused but impatient	Approach is unfocused but patient

ing conceptual entry into the mysteries and contradictions of particular countries. It is a starting point in cultural understanding.

ASSESSING CULTURAL DIFFERENCES

In this section, we turn from theory to practice. Specifically, how can global managers make use of the materials discussed here to better understand and succeed in foreign assignments? Two things are required to answer this question. First, it is necessary to have a relatively reliable means of identifying differences across cultures. We do this below by presenting one approach to classifying cultures based on the "big five" dimensions. Second, it is necessary to place individual managers into this equation so they can better understand their own personal values as they relate to global management. This, too, is discussed below.

ASSESSING NATIONAL CULTURES

A key problem with assessing national cultural differences involves the numeric scores suggested in the various models (e.g., Hofstede, Trompenaars).[13] Converting cultural differences into numeric scores is an imprecise science at best. Cultures by definition are qualitative, not quantitative, and attempts to attach numbers to various cultures only invite errors and misunderstandings. Moreover, as noted earlier, no culture is monolithic. Every culture consists of people who are different in many ways—sometimes stridently so—even if central tendencies can be differentiated between various nationalities. For example, while we may describe one culture as individualistic and another as collectivistic, in fact all people are individualistic. The difference is a matter only of degree; some are more individualistic than others.

Even so, various researchers have made earnest attempts to attach numbers to various cultures in order to facilitate country comparisons. Without such numbers, it is argued, comparisons by both researchers and managers become problematic. However, these ratings are based on research methods that have been widely criticized, and the accuracy of the results has frequently been questioned. Indeed, many of the estimates for specific countries and specific cultural dimensions do not agree with one another. For example, while Hofstede assigns Italy a score of 76 on individualism-collectivism (highly collectivistic), Trompenaars assigns it a 20 (moderately collectivistic). While Hofstede assigns Germany a score of 35 (egalitarian) on power distance, House and his GLOBE associates assign it a 5.25 (hierarchical).[14] Moreover, some country estimates by the same researchers change over time. For example, Trompenaars rated Thailand as somewhat individualistic in his first assessment, but collectivistic in his second.[15] Such differences call into question the entire rating system.

An alternative to quantitative measures is qualitative, or ethnographic, measures. But here, too, there are problems, largely because of possible rater bias in formulating both models and measures. While cultural anthropologists and other social scientists have made sincere attempts to differentiate across cultures using ethnographic or qualitative methods, room for error persists due to the possible cultural biases of the evaluators. For example, a U.S.-born, U.S.-educated anthropologist will likely view the world (and hence the cultures of different lands) through American eyes and may miss important cultural traits because he or she is not looking for them. Indeed, this occurred when Michael Bond and Peter Smith first noted that looking at cultures through an East Asian perspective leads to the identification of different cultural dimensions for purposes of assessment.[16] Such human bias in assessment and analysis is itself a natural outcome of cultural differences. As a result, as with quantitative assessments, ethnographic assessments of cultures do not always agree.

In order to operationalize the "big five" model, it is necessary to have a means of classifying cultures so general country comparisons can be made. Mindful of the limitations discussed above, we chose to estimate cultural differences using multiple measures and multiple methods. That is, we first assessed and then integrated a combination of quantitative and qualitative measures from available research in order to categorize cultures along the five dimensions used in the model. Moreover, instead of attempting to calculate specific numeric ratings that may appear to be more precise than they are, we attempted to develop a more qualitative rating, clustering cultures into four categories based on the relative strength of the various dimensions compared to other cultures. The results are shown in Exhibit 8.8. Note that these are only rough estimates based on available research and are designed to be used for general discussion, not research. In making use of this information, it is important to recognize that no particular rating is preferred over any other; they are just different.

While the results shown in the exhibit may appear to be less precise than assigning more specific numeric ratings, we believe that they are in fact both more accurate and more useful because they assume a more conservative stance in data analysis and because the assignment of cultures into the various categories is based on a comparison of multiple data points instead of one survey questionnaire. Still, room for error persists, and readers are cautioned to use their own judgment in interpreting results.

In interpreting the results shown in Exhibit 8.8, it must also be remembered that significant within-country differences can sometimes be found. For example, as noted

Exhibit 8.8

Country Ratings of National Cultures

Country	Relationship with the Environment	Social Orientation	Power Orientation	Rule Orientation	Time Orientation
Argentina	Harmony	Collectivist	Hierarchical	Relationship-based	Polychronic
Australia	Mastery+	Individualist+	Egalitarian+	Rule-based	Monochronic
Austria	Mastery	Individualist	Hierarchical	Rule-based+	Monochronic+
Belgium	Harmony	Individualist	Egalitarian	Rule-based	Monochronic
Brazil	Harmony	Collectivist	Hierarchical	Relationship-based	Polychronic+
Canada	Mastery	Individualist+	Egalitarian	Rule-based	Monochronic+
Chile	Harmony	Collectivist	Hierarchical	Relationship-based	Polychronic
China	Harmony	Collectivist+	Hierarchical	Relationship-based	Polychronic
Colombia	Harmony	Collectivist	Hierarchical	Relationship-based	Polychronic+
Costa Rica	Harmony	Collectivist	Egalitarian	Relationship-based	Polychronic
Czech Rep.	Mastery	Collectivist	Egalitarian	Rule-based	Monochronic
Denmark	Harmony	Individualist	Egalitarian+	Rule-based+	Monochronic
Ecuador	Harmony	Collectivist	Hierarchical+	Relationship-based	Polychronic+
Egypt	Harmony	Collectivist	Hierarchical+	Relationship-based	Polychronic+
El Salvador	Harmony	Collectivist	Hierarchical	Relationship-based	Polychronic+
Finland	Harmony	Individualist	Egalitarian+	Rule-based+	Monochronic
France	Harmony	Individualist	Hierarchical	Relationship-based	Polychronic
Germany	Mastery	Individualist	Hierarchical	Rule-based+	Monochronic+
Greece	Harmony	Individualist	Egalitarian	Relationship-based+	Polychronic
Guatemala	Harmony	Collectivist	Hierarchical	Relationship-based+	Polychronic+
India	Harmony	Collectivist	Hierarchical	Relationship-based	Polychronic
Indonesia	Harmony	Collectivist+	Hierarchical+	Relationship-based	Polychronic+
Iran	Harmony	Collectivist	Hierarchical+	Relationship-based	Polychronic
Ireland	Mastery	Individualist	Egalitarian+	Rule-based	Monochronic
Israel	Mastery	Individualist	Egalitarian	Rule-based	Monochronic
Italy	Harmony	Collectivist	Hierarchical	Relationship-based	Polychronic
Jamaica	Harmony	Collectivist	Egalitarian	Relationship-based	Polychronic+
Japan	Harmony	Collectivist+	Hierarchical	Relationship-based	Monochronic
Korea	Harmony	Collectivist+	Hierarchical	Relationship-based	Monochronic
Kuwait	Harmony	Collectivist	Hierarchical+	Relationship-based	Polychronic+
Malaysia	Harmony	Collectivist+	Hierarchical+	Relationship-based+	Polychronic
Mexico	Harmony	Collectivist	Hierarchical	Relationship-based	Polychronic+
Netherlands	Harmony	Individualist	Egalitarian+	Rule-based	Monochronic+
New Zealand	Mastery	Individualist	Egalitarian	Rule-based+	Monochronic
Norway	Harmony+	Collectivist	Egalitarian+	Rule-based+	Monochronic
Pakistan	Harmony	Collectivist	Hierarchical+	Relationship-based	Polychronic+
Panama	Harmony	Collectivist	Hierarchical	Relationship-based	Polychronic+
Peru	Harmony	Collectivist	Hierarchical	Relationship-based	Polychronic+
Philippines	Harmony	Collectivist	Hierarchical	Relationship-based	Polychronic+
Poland	Harmony	Collectivist	Hierarchical	Relationship-based	Monochronic
Portugal	Harmony	Collectivist	Hierarchical	Relationship-based	Polychronic
Russia	Mastery	Collectivist	Hierarchical	Relationship-based+	Monochronic
Saudi Arabia	Harmony	Collectivist	Hierarchical+	Relationship-based	Polychronic+
Singapore	Harmony	Collectivist+	Hierarchical	Rule-based+	Polychronic
Slovakia	Harmony	Collectivist	Hierarchical	Relationship-based	Polychronic
Spain	Harmony	Collectivist	Hierarchical	Relationship-based	Polychronic
Sweden	Harmony+	Collectivist	Egalitarian+	Rule-based+	Monochronic
Switzerland	Mastery	Individualist	Egalitarian	Rule-based+	Monochronic+
Taiwan	Harmony	Collectivist+	Hierarchical	Relationship-based	Polychronic
Thailand	Harmony+	Collectivist+	Hierarchical	Relationship-based	Polychronic
Tunisia	Harmony	Collectivist	Hierarchical	Relationship-based	Polychronic+
Turkey	Mastery	Collectivist	Hierarchical	Relationship-based	Polychronic+
United Kingdom	Mastery+	Individualist+	Hierarchical	Rule-based	Monochronic+
United States	Mastery+	Individualist+	Egalitarian	Rule-based	Monochronic+
Uruguay	Harmony	Collectivist	Hierarchical	Relationship-based	Polychronic
Venezuela	Harmony	Collectivist	Hierarchical+	Relationship-based+	Polychronic+

Note: All ratings are comparative. A "+" indicates a stronger tendency toward a particular dimension.

earlier, all Americans are not individualistic and all Chinese are not collectivistic. Differences can also be found between the various regions of a single country (e.g., north-south or east-west differences). While it is sometimes necessary to focus on central tendencies between cultures for purposes of general comparison, the role of individual and regional differences in determining attitudes and behaviors should not be overlooked.

Finally, it should not be surprising that cultural ratings for countries in the same geographic region (e.g., Denmark, Norway, and Sweden) tend to be closer than cultural scores for countries located in different regions of the world (e.g., Europe versus Latin America). This is a natural consequence of contiguous countries in various regions living side-by-side with their neighbors over centuries and sometimes millennia. Still, important cultural differences can be found across peoples inhabiting a particular region.

In interpreting these and other cultural assessments, Nancy Adler offers some sound advice on how to avoid making overgeneralizations or cultural stereotypes about the people from any culture:[17]

1. Cultural descriptions by their very nature contain limited information. Keep in mind that such generalizations often mask other useful information about cultural diversity (e.g., the existence of unique indigenous subgroups or regional variations).
2. Cultural descriptions should be limited to describing members of various groups as objectively as possible and should not include an evaluative component (e.g., this is good; that is bad).
3. Cultural descriptions should provide an accurate description of the beliefs, values, and social norms of a group.
4. Cultural descriptions should be considered a first best guess about the behaviors of a cultural group prior to developing more specific information about individual members of the group.
5. Cultural descriptions should be modified over time based on new information gained through observation or experience.

ASSESSING PERSONAL VALUES

To succeed in the global economy, managers must not only understand their environment; they must also understand themselves. They must know who they are and what they stand for, what they are willing to do and where they will draw the line. Without this understanding, managers run the risk of becoming lost in a sea of foreign cultures, not knowing which way to turn or what to do. One way to understand this is to examine the personal values held by individual managers as they approach their work and their careers. While there are many ways to assess personal values, we present one approach that is based on the "big five" model presented above. It is called the Personal Values Survey.

The Personal Values Survey is designed to assess the cultural profiles of individual managers, as opposed to entire cultures. It is through this type of assessment that individual differences within countries can be identified. That is, while a particular manager may be a citizen of a country that is largely hierarchical, he or she may in fact be more egalitarian. This information is important in considering overseas assignments. For example, an American with a strong sense of collectivism may have an easier time adapting to collectivistic countries such as China than a "typical" American, who is more individualistic. The Personal Values Survey is shown in Global Manager's Workbook 8.1 at the conclusion of this chapter. It is designed to provide a flavor of how individuals see themselves on five cultural dimensions. In completing this survey, it is important to recognize that individual scores reflect personal preferences and that there are no right or wrong answers.

MAPPING CULTURAL DISTANCES

Cultural distance refers to the degree of similarity or dissimilarity between two cultures.[18] This concept is important because it can influence both the preparation and the performance of global managers. That is, if a manager is traveling from his or her home country to a country that possesses relatively similar cultural traits (e.g., Canada and the United States, Peru and Bolivia, Sweden and Norway), the manager will likely experience few adaptation problems and can devote full energy to conducting business. On the other hand, if the cultural distance between the home country and the host country is sizable (e.g., Canada and Nigeria, Germany and Thailand, Sweden and Tunisia), more time and effort may be required to understand the local environment and how business is transacted before getting involved in the venture.

Cultural distance measures are qualitative in nature; precise numbers are simply unrealistic. Still, it is possible to estimate the relative magnitude of any differences between two cultures on various dimensions. For example, one culture may be highly relationship-based, while another may be highly rule-based. It is also possible to examine the fundamental nature of the differences between two cultures as they relate to social relationships and business practices. For example, if a country is highly relationship-based, what does this mean for establishing new business contacts; negotiating new contracts; hiring, managing, and compensating new employees; and so forth? Although estimates of cultural distance cannot provide precise measurements of cultural differences across national boundaries, they can provide managers with a valuable heads-up concerning what is in store when they travel to a new overseas assignment.

To illustrate how cultural mapping works, we return to the two country examples discussed above: China and the United States. The fundamental question is how the "big five" culture dimensions can be used to build a map of cultural differences as they relate to global business. In addition, we want to understand where or how individual managers fit into this picture. To accomplish this, we suggest a four-step procedure. Step 1 focuses on better understanding one's home country. Step 2 focuses on understanding the host country that is of interest. Step 3 then examines the cultural distance between home and host countries. For example, if an American manager is being sent to China, he or she could compare cultures in the United States (home country) and China (host country). Finally, step 4 uses the Personal Values Survey to better understand where individual managers fit into the equation.

STEP 1. HOME COUNTRY PROFILE

This chapter opened with some general observations about American culture. These observations are consistent with the cultural ratings shown in Exhibit 8.8. If this information is applied to the model for purposes of illustration, we develop a cultural profile of the United States as shown in Exhibit 8.9. As can be seen, while variations obviously exist, American culture tends to be mastery-oriented, highly individualistic, somewhat egalitarian, and rule-based compared to other cultures of the world. In addition, most Americans tend to be somewhat monochronic in their approach to work; indeed, many observers describe Americans in the business world as "linear workaholics." The picture that emerges from this profile is that of a culture that is control-oriented, assertive, democratic, change-oriented, and work-centered.

STEP 2. HOST COUNTRY PROFILE

Now, to continue our illustration, compare the profile of the United States with that of China. Based on the discussion in Chapter 7, we can summarize Chinese cultural trends as shown in Exhibit 8.10. The principal conclusion to emerge from this comparison is that it would be difficult to find two cultures that are more different than those of China and the United States. For starters, Chinese culture has historically emphasized harmony in social relations and relations with the environment, although this may be evolving over time (witness the Three Gorges Dam, for example). In addition, China is more tradition-oriented and takes a longer-term perspective in building social relationships.

In addition, Chinese culture is hierarchical, perhaps following from its Confucian heritage. Autocratic decision making is widely accepted, and people are often reluctant to challenge authority. While this may be changing slowly among China's young and successful entrepreneurs, the collectivistic norm remains strong across society. By contrast, the United States tends to be more egalitarian, although not as strongly as the Scandinavian countries or the Netherlands. Furthermore, compared to the United States, external social control in China is very high, with laws, regulations, and social norms that are rigidly enforced by government authorities, neighbors, and village elders. Under our definition of rule orientation, this places China more toward the relationship-based end of the dimension. That is, influential people largely enforce rules and control behavior more than the state on a day-to-day basis, and personal relationships and contacts often determine how business is done. Finally, Chinese tend to be somewhat more polychronic than typical Americans.

Exhibit 8.9

Cultural Profile: United States

Cultural Dimensions	Characteristics
Relationship with the environment	*Mastery-oriented:* Assertive; proactive; norms favor competition and the pursuit of personal goals; preference for performance-based rewards; high value on material possessions; change-oriented
Social organization	*Highly individualistic:* Individuals come first; strong belief in individual accountability and control; sanctions reinforce personal responsibility; low trust in others; contract-based relationships; low-context communication
Power distribution	*Moderately egalitarian:* Strong norms concerning democratic principles and equal rights; preference for participative decision making; people selected based on qualifications; resistance to autocratic practices; willingness to question authority
Rule orientation	*Rule-based:* Use of rules and policies to reduce uncertainty; high need for certainty; tendency to do things by the book; low tolerance for rule breaking; emphasis on legal contracts and record keeping; objective decision making.
Time orientation	*Monochronic:* Work activities organized in fairly linear ways; high degree of work-centeredness; impatient; separation of work and personal life; live to work

Exhibit 8.10

Cultural Profile: China

Cultural Dimensions	Characteristics
Relationship with the environment	*Harmony-oriented:* Passive; reactive; focus on living in harmony with nature and adjusting to one's environment; emphasis on social relevance; values relationships over achievement; cautious; skeptical of change
Social organization	*Collectivistic:* Group-centered; primary loyalty to family or group; focus on group goals; sanctions reinforce conformity to group norms; preference for preserving harmony over individual rights; relationship-based agreements; high-context communication
Power distribution	*Hierarchical:* Belief that power should be distributed hierarchically and that authority resides in institutions; emphasis on organizing vertically; preference for autocratic decision making; emphasis on who is in charge; high respect for authority
Rule orientation	*Relationship-based:* While on a societal level China makes extensive use of rules and policies to reduce uncertainty, at a group level personal contacts and relationships are more important; rule enforcement rests largely on control by influential people
Time orientation	*Moderately polychronic:* Simultaneous attention to multiple goals; nonlinear approach to work; relative concept of time; integration of work and personal life; patient; strong commitment to personal relationships

Exhibit 8.11

Mapping Cultural Distance: United States versus China

Cultural Dimensions	Home Country Profile (United States)	Host Country Profile (China)	Cultural Distance
Relationship with the environment	Mastery	Harmony	Large
Social organization	Individualistic	Collectivistic	Large
Power distribution	Egalitarian	Hierarchical	Large
Rule orientation	Rule-based	Relationship-based	Large
Time orientation	Monochronic	Polychronic	Large

STEP 3. ESTIMATING CULTURAL DISTANCE

With the information developed in steps 1 and 2, it is possible to estimate the cultural distance between the two cultures, as shown in Exhibit 8.11. The first thing one notices is that the differences between the two cultures are relatively large across all five dimensions, cautioning managers on both sides to be particularly alert to what they say and do. Offending a prospective partner is obviously not conducive to business success. By contrast, demonstrating genuine cultural sensitivity can establish a solid foundation upon which to build long-term and mutually beneficial business relations. It all begins with an understanding of how the other side approaches business.

What does all this mean for global managers doing business in China? China's high collectivism suggests that personal relationships may be more important than written contracts in solidifying business relationships. Networking is also critical, and most personal relationships demand continual nurturing. This requires more time and effort than many managers are used to devoting to business relationships. Hierarchical organizations and government bureaucracies also require more time and attention. Status and power are very important, as are good connections with people in influential positions. Communication must be carefully planned, since context can be as important as the message itself. Careful attention to message format, message presentation, and body language is critical. Efforts must be made to ensure that no one is embarrassed or loses face. If the manager is involved in running an overseas operation or managing people, employee incentive systems should not overemphasize individual performance as a basis for compensation and rewards.

Other countries can be compared for cultural distance using this same technique. For example, a comparison of France and Germany (in Exhibit 8.12) suggests that these two countries are relatively similar on two cultural dimensions (social organization and power distribution) but further apart on three others (relationship with the environment, rule orientation, and time orientation). While it is important to remem-

Exhibit 8.12

Mapping Cultural Distance: France versus Germany

Cultural Dimensions	Home Country Profile (France)	Host Country Profile (Germany)	Cultural Distance
Relationship with the environment	Harmony	Mastery	Large
Social organization	Individualistic	Individualistic	Small
Power distribution	Hierarchical	Hierarchical	Small
Rule orientation	Relationship-based	Rule-based	Large
Time orientation	Polychronic	Monochronic	Large

ber that within-country differences exist and that this analysis is very general, it nonetheless serves to highlight several clues to watch for in approaching interactions between people from these two cultures.

Step 4. Personal Values Survey

Finally, individual managers can use the Personal Values Survey (see Global Manager's Workbook 8.1 at the end of this chapter) to assess where they fit into this equation. In some cases, the managers may find that their personal value system matches well with the culture of the country they are going to. In other cases, they may find significant differences. Such information is useful in both instances. With this understanding, managers are in a better position to assess the degree of fit between themselves and various countries. While this survey provides only a rough estimate based on self-assessment, it is a good point of departure for better understanding oneself as a global manager.

With these four steps completed, a manager has in one location cultural profiles of the home and host countries, a personal values profile highlighting his or her own preferences, and a method to map differences across the two cultures. Based on this, the only remaining question is how managers will either respond to such differences or, perhaps more appropriately, prepare themselves to capitalize on them. In other words, an educated manager is far more likely to succeed in the turbulent global environment. Preparing oneself culturally adds one more valuable asset to the global manager's overseas tool kit. Successful overseas managers routinely educate themselves about how cultures can affect their business success. This preparation can include initiating a reading program focusing on the country involved, securing the services of a cross-cultural consultant, or working with other managers with host country experience. However it is accomplished, advance preparation is key to overseas success. We return to this topic later in the book when we examine staffing issues for overseas operations (see Chapter 13).

In summary, even a short analysis of cultural differences such as the one suggested here could assist managers in ways that can help them both avoid problems and capitalize on opportunities. It provides a useful beginning in cultural learning, as well as preparation for going overseas. Even so, it remains an important and universal caveat that all managers from a particular country will not necessarily behave in similar ways, so caution is still in order in building or developing new cross-cultural relationships. Expect the unexpected.

KEY TERMS

"big five" culture dimensions	polychronic
collectivistic	power distribution
cultural distance	relationship with the
egalitarian	environment
harmony-oriented culture	relationship-based cultures
hierarchical	rule orientation
individualistic	rule-based cultures
mastery-oriented culture	social organization
monochronic	time orientation

GLOBAL MANAGER'S WORKBOOK 8.1: PERSONAL VALUES SURVEY

This inventory provides an opportunity to assess your own views on culture and cultural differences. It is designed for self-assessment and discussion, not research. Please read the two descriptions for each question below and circle the number (1 through 5) that best describes your level of agreement. For each item, a 1 indicates that you strongly agree with the description on the left, while a 5 indicates that you strongly agree with the description on the right. A 3 indicates that you are equally divided between the two descriptions. In completing this survey, please remember that there are no right or wrong answers, so respond completely and truthfully.[19]

PERSONAL VALUES SURVEY

1. Societies grow and develop primarily through competition.   1 2 3 4 5   Societies grow and develop primarily through cooperation.

2. People should look after themselves; in the end, we are all responsible for ourselves.   1 2 3 4 5   People should look after each other; in the end, we all need the support of our group to survive.

3. It is usually wrong to question the authority of superiors. 1 2 3 4 5 It is usually acceptable to question the authority of superiors.

4. I believe things at work should be done by the book based on clear and published policies. 1 2 3 4 5 I believe things at work should frequently be done through informal channels.

5. I always try to focus on doing one thing at a time. 1 2 3 4 5 I often find myself doing many things at once.

6. It is important to harness nature in order to improve our general living conditions. 1 2 3 4 5 It is important to live in harmony with nature and modify our living conditions accordingly.

7. My principal responsibility is to myself. 1 2 3 4 5 My principal responsibility is to my family or group.

8. It is my responsibility to do what my boss tells me to do. 1 2 3 4 5 I have considerable freedom to do my job they way I think best.

9. The best way to reduce uncertainty in a society is to make and enforce rules governing people's behavior. 1 2 3 4 5 The best way to reduce uncertainty in a society is for people to follow the wishes of their superiors.

10. I usually assume that an appointment will begin on time. 1 2 3 4 5 I usually assume that an appointment will begin late.

11. Rewards should be based on performance. 1 2 3 4 5 Rewards should be based on seniority or need.

12. Protecting individual rights is more important than preserving group harmony. 1 2 3 4 5 Preserving group harmony is more important than protecting individual rights.

13. The best decisions are usually made at the top of the organization. 1 2 3 4 5 The best decisions are usually made toward the middle or bottom of the organization.

14. Decisions should usually be made based on objective criteria (e.g., rules, policies).   1 2 3 4 5   Decisions should usually be made based on subjective criteria (e.g., hunches, personal considerations).

15. Very few things distract me from my work.   1 2 3 4 5   I often get distracted from my work by other activities.

16. Most problems in society could be resolved quickly if people would assert themselves and take charge of the situation.   1 2 3 4 5   Most problems in society require patience and extensive consultation with others; there are no quick fixes.

17. Individual decision making usually leads to better decisions.   1 2 3 4 5   Group decision making usually leads to better decisions.

18. People should be promoted based on their status or position in society.   1 2 3 4 5   People should be promoted based on their accomplishments or merit.

19. Rule enforcement should be applied to everyone equally and without exception.   1 2 3 4 5   Rule enforcement should be modified based on individual circumstances.

20. I tend to be very impatient to get things done.   1 2 3 4 5   I am usually patient in trying to get things done.

21. Success comes through taking decisive actions to overcome new challenges.   1 2 3 4 5   Success comes through working with others in a collaborative way to meet new challenges.

22. The best way to do business is based on written contracts.   1 2 3 4 5   The best way to do business is based on personal relationships.

23. People at the top of an organization deserve to have most of the power.   1 2 3 4 5   Power should be evenly distributed throughout an organization.

24. Business should be based on legal contracts and meticulous record keeping.   1 2 3 4 5   Business should be based on personal relationships and interpersonal trust.

25. I try to keep a clear separation between my work and my personal life. 1 2 3 4 5 I often find that my work and my personal life tend to merge together.

26. Putting a man on the moon has had a greater impact on society than preserving a rain forest. 1 2 3 4 5 Preserving a rain forest has had a greater impact on society than putting a man on the moon.

27. People are usually known by what they accomplish. 1 2 3 4 5 People are usually known by which groups they belong to.

28. Effective organizations should be run from the top down. 1 2 3 4 5 Effective organizations should be run democratically.

29. I usually follow commonly accepted rules and policies without question, even if I know I won't get caught if I ignore them. 1 2 3 4 5 I frequently ignore rules and policies that make little sense to me, especially if I think I won't get caught.

30. Time is very valuable and should not be wasted on trivial issues. 1 2 3 4 5 People should not worry about time; there is sufficient time for most things.

31. Most people have friends, but a really successful person has many possessions. 1 2 3 4 5 Most people have possessions, but a really successful person has many friends.

32. Being myself is more important than fitting in with others. 1 2 3 4 5 Fitting in with others is more important than being myself.

33. People should go through proper channels at work to get things done. 1 2 3 4 5 People should talk with anyone they need to at work to get things done.

34. Societies are best run through the rule of law. 1 2 3 4 5 Societies are best run through interpersonal relationships.

35. I believe in making serious plans for the future. 1 2 3 4 5 The future is too uncertain to plan for seriously.

SCORING PROCEDURE

Step 1. Transfer the numeric scores for each question to the boxes below.

Column 1	Column 2	Column 3	Column 4	Column 5
1.	2.	3.	4.	5.
6.	7.	8.	9.	10.
11.	12.	13.	14.	15.
16.	17.	18.	19.	20.
21.	22.	23.	24.	25.
26.	27.	28.	29.	30.
31.	32.	33.	34.	35.

Step 2. Add each column and write the total scores in the boxes below.

Relationship with the Environment	Social Organization	Power Distribution	Rule Orientation	Time Orientation

SCORING KEY

Relationship with the environment: A score of 16 or lower indicates a preference for mastery and control over the environment; a score between 17 and 25 indicates a balance between mastery and harmony; a score of 26 or higher indicates a preference for cooperation, economy, and living in harmony with the environment.

Social organization: A score of 16 or lower indicates a preference for individualism; a score between 17 and 25 indicates a balance between individualism and collectivism; a score of 26 or higher indicates a preference for collectivism.

Power distribution: A score of 16 or lower indicates a preference for hierarchical relationships in society; a score between 17 and 25 indicates a balance between hierarchy and egalitarianism; a score of 26 or higher indicates a preference for egalitarian relationships in society.

Rule orientation: A score of 16 or lower indicates a rule-based orientation; a score

between 17 and 25 indicates a balance between rule-based and relationship-based orientations; a score of 26 or higher indicates a relationship-based orientation.
Time orientation: A score of 16 or lower indicates a preference for monochronic behavior; a score between 17 and 25 indicates a balance between monochronic and polychronic behavior; a score of 26 or higher indicates a preference for polychronic behavior.

INTERPRETING THE RESULTS

It is important to remember that individual scores reflect personal preferences and that there are no right or wrong answers. For more information concerning these dimensions and their role in global management, refer to this chapter and Chapter 7.

GLOBAL MANAGER'S WORKBOOK 8.2: MAPPING CULTURAL DISTANCES

1. Identify a prospective host country located on a different continent than where you live. Compare the culture of this country to that of your own home country using the materials discussed above, as well as any other information you can discover. Then estimate the cultural distance between the two cultures. Add any other critical issues that you believe differentiate the two cultures.

Cultural Dimensions	Home Country Profile	Host Country Profile	Cultural Distance
Relationship with the environment			
Social organization			
Power distribution			
Rule orientation			
Time orientation			

2. Based on your assessment, what predictions would you make concerning any possible differences in employee attitudes or behavior in the two cultures?
3. What predictions would you make concerning any possible differences in managerial style in the two cultures?
4. Based on your results on the Personal Values Survey (Global Manager's Workbook 8.1), compare your personal value profile against the host country cultural profile and estimate the level of fit.

5. Finally, what would be your biggest challenge if you were posted as a manager to the host country? Why?

NOTES

1. Phillip Harris, Robert Moran, and Sarah Moran, *Managing Cultural Differences,* 6th ed. (Amsterdam: Elsevier, 2004); Peter Lawrence, *Management in the U.S.A.* (London: Sage, 1996); Richard Lewis, *When Cultures Collide* (London: Nicholas Brealey, 1999); Edward T. Hall and Mildred Hall, *Understanding Cultural Differences: Germans, French, and Americans* (Yarmouth, ME: Intercultural, 1990).

2. Short descriptive titles such as these do not entirely capture the essence of each dimension; more complete definitions are offered below.

3. Fons Trompenaars and Charles Hampden-Turner, *Riding the Waves of Culture: Understanding Cultural Diversity in Global Business* (London: McGraw-Hill, 1998); Geert Hofstede, *Culture's Consequence: International Differences in Work Related Values* (Thousand Oaks, CA: Sage, 2001); Robert House, Paul Hanges, Mansour Javidan, Peter Dorfman, and Vipin Gupta, *Culture, Leadership, and Organizations: The GLOBE Study of 62 Societies* (Thousand Oaks, CA: Sage, 2004).

4. Edward T. Hall, *The Silent Language* (New York: Anchor Books, 1959); Edward T. Hall, *The Dance of Life* (New York: Anchor Books, 1983).

5. S.H. Schwartz, "A Theory of Cultural Values and Some Implications for Work," *Applied Psychology: An International Review* 48, no. 1 (1999): 23–47.

6. House, Hanges, Javidan, Dorfman, and Gupta, *Culture, Leadership, and Organizations.*

7. Steve Stecklow, "Helsinki on Wheels: Fast Finns Find Fines Fit Their Finances," *Wall Street Journal,* January 2, 2001, p. A1; "Rich Finn Gets Hefty Fine for Speeding," *Register-Guard,* February 11, 2004, p. A3.

8. Trompenaars and Hampden-Turner, *Riding the Waves of Culture*; Hofstede, *Culture's Consequence*; House, Hanges, Javidan, Dorfman, and Gupta, *Culture, Leadership, and Organizations.*

9. John Hooker, *Working Across Cultures* (Stanford, CA: Stanford Business Books, 2003).

10. House, Hanges, Javidan, Dorfman, and Gupta, *Culture, Leadership, and Organizations.*

11. Hooker, *Working Across Cultures.*

12. Trompenaars and Hampden-Turner, *Riding the Waves of Culture*; Hofstede, *Culture's Consequence*; House, Hanges, Javidan, Dorfman, and Gupta, *Culture, Leadership, and Organizations.*

13. Trompenaars and Hampden-Turner, *Riding the Waves of Culture*; House, Hanges, Javidan, Dorfman, and Gupta, *Culture, Leadership, and Organizations.*

14. Hofstede, *Culture's Consequence*; House, Hanges, Javidan, Dorfman, and Gupta, *Culture, Leadership, and Organizations.*

15. Trompenaars and Hampden-Turner, *Riding the Waves of Culture.*

16. Michael Bond and Peter Smith, "Cross-cultural Social and Organizational Psychology," *Annual Review of Psychology* 47 (1996): 205–35.

17. Nancy Adler, *International Dimensions of Organizational Behavior* (Cincinnati, OH: Southwestern, 1997).

18. Harry Triandis, *Culture and Social Behavior* (New York: McGraw-Hill, 1994).

19. This survey was developed using MBA students from thirty-two countries studying in both North America and Europe. It is designed for instructional use only.

Organizing for Global Business

ALL IN THE FAMILY, JAPANESE-STYLE

Honda Motor Company cofounder Takeo Fujisawa once observed that U.S. and Japanese management are 95 percent the same but differ in all important respects.[1] He was suggesting that while managers in both countries may appear to engage in similar activities and carry similar titles, the way they actually conduct business can be substantially different. Perhaps nowhere is this difference more pronounced than with respect to how organizations are put together. Both the United States and Japan have numerous large diversified corporations. In the West they are called conglomerates; in Japan they are called *keiretsu*. A principal difference between them, however, is that while both conglomerates and *keiretsu* consist of clusters of affiliated companies engaged in divergent businesses, in the West various member companies are typically run independently while in Japan they are not. That is, large Japanese companies typically consist of clusters of "sister companies" that actively help one another in both good times and bad. This help can take many forms, including mutual purchasing agreements, cross holdings of stock, loans from one company to another, exchange of management talent, and so forth. When a sister company is in trouble, other companies in the *keiretsu* step forward to offer assistance. However, there is a downside to this mutual assistance arrangement: when a sister company is either unwilling or incapable of turning itself around, the prosperity of the entire group can be threatened.

Consider the case of Mitsubishi Motors, part of the huge Mitsubishi Business Group. Mitsubishi Motors fell on hard times with poor car designs, poor manufacturing quality, and a string of recalls that the company worked hard to cover up. Car sales plummeted and costs rose sharply as company management refused year after year to make necessary changes. Many economists questioned whether the car company would survive. Even German automotive giant DaimlerChrysler, which owns a 37 percent stake in Mitsubishi Motors from an earlier bailout, refused in 2004 to invest any more capital in what was described as an overstaffed and poorly run operation.[2] So, what happened? After their German partners stepped back, Mitsubishi-owned Bank of Tokyo and Mitsubishi Trust Bank agreed to a major infusion of capital to bail out the ailing company. Press releases noted that the entire Mitsubishi group of companies would intervene and lead a "major turnaround" of the company. However, no specifics were provided and many questioned whether any real change would follow.[3]

About the same time, Toyota Motor Company agreed to two major bailouts of Tomen Corporation, a Japanese trading company with ties to Toyota. Tomen had been losing money for several years but was able to secure help because of its connections with the Toyota group. As one observer noted, Toyota's bailout was "adding ballast to a bankrupt corporate model in which good companies help bad ones survive—to the ultimate detriment not only of their shareholders but also the struggling Japanese economy."[4]

Globalization presents many challenges for managers, and cultures often differ in the ways they respond to them. Mitsubishi and Toyota, both highly successful business groups, have apparently chosen to continue the long-standing Japanese tradition of protecting affiliated companies at almost any cost, even when these firms prove to be inefficient and unprofitable. As we shall see later in this chapter, another major Japanese firm, Nissan, chose an alternative course of action.

ORGANIZING FOR GLOBAL COMPETITION

The choice of an appropriate organization design for conducting global business typically evolves over time as firms increase their involvement in global activities (see Chapter 1). This evolutionary process often begins with some form of domestic organization design, where international activities are largely an appendage to the more central domestic activities, and evolves over time into a more integrated global organization design that places international business at the center of the organization's strategy.

DOMESTIC ORGANIZATION DESIGNS

Domestic organization designs are most commonly found when a national firm initially begins to export a product is has long made for the home market.[5] This endeavor requires some structure to oversee successful implementation, but because the venture is new and may not be successful, most organizations approach with caution, using trusted local managers. Domestic organization designs for international business include the following (see Exhibit 9.1):

• *Corollary model.* The *corollary model* of organization design is used when a local firm receives only a few orders from abroad and uses its existing organization design to fill these orders. For example, when Burley Design of Eugene, Oregon, received its first requests to sell some of their bicycle carts in Switzerland, it used its local departments to fill the order. That is, the marketing people handled the marketing, while the finance people handled the finance. No new structure was established. Most of these transactions are done in an ad hoc fashion as international sales come into the company.

• *Export department.* Once a firm gets more serious about selling its products

Exhibit 9.1 **Domestic Organization Designs for Global Business**

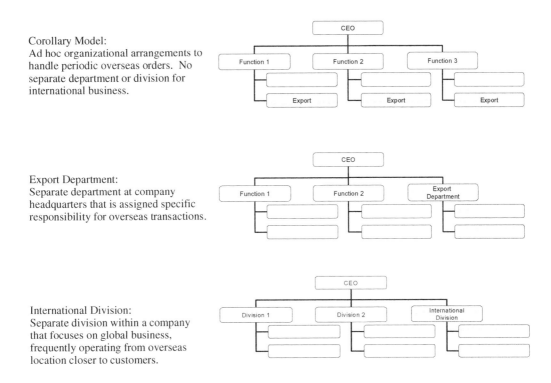

Corollary Model:
Ad hoc organizational arrangements to handle periodic overseas orders. No separate department or division for international business.

Export Department:
Separate department at company headquarters that is assigned specific responsibility for overseas transactions.

International Division:
Separate division within a company that focuses on global business, frequently operating from overseas location closer to customers.

abroad, or when its overseas sales volume increases, it frequently establishes an export department. The *export department model* uses a separate department within the home company's headquarters that is assigned specific responsibility for overseas transactions. Again, this is simple to establish and run.

• *International division.* As companies become more sophisticated in differentiating among their global markets, they soon realize that localized expertise represents a strategic asset for satisfying local customer demands. In such cases, firms frequently follow the *international division model*. While export departments are usually located in corporate headquarters in the home country, international divisions are most often located overseas near the firm's principal global markets. Local managers are hired, again to get close to principal customers and markets, and to provide a worldview for headquarters on future business opportunities abroad.

GLOBAL ORGANIZATION DESIGNS

When international activities become a more prominent aspect of the business as a whole, most companies reorganize to capitalize on this growing business sector. They then select one of the typical global organization designs (see Exhibit 9.2). Companies go to great lengths to identify a design that will support the firm's strategic objectives.

Exhibit 9.2   **Global Organization Designs**

Global Product Design:
Organizing a company's global
business based on product lines (e.g.,
creating separate divisions for
consumer products and industrial
products worldwide).

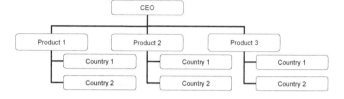

Global Area Design:
Organizing a company's global
business based on geographic regions
of the world (e.g., Pacific region,
Latin American region).

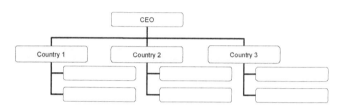

Global Functional Design:
Organizing a company's global
business based on company functional
areas (e.g., finance, operations,
marketing).

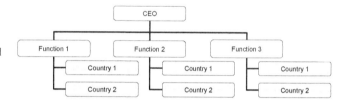

Global Customer Design:
Organizing a company's global
business based on the unique needs of
customers (e.g., B2B business,
franchise businesses).

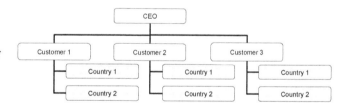

Global Matrix Design:
Organizing a company's global
business based on a combination of
any two of the above designs (e.g.,
integrating global area with global
product design).

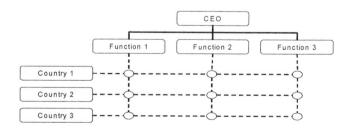

An appropriate global organization design should help the firm integrate four types of strategic information to facilitate successful competition:

1. Area knowledge, including an understanding of the local area's culture, economics, and social conditions;
2. Product knowledge, including an understanding of local customer needs and possible markets for company products;
3. Functional knowledge, including local access to expertise in the various functional areas of business (e.g., finance, production, etc.); and
4. Customer knowledge, including an understanding of each customer's particular needs for sales and service.

The principal global organization designs include the following:

• *Global product design.* The most common global organization design is the *global product design.* In this design, worldwide responsibility for specific product groups is assigned to separate operating divisions within the firm. Thus, Unilever might assign its soap and laundry products to one division that is responsible for worldwide sales, while another division is given worldwide responsibility for baby products, and so on. Companies that stress product development and marketing (e.g., consumer products companies) frequently use this form of organization.

• *Global area design.* The *global area design,* another common form of global design, organizes a firm by geographic region. Regional headquarters are established in various parts of the world, and each headquarters is responsible for all products sold and distributed in that region. This model is frequently used when a firm's products are not easily transferable across regional boundaries. Cadbury Schweppes, the British candy and soft drink manufacturer, uses a global area design due to variations is taste for such products across regions. Candies that are popular in the United Kingdom differ from those that are popular in the United States or Japan, and a global area design allows each region to focus its energies on meeting local tastes. The German publishing giant Bertelsmann AG also uses this design due to the language and cultural differences across its various publications (*Der Spiegel* in Germany; *Parents* magazine in the United States).

• *Global functional design.* A *global functional design* is typically used by companies that have relatively narrow product lines that are easily transferred around the world. In this model, each functional department within a company creates departments or divisions in various regions of the world. British Airways, for example, sells the same "product" around the world. Its efforts are supported by a global marketing department responsible for worldwide sales, a public affairs department responsible for advertising and customer relations around the world, and so forth. In this way, the key functional areas are coordinated to allow the airline to project one global brand image and one uniform level of service.

• *Global customer design.* A *global customer design* is a unique design that tailors a firm's organization to meet the needs of specialized global customers. Kodak, for example, organizes its international operations into commercial business and consumer business groups. These are very different markets, requiring different products, different levels of technical support, and different approaches to marketing and distribution. Automobile tire companies, such as Goodyear and Michelin, also follow this pattern, establishing one division to sell new tires in bulk to auto manufacturers and another to sell to individual auto customers seeking tire replacements.

• *Global matrix design.* The most complex international organization design, the *global matrix design,* represents a blend of two of the above global designs working in tandem (e.g., integrating a global functional design with a global product design, as does Texas Instruments). As with any matrix organization, each manager would have two supervisors, leading to improved communications and flexibility but reduced accountability and job clarity.

Beyond these standardized forms of organization, many companies develop their own unique *hybrid organization design* to suit their own particular global needs. The global auto giant Nissan, for example, uses a global area design to sell and service its cars around the world. However, its U.S. market is so large that in this case Nissan uses a functional organization design to successfully meet market demand.

CULTURE, ORGANIZATION, AND MANAGEMENT: INSIDE THE JAPANESE *KEIRETSU*

One way to develop a clearer understanding of variations in organization design as they relate to international business is to compare typical designs across countries. Cultural differences can significantly influence how organizations are put together. As noted above, perhaps nowhere is the difference more apparent than between typical Western and Japanese corporations. Japan's large vertically integrated *keiretsu* organizations (e.g., Sumitomo, Mitsui, Mitsubishi) represent a unique approach to organization that has served their companies and their country well over the years.[6] The design of these organizations is rooted in Japanese history and is successful largely because it is congruent with the national culture. The effects of this congruence can be seen in the unsuccessful attempts of many Western firms to imitate the basic *keiretsu* design. In view of the importance of Japan in the global economy, we turn now to an examination of how typical Japanese firms are organized to succeed.

WESTERN VERSUS JAPANESE APPROACHES TO ORGANIZATION AND MANAGEMENT

As a point of comparison for understanding Japanese organization design, it is helpful to review how typical Western firms are organized and managed. While wide variations obviously exist across companies, Western firms typically represent loosely coupled systems with many key parts actually located outside of the company for purposes of efficiency and flexibility (see Exhibit 9.3). Western CEOs tend to have considerable power as decision makers and leaders so long as they succeed. Partly as a result of this, many Western firms tend to have a top-down decision-making style. When Western companies need capital for expanding their business, market research for a new product, or in-depth legal advice, they typi-

Exhibit 9.3

Typical Management Structures in Western and Japanese Firms

Characteristics	Typical Western Firms	Typical Japanese Firms
Role of CEO	Powerful decision maker	Moderately powerful consensus builder
Center of power	CEO and board of directors	CEO and president's club
Decision making	Generally top-down	Top-down or bottom-up; autocratic but benevolent
Financing and performance emphasis	Largely external financing in capital markets where outside investors and financial analysts prefer, short-term results	Company-based financing, long-term investment strategies, limited dividends, and little pressure for short-term results
Market research	Frequently outsourced	Typically handled in-house
Legal services	Frequently outsourced	Seldom outsourced
Basis of agreements	Legal contracts	Personal agreements
Production facilities	Increasingly outsourced to independent overseas firms	Increasingly moved to overseas locations under company control
Supplier strategy	Typically outsourced to independent suppliers	Typically outsourced to affiliated suppliers
Distribution strategy	Often outsourced to independent distributors	Typically handled in-house
View of employees	Employees as factors of production	Employees as members of the organization
Human resources management	Increasingly outsourced; reports to upper management	Seldom outsourced; reports to top management
Corporate culture	Influenced by American culture of individualism, hierarchy, and competition	Influenced by Japanese culture of collectivism, inclusion, and participation
Type of union	Independent unions	Company unions

cally go outside the company. Likewise, both manufacturing and service companies often rely on outside suppliers and distributors that have only a tenuous relationship to the company. And even inside the company, employees are often viewed as factors of production more than members of the organization. Indeed, in some Western companies, employees are routinely hired and fired based on variations in workloads.

All of this contrasts sharply with the typical Japanese firm.[7] In Japan, employees are treated as fixed costs, not variable costs, and relationships with suppliers tend to be closer and more stable over time. Executives have less power, and decision making is distributed throughout the firm. Financing is more likely to come from inside the Japanese conglomerate's own financial institutions (e.g., company-owned banks or insurance companies), while market research and even legal advice frequently is done within the firm. Finally, Japanese unions tend to be company unions (referred to as *enterprise unions*) and are more closely associated with company interests than is the case in the West.

INSTITUTIONAL DIFFERENCES AND COMPETITIVE STRATEGIES

If there is a principal difference in the business strategies of Japanese firms compared to their U.S. counterparts, it is their preoccupation with gaining market share instead of net profits or higher stock prices.[8] This fundamental difference results from several institutional differences in the two business environments that allow many Japanese firms to take a longer-term perspective than do their U.S. competitors (see Exhibit 9.4).

As a result of these differences, Japanese firms are better positioned to focus their attention on attaining strategic objectives (such as beating competitors) instead of financial objectives (such as keeping stockholders happy). This competitive advantage occurs for three principal reasons: First, low profits and high retained earnings support growth. Second, close relationships with banks allow the use of heavy debt to support growth. And finally, Japanese stockholders routinely accept low dividends and management's absolute control of the firm.

Within this institutional framework, many Japanese firms are able to develop strategic plans to compete against Western firms by using one or more of the following three strategies. First, Japanese firms often compete with high-value products where the company can add value with knowledge instead of some other factor. For example, many Japanese firms tend to compete based on superior technology instead of cost (e.g., cameras). With a highly educated—but also highly paid—workforce, this represents a smart strategy. Second, such firms often continually stress productivity improvements to minimize costs and remain ahead of competitors. Japan's use of just-in-time production and TQM quality control systems is legendary. And finally, many Japanese firms capitalize on the resources of the *keiretsu* network. For example, Japanese companies routinely get financing from group banks and use group-based trading companies for distribution.

Using these strategies, Japanese firms generally follow an incremental sequence of tactics to capture targeted markets. First, they enter a market at the low end with high-quality products. Through continuous improvement, they then move to penetrate the market and build customer loyalty. Next, they move to the upscale portion of the market, where profit margins are more substantial. Overseas manufacturing facilities are opened when a sufficient overseas market exists to ensure manufacturing economies of scale. Finally, profits from the venture are reinvested into improving existing products or developing new ones to remain one step ahead of competitors. The end result of this strategy is to force competitors to play a never-ending game of catch-up until their resources are depleted and they leave the market.

Exhibit 9.4

U.S. and Japanese Institutional Environments

U.S. Institutional Environment	Japanese Institutional Environment
Business-government relations are distant and oftentimes adversarial, with the government acting as principal regulator.	Business-government relations are cooperative, with the government targeting strategic industries and supporting local industries.
The principal purpose of a company is to maximize stockholder wealth.	The principal purpose of a company is to build value over the long term to benefit investors, employees, and the nation.
Investors stress short-term transactions and returns on investment.	Investors stress long-term growth. Dividends are paid at a constant rate as a percentage of par value of stock, not as a percentage of profits.
A clear link exists between earnings per share and stock price.	Investors stress long-term stock appreciation instead of earnings per share.
Managers are frequently offered stock options and large bonuses for superior performance.	Managers are seldom offered stock options of large bonuses for superior performance.
Undervalued companies are frequently subject to hostile takeovers.	Companies maintain few outside board members to defend stockholder interests. Undervalued companies typically are protected by sister companies from outside takeovers.

TYPES OF *KEIRETSU* STRUCTURES

To succeed in business, various Japanese companies (*kaisha* in Japanese) join together to form a *keiretsu* network, as discussed above. The *keiretsu* provides financial, organizational, legal, and logistical support for its sister companies. For example, when Mitsubishi Motors (a *kaisha*) needs glass, sheet metal, electrical components, or fabric for its automobile assembly line, it is likely to secure most if not all of these materials from other companies within the Mitsubishi Business Group (a *keiretsu*). Obviously, not being a *keiretsu* member can lead to isolation and missed business opportunities. It is this isolation from the market—not being allowed membership in key business relationships—that many Western companies object to in attempting to conduct business in Japan.

Japanese *keiretsu* can be divided into two basic types: horizontal (*yoko*) and vertical (*tate*). A *horizontal keiretsu* consists of a group of interlocking companies typically clustered around a lead manufacturer, a main bank, and a trading company, and overseen by a presidents' council consisting of the presidents of the major group companies. Exhibit 9.5 illustrates how a horizontal *keiretsu* is organized. The "big six" horizontal *keiretsu* are Mitsui, Mitsubishi, Sumitomo, Fuyo, Sanwa, and Dai-Ichi Kangyo Bank (or DKB) Group. By contrast, a *vertical keiretsu* consists of a large manufacturing company surrounded by numerous small and subservient suppliers and distributors that keep the op-

Exhibit 9.5 **Structure of a Typical Horizontal Keiretsu**

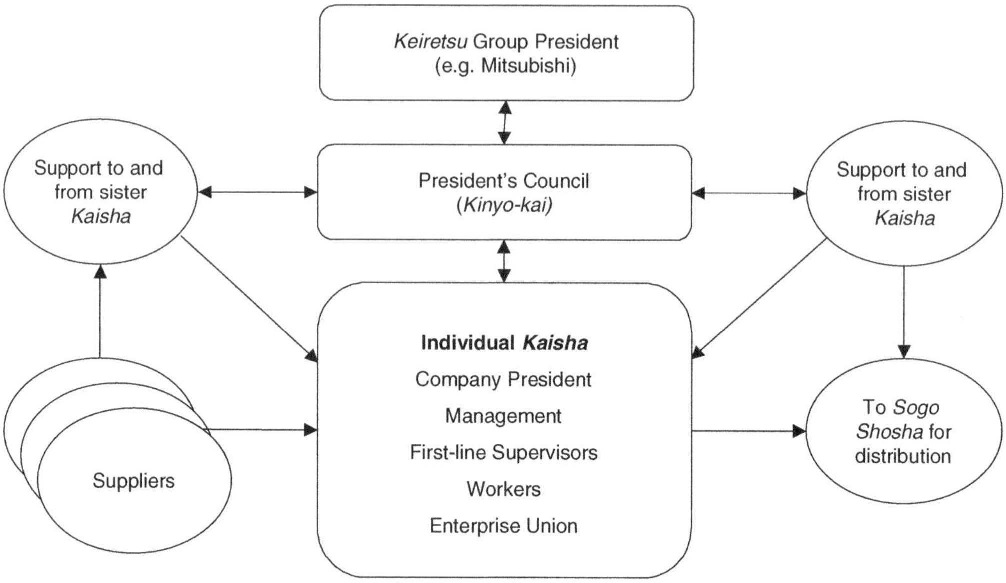

erations running smoothly, typically through a just-in-time (or *kanban*) production system. Toyota Motor Company is a good example of a vertical *keiretsu.*

HORIZONTAL *KEIRETSU*

An example of a horizontal *keiretsu* can be seen in the Mitsubishi Business Group (see Exhibit 9.6). Here we see a main bank (Mitsubishi Bank), a trading company (Mitsubishi Shoji), and a flagship manufacturer (Mitsubishi Heavy Industries). In addition, three financial firms are clustered around these three key companies: a life insurance company, a business insurance company, and a trust bank. Together, these financial firms, the trading company, and the group's key manufacturers give the *keiretsu* its unique identity. Beyond this are hundreds of large and small companies that are associated with the group. Senior managers from the principal companies are frequently assigned to serve in management positions in the smaller firms to assist with intercompany coordination support. Interlocking directorates are common to reinforce this family system.

Main Bank

Within each horizontal *keiretsu,* the *main bank* performs several functions. Its most important role is providing funds for company operations, expansion, and research and development. These banks provide more than two-thirds of the financial needs of *keiretsu*-affiliated companies. Second, member companies frequently hold stock

Exhibit 9.6

Mitsubishi's Horizontal *Keiretsu*

Annual sales	$433 billion worldwide
Number of employees	400,000 worldwide
Group chairman	Principal coordinator and consensus builder for group activities
President's council (*kinyo-kai*)	Principal decision-making body for the group, consisting of the presidents of the top twenty-five companies; meets monthly to discuss long- and short-term group strategies and facilitate coordination actions across sister companies
Mitsubishi Heavy Industries*	World's largest heavy industries companies (61,000 employees, $22 billion annual sales), involved in shipbuilding, industrial machinery, aerospace and aircraft manufacturing, construction, power plants, and mining
Mitsubishi Bank*	Provides funds for company operations, maintains cross holdings of sister companies' stocks, audits sister companies, provides venture capital for new endeavors, and rescues sister companies facing bankruptcy
Mitsubishi Shoji* (*sogo shosha*)	Provides sister companies with easy access to global markets and distribution networks, collects and analyzes market and economic data, assists sister companies with marketing, helps nonmember trading partners import into Japan, and provides credit for affiliated companies
Other *kaisha* members	200 principal companies, plus numerous smaller ones, that comprise Mitsubishi Group
Enterprise union	Company union representing blue-collar and lower-level white-collar employees
Suppliers	1,000 affiliated suppliers providing parts and component subassemblies to various group companies, typically using a *kanban* system

Source: Mitsubishi Corporation Website, 2004, www.mitsubishi.com.
*The "big three" (i.e., most powerful) companies of the Mitsubishi Group.

in sister companies (known as stable cross-shareholdings). Main banks are among the nation's largest shareholders for such firms, providing considerable stability for company management interested in long-term growth strategies. Third, main banks provide an important audit function for member companies in monitoring corporate performance and evaluating risk. Fourth, main banks provide the best source of venture capital for member companies interested in launching new but risky ventures. For instance, Sumitomo Bank provided massive start-up investments in member company NEC's initiative to capture the semiconductor market. Finally, main banks serve as the "company doctor" in rescuing companies that are facing bankruptcy. Since corporate bankruptcy can threaten public confidence in Japan's economic system, not just a specific business group, main banks often quietly provide financial support to keep ailing companies going until the firm can be reorganized or the problem resolved. This financial commitment to member companies can also create trouble for the *keiretsu,* however, when the main bank is required to bail out a noncompetitive company that should perhaps be sold off or dissolved.

Sogo Shosha

The trading company, or *sogo shosha,* provides member companies with ready access to global markets and distribution networks. These companies (e.g., Mitsubishi Shoji or Sumitomo Busan) maintain offices throughout the world and are continually on the lookout for new or expanded markets. At the same time, their field offices collect and analyze market and economic intelligence that can be used by member companies to develop new products or otherwise get a jump on the competition. They frequently assist member companies with various marketing activities as well and facilitate imports into Japan for their business customers. In fact, historically, Japanese trading companies have been responsible for almost half of Japan's imports and three-fifths of its exports. Finally, the *sogo shosha* often provide significant credit (through the group's main bank) for small and medium-sized companies involved in business activities with member companies, again getting a jump on competitors that operate further from lines of credit.

President's Council

Although hundreds of companies may be affiliated with one *keiretsu,* only the principal companies are allowed to join the *presidents' council (shacho-kai,* or *kinyo-kai* in the case of Mitsubishi). This council (typically consisting of the CEOs of the top twenty to thirty group companies) meets monthly to discuss principal strategies for the group, as well as issues of coordination across the various sister companies. Since council meetings are private and no records are maintained, little is understood about how such councils actually work. At the very least, however, these meetings facilitate extensive cooperation across member companies on developing group strategy and group solidarity, as well as mediating disagreements across member companies.

VERTICAL *KEIRETSU*

When most Westerners think of a *keiretsu,* they have in mind the horizontal variety discussed above. However, the vertical (or pyramid) *keiretsu* can be just as powerful. Key vertical *keiretsu* include the major Japanese automobile firms, such as Toyota, Nissan, and Honda, as well as some of the major electric giants, such as Matsushita (including Panasonic, Quasar, and National brands) and Sony. An illustration of the organization structure of a vertical *keiretsu* is shown in Exhibit 9.7. More specific information on the Toyota vertical *keiretsu* is shown in Exhibit 9.8. As noted above, a vertical *keiretsu* consists of a major company surrounded by a large number of smaller firms that act as either suppliers or distributors for the big firm.

  In point of fact, there are two kinds of vertical *keiretsu:* a *production keiretsu,* in which a myriad of parts suppliers join together to create subassemblies for a single end-product manufacturer (such as Toyota), and a *distribution keiretsu,* in

Exhibit 9.7   **Structure of a Typical Vertical Keiretsu**

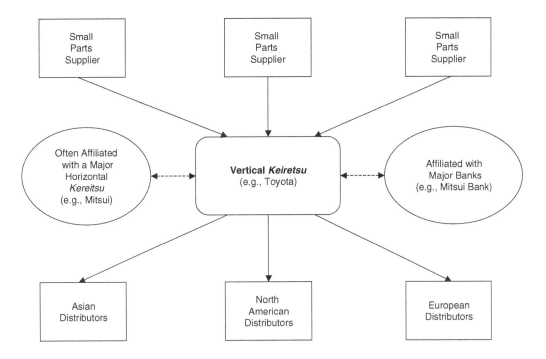

which a single large firm, usually a manufacturer, moves products to market through a network of wholesalers and retailers that depend on the parent company for goods. Since most manufacturers have both *keiretsu* types (production and distribution), we can envision the two like an hourglass: an upside-down (production) pyramid on top, in which individual parts suppliers provide various parts (e.g., fabric for car seats) to subcomponent assembly companies, which ultimately provide subassemblies (e.g., completed seats) to the parent company in the center of the hourglass. Then the parent company assembles the end products and prepares them for market. Next, these products are passed down into another (distribution) pyramid, where they are distributed to wholesalers and ultimately to retail consumers.

In some cases, a leading company from a vertical *keiretsu* will form an alliance with a horizontal *keiretsu* to ensure solid financing and improved trading capabilities. Toyota is a member of the Mitsui Group, for example, in addition to running its own vertical *keiretsu*. Finally, numerous small supplier firms become quasi members of the group and receive long-term purchasing contracts, as well as assistance with financing and sometimes research and development. These suppliers support the famous *kanban* (or just-in-time) inventory system that Japan is noted for and must remain loyal to one group. That is, when supplies on an assembly line get short, suppliers are automatically notified and replenish the factory in short order.

Exhibit 9.8

Toyota's Vertical *Keiretsu*

Annual sales	6,780,000 cars worldwide
Annual revenue	$133 billion worldwide
Number of employees	264,000 worldwide
Number of global markets	140 countries worldwide
Number of plants in Japan	12 plants and 11 principal manufacturing subsidiaries
Number of plants outside Japan	46 manufacturing plants in 26 countries
Affiliated *keiretsu*	Affiliated with Mitsui Group (a horizontal *keiretsu*)
Enterprise union	Company union representing blue-collar and lower-level white-collar employees
Suppliers	Hundreds of affiliated suppliers providing parts and component subassemblies to various group companies, typically using a *kanban* system

Source: Toyota Motor Company, *2004 Annual Report: To New Frontiers*, March 31, 2004, pp. 70–74.

COMPETITIVE ADVANTAGE AT KIRIN BREWERY

Whether we are talking about a horizontal or vertical *keiretsu,* many observers have argued that the very structure of these conglomerates provides an unfair advantage in global competition. To see how this might work, consider the example of Kirin Brewery, a member of the Mitsubishi *keiretsu.* To produce, bottle, and distribute beer, Kirin needs help from a multitude of sources. In many cases, it can get this help from sister companies in a long-term, reliable manner. Consider:

- When Kirin needs glass for its bottles, it contacts Asahi Glass, a Mitsubishi company.
- When Kirin needs aluminum for its cans, it contacts Mitsubishi Aluminum.
- When Kirin needs plastic to bottle its soft drinks, it contacts Mitsubishi Plastics.
- When Kirin needs paper for labels, it contacts Mitsubishi Paper.
- When Kirin needs financing for its operations, it contacts Mitsubishi Bank.
- When Kirin needs to construct new facilities, it contacts Mitsubishi Construction.
- When Kirin needs cars and trucks to help distribute its products, it contacts Mitsubishi Motors.
- When Kirin needs global distribution of its products, it contacts Mitsubishi Shoji.

You get the picture. The interlocking companies that comprise *keiretsu* such as Mitsubishi can create a considerable competitive advantage in global business, and it is precisely this organizational format that many Western companies point to when claiming that Japanese companies have an unfair trade advantage.

It has been suggested by some that the *keiretsu* model is beginning to emerge in the United States. Ford Motor Company is frequently cited as an example of an American *keiretsu*. It is true that Ford now focuses almost exclusively on automotive and financial services and has divested itself of most other unrelated businesses. In the process, Ford organized a network of affiliated companies that support Ford in such areas as R & D, parts manufacture, vehicle assembly, marketing, and financial services. In research, for example, Ford belongs to eight consortia that engage in research and development for such items as improved engineering and quality control techniques, materials, and electric car batteries. In the area of parts manufacture, Ford holds equity stakes in Cummins Engine (engines), Excel Industries (windows), and Decoma International (body parts and wheels) and relies on these firms as major suppliers for Ford's final assembly line. In vehicle assembly, Ford has ownership interests in Europe, South America, and Asia. It uses these sister companies to both manufacture and market cars in these regions. And in financial services, Ford has seven wholly owned subsidiaries that range from consumer credit to commercial leasing.

However, while Ford and other Western companies may be embracing global sourcing, integrated manufacturing, and multinational marketing, it is questionable whether such companies actually resemble the *keiretsu* model. Western companies have always pursued vertical integration of manufacturing and distribution when it led to reduced costs or expanded markets. There is nothing new in this. By contrast, the Japanese *keiretsu* represents an entire social system in which national culture, government policies, corporate strategies, and management practices are fully integrated, mutually supportive, and reinforced through incentives and rewards that make the entire enterprise run smoothly over the long run. This is not the case in most Western companies. At Ford, for example, consider what happens to suppliers—or employees, for that matter—when the company experiences economic downturns. Thus, while clear similarities exist, and while multinationals pursue vertical integration to achieve operating efficiencies, it would be misleading to claim that many Western companies have adopted the Japanese business model as their own. Their cultures, and in many cases their governments, would not allow it.

MANAGEMENT IN A JAPANESE *KEIRETSU*

Many aspects of managing in a Japanese *keiretsu* can be significantly different than the process typically found in Western firms. Of particular note are significant differences in how many Japanese firms approach human resources management (HRM), make decisions, and manage the collective bargaining process. Each of these aspects of management will be examined, beginning with HRM practices.

HUMAN RESOURCES MANAGEMENT PRACTICES

Japanese *kaisha* tend to view all regular employees as part of their permanent cost structure. As a result, during difficult financial periods, most Japanese companies will go to great lengths to retain their workers. This contrasts with the situation in the

Exhibit 9.9

U.S. and Japanese HRM Practices

Characteristics	United States	Japan
Selection criteria	Personable, assertive, competitive, capacity to make immediate contributions to company, willingness to take risks	Team player, disciplined, eager to learn, capacity for long-term personal growth, absolute loyalty, obedience
Employment contract	Employment only as long as individual contributes and sufficient work exists	Employment for life for most managers and senior male production workers
Specialization	Emphasis on specialization (e.g., finance, marketing) with only limited cross training for people on a general management track	Considerable cross-functional training for all managers, with emphasis on becoming a generalist
Decision making	Individual top-down decision making	Relatively high level of multilevel consensus building in decision-making
Responsibility	Emphasis on individual responsibility	Emphasis on group responsibility
Concern for employee	Little concern for employee as a total person	Considerable concern for employee as a total person
Control systems	Explicit formal control systems from supervisor	Implicit, less formal control systems from supervisor and colleagues
Performance feedback	Objective, critical feedback from supervisor	Intuitive, informal feedback from supervisor and colleagues
Promotion rate	Moderate to rapid, depending on performance	Slow, regardless of performance

United States, where layoffs are frequently seen as an easy solution to financial exigency. If workers are seen as a fixed resource, it makes sense to invest heavily in their training. Long-term employment will allow for sufficient payback of such training expenses. In this sense, Western observers have suggested that Japanese companies treat their employees more like family members than employees. A comparison between traditional U.S. and Japanese management practices is shown in Exhibit 9.9. Note, however, that these exhibits summarize only very general characteristics for the two countries and that numerous exceptions exist. (Consider, for example, the HRM practices of General Motors versus those of Google.) Even so, they should provide a rough overview of the differences between the two cultural systems.

Concern has frequently been expressed in the Japanese media that employees' commitment to their companies in Japan may be too strong. For example, many Japanese refuse to take all of the vacation time to which they are entitled—a practice seldom witnessed in the West. A commonly used Japanese word, *ganbatte*, typifies this overzealous commitment to work.[9] Indeed, Japanese employees and even school-children will often be heard to say to their friends or colleagues, "*Ganbatte kudasai*"—never give up, try harder, do your best. On the positive side, *ganbatte* shows strong commitment to succeed on behalf of one's company or family. On the negative side, it often manifests itself in large numbers of work-related health problems. Health care professionals express concern about the large number of Japanese employees who overwork themselves to the point of becoming ill.

Finally, it is important to note that in view of Japan's long-running economic problems and increased global pressures for efficiency, several Japanese companies (e.g., Hitachi) have recently begun to back away from their former policies of iron-clad job security and lifetime employment.[10] Other companies are beginning to place greater emphasis on individual performance and performance appraisals, referred to as the *nenpo* system.[11]

Even so, the general characteristics of Japanese HRM systems remain relatively constant. Concern for the group, respect for age and seniority, and devotion to the company remain hallmarks of the typical Japanese firm. Indeed, Fujitsu recently decided to discontinue its much-heralded Western-style performance-based pay system because it proved to be a poor fit with Japanese culture. Fujitsu's new system will emphasize worker enthusiasm and energy in tackling a job instead of actual goal accomplishment in annual performance evaluations.[12] Moreover, when Fujitsu announced that it was laying off 15,000 workers, or 9 percent of its workforce, it made it clear that all involuntary layoffs would take place in operations outside Japan. Any Japanese workforce reductions would be accomplished through retirements and normal attrition.

RINGI-SEI DECISION PROCESS

Decision making in a typical Japanese *kaisha* reflects Japanese culture and is seen by many observers as being quite distinct from decision making in the West. Not surprisingly, Japanese firms endorse the concept of decision making based on consensus up and down the hierarchy.[13] The system by which this is done is usually called *ringi-seido* (often shortened to simply *ringi-sei*), or circle of discussion. *Ringi* means to circulate something and accurately describes the basic process. The *ringi-sei system* generally consists of two parts: *nemawashi,* or general discussions and putting out feelers, and *ringi-sho,* or putting forth a specific written proposal for discussion, modification, and approval. This process is illustrated in Exhibit 9.10.

When a particular problem or opportunity is identified, a group of workers or supervisors will discuss various parameters of the problem and try to identify possible solutions. At times, technical experts will be brought in for assistance. If the initial results are positive, employees will approach their supervisor for more advice and possible support. This entire process is generally referred to in Japan as *nemawashi.* The word *nemawashi* is derived from a description of the process of preparing the roots of a tree for planting. The concept here is that if the roots are properly prepared, the tree will survive and prosper. Similarly, if a proposal is properly prepared, it, too, should survive and prosper.

When a group has achieved informal consensus, a formal proposal is then drafted for submission up the chain of command. This formal document, known as a *ringi-sho,*

Exhibit 9.10

Japanese *Ringi-sei* Decision Process

Step in Process	Decision-Making Process	Organizational Activities
1	*Nemawashi* (informal consultations)	Lower-level employees in a section or department work together to solve a problem and to gain informal consensus around a possible solution.
2		Department heads, section chiefs, and supervisors meet informally to discuss and modify the proposal. Technical experts are consulted where needed to improve the proposal.
3		Departmental consensus is reached on a specific proposal or plan of action. At this stage, considerable planning on the project has been completed.
4	*Ringi-sho* (document system; formal authorization process)	A formal written proposal (*ringi-sho*) is then drafted and passed up the chain of command for approval or rejection. Managers who approve of the plan stamp their name on it; managers who do not approve either refrain from stamping or stamp it on the reverse side.
5		If the *ringi-sho* document makes it to top management, it is highly likely to be approved, since rank-and-file managers up the chain of command have already agreed to it.

is reviewed by successively higher levels of management. If a manager agrees with the proposal, he stamps his name on it; if not, he either refrains from stamping it or stamps it on the reverse side. By the time the document reaches upper management, it has become clear whether it has broad-based support or not. If it does enjoy support, in all likelihood top management will formally adopt the proposal. In this way, upper management frequently has little input into the decision making process. If a proposal has universal support up the chain of command, top managers will often be hard-pressed to oppose it. (Consider how this process differs from typical Western decision making, where top managers usually have the final word on all critical—and, indeed, not so critical—decisions.)

While discussions concerning a particular decision or course of action are proceeding, two seemingly contradictory processes often occur that tend to confuse many Westerners. In Japan, doing or saying the right thing according to prevailing norms or social custom is referred to as *tatemae,* while doing or saying what one actually prefers to do (which may be difficult) is referred to as *honne.* Thus, in a conversation or meeting, to some Westerners a Japanese manager may speak in contradictions or, worse, speak insincerely. In reality, the manager may simply be saying what he believes he is obliged to say, while hoping that through subtle signals the recipient of the message will discover his true desire or intent. This can be confusing to many Westerners and requires them to listen carefully and observe body language

Exhibit 9.11

Labor Relations in the United States and Japan

Characteristics	United States	Japan
Percentage of workers unionized	14	24
Common form of union	Multi-industry	Company-based
Contract coverage	Parties to contract	Specific firm
Largest national union*	AFL-CIO	Rengo
Union-management relations	Frequently adversarial	Typically cooperative
Focus on collective bargaining	Wages, hours, and benefits	Wages, hours, and benefits
Bargaining strategy	Often decentralized	Typically decentralized
Grievance resolution procedures	Typically voluntary arbitration	Typically agreed-upon rules
Union participation in management	Little or no consultation with unions	Frequent management consultation with unions

*AFL-CIO: American Federation of Labor–Congress of Industrial Organizations; Rengo: Japanese Trade Union Confederation.

(for example, reading someone's face) as well as formal speech. After all, Japan is a high-context culture, while most Western nations are not.

A key point to remember: The *ringi-sei* process tends to result in slow decisions, often a disadvantage in a fast-paced competitive global business environment. However, this process yields considerable support for and commitment to the emergent solution when it is achieved. By contrast, many Western decisions are typically made unilaterally much higher up in the management hierarchy but, once made, frequently face considerable opposition or apathy as managers and workers attempt to implement them. As a result, strategic planning is frequently accomplished more quickly in the West, while strategic implementation is frequently accomplished more quickly in Japan.

ENTERPRISE UNIONS AND LABOR RELATIONS

There are more than 70,000 labor unions in Japan, most of which are company-specific. These enterprise unions tend to include both workers and lower- and middle-level managers. This situation differs from that in the United States, for example, where most unions are industrial unions that have members in several companies in the same industry.

Although many enterprise unions are affiliated with national labor federations (which facilitate the annual spring wage negotiations, or *shunto*), these organizations are more decentralized than those in the United States. As a result, Japanese workers in enterprise unions typically do not experience the same degree of divided loyalties (union vs. company) that is often seen in the United States among unionized workers. In addition, it is not uncommon for union members in Japanese companies to rise through the management ranks—even to the position of company president in some cases. This seldom occurs in the United States, where the managerial hierarchy is separate and distinct from the blue-collar class and where junior managers are typically hired from among recent college graduates, not rank-and-file production workers.

Even though enterprise unions are often linked to large, nationwide industrial unions, industrial action (e.g., strikes) is rare, and most disputes are settled relatively amicably. A comparison of Japanese industrial relations systems with those of the United States is shown in Exhibit 9.11.

The lack of clear divisions between labor and management in Japanese firms often makes it possible to enlist workers at all levels in efforts to improve productivity and product quality. Quality and service are companywide concerns from the top to the bottom of the organization, not just management concerns. Japan is noted for its widespread use of *quality circles* (QC, or QCC for quality control circles), small groups of workers who spend time (frequently their own) trying to improve operational procedures or product quality in their own area.[14] These efforts help Japanese firms with their *kaizen,* a philosophy of continuous improvement that is also a hallmark of Japanese manufacturing firms.[15]

In summary, the typical Japanese approach to organization and management is both different and effective, and it represents a formidable threat to global competitors. Japanese firms have found a way to build their organizations in ways that draw support from the local environment and culture and mobilize their resources in ways that many Western firms have difficulty understanding, let alone responding to. It is a model that prizes cooperation and mutual support among friends and all-out competition against all others.

KEY TERMS

corollary model
distribution *keiretsu*
enterprise unions
export department model
global area design
global customer design
global functional design
global matrix design
global product design
horizontal *keiretsu*
hybrid organization design
international division model
kaisha

kaizen
kanban
keiretsu
main bank
nemawashi
presidents' council
production *keiretsu*
ringi-sei system
ringi-sho
quality circles
sogo shosha
vertical *keiretsu*

GLOBAL MANAGER'S WORKBOOK 9.1: ORGANIZING IN THE UNITED STATES AND JAPAN

Based on what you have learned about the cultures and business practices of Japan and the United States, consider the following questions about organizing for global business:

1. In your judgment, what are the principal differences in typical Japanese and U.S. approaches to organizing for global business? What are the advantages and disadvantages of each?
2. What are the key differences in the way typical Japanese and U.S. firms approach staffing (or HRM) decisions? What are the advantages and disadvantages of each?
3. What are the principal differences in the way typical Japanese and U.S. firms approach decision making? What are the advantages and disadvantages of each?
4. What might typical U.S. firms learn from their Japanese counterparts about doing global business more effectively? What might typical Japanese firms learn from their U.S. counterparts?
5. In your view, what is the worst mistake a global manager could make in trying to do business with a Japanese firm? What is the worst mistake a global manager could make in trying to do business with a U.S. firm?

GLOBAL MANAGER'S WORKBOOK 9.2: REINVENTING NISSAN

Throughout the 1980s, it was hard to pick up a Western business magazine or newspaper without seeing an article on the virtues of Japanese management techniques or the way of doing business in Japan. The charge to the West was clear: Learn from Japan. North American and European companies were urged to adopt Japanese corporate policies, such as lifetime employment, group-based compensation, reliance on close customer-supplier networks such as those found in the *keiretsu* system, and even morning group exercises. Nowhere was this admiration more visible than with Japan's automobile companies, including Toyota, Honda, and Nissan.

In the early 1990s, however, the economic bubble burst, and Japanese industry began a tailspin that continues to this day. Corporate growth rates slowed, the stock market stagnated, and many Japanese industrialists began to lose confidence in the Japanese "economic miracle." Among the corporate elite, Nissan suffered the greatest fall.[16] Significant expansion of its domestic markets during the 1980s left the company with too many factories and workers as it was forced to battle for market share in the crowded Japanese auto market by keeping its prices down. Nissan also suffered from excess capacity in its European markets, while the high value of the yen made it difficult to export its way out of trouble. Meanwhile, the Asian currency crisis of 1997–98 dried up demand for its cars throughout much of East and Southeast Asia. As a result, the company failed to make a profit from 1992 onward.

In an effort to turn Nissan around, company executives initiated a cost-cutting program in 1994. Nissan announced that it would cut the number of suppliers it would use in the future, thereby increasing the size and reducing the cost of orders from remaining suppliers. The company also decided to trim its workforce and reduce the number of parts used in manufacturing to simplify its procurement procedures and reduce its inventory costs. Unfortunately, these efforts largely failed to reduce costs or return Nissan to profitability.

Unable to overcome its mounting problems, Nissan finally suffered the ultimate indignity for a Japanese company: It was essentially taken over by a foreigner. In May 1999, Renault bought 37 percent of Nissan's common stock for $5.4 billion, thereby transferring control of Japan's second-largest automobile company to the French firm. Renault sent one of its most highly respected executives, Carlos Ghosn, to Tokyo to assume control over the ailing company. After spending five months reviewing Nissan's operations, Brazilian-born Ghosn announced a revival plan for the company that was designed to reduce annual operating costs by nearly $10 billion. To accomplish this goal, Ghosn planned to close five Japanese factories and eliminate 21,000 jobs. About 16,000 jobs would be cut in Nissan's domestic operations. Mindful of Japan's distaste for layoffs and labor laws that make firing employees expensive, Ghosn decided that employment reductions would be achieved largely through attrition, which averaged close to 2,000 domestic employees per year. Early retirements were also considered but ruled out when local labor unions objected.

Other cost reductions included closing regional offices in New York and Washington and reducing the number of models produced. To reinforce the critical challenges facing the company, Ghosn announced that no one in purchasing, engineering, or administration would receive a pay raise until they showed what their contribution was to cost cutting. To cut Nissan's massive debt, Ghosn also began efforts to streamline the company's dealership networks in both Japan and North America. In Japan, one-half of the dealerships were closed, leading to considerable local protests.

Another problem emerged when Ghosn realized that Nissan had a product image that differed across countries, thereby making it difficult to launch cost-effective cross-border advertising campaigns. Worse still, he discovered that Nissan suffered from a brand deficiency, leading customers to value rival products more highly than his company's products. Thus, comparable products manufactured by Toyota, Honda, and Ford could charge more than $1,000 more per car than Nissan. Ghosn responded by giving one firm exclusive worldwide advertising rights for Nissan in an effort to begin building a unified brand image. This move was intended to give Nissan some breathing room while it developed and launched new and more appealing products.

Ghosn then attacked the parts procurement process. He estimated that Nissan's parts procurement costs were 10 percent higher than Renault's, and that by combining, centralizing, and globalizing Renault's and Nissan's parts procurement he could achieve a cost reduction of 20 percent. To do so, however, he had to attack the very *keiretsu* system on which Nissan was built. This plan represented a major risk in view of the financial stake Nissan held in most of its *keiretsu* partners. His criticism of the *keiretsu* system was blunt. He argued that Nissan's purchase of parts through the *keiretsu* system promoted inefficiency and mediocrity. Since the suppliers were guaranteed business, they often failed to innovate or cut costs. As Ghosn noted at the time, about 60 percent of Nissan's costs were attributed to suppliers. Nissan needed suppliers that were innovative. That wouldn't happen with *keiretsu* companies, he concluded.

As a result, Ghosn announced that Nissan would liquidate its holdings in all but 4 of its 1,400 *keiretsu* partners. In addition, Nissan would cut the number of its suppliers in half—to about 600. Instead of purchasing the same part from several suppliers, the company would henceforth concentrate its purchases among a smaller number of suppliers, allowing them to achieve greater economies of scale and reduce their costs. Suppliers that could cut their costs by at least 20 percent would be guaranteed orders; others would not. The Japanese government—and many labor unions—were horrified. It was predicted that Ghosn's controversial plan would lead to tens of thousands of job losses as the small, inefficient suppliers closed their doors. Others predicted that Ghosn himself would be gone with a year.

Next, Ghosn attacked Nissan's own corporate culture. After concluding that many executives were more interested in protecting their own turf than promoting overall corporate objectives and that communication across divisions was poor, he set about initiating major changes in the way Nissan ran itself as a corporation. To accomplish this, he moved swiftly to redirect company managers by refocusing their efforts on improving profits and enhancing customer satisfaction. He established a network of multinational, cross-functional teams to reexamine and reinvigorate each of the firm's principal activities, ranging from research and development to purchasing to manufacturing to distribution. These teams were also charged with the responsibility of tearing down divisional walls and building a global partnership for the future. Ghosn is now talking about implementing U.S.-style pay-for-performance compensation plans, including stock options and bonuses based on profitability and performance—for managerial and nonmanagerial employees alike. This will replace the current seniority system so deeply entrenched in Japanese work culture. And to drive the point home that Nissan will become a truly global firm, not just a Japanese firm operating internationally, Ghosn announced that henceforth the company's official language would be English, not Japanese.

Where did all of this end? By 2002, Nissan was operating in the black, with several new models and a new global marketing strategy that seems to be working. Between 1999 and 2002, Nissan posted the following results:

- Following eight straight years of operating losses, Nissan returned to profitability. Since 2001, operating profits have been at an all-time company high.
- Net automotive debt is at a twenty-four-year low.
- Eight new car models have been developed and successfully launched.
- Supplier costs have been reduced by 20 percent.
- The number of parts suppliers has been reduced by 40 percent, while the number of service providers has been reduced by 60 percent.
- Five unprofitable Nissan plants have been closed.
- More than 21,000 employees have been made redundant.

- The number of profitable car models increased from four out of forty-three to eighteen out of thirty-six models.

Despite this record of success, critics continue to say that Ghosn's changes will be temporary and that Japanese culture will eventually reassert control over the firm after the current crisis ends. Some suggest that no outsider—especially a Brazilian-born French executive—will ever understand the Japanese business culture. Nor will he have the credibility to motivate Japanese managers and workers. Others are not so sure.

As for Carlos Ghosn, he was promoted to run the entire Renault group, beginning in 2005. He immediately announced that despite his promotion he would continue to run Nissan by himself, dividing his time between Paris and Tokyo. Shortly after this announcement, he also assumed direct command of both the Chinese and North American operations for Nissan. Ghosn apparently plans to be a very busy global manager.

QUESTIONS FOR DISCUSSION

1. What are the principal political, social, and economic risks associated with Nissan's new approach to manufacturing and management under the leadership of Carlos Ghosn?
2. Compare and contrast U.S. and Japanese decision-making strategies. How might these differences influence Ghosn's ultimate success?
3. What potential problems might emerge as a result of Nissan's elimination of the *keiretsu* system for sourcing parts and supplies?
4. What potential problems might Nissan face if it goes ahead with its pay-for-performance compensation system? How might the problems be reduced?
5. What special problems face Japanese firms such as Nissan, with their enterprise unions, compared to Western-style industrial unions?
6. Do you agree with the assertion that any foreign executive who tries to turn around a Japanese firm is doomed to failure due to a lack of understanding of Japanese business culture and traditions? Or do you believe that being an outsider is actually an advantage? Why?
7. Do you agree with Ghosn's decision to make English the official language of Nissan as part of his globalization efforts?
8. Does the Nissan model as implemented by Ghosn represent the future of Japanese business practices in the highly competitive global environment? Is this possible in view of Japan's culture and traditions?

NOTES

1. David Thomas, *Essentials of International Management: A Cross-Cultural Perspective* (Thousand Oaks, CA: Sage, 2002), p. 147.

2. Martin Fackler, "Mitsubishi Motors to Review Products, Overhaul Its Culture," *Wall Street Journal*, May 3, 2004, p. A12.

3. Gail Edmondson, "Japan: A Tale of Two Mergers," *Business Week,* May 10, 2004, pp. 42–43.

4. Chester Dawson, "Stop Feeding Losers, Toyota," *Business Week,* January 13, 2003, p. 48.

5. Ricky Griffin and Michael Pustay, *International Business: A Managerial Perspective* (Upper Saddle River, NJ: Prentice Hall, 2003).

6. James Abbeglen and George Stalk, *Kaisha: The Japanese Corporation* (New York: Harper and Row, 1985).

7. Toyohiro Kono and Stewart Clegg, *Trends in Japanese Management: Continuing Strengths, Current Problems, and Changing Priorities* (London: Palgrave, 2001); Masahiko Aoki and Ronald Dore, eds., The Japanese Firm (Oxford: Oxford University Press, 1994).

8. Kono and Clegg, *Trends in Japanese Management.*

9. Christopher Meek, "Ganbatte: Understanding the Japanese Employee," *Business Horizons,* January–February 1999, pp. 27–36.

10. Kono and Clegg, *Trends in Japanese Management.*

11. John Cullen and K. Praveen Parboteeah, *Multinational Management: A Strategic Approach* (Cincinnati: Southwestern College Publishing, 2005).

12. Miki Tanikawa, "Fujitsu Decides to Backtrack on Performance-based Pay," *New York Times,* March 22, 2001.

13. Hiroki Kato and Joan Kato, *Understanding and Working with the Japanese Business World* (Englewood Cliffs, NJ: Prentice Hall, 1992).

14. Kono and Clegg, *Trends in Japanese Management.*

15. Paul Lillrank and Noriaki Kano, *Continuous Improvement: Quality Control Circles in Japanese Industry* (Ann Arbor: Center for Japanese Studies, University of Michigan, 1989).

16. Arran Scott and Norihiko Shirouzu, "Nissan's Chief to Steer U.S. Operations," *Wall Street Journal,* March 24, 2004, p. A2; "Nissan's Boss," *Business Week,* October 4, 2004, pp. 50–60; Chester Dawson, "The Zen of Nissan," *Business Week,* July 22, 2002, pp. 46–49; John Milliken and Dean Fu, "The Global Leadership of Carlos Ghosn at Nissan," Thunderbird Case Series #A07-03-0014, 2003, http://www.thunderbird.edu/faculty_research/case_series/cases_2003/carlos_ghosn.htm.

10 Developing Global Business Strategies

WAL-MART GOES TO MEXICO

When Wal-Mart decides to enter a market, local competitors soon realize that their future prospects are clearly under threat. Both at home and abroad, Wal-Mart has both the resources and the reputation for sucking the air (and the customers) out of any local market it enters. Few can compete against the merchandise giant on price. Within ten years of entering the Mexican market, Wal-Mart (referred to as "Wal-Mex" by its competitors) had captured half of all supermarket sales in the country.[1] It now boasts more than six hundred stores and wholesale outlets nationwide and annual sales of more than $10 billion.

Wal-Mart competes in Mexico much the same way it does north of the border. It squeezes its suppliers on price and readily drops suppliers that do not comply. In one case, Wal-Mart reputedly pulled a brand of yogurt off its shelves when the supplier refused to offer permanent discounts that the supplier claimed were below its cost. While the supplier described Wal-Mart's practices as "aggressive and abusive," a Wal-Mart representative replied, "If we stop doing business with a supplier, it's because his costs don't allow him to sell at prices we've established."[2]

Can Mexican companies compete against this onslaught? At least two are trying very hard. Retailers Comerci and Grupo Gigante have lowered prices and launched aggressive advertising campaigns, often with anti-foreign "Buy Mexican" themes. At the same time, they have asked the Mexican government to investigate unfair trade practices and allegations of fraud and misrepresentation against Wal-Mart. Both local companies have aggressively sought to open new stores around Mexico to build their customer base. Even so, sales and profits at both Comerci and Gigante have fallen significantly in recent years, and both are looking for foreign partners with major resources. As one Comerci's executive notes, "If we don't have a partner with a lot of resources . . . Wal-Mex will be eight to ten times bigger than us in five years."[3]

CULTURE AND STRATEGY: WAL-MART, CARREFOUR, AND ALDI

A firm's *strategy* represents the set of actions it takes to adjust to external pressures, threats, and opportunities. Strategy is the means used to achieve an end, whether it is growth, market share, or profitability. A firm's strategy also highlights its business perspective, its way of doing things. Either way, it is important to keep in mind that in the final analysis strategy is all about trade-offs. Organizations cannot do everything at the same time; they need to focus on some things and ignore others. It is therefore helpful to think of strategy as a pattern of attention by which organizations choose to focus their limited resources on certain specific opportunities or threats in the business environment while ignoring others.[4] Strategy is the means to focus organizational energies and resources toward specific objectives that have either short-term or long-term payoffs for the organization.

When managers make strategic decisions—that is, when they choose what to emphasize and what to ignore—they draw upon their personal beliefs and values.[5] These beliefs and values are often influenced by the cultures in which the decisions are made. Therefore, it is not unusual to see similar firms from different nations following different strategic objectives. For example, return to the Wal-Mart example above and contrast its strategy with that of two other large global retailers: the French Carrefour and German Aldi. These three companies are successful global retailers, and each follows a different global strategy. The different cultural backgrounds of these firms can help explain these different strategies.

As the example above shows, Wal-Mart's international expansion strategy is to replicate in foreign countries a formula that has worked very well in the United States, including standardized store layouts, its "everyday low prices" concept, and its approach to managing suppliers and technological integration. This strategy has worked well in several markets, including Mexico, Canada, and the United Kingdom, but is not without its problems. Consider the difficulties faced by Wal-Mart in its efforts to expand into Germany, the third largest retail market after Japan and the United States. In the late 1990s, Wal-Mart bought two local chains, Wetkauf and Interspar, for $1.6 billion. It faced several problems in Germany, including price controls that prevented retailers from selling below cost, rigid labor laws, and zoning controls that banned Wal-Mart from building its typical jumbo stores. In addition, Wal-Mart was not ready to compete with local rivals in Germany that were comfortable with thin profit margins. In Germany, many competing stores are owned by wealthy families whose primary goal is long-term shareholder value instead of short-term profit. As a result of these problems, Wal-Mart has lost money in Germany since its arrival.[6]

France's Carrefour, the second largest retailer in the world, uses a global strategy very different from that of Wal-Mart. Instead of using a standard store model, Carrefour adapts its stores and products to local tastes.[7] Retail experts suggest that Carrefour's strategy has resulted in fewer major mistakes, such as Wal-Mart's failure in Germany, but in more minor ones. Despite being the number one retailer in Asia, Carrefour had to pull out of Hong Kong, where it could not find a window between the two leading local competitors. In other instances, it has been criticized for locating stores in the wrong places and for being "too French," despite its efforts to adapt.[8] And while Carrefour has achieved a strong presence in much of Asia, Europe, and Latin America, it is largely absent from the three most important retail markets in the world: Japan, Germany, and the United States. A major push into Japan led to only modest results after the company refused to join with a local Japanese partner.[9]

Meanwhile, another major global retailer, Germany's Aldi, approaches the market as a *hard discounter;* that is, it sells its products for less than traditional discounters, including both Wal-Mart and Carrefour. To accomplish this, Aldi's stores typically carry only 700 items, compared to as many as 150,000 for some Wal-Mart stores. They do not carry major brand names such as Nestlé or Nivea; they simplify their shipping and handling procedures; and they cut prices in every possible way. The merchandise is stacked up in boxes in the stores, lines at the register are long, and customers pack their own purchases. Nevertheless, prices are very low. Many German customers like it, as do customers in several other European countries where Aldi does business. Aldi is now building a presence in the U.S. market. Its expansion strategy is to start in niche markets, under the radar of the competition, and expand without being noticed. For instance, Aldi has been in the United States since 1976 and plans to reach 1,000 stores by 2010, but it is still hardly recognized as a competitor outside of the particular neighborhoods where it does business.[10]

The core issue here is not which strategy is better, but why they are different. Clearly, there is no right or wrong strategy, as all three retailers are highly successful. They have made different trade-offs, guided by different values and beliefs. For instance, Wal-Mart takes a more aggressive approach when entering new markets, trying to change the market consumption behavior rather than adapting to it, as Carrefour does. These different decisions may be an outcome of different cultural values. As noted in Chapter 8, cultures can vary in the extent to which they seek mastery or harmony with their environment. Some cultures, such as that typical of the United States, are mastery-oriented and stress control over the environment, while others, such as that typical of France, stress harmony and adaptation. Such cultural characteristics are likely to influence these firms' overall global strategies.

Similarly, cultural differences can also influence a retailer's time frame for international expansion. As discussed in Chapter 7, some cultures emphasize planning and taking a long-term perspective, while others focus on the present and make decisions based on the short term. This cultural value may have influenced the three retailers' approach to international expansion. Aldi, for example, consistently takes a long-term perspective in market penetration, growing slowly under the radar of the competition. Carrefour and Wal-Mart, on the other hand, tend to focus on more rapid growth.

In the end, the important point to remember is that culture can serve as a perceptual filter, helping managers make sense of their environments and decide what is worthy of attention and action. As a result, different firms may make different decisions when faced with the same problem or opportunity. With this in mind, we turn now to an examination of several key issues facing global firms as they consider entering new overseas markets.

STRATEGIES FOR GLOBAL COMPETITION

Gucharan Das, former chairman of Procter & Gamble in India, speaks from experience when he says, "Globalization does not mean imposing homogeneous solutions in a pluralistic world. It means having a global vision and strategy, but it also means cultivating roots and individual identities."[11] Above all, it means tailoring corporate strategies to fit local conditions.

Many companies operating in a global market typically must deal with two opposing forces. On one hand, they face pressures for cost reduction, as customers want quality products at low price. This suggests that firms should manufacture global products that can maximize the company's economies of scale. On the other hand, many companies face pressures for local adaptation, as customer tastes vary across geographic regions. Customers in Mexico, Canada, and Thailand often prefer different versions of the same basic product (e.g., smaller cars vs. bigger cars). These two opposing forces—pressures for cost reduction and pressures for local adaptation—lie at the heart of decisions about strategic planning and implementation.

On a general level, global organizations can choose among four main strategies to deal with these two market pressures: international, multidomestic, global, and transnational (see Exhibit 10.1).[12] Obviously, some organizations may choose a hybrid strategy and may not fit neatly into any of these categories.

INTERNATIONAL STRATEGY

With an *international strategy,* firms choose to replicate a successful home product strategy in new markets overseas, using the core competency advantage they developed for their home markets in their overseas markets. That is, they offer the same products the world over to a customer base that presumably values what the products have to offer. This strategy works best when the pressures for cost reductions are low and when the customer wants the original product. For example, Mercedes-Benz has an internationally recognized brand name and exploits this recognition throughout the world. It is under little pressure for global efficiencies (indeed, it can charge almost whatever it wants for its product) and little pressure to adapt its products to local markets. It generally believes that a Mercedes is a Mercedes, and this is what many global customers want.

MULTIDOMESTIC STRATEGY

Firms using a *multidomestic strategy* choose to focus attention on local markets and product adaptation at the expense of global efficiencies and cost reduction. These firms often view themselves as a collection of relatively independent operating subsidiaries, each focusing on a specific local market. Each subsidiary is free to customize its products, marketing campaigns, and operating techniques to meet local needs. This strategy works best when there are clear differences among local markets, when economies of scale are not critical, and when costs of coordination between the parent firm and its various foreign subsidiaries are high. British food and soft drink

Exhibit 10.1   **Organizational Strategies for Multinational Firms**

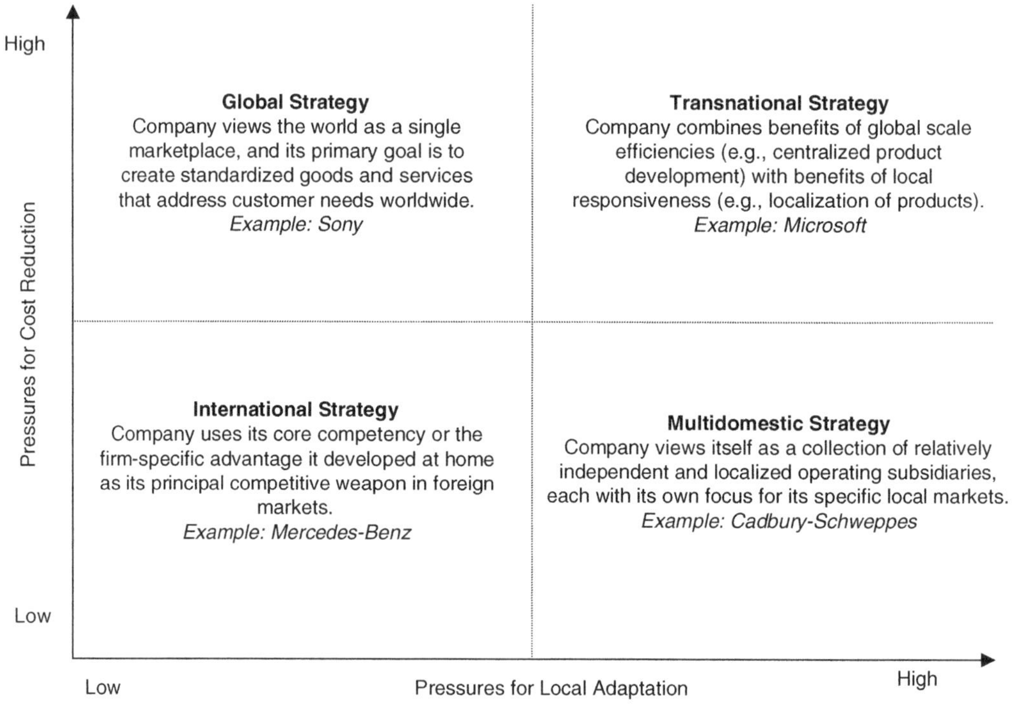

High

Global Strategy
Company views the world as a single
marketplace, and its primary goal is to
create standardized goods and services
that address customer needs worldwide.
Example: Sony

Transnational Strategy
Company combines benefits of global scale
efficiencies (e.g., centralized product
development) with benefits of local
responsiveness (e.g., localization of products).
Example: Microsoft

International Strategy
Company uses its core competency or the
firm-specific advantage it developed at home
as its principal competitive weapon in foreign
markets.
Example: Mercedes-Benz

Multidomestic Strategy
Company views itself as a collection of relatively
independent and localized operating subsidiaries,
each with its own focus for its specific local markets.
Example: Cadbury-Schweppes

Pressures for Cost Reduction

Low

Low   Pressures for Local Adaptation   High

producer Cadbury-Schweppes uses this strategy when it sells different soft drinks
and candies in the United States and the United Kingdom depending on local tastes
and preferences.

GLOBAL STRATEGY

Firms employing a *global strategy* choose to focus attention on cost reduction and
efficiencies at the expense of local adaptation. This strategy assumes that the world
is one interconnected market. Based on this assumption, firms try to create standardized goods and services that will meet world demand. A good example is the Sony
PlayStation 2, which was introduced to acclaim around the world. (Portable DVD
players, iPods, and MP3 players are also good examples of this strategy.) There is
little need to tailor these products to various local needs. Manufacturing economies
of scale are important here, however, to keep prices down and possible competitors
out of the market.

TRANSNATIONAL STRATEGY

Finally, firms employing a *transnational strategy* recognize that both cost efficiencies and local adaptation require attention. The transnational strategy tries to achieve
the best of both worlds by combining the benefits of global scale efficiencies with

the benefits of local responsiveness. Firms using this strategy try to combine operating efficiency with adaptation by globalizing some activities while localizing others. Activities that are downstream (or close to the customer) are decentralized to allow adaption to local markets. Activities that are upstream (or further away from the customer) are centralized to achieve economies of scale.[13]

An example of a transnational strategy can be seen in Microsoft, which centralizes its product development in the United States but adapts each product for local needs. It then establishes a strong market presence in various countries to both push the product and determine how the firm can better adapt its products for local consumption. As a result, Microsoft Office is a standard global product, with considerable economies of scale in both development and manufacturing. However, with a few clicks, the software is adapted to native French speakers, Spanish speakers, Japanese speakers, and so forth. Moreover, local marketing representatives can adapt their advertising strategies to reinforce the "local-ness" of the product. The strategy therefore succeeds in achieving both global efficiencies and local responsiveness and flexibility.

STRATEGIES FOR MARKET ENTRY

Once a global business strategy has been established, the next challenge facing international firms is how best to enter the targeted markets. This challenge consists of two key decisions: First, what is the best location or locations for expansion? And second, what is the best way to enter these markets? Together, these decisions will in no small way determine the success or failure of any new venture.

LOCATION DECISIONS

The first critical decision managers must make when entering foreign markets is where to locate. This is especially true for foreign direct investment (FDI) decisions. In deciding where to go, managers typically consider five factors:[14]

1. *Cost factors.* When selecting a location for expansion, global firms need to consider the costs associated with doing business in the host country. Cost factors include transport to and from the host country, labor costs, land and construction costs, cost of resources and raw materials, financing costs, taxes, and any financial incentives that are required.
2. *Demand factors.* Global firms also need to assess the demand available in the host country, including the available market size and potential growth, the existence of current customers, and the intensity of the local competition.
3. *Strategic factors.* Besides cost and demand factors, global firms need to consider characteristics of the location that may increase or decrease the chances of success. Strategic factors include the country's infrastructure, manufacturing concentration, existence of complementary industries, quality of the workforce, and proximity to buyers and suppliers.

Exhibit 10.2 **Entry Modes for Foreign Markets**

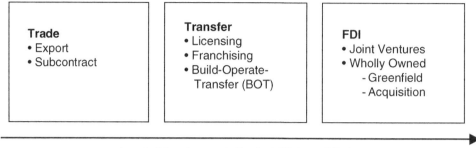

Level of Involvement, Control, Risk, and Return

4. *Regulatory and economic factors.* Regulatory and economic factors, such as the existence of industrial policies or FDI policies, may influence the ability of the firm to operate. These regulations may favor some businesses over others and limit the choices of entry modes that are available.
5. *Sociopolitical factors.* Finally, global firms need to evaluate the potential host country regarding its sociopolitical environment. Political instability, cultural differences, corruption, and other social characteristics may hinder the ability of the firm to succeed in the new market (see Chapter 5).

MODE OF ENTRY DECISIONS

Once a location has been identified, firms must decide how to enter the targeted market. Firms typically choose from among three types of *market entry mode:* (1) trade-related; (2) transfer-related; and (3) foreign direct investment–related. As shown in Exhibit 10.2, the resource commitment, organizational control, involved risk, and expected return on investment tend to increase as firms move from trade to transfer to FDI mode. We will examine each of these briefly and compare the benefits and drawbacks of each strategy.

Trade-Related Market Entry

There are two basic types of *trade-related market entry:* exporting and subcontracting. The simplest form of internationalizing a domestic business is exporting. Indeed, this remains the most common form of international business expansion. *Exporting* generally takes one of three forms:

- *Indirect exporting,* where a company sells its products to another firm that exports the products to the final market
- *Direct exporting,* where a firm exports its products directly to the foreign market
- *Intracorporate transfers,* where a firm sells its products to an affiliated firm, which then handles the export

At times, a company will contract with an *export management company (EMC)* to represent it in its exporting. EMCs act like export departments for firms and are specialized in handling all the intricacies of cross-national trading. Some larger companies—especially the major Japanese *keiretsu*—use *trading companies* to handle this responsibility. Finally, *freight forwarders* are private companies that specialize in transporting the goods, arranging customs documentation, and getting transportation services for their clients. The advantages and disadvantages of exporting compared to other modes of entry are reviewed in Exhibit 10.3.

The second trade-related mode of entry involves subcontracting. *Subcontracting* is the process by which a foreign company provides local manufacturers with raw materials, semifinished products, or technology for producing goods that will be bought back by the foreign company. Subcontracting is the preferred mode of entry when the multinational is seeking lower labor costs. Nike is a typical example. Nike provides technology and raw materials to contractors in Vietnam, China, Thailand, Indonesia, and Bangladesh, controls product quality and production processes, and pays a fee to local factories.

Transfer-Related Market Entry

Transfer-related market entry involves entering a foreign market through the transfer of assets or the rights to use assets to a second (usually local) party in exchange for royalties or other forms of payment. Examples include licensing, franchising, and build-operate-transfer (BOT) projects.

Licensing occurs when a company leases the use of its *intellectual property rights* (including intangible rights such as copyrights, patents, brand names, trademarks, technology, or manufacturing methods) to local companies for a fee. Licensing is a popular means of market entry because it involves little out-of-pocket expense for the licenser. Compensation from a licensing agreement is called *royalties,* and can be paid as a flat fee, a fixed amount per unit sold or, most commonly, a percentage of sales of the licensed product.

Franchising is a special form of licensing that allows the franchisor (the owner of the product or service) greater control over how the product is used or marketed. A franchising agreement allows a local entrepreneur (a franchisee) to operate a business under the name of the franchisor in exchange for payment of fees. The franchisor provides the trademarks, operating systems, and brand name, as well as continuous services such as advertising, training, and quality assurance programs. The best examples of franchising are the fast-food restaurants that are currently spreading around the world. Fees are usually paid as a fixed payment plus a royalty on sales.

Build-operate-transfer (BOT) is a type of *turnkey project,* where one company designs, builds, and equips an entire factory or production system and then turns it over to the purchaser for a predetermined price. A BOT project occurs when a firm builds a facility, operates it for some time, and then transfers ownership of the facility to another party. The BOT model is particularly popular in massive construction projects where local firms or local governments want to establish an industry but lack either the capital or the know-how to succeed in the short run. This approach

Exhibit 10.3

Strategies for Market Entry

Strategies	Best Used When Firm Wants	Cautions or Limitations on Use
Exporting	Low financial exposure	Vulnerable to tariffs and nontariff barriers
	Gradual market entry	Logistical complexities
	Knowledge about local markets	Potential conflicts with distributors
	Avoidance of foreign investment restrictions	
Subcontracting	Low financial risk	Reduced control over quality, delivery schedules, and so on
	Minimal investment in manufacturing	Reduced learning potential
		Potential public relations problems if contractor cuts corners
Licensing	Low financial risk	Limited market opportunities
	Inexpensive way to assess market potential	Dependence on licensee
	Avoidance of tariffs and restrictions on foreign investment	Potential conflicts with licensee
	Licensee to provide local market knowledge	Possibility of creating future competitor
Franchising	Low financial risk	Limits market opportunities and profits
	Inexpensive way to assess market potential	Dependence on franchisee
	Avoidance of tariffs and restrictions on foreign investment	Potential conflicts with franchisee
	More control than licensing	Possibility of creating future competitor
	Franchisee to provide local market knowledge	
Build-operate-transfer	Firm's limited resources focused on its area of expertise	Risk of cost overruns
	Avoidance of long-term operating costs	Construction delays with suppliers and contractors
Foreign direct investment	High potential profit	High financial investments
	Control over operations	High exposure to political risk
	Knowledge of local markets	Vulnerable to restrictions on foreign investment
	Avoidance of tariffs and nontariff barriers	Increased managerial complexity

Sources: Ricky Griffin and Michael Pustay, *International Business,* 4th ed. (Upper Saddle River, NJ: Prentice-Hall, 2005); Oded Shenkar and Yadong Luo, *International Business* (New York: Wiley, 2004).

allows the contractor of the BOT to regain its investment and allows the purchaser to learn how the facility operates over time.

Foreign Direct Investment Market Entry

Finally, *foreign direct investment* (FDI) occurs when a firm wants to secure an ownership stake in a foreign enterprise. Ownership control is important when firms need to closely coordinate overseas operations with headquarters activities or when firms seek to fully exploit the economic potential of proprietary technology, manufacturing expertise, or some other intellectual property right. FDI can take one of two forms: joint ventures and wholly owned subsidiaries.

A *joint venture* is collaboration between two firms who intend to work together to create a jointly owned enterprise that promotes their mutual interest. (Joint ventures are discussed in Chapter 11.) By contrast, a *wholly owned subsidiary* is an entry mode in which the foreign country owns 100 percent of the new entity in a foreign country. Companies using this entry mode usually follow two strategies. A *greenfield strategy* is a form of investment in which a company designs and builds a new factory from scratch, starting with nothing but a "green field." An *acquisition strategy* (also known as *brownfield strategy)* is a form of foreign direct investment in which a company acquires an existing factory or facility in a foreign country and then modernizes or rebuilds the facility for a new business.

When a factory is built using these strategies and where little transformation of the product is undertaken (e.g., only final assembly of parts), it is referred to as a *screwdriver plant*. Screwdriver plants, such as those often used in Mexico's *maquiladora* facilities, are often created as a means to avoid paying tariffs by putting the finishing touches on completed products and then exporting them as being made in the country where the final assembly was performed (see Chapter 6).

Entry Mode Decision Factors

A decision about the best mode of entry into foreign markets obviously depends on the targeted country, the products, and the philosophy and strategy of the firm. Several key factors enter this decision:

• *Ownership advantages.* A key question in starting any new venture is whether a company is better off owning the new venture or at least owning the rights to the product. If a product has proprietary technology or a widely recognized brand name, ownership has clear advantages. For example, McDonald's offers to sell its clearly recognizable brand name and golden arches trademark to franchisees throughout the world in exchange for lucrative fees. On the other hand, if the product is essentially a commodity (e.g., memory chips), these advantages may disappear.

• *Location advantages.* The location decision focuses on the relative advantages of making the product in a company's home country and exporting it to the new market or making it in the host country. If home country manufacturing is more advantageous, then the firm will likely export the finished product to the new market. If local production is better, the company will likely license the technology and invest in local facilities to oversee quality of production.

• *Internalization advantages.* The question of internalization is whether a firm should manufacture the product itself or join forces with local firms. The transaction costs are critical. *Transaction costs* include costs of negotiating, monitoring, and enforcing the agreement between potential partners. If such costs are high, a firm will likely rely on FDI or a joint venture for purposes of market entry, as Toyota does with FDI. On the other hand, if transaction costs are low, firms will likely use franchising, licensing, or contract manufacturing, as McDonald's does.

• *Other factors.* Other factors included in the decision to select an entry mode include a firm's need to control sensitive technologies, availability of resources, the firm's overall global business strategy, local policies that impede the firm's entrance as a wholly owned subsidiary, and cultural distance between home and host country. These issues were discussed in previous chapters.

DOING BUSINESS IN MEXICO: INSIDE THE MEXICAN *GRUPO*

With these considerations on competitive strategies and market entry modes in mind, we turn now to look at the culture and business practices of Mexico as an example of how companies can apply global strategies to succeed in local cultures.[15] In recent years, Mexico has become a location of choice for companies interested in both offshore manufacturing and overseas sales. However, many of these ventures have failed due to a lack of genuine understanding of the local realities or, worse, a presumption about local realities that proved to be incorrect. We therefore ask the question, What does it take to succeed in the Mexican business environment?

THE MEXICAN BUSINESS ENVIRONMENT

Business in Mexico is concentrated in its three largest cities: Mexico City, Monterrey, and Guadalajara. Of these three, Mexico City stands out with nearly 25 percent of the country's population, many of its major firms, and most of its key government offices. Monterrey is Mexico's principal industrial city and is headquarters to many major firms. Guadalajara is the commercial and industrial center of the western coastal region of Mexico. Its business community is somewhat more conservative and is neither as sophisticated as that of Mexico City nor as aggressive as that of Monterrey. While there are powerful individuals and large corporations in Guadalajara, their influence and power are generally less than is found in Monterrey or Mexico City.

As Mexico industrialized throughout the twentieth century, government policy routinely created local monopolies and insulated domestic producers from foreign competition. This led to highly inefficient production methods, overstaffed operations, and an uncaring approach to quality control or product delivery schedules. As a result, Mexican products developed a reputation for poor quality, and many companies could not be relied upon to deliver on their promises or contracts.

Today, however, Mexican industry is being forced to improve its competitive position to compete in the global economy. As a result, Mexico has been increasingly recognized for producing high-quality products—most notably in the fields of electronics and automobiles. Indeed, some of the highest-rated U.S. cars in terms of quality are made in Mexico. Likewise, Japan and Germany manufacture large numbers of equally high-quality cars in Mexico for export and domestic consumption. (Mexico is the exclusive producer of both the Volkswagen Beetle and the Chrysler PT Cruiser.)

Mexico's competitive strength is in its low-priced workforce and rising manufacturing quality. Individual worker productivity varies widely throughout Mexico. In many key industrial clusters, the country has developed a level of labor productivity that compares favorably with that of many heavily industrialized countries. In recent years, the Mexican government has been active in raising the level of productivity of the Mexican workforce, including the widespread use of government-sponsored training programs and reinvestment programs.

The Mexican economy is also increasingly open to foreign direct investment. Currently, 73 percent of its economy is open to 100 percent foreign ownership, without prior governmental approval. This represents a reversal of decades of some of the strictest indigenization laws (laws requiring local ownership of companies) in the world. Government approval is still required, however, in certain strategic industries (e.g., petroleum) or where the investment exceeds $100 million. Mexico remains concerned about being economically (or even politically) absorbed into the wealthy and powerful U.S. economy to the north. Indeed, there is an old Mexican saying: "Poor Mexico: So far from God and so near the United States." National sovereignty remains a critical issue.

For those doing business in Mexico, proper contacts with various government departments can be vital for success. Like their U.S. counterparts, most Mexican businesspeople tend to be somewhat scornful of the effectiveness of political officials in general and often claim that they want little to do with them. However, in Mexico (as elsewhere) when a cabinet official, governor, or mayor launches a new program, those same businesspeople often race to see who can be first on the scene to lend a hand and participate in the program. There is a reason for this. No political office in the United States can compare in terms of raw power to that wielded by government officials in Mexico. Top government officials preside as if over a fiefdom, and their decisions can have a significant impact on any business. Official contacts are of tremendous help to any business endeavor. Another benefit is that one's credibility within the business community increases proportionally to the depth and breadth of one's access to government officials.

In recent years, the Mexican government has taken significant steps to crack down on bribery and corruption at all levels. This is not to say major bribery no longer exists, but it is much more subtle and is less likely to involve visitors from other countries. The tradition of bribery, or *mordida* (the bite), predates the Mexican Republic, and one may still be asked for a "contribution" from time to time. Small-scale bribery often involves minor officials that regularly deal with foreign businesspersons or tourists who expect a small cash payment in return for their providing a service (e.g., extending a tourist card or visa). Paying the *mordida* is straightforward but discreet.

In the United States, membership in trade or business associations offers many advantages, including opportunities for networking and career advancement. The same holds true for Mexico. In fact, membership in trade associations may be even more essential in Mexico, where the value of personal relations in business is critical. In Mexican culture, where connections within an industrial sector can mean the difference between success and failure, trade associations provide essential networking opportunities and forums for deepening business relationships into friendships. The most important business association for U.S. businesspersons in Mexico is the American Chamber of Commerce. The chamber boasts more than 2,500 member companies and actually has more Mexican company members than American.

The Mexican chambers of commerce are also powerful organizations and offer fertile hunting ground for contacts. Mexican law has long mandated that every business must belong to one of the officially sanctioned chambers of commerce. There are dozens of specialized chambers, including the two principal ones: Canacintra (Chamber of Industry) and Canaco (Chamber of Commerce). Canacintra represents eleven major industrial manufacturing sectors and has more than 86,000 members. Canaco represents mostly retail merchants and the tourism industry, and in Mexico City alone has more than 50,000 members. The national presidents of these chambers have direct access to the Mexican president, the cabinet, and many high-level officials.

MEXICAN CULTURE AND SOCIAL PATTERNS

Anthropologists tend to describe the Mexican culture as being collectivistic, hierarchical, polychronic, paternalistic, group-centered, security-oriented, somewhat formal, and at times fatalistic.[16] This certainly does not apply to all Mexicans; indeed, it doesn't even recognize that Mexico is a multicultural society with both European and native influences. Even so, foreign visitors frequently observe that Mexicans will at times go to great lengths to protect their dignity, uphold their honor, and maintain their good name (see Exhibit 10.4). The uniqueness of the individual is honored in Mexico, and people are judged on their individual achievements, demeanor, trustworthiness, and character. Personal respect is a very important element in any relationship. Even a relatively insignificant comment or action can be interpreted in a negative or deprecating manner and can destroy the trust between two people.

Mexican business culture operates under a strict caste system. Most business is conducted between equals, and titles and social position are important. As a result, it is unlikely that a Mexican company president would meet with a midlevel representative of another firm, even an important foreign firm. Thus, smart international companies send presidents to meet presidents, vice presidents to meet vice presidents, and so forth. In addition, a personal introduction through a mutual friend is always helpful, as it is in many parts of the world.

Mexicans are polite in formal business situations but become more relaxed once the parties have established their relative positions within the hierarchy and begin to get to know each other. For this reason, it is crucial for global managers to determine

Exhibit 10.4

Cultural Trends in the United States and Mexico

U.S. Cultural Trends	Mexican Cultural Trends
Individualistic	Collectivistic
Egalitarian	Hierarchical
Mastery	Harmony
Monochronic	Polychronic
Risk-tolerant	Risk-averse
Strong competitive spirit	Strong cooperative spirit
Personal responsibility important	Group or family responsibility important
Future orientation	Past and present orientation
Decisions typically based on facts	Decisions often based on intuition and ideas
Emphasis on the practical	Emphasis on the artistic
Change seen as positive	Change often viewed with concern
Strong belief in self-help and initiative	Belief in group or family support
Heavily work-oriented	Emphasis on balance of work and leisure
Informal working style	Formal working style
Strong materialism	Moderate materialism

and acknowledge the status of the person they are dealing with when preparing for a face-to-face meeting, as well as to convey their own position. People are also evaluated on their outward displays, their personal image (*imagen*), so they should dress well. In Mexico, formality rules.

ORGANIZATION AND MANAGEMENT IN MEXICO

A typical Mexican business group (or *grupo*) consists of several highly diverse companies that operate in a climate of familial ties, mutual trust, and overall cooperation. *Grupos* are typically led by strong, powerful CEOs who are often also the principal stockholders. Member companies typically share operating philosophies, channels of distribution, marketing intelligence, and efficiencies of scale, even though they are legally separate entities.

Foreign executives observe that U.S. and Mexican managers frequently approach business matters in very different ways. Many of these differences are based on contrasting beliefs concerning what constitutes good management.[17] For starters, consider the following:

• Many Mexican managers see U.S. managers as being too direct, too impatient, and too reticent to accept blame. On the other hand, many U.S. managers see Mexican managers as being too polite, too indecisive, and too slow to act.

• Many Americans seek rational, linear decisions based on concrete and business-related evidence. By contrast, many Mexican managers use a more nonlinear approach, considering other issues (e.g., personal relationships, traditions, and personal loyalties) and reaching decisions through extended discussions with various parties.

• Many Americans see no problem in criticizing others in public or placing blame or responsibility for failure on specific individuals. By contrast, many Mexicans prefer to avoid placing blame and instead focus on the positive aspects of individual behavior or performance.

• Many Mexicans value strong interpersonal relationships, human dignity, and the full enjoyment of life. There is a strong belief in the importance of achieving a suitable balance between home life and work life. By contrast, many Americans seem to value aggressively attacking problems, egalitarian conduct, and accomplishing tasks at almost any price. Working long hours is assumed and, for many, a rich family life can be a detriment to career success.

• Mexican businesspersons typically negotiate contracts and deals in restaurants, hotels, conference rooms, or other neutral territory. Rarely will a Mexican company conduct extensive negotiations at its own place of business.

Foreign observers also suggest that management in Mexico tends to be somewhat more autocratic than is typically found in the United States. However, while a manager in Mexico must be respected by his or her subordinates for being tough and decisive, he or she must also be seen as *simpático*, or understanding. Managers in Mexico tend to exhibit a strong sense of paternalism, a caring for the personal side of their employees that is often absent and at times even resented north of the border. They must act like a *patron* and treat their subordinates like an extended family, as Japanese managers do. Along with this, managers must also treat their employees with a strong sense of respect; personal slights frequently bring strong resentment. Mexican workers often need more communication, relationship building, and reassurance than employees in the United States.

Networking is very important in Mexico. Cultivating personal relationships with those who may be in a position to help you is crucial to successful business in Mexico. These relationships are typically built on complex personal ties rather than on legal contracts as is typical in the United States. Being accepted as part of a network also entails reciprocity. This requires you to use your own contacts and connections (called *palancas*) to help others when called upon for assistance. This is similar to the Chinese concept of *guanxi,* which was discussed in Chapter 7. Your success depends in part on whom you know. As part of this relationship building, gifts are traditionally exchanged during formal ceremonies, especially during official visits by governmental authorities. For Mexicans, typical gifts include regional handcrafts, books, or pieces of art.

A key issue for success in managing in Mexico is flexibility. Recognizing cultural norms, particularly the importance of holidays and festivals, is essential. In addition, many Mexican companies take a more paternalistic approach in their relations with their employees. This often means providing services that are not traditionally considered the responsibility of employers in the United States. For example, many Mexican employees expect the company to provide transportation to the work site. This is often accomplished by subcontracting privately owned buses to travel through the neighborhoods of the employees and gather the workers each morning. Many firms also provide cafeterias and feed their employees lunch each day. These provisions are particularly important at the U.S.-Mexico border in the *maquiladoras,* where the influx of workers has far exceeded the capacity of the supporting infrastructure.

Mexican firms are characterized by strong centralized decision making. While the necessity to decentralize many functions and responsibilities is recognized, it is clearly understood that the boss has the final say. Today, particularly in the larger firms, a new generation of younger and highly educated managers is beginning to gain prominence. This new generation is beginning to change corporate cultures to be more receptive to decentralization of decision making.

In any culture, the use of time can tell us a great deal about how organizations (and societies) work. This is clearly true in Mexico. Time is frequently used intentionally to demonstrate who is more important. Making someone wait shows power, prestige, and status. At the same time, managers must be careful not to offend their counterparts and thereby risk losing business.

Another aspect of time is the sense of urgency with which business is done. Mexico is famous for the concept of *mañana*. The idea here is that there is always another day to complete today's work. While putting things off is commonplace, it would be incorrect to equate this phenomenon with laziness or an unprofessional work attitude. Rather, it represents a different approach to doing business—one that seeks to prioritize conflicting requirements. Mexicans believe that there are other priorities in life than just work and that conditions often conspire to prevent the realization of plans as envisioned. Rather than get unduly stressed about multiple and often conflicting demands, they often take a more relaxed attitude, assuming that things will eventually get done. This is a hard concept for many Americans, Asians, and Europeans to comprehend. Foreigners must understand that when Mexicans promise something will be done by a certain time or date, they are often saying this to please the person they are dealing with rather that giving an straightforward appraisal of when the work will be done. In Mexico, unlike in many other countries, such promises are not considered a contract or firm obligation. Time commitments are more likely to be made out of politeness and the need for having a ballpark idea of when the work will be completed. Therefore, foreigners should not expect that work will actually be finished when promised and should plan accordingly.

In summary, doing business in Mexico requires not just an understanding of the local culture but a genuine willingness to adapt to customs and patterns of behavior that many visitors are not used to. Without this sensitivity, business strategies to enter the Mexican market will likely be far less successful. The prudent manager adapts, and builds the business based on true partnership.

KEY TERMS

acquisition strategy
brownfield strategy
build-operate-transfer (BOT)
direct exporting
exporting

export management company
  (EMC)
foreign direct investment
franchising
freight forwarder

(continued)

global strategy
greenfield strategy
grupo
hard discounter
indirect exporting
intellectual property rights
international strategy
intracorporate transfers
joint venture
licensing
market entry mode
multidomestic strategy

royalties
screwdriver plant
strategy
subcontracting
trade-related market entry
trading company
transaction costs
transfer-related market entry
transnational strategy
turnkey project
wholly owned subsidiary

GLOBAL MANAGER'S WORKBOOK 10.1: MEXICAN COKE

In Lawrenceville, Georgia, just thirty miles from the world headquarters of Atlanta-based Coca-Cola Company, Las Tarascas Latino Supermarket sells Coca-Cola made and bottled in Mexico.[18] They also sell Coke made in the United States at a lower price, but few customers buy it. Why? Local customers from both the Anglo and Latino communities give the same answer: Mexican Coke tastes better. Mexican Coke is made from Coca-Cola's original formula using cane sugar. According to customers, cane sugar produces a sweeter, cleaner flavor than the high-fructose corn syrup in the American version. While cane sugar is plentiful and inexpensive in Mexico, corn syrup is cheaper in the United States. As a result of this taste preference, Mexican Coke has increased its customer base in several regions along the U.S.-Mexican border, especially among baby boomers who can recall when their cola was made with cane sugar before rising costs drove U.S. bottlers to switch to corn syrup in the 1980s.

So what is Coca-Cola doing about this? The global soft drink giant and its bottlers are quietly trying to block the shipment of Mexican Coke across the border. Why? Because the regional bottlers in the United States do not profit from its import or sale. Mexican Coke is produced by independent Mexican bottlers and then brought across the border and distributed in the United States by third-party distributors and retailers. "We believe that those territory rights belong to the rightful bottlers," said a Coke spokesperson.[19] An industry analyst added that Coke might also want to quell any potential demand for a formula that would cost more to produce. The irony here is that many U.S. bottlers make a cane sugar Coke each year for Passover, since many Jewish customers don't eat or drink corn products during the holiday. Even so, the company said it has no plans to begin producing for a wider market.

Coca-Cola is in a difficult position. Its bottlers have contracts guaranteeing them exclusive rights to make and sell Coke within their regions. However, the company can do little beyond trying to discourage the imports, because Mexican bottlers legally produce the drink across the border and third-party distributors and retailers who bring the Mexican Coke to market are not bound by contracts between Coke and its U.S. bottlers. Meanwhile, more and more Americans are eager to buy the cola from south of the border.

Based on what you have read, consider the following questions:

1. Is Coca-Cola using an international, multidomestic, global, or transnational strategy? Is this the most appropriate strategy for them to use? Why or why not?
2. Coca-Cola presumably wants to make as much money as it can from the sale and distribution of its cola. In doing so, however, it must balance the needs of its U.S. regional bottlers and its Mexican bottlers. What would you recommend they do now to help resolve this strategic conflict?
3. The U.S. regional bottlers presumably want as much market share and cola sales in their regions as they can get. What would you recommend they do now as their next strategic move?
4. The Mexican producer presumably wants as much market share and cola sales in the United States as it can get. At the same time, however, it does not want to alienate Coca-Cola, which can cancel its Mexican production rights. What would you recommend they do now as their next strategic move?

GLOBAL MANAGER'S WORKBOOK 10.2: EMBRAER

People often associate Brazil with World Cup soccer and beautiful sunny beaches, but not commercial aircraft manufacturing. But Brazil is one of the world's leading manufacturers of small commercial jets, with offices in Australia, China, France, Singapore, and the United States and an order backlog totaling $11 billion. The company that achieved this status is Embraer (Empresa Brasileira de Aeronáutica S.A.). While Embraer may not be a household word in many parts of the world, most airline passengers in North and South America, Europe, and much of Asia have probably flown on one of their planes at one time or another. In the United States, for example, Embraer, along with Canadian rival Bombardier, jointly controls most of the market for regional jets.

Embraer was established in 1969 by the Brazilian government to provide the country with its own aircraft-manufacturing capability. But government sponsorship did not ensure success, and by 1994 the company had lost more than $300 million. Privatization was the only way to avoid bankruptcy. Since then, Embraer has transformed itself from a near-bankrupt state-run enterprise into one of Brazil's leading export companies and the world's fourth largest aircraft manufacturer after Airbus, Boeing, and Bombardier. This impressive turnaround is credited to its smart strategic positioning. While Airbus and Boeing invested heavily in larger aircraft, Embraer focused on the small commercial jet market, initially targeting regional carriers, such as American Eagle, United Express, Luxair, and British Midland. These regional jets (ERJ 135, 140, and 145 series) seated between thirty and fifty passengers.

But beginning in 1999, Embraer launched a new and larger family of commercial jet aircraft with seating capacities ranging from seventy to one hundred passengers

(Embraer 175, 190, and 195 series). Advanced engineering, superior operating efficiency, spacious cabins, and competitive prices characterize the newer planes. This new series placed the Brazilian company in a head-to-head competition with both Airbus's A318 and Boeing's 717 (formerly the DC9) for mainline carriers such as Air Canada, US Airways, Jet Blue, Finnair, and Continental. As Mauricio Botelho, Embraer's president and the chief architect of its turnaround, explained,

> Some of the mainline carriers are focused on the 100-seater, while the regional airliners are focused on the 70-seaters. What is interesting is the expansion of the regional airlines and downsizing of the mainline carriers. [The Embraer 190 and 195] are perfect for this market. They are not regional jets; they are big aircraft. Look at it in terms of the comfort they provide, the seating, the cabin height, the baggage compartment, and the performance. This is much more compatible with mainline airline requirements than what is known today as a regional jet. When you see the regional airlines growing their fleets to 70-seat aircraft and the major carriers coming down to 100-seat aircraft, and the level of comfort expected by passengers, this is the perfect aircraft.[20]

As one of Brazil's leading export companies, Embraer has as its principal business strategy the building of aircraft in Brazil for export to other countries. In this way, Embraer maintains tight control over both technology and quality control. In late 2002, however, the company decided to increase its international presence by building a factory in China. To accomplish this, Embraer committed $25 million and formed a joint venture with the state-run China Aviation Industry Corporation II, or AVIC II. The new joint venture, Harbin Embraer Aircraft Industry, is controlled by Embraer, which holds a 51 percent stake in the new company, with the remaining 49 percent held by AVIC II. Chinese leaders were quick to endorse the new venture. Guan Dongyuan observed, "Embraer sees the strengthening of air transportation in China as a key component of the country's development, and the Harbin assembly line is a clear sign of our long-term commitment to the progress of the Chinese aeronautical industry. . . . The establishment of the Harbin Embraer facility places Embraer in a privileged position to serve Chinese operator customers."[21]

Harbin Embraer began production in 2003, producing one ERJ 145 aircraft per month, but with plans to double production shortly. The company believes that the Chinese aviation market will grow substantially and has a capacity to absorb about three hundred aircraft in the coming ten years. Its 258,000-square-foot production facility in Harbin employs 220 Chinese employees; only 15 Brazilians were expatriated to China to work on the venture.[22] Eventually, Harbin Embraer plans to manufacture the larger 170/190 series of jet aircraft.

The joint venture in China was a landmark for Embraer—its first offshore manufacturing facility. But company president Botelho said the company has no interest in establishing additional joint ventures in Asia. "The joint venture model only applies to China. We will continue to export Brazilian-made aircraft to the other countries in Asia," he noted.[23] Even so, offshore facilities will be built elsewhere. In 2003, Embraer formed an alliance with Lockheed Martin of the United States to build next-generation surveillance planes for the U.S. Army. Then, in August 2004, Embraer closed a deal to sell ERJ 145 jets to the U.S. military for use in battle camps. The initial contract is worth $879 million but may eventually reach $7 billion. As part of the contract, Embraer announced plans to construct a major new facility in Jacksonville, Florida, to manufacture the aircraft.

Based on what you have learned, answer the following questions:

1. What business strategy does Embraer follow? Do you agree with this strategy? Why or why not?
2. Traditionally, Embraer has relied on exports from Brazil as a mode of entry into foreign markets. However, when entering the Chinese market the company chose to use a joint venture. Why do you believe it decided to establish a joint venture in China rather than simply exporting planes from Brazil? What are the advantages and disadvantages of each? Why do you believe Embraer chose not go solo and establish an Embraer subsidiary in China?
3. Embraer's Mauricio Botelho said the joint-venture model would apply exclusively to China; other Asian aircraft markets would be served from Brazil. What is the logic behind this statement? What makes China different from other Asian markets?
4. In view of the technological and manufacturing strength of the U.S. aircraft industry, why do you think the U.S. military contracted to buy planes from a Brazilian firm?
5. As a strategy consultant to Embraer, where would you advise Embraer to move next? Explain your choice.

NOTES

1. Jack Ewing, "The Next Wal-Mart," *Business Week,* April 26, 2004, p. 60.
2. Geri Smith, "War of the Superstores," *Business Week,* September 23, 2002, p. 60.
3. Ibid.
4. W. Ocasio, "Towards an Attention-based View of the Firm," *Strategic Management Journal* 18, no. 6 (1997): 187.
5. Susan Schneider and Jean-Louis Barsoux, *Managing Across Cultures,* 2nd ed. (London: Prentice Hall, 2003).
6. "How Big Can It Grow?" *Economist,* April 17, 2004, p. 67.
7. Charles Rarick, "Wal-Mart or Carrefour?" in *Cases and Exercises in International Business,* ed. Charles Rarick (Upper Saddle River, NJ: Prentice Hall, 2002).
8. "A Hyper Market," *Economist,* April 7, 2004, p. 68.
9. Ginny Parker, "French Retailer Carrefour May Pay a Price for Going Solo in Japan," *Wall Street Journal,* October 13, 2004, p. A14.
10. Ewing, "The Next Wal-Mart."
11. David Thomas, *Essentials of International Management: A Cross-Cultural Perspective* (Thousand Oaks, CA: Sage, 2002), p. 189.
12. Sumantra Ghoshal and Natin Nohria, "Horses for Courses: Organizational Forms for Multinational Corporations," *Sloan Management Review* (Winter 1993): 27–31.
13. Gregory Dess, G.T. Lumpkin, and Marilyn Taylor, *Strategic Management: Creating Competitive Advantages* (New York: McGraw-Hill, 2005).
14. Oded Shenkar and Yadong Luo, *International Business* (New York: Wiley, 2004).

15. The authors are indebted to Wendy Gamboa and Martha Larragoity for their research assistance on this section.

16. Christopher Engholm and Scott Grimes, *Doing Business in Mexico* (Upper Saddle River, NJ: Prentice Hall, 1997); Eva Kras, *Management in Two Cultures: Bridging the Gap Between United States and Mexican Managers* (Yarmouth, ME: Intercultural, 1989).

17. Engholm and Grimes, *Doing Business in Mexico*.

18. Louise Chu, "For Many Immigrants, Only Mexican Coke Can Quench," *Register-Guard,* November 6, 2004, p. B5.

19. Ibid.

20. Paul Lewis, "Face the Facts with . . . Mauricio Botelho," *Flight Daily News,* June 15, 2003, p. 36.

21. "Embraer Participates in the 2004 China Air Show," www.embraer.com, November 12, 2004, p. 1.

22. "Embraer Abre Fábrica na China, Mas Descarta Novas Parcerias na Ásia" (Embraer Opens New Factory in China, But Discards New Partnerships in Asia), *Exame,* December, 2, 2002, http://portalexame.abril.com.br/empresas/conteudo_19158.shtml.

23. Ibid.

11 | Building Global Strategic Alliances

KOREAN FIRMS CAPITALIZE ON STRATEGIC ALLIANCES

Beginning in the early 1970s and continuing through the mid-1990s, Korea was routinely mentioned as a textbook example of an economic miracle. Aggressive Korean companies captured an increasingly larger share of key global markets including automobiles, electronics, semiconductors, shipbuilding, construction, and textiles. With a highly motivated and disciplined workforce, borrowed technology, government funding, corporate entrepreneurial talent, and protected local markets, Korean industry thrived. Then, in 1997, the bottom fell out of the Korean financial markets, as it did in several other Asian countries, and a decade of economic progress disappeared overnight.

To regain their status as key players in the global economy, Korean companies needed a new approach to strategic management, particularly as it related to technology. If they were going to come back, their strategic partners would again play an important, albeit somewhat different, role. Companies such as Samsung Electronics and Hyundai Motors had always used strategic partners. Indeed, this is how both companies initially gained the technologies necessary to enter global markets. In the past, however, their international partners held the upper hand and frequently sold the Koreans dated technologies. The Koreans then used this knowledge to manufacture inexpensive products for low-end markets.

But by the beginning of the twenty-first century, as Korea was climbing out of its financial crisis, the world of business had changed. The new global markets the companies now faced were not as forgiving as those in the past. Korea could no longer compete with countries such as China at the low end of the market. Nor could Korea retain its protected local markets. Now Korean companies would have to compete based on technological sophistication (not cost), and for this they would need to leapfrog the competition. To succeed, they needed to redefine their roles in their relationships with their strategic partners from that of subordinates to that of equal partners. The turnaround began in earnest around 2000.

223

In the case of Hyundai Motor Company, the company capitalized on its alliance first with DaimlerChrysler to build increasingly technologically sophisticated cars for the global marketplace.[1] Four key strategies were used. First, Hyundai purchased competitor Kia Motors to increase its size and scope in the marketplace and bargaining position with suppliers. Then, learning from its German partner, Hyundai focused relentlessly on improving product quality. At the same time, it opened design studios and research centers in the United States, Europe, and Japan and invested more than $5 billion in developing new models. Finally, it began opening new production facilities overseas (including in the United States) with a targeted global output of 5 million cars by 2010. As a result of these efforts, Hyundai Motors was recognized in 2004 in the J.D. Powers customer satisfaction survey for making some of the best-quality cars sold in the U.S. market.

In the case of Samsung Electronics, the story was much the same. Samsung capitalized on its alliances with Sumitomo Chemical, Dell Computer, Microsoft, Nokia, T-Mobile, and Sprint PCS and distribution alliances with Best Buy and Circuit City to develop and sell products for higher-end markets.[2] Samsung made extensive use of vertical integration in developing and capitalizing on four key technologies: semiconductors, telecommunications, digital appliances, and digital media. As a result, today Samsung Electronics is a global leader in a wide variety of forward-looking technology-based industries, including cell phones, plasma and LCD displays, flash memories, DRAMs, MP3 players, and DVD players. In past years, Samsung acquired technology from its strategic partners; now it sells its own technologies to these same partners.

In both cases, the Korean firms learned from their strategic partners and went on to become equal if not superior partners in the alliance. Today, both companies are widely respected for their product innovation, locally developed technologies, and manufacturing quality. For such companies, the future looks bright.

TYPES OF GLOBAL STRATEGIC ALLIANCES

Cooperation between firms doing business in the global arena can take many forms, including cross licensing of proprietary technology, sharing production facilities, joint R and D projects, and marketing of each other's products under joint distribution agreements. These forms of cooperation are called strategic alliances. A *global strategic alliance* is a business arrangement through which two or more firms agree to cooperate for their mutual benefit in global markets. Global strategic alliances can be divided into two types: equity alliances and nonequity alliances.

EQUITY ALLIANCES

Equity alliances (also called equity partnerships) are agreements between two or more firms where the parties have a financial stake and assume an ownership interest in the success of the venture. Nonequity ventures require no such ownership investment. Equity alliances come in two forms: international joint ventures and international mergers or acquisitions, as illustrated in Exhibit 11.1.

Exhibit 11.1 **Types of Global Strategic Alliances**

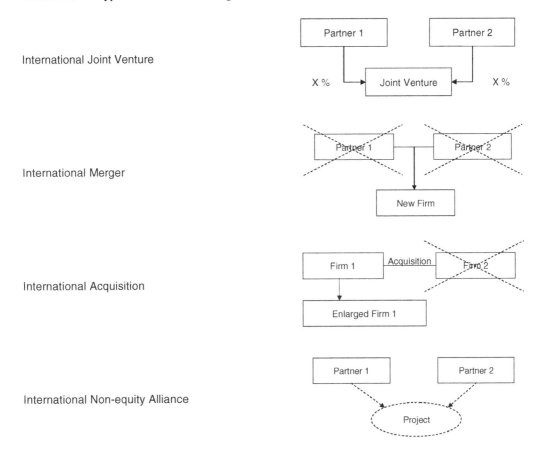

International Joint Venture

An *international joint venture (IJV)* occurs when two independent companies join forces and create a separate legal organizational entity (i.e., a new company) representing the partial holdings of the parent firms. Such ventures are subject to joint control by the parent firms. Since international joint ventures are legal entities, they must have their own management and boards of directors. Because of this, such alliances are typically used in international business only when both partners seek a long-term and stable business relationship. Otherwise, a more casual strategic alliance, such as a nonequity alliance, is usually preferred. A good example of an international joint venture can be seen in the partnership between Samsung Electronics and Corning Glass to produce specialty glass for the Korean television market. This partnership has proven to be successful for more than thirty years, largely because both parties trust, nurture, and coordinate the venture for the benefit of both parent companies.

International Merger or Acquisition

A second form of equity alliance occurs when two firms agree to merge to create a new, larger, and they hope more competitive global firm or when one firm acquires another for the same purpose. As the trend toward globalization continues, competitive pressures to become both large and lean have pushed many companies such as Daimler Benz and Chrysler Corporation (now DaimlerChrysler) and Pfizer and Warner Lambert (now Pfizer) to merge. The new companies hope to be in a better position to compete worldwide but often suffer from integration problems resulting from trying to merge two distinct corporate cultures. The turbulent case of the DaimlerChrysler merger is a case in point.

Nonequity Alliances

A *nonequity alliance* is an investment vehicle used by two or more firms when responsibilities and profits are assigned to each party according to a contract. No new firm is created. Each party enters the alliance as a separate legal entity and bears its own liabilities. This arrangement provides all parties with considerable freedom to structure their assets, organize their production processes, and manage their operations. Nonequity alliances can take many different forms, including the following:[3]

• *Exploration consortium.* An *exploration consortium* is an alliance formed by two or more companies to share exploration and development costs for locating and extracting natural resources that have commercial application. Most oil and gas exploration is done in this way in order to spread huge development costs among several companies.

• *R&D consortium.* An *R&D consortium* is formed when two or more entities share research and development costs but then go their separate ways in applying or marketing the benefits of the consortium. For example, Microsoft teamed up with China's Qinghua University to develop Chinese-based software technologies. After these technologies were developed, each went its own way in developing applications software based on the new technology.

• *Coproduction agreement.* A *coproduction agreement* is an agreement between two or more companies to share production expenses for a major manufacturing project. Boeing formed such an alliance with Mitsubishi Heavy Industries and Fuji Heavy Industries to help coproduce its new 7E7 commercial jetliner.

• *Coservice agreement.* A *coservice agreement* is an agreement between companies to share services that benefit both parties. Delta Air Lines and Air France, for example, share ticketing, customer service, and frequent flyer programs in a partnership that is mutually advantageous.

• *Comarketing agreement.* A *comarketing agreement* is an agreement to share marketing efforts. In one such agreement, American-based Praxair agreed to share its U.S. distribution channels in exchange for access to German-based Merck KGA's distribution channels in Europe and Asia.

• *Comanagement agreement.* A *comanagement agreement* is an agreement to share management expertise in such areas as production management, supply-chain management, employee training and development, and information systems development. This type of agreement is frequently seen between small local companies in developing countries and the major Japanese trading companies. While the trading companies want access to the local economies, the local firms often want improved management systems to help them gain access to major markets such as those in Japan.

• *Long-term supply agreement.* A *long-term supply agreement* is one company's agreement to supply another company on a long-term basis in exchange for information updates on changing products and emerging technologies. IKEA, for example, provides its major suppliers with product updates and information on changing consumer trends in exchange for a long-term commitment to work with the company to stay ahead of the competition.

ORGANIZING GLOBAL STRATEGIC ALLIANCES

Strategic alliances are usually organized in one of three ways. In some cases, they use what is called a *shared management agreement,* where all partners to the venture actively participate in the management of the alliance. This is the case with the Samsung–Corning Glass partnership. Under such arrangements, alliance managers usually have little power since all partner companies are continually looking over their shoulder and actively participating in the management of the venture. To succeed in this type of arrangement, however, all partners must be very skilled in making cooperative arrangements work.

A second approach to management is an *assigned arrangement,* whereby one partner is assigned responsibility for running the venture. In this type of situation, the lead partner has significant control over the operating decisions of the venture, although there is still joint oversight of the venture by the other partners. NUMMI, the successful Toyota–General Motors (GM) joint venture discussed below (see Benefits of Strategic Alliances), is an example of this.

Finally, some alliances are run using a *delegated arrangement.* This type of arrangement applies only to joint ventures, where the entity has legal status as a corporation. In this case, the joint venture managers are hired or assigned to run the venture, and the partners to the alliance agree to delegate management control to these managers. Venture managers are responsible for day-to-day decisions and for implementation of the strategic objectives of the firm. Even so, they are still accountable to the partners that own the joint venture.

BENEFITS OF STRATEGIC ALLIANCES

The types of strategic alliances discussed here can bring significant advantages to firms interested in expanding in the international marketplace. At least four benefits can be identified (see Exhibit 11.2):[4]

Exhibit 11.2

Benefits and Drawbacks of Global Strategic Alliances

	Explanation
Potential Benefits:	
Ease of market entry	Local partners understand local markets.
Shared risks	Partners can underwrite some of the investment risks.
Shared knowledge	Partners can learn from each other, making both better competitors.
Synergistic payoffs	Two companies can often achieve more working together than each can working separately.
Potential Drawbacks:	
Conflicting goals	Incompatible personal or corporate goals can cause partners to seek achievement of their goals elsewhere.
Lack of openness or trust	Mistrust or hidden agendas can cause both partners to lose faith in the partnership and/or withdraw prematurely.
Disagreement over income distribution	Conflict over distributing partnership gains can cause partners to reassess their commitment to the venture.
Loss of local control	Entrepreneurs who created the circumstances for the partnership may lose control over the enterprise they created.
Changing circumstances	Changes in economic conditions or customer preferences can negate the original purpose of the partnership.

EASE OF MARKET ENTRY

The first advantage of global strategic alliances is ease of market entry, since a local partner in the host country can often overcome government impediments or other local challenges to outside companies. For example, Otis Elevator has five joint ventures in China alone. Its Chinese partners have helped Otis win local installation and service contracts that would not have otherwise been available to outside firms that were not affiliated in some way with key leaders in Chinese government and industry. Otis brought technology, training, and equipment to the partnership, while its Chinese partners brought knowledge of local customs, policies, and business practices. But most important, the local partners brought access to China's vast markets.

SHARED RISKS

Strategic alliances can also help share the risks associated with a new venture, through pooling either development costs or manufacturing and distribution costs. As noted earlier, Boeing did this with their new—and very expensive—Boeing 787 Dreamliner, taking on two principal Japanese partners, who provided both investment capital and technical and manufacturing expertise in exchange for an equity stake in the project.

SHARED KNOWLEDGE

Companies that form strategic alliances can often benefit from shared knowledge and expertise, since each partner brings to the table different competencies that collectively make the partnership stronger. When GM and Toyota created a joint venture called *NUMMI* (New United Motor Manufacturing, Inc.) in Freemont, California, to jointly produce compact cars, both firms benefited. Toyota learned more about American markets and labor relations, while GM learned useful skills in improved manufacturing. Toyota manages the facility and manufactures cars for both companies on the same assembly line.

SYNERGISTIC PAYOFFS

Finally, strategic alliances often lead to synergistic outcomes that facilitate competitive advantage. By working together, both companies can achieve more than if they tried to work separately. High-tech firms such as those in the semiconductor industry often form alliances to jointly develop cutting-edge technologies that can then be distributed among the partners. Individual company costs for research and development are thereby reduced, and all partners to the consortium benefit.

DRAWBACKS OF STRATEGIC ALLIANCES

At the same time, global strategic alliances are not without their problems.[5] These problems include the following:

CONFLICTING GOALS

In the history of strategic alliances, numerous incompatibilities have emerged between the partners as they grew and evolved over time. For example, General Electric's (GE) alliance with Germany's Siemens struggled because GE management stressed financial management while Siemens stressed engineering. Such incompatibilities can result from differences in corporate or national cultures, disagreements over goals and objectives, personality conflicts between key players, and so forth.

LACK OF OPENNESS OR TRUST

In addition, alliances can flounder because one or more partners resist providing key information—often proprietary information—relating to the operations of the venture to other stakeholders. A joint venture between Ford and Mazda stalled when Mazda refused to allow its Ford engineering counterparts access to its research laboratory, despite the fact that Ford owned 33 percent of Mazda. The conflict was finally resolved by allowing Ford engineers into the Mazda laboratories, but only for short periods of time.

DISAGREEMENT OVER INCOME DISTRIBUTION

Conflicts can also emerge over how earnings are distributed. Some partners may wish to reinvest earnings in research on future products, while others may wish to return all earnings to stockholders or equity partners. This happened when Rubbermaid broke off an alliance with Dutch DSM Group to manufacture and distribute its products throughout Europe, Africa, and the Middle East because DSM refused to reinvest earnings in future product development, a key to the long-term success of the venture as Rubbermaid saw it.

LOSS OF LOCAL CONTROL

A fourth pitfall to global strategic alliances is a loss of local control. Any partnership involves some loss of autonomy, and in many cases a partner realizes—sometimes too late—that it has lost control over decisions that it values. One partner may wish to continually introduce new products, while the other partner may wish to push older products as long as possible. In other cases, joint ventures can lead to one partner buying out the other. One study found that of 150 terminated joint ventures involving Japanese firms, three-fourths ended because the Japanese partner bought out the other partner.[6] In another case, when French-based Thompson Electronics (RCA in the United States) sought an alliance with China-based TCL to lower production costs for their television business, they soon learned that their Chinese partner's larger size and stronger financial position gave TCL, not Thompson, majority control over the new venture. Only one Thompson executive was appointed to the new board of directors.[7]

CHANGING CIRCUMSTANCES

Finally, some alliances falter because the business environment changes. Economic conditions or customer tastes require companies to reassess their business practices, and at times previous cooperative arrangements no longer serve the needs or objectives of the firm. In 1987, Ford and Volkswagen formed Autolatina, which became the largest car manufacturer in Latin America. The two companies believed that by working together they could surmount both the poor economic conditions and the government import restrictions throughout Latin America. However, by the mid-1990s, import tariffs in Latin America had been reduced and the economy had improved. In light of these changes, both auto firms decided that they were better off trying to capture market share in the region working individually rather than collectively. The partnership disbanded and the two companies went their separate ways.

To better understand how culture can influence the success or failure of strategic alliances and international joint ventures, we turn now to a look at two very different environments: Spain and Korea. Consider the key ingredients for success if the company you worked for was forming an alliance with a strategic partner from one of these two countries.

MANAGING STRATEGIC ALLIANCES: INSIDE THE SPANISH *EMPRESA*

Spain is an interesting country, not only because of its *fiestas* and Mediterranean culture, but also because of its accomplishments. Modern Spain was born in 1975 with the death of General Franco and accession of King Juan Carlos to the throne. Over the past thirty years, Spain has been transformed from an ultra-Catholic, isolated, fascist dictatorship into a modern parliamentary democracy. Today, it is the second largest country in the European Union in landmass and the second most important tourist destination in the European Union, and it is gaining in economic power. Spaniards today are 30 percent richer than they were in 1975, and their economy has been growing faster than the European average for nearly a decade.[8]

Spain's 40 million people are spread into seventeen autonomous regions. Regionalism in Spain is taken very seriously and influences both business and politics. The regions of Spain have their own distinctive histories and cultures and have experienced increasing autonomy since 1975. In the past thirty years, regional governments have stressed local autonomy and uniqueness through policies that foster local languages, arts, and traditions. In some regions of Spain, regional identity and loyalty are more important than national identity and represent a major political issue. Spanish regionalism is a critical part of Spanish culture and needs to be considered when doing business in Spain.[9]

Besides Castilian (Spanish), Galician, Catalan, Valencian, and Euskera are official languages in Galicia, Catalonia, Valencia, and the Basque country, respectively. Additional languages and dialects are spoken in other regions. These languages receive equal status with Castilian in their respective regions, are used widely, and are taught in schools. Even though most Spaniards in these regions are bilingual, many take pride in speaking their local language and often revert to their local language in the presence of friends and colleagues. Short-term visitors are expected to speak Castilian, if anything, but long-term expatriates are advised to learn the local language. Many Basques, Catalans, and Galicians think of themselves as members of a nation conquered by Spain, and separatist movements remain strong, particularly in the Basque country. A recent survey suggested that close to 35 percent of Basques and Catalans and 12 percent of Galicians want full independence from Spain.[10] Indeed, the issue of regionalism (or local nationalism) may be one of the most intractable challenges for Spain's government.

SPANISH CULTURE AND SOCIAL PATTERNS

Despite significant regional variations, it is still possible to identify several important common cultural trends across Spain that stem from a common Mediterranean and Catholic influence. These trends are summarized in Exhibit 11.3, with comparisons to the United States as a point of reference.

Arriving in Spain, foreigners immediately notice an intensity of life on the streets. Spaniards like to be on the streets, in bars, cafés, restaurants, and public spaces. It is no wonder that Spain has more cafés and bars per capita than anywhere else in the world.[11] Spain is often described as the land of *fiestas,* and Spaniards spend consid-

Exhibit 11.3

Cultural Differences Between the United States and Spain

United States	Spain
Uncomfortable with emotional outbursts, especially in business relations	Highly emotional in both business and personal life
Low-context culture; linear and direct communications; general preference for sticking to a topic when discussing business	High-context culture; issues often discussed at length and unrelated information often included in the conversation
Assertiveness valued; emphasis on accomplishments: people are often proud to tell others about their achievements	Modesty valued; tendency to understate achievements: people who boast about themselves or their achievements tend not to be respected
Value placed on accuracy and objectivity over personal pride	Personal pride and honor take precedence over objectivity and accuracy
Decision making often based on "objective" quantitative data; decision making should be impersonal	Decision making often based on qualitative information (e.g., talking to people the decision maker trusts)
Personal accomplishments critical in hiring decisions and establishing business relationships	Trust and knowing a person critical in hiring decisions and in establishing business relationships
Nepotism discouraged and often illegal; emphasis on hiring the best candidate	Nepotism preferred to ensure trust in employees
Nuclear family important, while extended family often unimportant	Extended family important and frequently involved in business relationships
Monochronic; time is important; task-oriented	Polychronic; time is fluid and delays are common; relationship-oriented
Emphasis on thinking big; preference often for initiating a new venture with a major contract, signaling success	Emphasis on thinking small; preference often on starting with a small contract and increasing business later when trust is established
Moderately egalitarian; hierarchies only moderately important	Hierarchical; hierarchies very important in establishing relationships
Future-oriented; forecasts and planning important	Short-term-oriented; emphasis on living for today, not on planning
Idealistic; belief that individuals and societies can improve through effort	Cynical; fatalistic; somewhat pessimistic about prospects for improvement
Adherence to rules and regulations; do things by the book	Casual attitudes towards rules and regulations; close supervision required
Status based on achievement and material possessions	Status based on position, title, and personal image

erable amounts of money in celebrations every year. Indeed, many observers see the Spaniards as the "party animals" of Europe.

Even so, these same observers are puzzled by the seeming seriousness of Spaniards. In Spain, public decorum implies seriousness, and except during *fiesta* time, Spaniards often go about their daily lives in what appears to be a somber mood. However, this seriousness is usually not a reflection of thoughts and feelings, but the expected behavior toward anonymous people. For many Spaniards, strangers are not entitled to the same friendliness as the people they know. This logic also applies to customers, mainly in the Spanish bureaucracy, where attendants may seem unhelpful and at times even rude. Establishing personal relationships is critical to making any progress. Spaniards are gregarious people and value the support and approval of family and friends. They tend to form long-term relationships and value belonging to a group, town, or organization. Thus, sometimes outsiders need to make an extra effort to fit into a group of some kind to be accepted.

More important, outsiders need to be patient. Spaniards take a relaxed attitude toward time, spending it on issues that may seem irrelevant to a time-conscious foreigner. They do not value detailed schedules, and meetings seldom begin on time. Spaniards believe that too much planning leads to loss of spontaneity and flexibility, which are regarded as more important.

ORGANIZATION AND MANAGEMENT IN SPAIN

The relatively recent appearance of modern Spain has left marks of underdevelopment on the nation that still plague the business environment. Spanish businesses, referred to as *empresas,* are still relatively timid and deferential toward government. Spanish multinationals are usually active players in the Spanish-speaking world, but few have ventured outside Latin America.

Part of the problem is that businesses in Spain have to deal with a rigid labor environment, a vestige of the old dictatorship. Franco fostered employment by making it difficult for employers to dismiss workers. With the arrival of democracy, unions were able to increase low wages as well as keep several of workers' earlier privileges. A decade ago, unemployment in Spain was close to 20 percent, but it has been reduced significantly in recent years, as Spain became the low-wage country of choice for firms wanting to establish operations in Europe. With the enlargement of the European Union (see Chapter 6), however, this is about to change, as Eastern European countries are becoming more attractive for businesses. The Spanish government is working on labor reforms, but their success is yet to be seen.

The European Union's enlargement is also impacting the Spanish economy in other ways. Until recently, Spain was the largest beneficiary of EU funds (just ahead of Ireland), which helped it achieve its economic success. However, as new, poorer members enter the European Union, Spain will become a net contributor to the European Union. Spain is now going through a transition period and considerable effort will be required to keep Spain's economy strong despite reduced EU support. For example, the Spanish tax system needs significant reform. Spain's underground economy is strong, and people complain that the national tax burden favors the wealthy at the expense of the poor. Also, Spain lags behind in its use of technology. Even though Spain's major banks and businesses use state-of-the-art technology in their operations, Spaniards in general have been slow to embrace the Internet, and the universities are weak in science and technology. This resistance to technology is likely to make Spain less productive and undermine its competitiveness.[12]

Generally speaking, Spain is slowly becoming more "European." For instance, even though the Spaniards' notion of time is still more flexible than that of most Europeans, it is slowly adjusting to the European time schedule. Major businesses no longer close during the day, and workers in major business centers can no longer afford to go home for a *siesta*. Still, everything in Spain begins later and finishes later. A typical workday starts at 9 A.M. and can easily finish after 8 P.M., with a long lunch break. Outside large commercial centers, Spaniards still enjoy a daily *siesta* lasting between two and three hours. During the summer months, when most Spaniards take vacation, some companies adopt a summer schedule in which people work straight through until about 3 P.M. and then leave for the day.

In such a sociable country as Spain, business and leisure are intertwined. Businesspeople often prefer to make important business decisions outside the office over a meal, coffee, or *tapas* (appetizer-like food served throughout the day). These meetings are usually impromptu: people are often expected to drop everything and go. Not surprisingly, developing trust (*confianza*) and building social relationships are critical. Business associations are commonly supported by social relationships, and it is common to rely on family networks. What many Westerners see as nepotism and intentional inefficiencies are normal business practice in Spain. Most Spaniards would agree that unqualified people sometimes secure undeserved positions because of *enchufes* (contacts), but trust remains more important than achievement when hiring and doing business. Trust is also critical when making decisions. Spaniards are more likely to seek the advice of someone they trust than to collect so-called hard data.

Spaniards believe in building trust over time, and they value long-term relationships. Therefore, they prefer to start small when doing business with a stranger and grow the business as trust levels grow. The process of building trust and developing relationships is accompanied by long—frequently off-the-subject—conversations. Spaniards talk about several subjects besides business in a meeting, and when talking about business they frequently deliver messages indirectly. They like to discuss issues at length and may repeat themselves two or three times. If disagreements arise, they are likely to raise their voice and interrupt often. This behavior is not intended to be rude and is not a sign of anger; rather it displays interest. However, for most Spaniards, honor and personal pride are important, and criticisms may be interpreted as personal rather than objective feedback, especially when prior trust has not been established.[13]

At work, Spaniards adopt a more relaxed attitude than most Westerners. It is said that Spaniards work to live and do not want to look too driven. Work is often interrupted to catch up with office gossip, have coffee in a nearby café, or run small errands. At the same time, however, absenteeism is low, as Spaniards will most likely take a few hours off and go back to work rather than miss the whole day.

Status and hierarchical position are valued more than money and personal satisfaction. Thus, Spaniards are frequently unwilling to change jobs for a higher salary or more interesting work, especially when it implies starting over or losing status. For this reason, as well as legal difficulties associated with dismissing workers, Spaniards tend to remain in organizations for a long time. Work relationships often evolve into family-like relationships.

In general, Spaniards are generous and hospitable. To the amusement and sometimes embarrassment of foreigners, Spaniards may get into intense arguments over who pays the whole tab in a restaurant. Splitting the bill is considered impolite; rather, reciprocity at the next meal is expected as the relationship continues.

In summary, when working with Spaniards, it is important to make an effort to understand their unique behavior. They are proud of their culture, and efforts to adapt to the Spanish way of life are taken as a sign of respect. These efforts represent an effective way to gain acceptance, and in Spain this is the first step toward business success.

MANAGING STRATEGIC ALLIANCES: INSIDE THE KOREAN *CHAEBOL*

If people are looking for a contrast to the seemingly laid-back Spaniards, especially as potential strategic alliance partners, they need look no further than Korea. Korean companies initiated a myriad of strategic alliances early in their economic development efforts in order to gain needed technologies from both Japan and the West.[14] Many of these alliances continue today, and new ones are added frequently. But building a partnership in Korea means something very different than it does in Spain.

KOREAN CULTURE AND SOCIAL PATTERNS

Korean conglomerates are typically referred to as *chaebol*. This translates roughly into "fortune cluster." A *chaebol* typically consists of a largely family-controlled business conglomerate with numerous often highly diversified companies. The *chaebol* is not unlike the Japanese *keiretsu* in organization design, but it can be very different in terms of ownership and management practices. Until the late 1990s, there were perhaps a dozen genuinely powerful *chaebol* groups in Korea, including Samsung, Hyundai, Lucky-Goldstar (now LG), Sunkyong (now SK), and Ssangyong. Over the past several years, however, as a result of increased economic turmoil and government restrictions, several of these groups have broken up into smaller and leaner firms. Hyundai Business Group, for example, broke into the relatively independent Hyundai Heavy Industries, Hyundai Motor Company, Hyundai Construction Company, Hynix Semiconductor, and so forth. Daewoo Business Group disintegrated, although some of its companies, such as Daewoo Shipbuilding, remain strong. Despite these changes, or perhaps because of them, Korea's major companies remain strong competitors on the world stage, especially in heavy industries and consumer electronics.

At the risk of oversimplification, we can say that Korean *chaebol*s have tended to exhibit several common characteristics, especially during their formative stages. Most

Exhibit 11.4

Characteristics of Traditional Korean *Chaebols*

Characteristics	Strategic Value
Family control	Guarantees that corporate management speaks with one voice on both strategic and operational issues; reduces potential for disagreements among divergent stakeholders; allows for the development of second-generation owner-managers
Strong entrepreneurial orientation	Encourages companies to be first to market and continually alert for new and promising business ventures; facilitates creativity and innovation throughout the organization
Paternalistic leadership	Minimizes potential disagreements over strategic directions of the firm; assures customers (including the government) that company can deliver; provides employees with charismatic role model
Centralized planning and coordination	Ensures tight management controls over all funding and investment decisions; allows company to pursue numerous divergent business ventures simultaneously
Close business-government relations	Facilitates access to government-controlled capital, foreign technologies, and export licenses

of these characteristics follow from the national culture in which they operated. These include: (1) tight family control over the management structure of the firm; (2) a strong entrepreneurial orientation that drives these firms to continually pursue new business opportunities; (3) a strong paternalistic leadership in which the directives of the chairman and other managers are to be followed without question; (4) centralized planning and coordination, usually through a central planning office for the entire group; and (5) close cooperation between the firm and the government. These five characteristics are summarized in Exhibit 11.4, along with the strategic value of each. Note the differences here between the typical *chaebol* and its Japanese counterpart, as discussed in Chapter 9.

ORGANIZATION AND MANAGEMENT IN KOREA

Organizational analysts have long argued that the real soul of a business enterprise is found in its culture. Nowhere is this more accurate than with respect to Korean firms. Korean culture tends to be characterized by a ruthless dedication to hard work, the importance of group harmony, a willingness to accept challenges without question, and an ability to silently read the moods and intentions of people throughout the organization.

The picture that emerges from the above analysis is one of compromise and perhaps evolution. Korean corporate culture is both strong and flexible. It is rooted in Eastern traditions yet has learned from the West. It is highly collectivistic but has touches of individualism. This paradox is illustrated in a comparison of Korean management practices and those of the typical U.S. firm (see Exhibit 11.5).

Exhibit 11.5

Typical U.S. and Korean Corporate Cultures

Characteristics	Typical U.S. Firm	Typical Korean Firm
Basis for relationships	Written contracts	Personal relationships
Social contract	Individual rights dominant	Harmony dominant
Individual versus group	Individual dominates	Group dominates
Context	Low	High
Basis of achievement	Individual	Group
Company loyalty	Frequently weak	Very strong
Decision-making style	Varies considerably	Highly autocratic
Basis of work commitment	Protestant work ethic	Confucian work ethic
Vertical relationships	Impersonal; bureaucratic	Highly paternalistic
Job descriptions	Very specific	Very general
Employment	No guarantees	No guarantees
Employee turnover	High	Low

Sources: Adapted from Gerardo R. Ungson, Richard M. Steers, and Seung-Ho Park, *Korean Enterprise: The Quest for Globalization* (Boston: Harvard Business School Press, 1997); Richard M. Steers, *Made in Korea: Chung Ju Yung and the Rise of Hyundai* (New York: Routledge, 1999).

Korean management is perhaps best described as a blend of East and West with a clear Eastern bias. However, some argue that the new realities of global competition are pushing Korean firms to move somewhat more to the West along this continuum in order to become true global corporations instead of just Korean firms doing business internationally.

As Korean industry grew and developed, it had what many Westerners call a "secret weapon": the *salaryman,* or white-collar employee. Highly motivated, highly skilled, unquestioning in obedience, and unyielding in determination, salarymen (more than 95 percent of Korean managers are men) are the frontline troops that carry out company objectives around the world. They are the original "road warriors" in every sense of the word.

As in Japan, prospective job applicants to Korea's prestigious firms pass through a grueling series of personal and intellectual hurdles to prove that they are worthy of joining the organization. This includes a company-sponsored entrance examination that covers English-language proficiency, as well as technical and management skills. Good university grades are also important factors in the selection process. In addition, applicants pass through extensive personal interviews and reference checks. In hiring decisions, new college graduates are preferred over people with experience. Once hired, they are typically rotated through such core departments as planning, finance, and accounting after a period of training and indoctrination. This practice contrasts with the typical U.S. approach, in which previous work experience is highly valued and new employees are typically assigned to a functional department based on their specialty. It also contrasts somewhat with Japanese companies, where new employees are more likely to begin their jobs in the field rather than at corporate headquarters.

One study sought to identify how major Korean companies describe their ideal manager.[15] In other words, what are the keys to managerial success and how do companies identify these characteristics when hiring new employees? The ideal young candidate for most companies is described as both smart and highly motivated. He exhibits a strong work ethic and a positive attitude toward hard work for both company and country. Personal initiative is important. He has a good character and background and is willing to learn. Finally, he presents himself well and is comfortable to be around. Some companies also indicate that the ideal candidate is a risk taker who has the capacity to make rapid and incisive decisions under pressure.

New hires quickly discover that working for Korean firms is not unlike being in military service. To begin with, companies demand absolute commitment and dedication to the firm; they tolerate no criticism. All employees are expected to follow orders without question. They are expected to think and behave in ways that are consistent with the firm's guiding philosophy. And they are expected to make whatever sacrifice is required to help the firm succeed. Indeed, during the 1980s, a number of Korean managers went to jail for extended periods of time, not necessarily because they were guilty of any legal infraction, but because explaining their plight in public might have put the company in a bad light. Colleagues become comrades, and companies become families.

Working for a Korean *chaebol* is not for the weak in spirit. Working hours are long, and salarymen often look tired as they sit through meeting after meeting throughout the day.[16] It is better than it used to be, however. Before the labor reforms of the late 1980s and early 1990s, many salarymen routinely worked all day long six and sometimes seven days a week. As one senior executive described his work life in the early days, "I worked sixteen hours a day, seven days a week, for sixteen years. No holidays. If the chairman was working, so were we." And the chairman was always working. "We didn't mind, however. We learned from the chairman; we respected him. He was always very demanding, but he was a good teacher."[17]

Today, while everyone still puts in long hours, current work schedules have improved over earlier times. The typical midlevel salaryman rises at about six in the morning, six days each week. After a quick traditional breakfast of rice, soup, and fresh fruit, he catches a crowded subway at about 7 A.M. for the downtown headquarters building, usually arriving at about 8 A.M. He spends his days at a small desk in a room filled with other small desks, always alert to the comings and goings of his supervisor. He frequently does not leave work until after 6 or 7 P.M.

Much of his work involves a team effort. Indeed, many Korean firms have no individual job descriptions like those found in the West. Instead, employees' assignments and areas of responsibility change and evolve depending on circumstance. On one occasion, for example, an entire management training class at Hyundai Motor Company was suspended for two weeks because several taxi companies announced they would make a major purchase of new cars. The managers were sent scurrying out to sell as many new cars as they could. The instructor was sent home. After achieving their goal, they returned to their training program. The successful salaryman does whatever is called for. Nowhere throughout the corporation would a visitor ever hear the words "That's not my job." Everything is every employee's job.

While teamwork is important, so, too, is discipline. Indeed, the term "top-down" may represent an understatement in describing Korean management style. Instructions from above are to be followed to the letter and without question. Employees from senior executives down to the newest trainee carefully watch those above them for signs of impending action. Indeed, perhaps the greatest challenge for a salaryman is to figure out whether the manager a notch or two above him approves of what he is doing. In some cases, this results in little being accomplished until a salaryman has been given direct orders. Then activity reigns supreme as he tries to meet his assignment in the smallest possible amount of time. Once a task is assigned, failure to complete it is not an acceptable alternative. While this military style of management has softened somewhat in recent years, discipline and compliance with directives remain an important hallmark of Korean firms.

As has been shown, Spain and Korea approach their work in very different ways. This dichotomy poses very different challenges for managers trying to make global strategic alliances work. To succeed, managers must understand their particular situation and respond with both cultural sensitivity and managerial competence. Above all, a global manager must add value to any partnership, regardless of the partner's home country, or risk becoming either ineffective or obsolete. In short, working with strategic partners is not always for the timid or weak in spirit.

KEY TERMS

assigned arrangement	exploration consortium
chaebol	global strategic alliance
comanagement agreement	international joint venture (IJV)
comarketing agreement	long-term supply agreement
coproduction agreement	nonequity alliance
coservice agreement	NUMMI
delegated arrangement	R&D consortium
empresa	salaryman
equity alliance	shared management arrangement

GLOBAL MANAGER'S WORKBOOK 11.1: SECOINSA

When Japan's Fujitsu joined forces with Spain's recently privatized national telephone company, Telefónica, and several local banks to create Secoinsa (Sociedad Espanola de Comunicaciones e Informatica S.A.), everyone knew that it would be a challenging alliance, but few realized just how challenging.[18] The Japanese managers that arrived to help run the new partnership seemed totally unprepared for the Spanish culture or way of doing business. At the same time, their Spanish partners were equally perplexed about how to work with the Japanese. Problems began almost immediately.

The first problem involved language. Both partners relied on English, since few Japanese partners could speak Spanish and no Spaniards could speak Japanese. The Japanese soon became frustrated because they could not express their true feelings in English, while the Spaniards were equally frustrated with what they considered to be the Japanese's "all business all the time" approach to interpersonal relations. The Spaniards concluded early on that their Japanese counterparts were not well rounded because all they talked about was business. They also felt that the Japanese were looking down on their local Spanish traditions and customs. The Japanese, in turn, questioned the work ethic of their Spanish counterparts because of their excessively long meals and time away from work. Neither side had an easy time building rapport, and numerous misunderstandings emerged. Stress levels increased on both sides.

Substantial disagreements also arose over the ways in which decisions were made at the new company. The Japanese tried to use a consensual decision process that required considerable time but led to broad-based support for final decisions. The Spaniards preferred to have senior managers make decisions more autocratically and lost patience with the endless rounds of discussions requested by their partners.

Finally, problems arose in manufacturing and quality control. Fujitsu managers insisted on maintaining strict controls over production processes to ensure quality control and prevent imitation by their competitors. They wanted all components used in the manufacturing process to be manufactured in Japan. If this proved to be infeasible, they wanted all the parts at least to be tested in Japan at Fujitsu's testing facilities. Their Spanish partners preferred using components manufactured in Spain (or at least the European Union) and saw no reason to ship them to Japan for testing. Fujitsu finally agreed to this arrangement so long as the components were manufactured by Secoinsa and not by an outside vendor. Both sides came to see the other as difficult, narrow-minded, inflexible, and overly nationalistic, but the venture continued because Fujitsu wanted access to the Spanish (and European) market and the Spanish wanted access to Japan's leading-edge technology. But neither side was happy.

QUESTIONS FOR DISCUSSION

1. What is the fundamental problem in this strategic alliance? Why did this occur?
2. What could the Japanese managers at Fujitsu do now to rebuild trust and get the partnership back on track?
3. What could the Spanish managers at Secoinsa do now to rebuild trust and get the partnership back on track?
4. If the two companies could start over, how might each side have approached the alliance differently in order to enhance the chances of long-term success?

GLOBAL MANAGER'S WORKBOOK 11.2: AMKOR TECHNOLOGIES

American Biotechnology, Inc. (ABI), was founded in 1980 and is today one of the fastest-growing biotechnology firms in the United States.[19] ABI is headquartered in San Jose, California, in the heart of Silicon Valley. In addition to its corporate headquarters and central research and manufacturing facilities in San Jose, ABI has branch offices in twelve North American cities, as well as both marketing and manufacturing facilities in England, Germany, Argentina, Japan, and Korea. Its competitive position in the marketplace depends heavily on maintaining its lead in research and development, as well as on its ability to rapidly convert its technological advances into marketable products. The company exists in a fast-paced business environment, and management must continually work to maintain its product leadership.

Also in 1980, entrepreneur Lee Seung-Ho founded the Hangul Business Group, in Korea. To help establish the company, the Korean government gave Hangul financial assistance, access to technology, and a local monopoly in return for its commitment to develop the industry. With this help, the Hangul Group soon emerged as a leader in the chemical and pharmaceutical industries. By 1985, it had become Korea's largest producer and distributor of drugs and pharmaceuticals.

While ABI and the Hangul Group share similar goals and objectives as major corporations in a highly competitive world, they exist in fundamentally different business and cultural environments. Americans tend to place a high value on change and dynamism and consider themselves to be largely future-oriented, while Koreans tend to exhibit greater respect for tradition. Americans are often described as living in a youth-oriented culture where independence and individual achievement are valued. By contrast, Koreans exhibit greater respect for age and believe in the preeminence of the family group over the individual.

CREATION OF AMKOR TECHNOLOGIES

American Biotechnology, Inc., initially entered Korea in 1990 through a distributorship arrangement with the Hangul Group. This arrangement initially suited both partners in that ABI acquired access to the Korean marketplace while the Hangul Group acquired experience in both international trade and high-technology manufacturing. As the relationship continued, it became evident that both companies could benefit from merging their efforts into one cohesive and integrated Korean-based firm. As a result, in 1995, AmKor Technologies was established as a joint venture between ABI and the Hangul Group. AmKor grew rapidly into a successful manufacturing concern, as well as a marketing operation. Within both the American and Korean business communities in Seoul, the company was widely considered to be a success story of Korean-American business cooperation. Each year saw increased sales and profitability, despite a highly competitive marketplace.

With the combined efforts of both partners, AmKor soon began to manufacture sufficiently broad product lines to fill the general demands of the Korean marketplace. Production levels also allowed for some export to countries in Southeast Asia. AmKor also began investing heavily in research and development. These efforts were coordinated through a joint committee from both parent companies to avoid unnecessary duplication of effort. Several successful new products emerged from this endeavor. ABI considers the Korean operation to be one of its most successful in the international arena and feels that the company's future prospects are quite promising, especially since Korea continues to experience economic prosperity and reasonable political stability. The steady improvement in Korea's standard of living also opens new opportunities for the company's products.

KEY PERSONNEL AND ORGANIZATION

Since its establishment in 1995, AmKor Technologies has been led by Lee Sanghoon, eldest son of Hangul's founder. However, while Lee serves as president and is largely responsible for relations with the Korean business community, he has little experience in the biotechnology industry. As a result, the day-to-day operations of AmKor are managed by Mathew Davenport, an American appointed by the American partner. Reporting to Davenport are five Korean senior managing directors, who oversee the functional areas of managing the enterprise (e.g., local manufacturing, sales, finance, etc.), and one American executive assistant, Alan Bird. While several other Americans are assigned to the joint venture, they are concerned primarily with research and development and have no overall management responsibilities. Key personnel at AmKor Technologies are as follows:

Lee Sanghoon, President

Lee Sanghoon studied economics at the prestigious Seoul National University. After graduation, he went to the United States and received an M.B.A. from Georgetown University. He then returned to Korea and joined the Hangul Group as a special assistant to his father. Several managerial assignments within the group followed until he was appointed vice president and later president of the group's small cosmetics company in 1986. When AmKor was created in 1995, his father appointed Lee as its founding president.

   The Lee family is well connected in the business community. Chairman Lee (the senior) has served as honorary chairman of the powerful Federation of Korean Industries and is an active supporter of the current ruling political party. He and his son are both active in the Korean international business community and are members of the American Chamber of Commerce in Seoul, as well as several elite business clubs. Such connections are clearly important to the success of any business venture in Korea. As the chairman's eldest son, it is widely assumed that Lee Sanghoon will one day assume control of the entire Hangul Group after his father's retirement.

Matthew Davenport, Vice President and General Manager

In 1999, shortly after its founding, AmKor's general manager announced his retirement from the company. Based on the terms of the joint venture agreement, ABI was responsible for selecting his replacement. After a careful internal search, the company selected Matthew Davenport for the job. Davenport was an experienced international executive, having spent most of his career with ABI in its international division. He had a B.S. in chemical engineering from the University of Minnesota and had served with the company in Germany, England, and Argentina. In addition, Davenport had spent several years in the home office's international division in San

ORGANIZATION AND KEY PERSONNEL OF AMKOR TECHNOLOGIES

Equity joint venture partners (50 percent share each):

- American Biotechnology, Inc., San Jose, California, United States (founded 1980)
- Hangul Group, Seoul, Korea (founded 1980)

AmKor Technologies founded: 1995
Head office: Seoul, Korea
Number of AmKor employees: 3,560
Primary AmKor business: Manufacture, distribution, and sales of bio-technology-based pharmaceuticals and drugs; some research and development in association with parent companies
Primary markets: 90 percent of sales within Korea; 10 percent to other countries in Southeast Asia

Key AmKor officers:

- Lee Sanghoon: president; age forty-eight; with Hangul Group since 1980; with AmKor since 1988
- Matthew Davenport: vice president and general manager; age fifty-four; with ABI since 1983; with AmKor since 1999
- Alan Bird: executive assistant; age twenty-nine; with ABI since 1998; with AmKor since 2002
- Senior managing directors: five; all Korean

Jose, California. Davenport was well known for his technical expertise and for his no-nonsense approach to turnaround management. In particular, he was credited with reorganizing both the British and Argentine operations through corporate streamlining and cost-cutting procedures.

In September 1999, Davenport arrived in Korea to become the new vice president and general manager. He was delighted with the challenge to expand the Korean operations. Davenport was also pleased with the growth and development of ABI and felt he had played a major part in this success. If he could further improve the growth and performance record of AmKor, he could then return to headquarters with an inside track to becoming ABI's next corporate vice president for international operations.

Alan Bird, Executive Assistant

Alan Bird was born and raised in Seattle, Washington. After high school he attended the University of Washington and majored in East Asian studies. During this time, he acquired a moderate degree of fluency in the Korean language. After graduation, he entered the University of Arizona and received an M.B.A. Bird then entered the U.S. Army and, because of his language expertise, was stationed in Korea. While there, he continued to study Korean language and culture at Yonsei University in Seoul. He made many Korean friends, developed a strong affection for the country, and vowed to return there to live.

When he was discharged from the army, he returned to the United States and went to work for ABI as a management trainee in 1998. He was quickly recognized as a bright, highly motivated manager who consistently brought new ideas and strategies to the assignments he was given. The company was pleased that Bird had chosen ABI as a place to make his career. When the company needed a new executive assistant for its AmKor joint venture in 2001, Bird was the obvious choice to send to Seoul to help with the venture.

Bird was pleased to return to Korea, not only because of his admiration for the country, but also because it gave him an opportunity to improve what he considered to be the "ugly American" image abroad. Because of his language ability and interest in Korea, he was able to mix with broad segments of the local population. He noted that Americans frequently had a tendency to impose their own value systems, beliefs, and ideals upon foreigners, believing that anything American was universally superior and always applicable. He was embarrassed by many of these American attitudes and was determined to do something about it.

At AmKor, Bird's responsibilities included troubleshooting with major Korean customers, attending trade meetings, negotiating with government officials, conducting marketing research projects, and helping with day-to-day administration. He reported directly to Davenport. During his early assignments in Seoul, Bird was seen as highly successful by the company. He moved easily among both Koreans and Americans and was respected by both groups for his honesty and integrity, as well as for his ability to compromise and reach consensus.

PROBLEMS AT WORK

When Bird arrived in Seoul in 2001, Davenport was initially very pleased to have him on board. He knew that Bird was energetic and could communicate with the "locals." Davenport realized that Bird had considerable expertise about Korean business and culture and from the beginning sought Bird's advice on several difficult and complex interpersonal and administrative problems. However, after a few months on the job, Davenport became concerned about what he felt were subtle yet important changes in Alan Bird's attitude and behaviors. Davenport felt that Bird was becoming too absorbed in the local Korean culture and was reaching a point where he was losing his American identity. Bird seemed to have "gone native," and this change resulted in a substantial loss of his administrative effectiveness, according to Davenport.

As Davenport reflected on these changes, he noted several examples of what he felt was Bird's "complete emotional involvement" in the culture of Korea. First, he observed that Bird increasingly spoke Korean instead of English to other AmKor employees, despite the fact that all Korean employees of the joint venture were bilingual. In addition, Bird had recently met and married a young Korean woman from

Ewha Women's University. After his marriage, Bird moved into a Korean neighborhood and spent much of his free time with his Korean neighbors. Finally, although ABI had a company policy of granting its American employees a one-month fully paid home leave every year, Davenport noted that Bird had never taken such trips, preferring instead to spend his holidays visiting remote parts of Korea to study Korean history and religion.

At work, Bird had assumed many of the characteristics of a typical Korean executive. He spent considerable time listening to the personal problems of his subordinates and maintained close social ties with many of the men in the organization. After work, he frequently went out drinking and socializing with several Korean colleagues. He even helped to arrange a marriage for one of his Korean subordinates. As a result, many employees sought Bird's advice when they had complaints or concerns about management. Recently, several employees had complained to Bird about personnel policy changes made by Davenport. One such change involved a shift from seniority-based promotion to performance-based promotion. Initially, AmKor followed traditional Korean HRM policies, including the practice of promoting employees based largely on seniority within the organization. Shortly after his arrival, however, Davenport instituted a new Western-style promotion policy based largely on annual employee performance appraisals. These appraisals were conducted for all salarymen by their immediate supervisors, in consultation with the Human Resources Department.

Some employees felt that this shift to performance-based promotion would create conflicts and disturb corporate harmony, especially if younger employees began being promoted above more senior employees. Confucian principles dictated that age was to be respected and honored, and challenging this tradition could jeopardize existing harmony among the employees. The employees asked Bird to intercede on their behalf. Bird approached Davenport with the problem and insisted that the employees' concerns were justified in view of traditional Korean practices. However, Davenport defended the new policy, arguing that the new demands of global competition required a high-performance corporation and that basing employee promotion on actual job performance instead of seniority was the best way to ensure a highly motivated and competitive workforce.

While Davenport had initially found it helpful to learn the feelings of local managers from Bird, he increasingly began to resent having to deal with Bird as an adversary instead of an ally. Davenport became increasingly reluctant to ask Bird's opinion because he invariably raised objections to proposed changes or innovations that were contrary to traditional Korean norms and customs. From Davenport's point of view, significant changes were emerging in Korean customs and society, and he was confident that many of the points Bird objected to were not tied to existing cultural patterns as rigidly as Bird seemed to think. Davenport's assessment of the situation was bolstered by his observation that many Korean subordinates were, in fact, quite progressive in terms of their approach to management. In fact, as Davenport saw it, the Koreans were frequently more willing than Bird to try out new ideas in the workplace. For example, Davenport felt it was time to begin promoting women into the traditionally male managerial ranks. When he suggested this to several Korean managers, they did not object, yet Bird cautioned against taking the lead with such a "revolutionary" change in an Asian country. Davenport believed further that there was no point in a progressive American company's merely imitating local customs. Indeed, a socially responsible company's real contribution to Korean society was to introduce new ideas and innovations and facilitate economic development for this newly industrialized country.

The more Davenport reflected on Bird's recent behavior, the more concerned he became about the soundness of Bird's overall judgment as an AmKor manager. For instance, when Davenport wanted to dismiss a Korean manager who in his opinion lacked initiative, leadership, and general competency, Bird defended the manager, noting that the company had never before fired a manager. Bird also argued that the manager had been loyal and honest and that the company was partially at fault for having retained him for the past five years without helping the man to improve. But Davenport fired the manager anyway, only to discover two weeks later that Bird had interceded on behalf of the manager to get another Hangul Group company to hire him. When confronted, Bird simply said that he had done what was expected of a superior in any responsible Korean company.

Davenport concluded that such incidents were symptomatic of a serious problem. Bird had been an effective and efficient manager. His knowledge of the Korean language and people had proved invaluable. On numerous occasions, his American friends envied Davenport for having a man of Bird's qualifications as an assistant. Davenport also knew that Bird had received several outstanding offers to work for other companies in Korea. Davenport felt that Bird would be far more effective if he could take a more emotionally detached attitude toward Korea. In Davenport's view, the best international executive for both AmKor and ABI was one who retained his belief in the fundamental American values that made the company so successful, while simultaneously being sympathetic to local customs and attitudes. A good manager was, first and foremost, committed to the company and its development.

DAVENPORT'S DECISION

After a thorough review of the situation, Davenport decided that it was in the best interest of both AmKor and ABI to transfer Alan Bird back to corporate headquarters in California. While this was a difficult decision, Davenport felt that Bird's presence in Seoul had become divisive and threatened the continued growth and development of AmKor. While Bird had considerable management potential, his career would benefit from a new assignment in the home office, where he could be reacquainted with the norms, values, and management practices of the larger company. With proper care and attention, Bird had the potential to continue his career with the company once he clearly understood the role of an international manager in a highly competitive global environment.

In the meantime, Davenport felt that AmKor would benefit if a new executive assistant were sent from San Jose. This would provide valuable experience for another junior American manager from the company and would simultaneously send a clear message to local AmKor employees that Davenport was committed to continuing his improvements in the management and operations of the Korean venture.

Davenport sent a letter to the president of ABI informing him of his decision and then informed both Bird and AmKor president Lee. While Bird made no initial response to the transfer, Lee expressed considerable concern with the decision. Lee noted that Bird had been a good employee and had done much to further Korean-American relations within AmKor. The Korean employees admired and respected Bird and would not understand his transfer back to the United States In addition, in Lee's mind, asking Bird to relocate to California and sever his Korean ties might force him to resign and join another Korean-based company. With his acquired expertise in biotechnology, he might even end up working for a competitor such as Samsung or LG.

In a conversation the following morning, Lee told Davenport that, while he understood that the accords of the joint venture gave control over American AmKor employees to Davenport, he hoped that Davenport would reconsider his decision and keep Bird in Seoul. Davenport replied that, in good conscience, he could not agree to this; his decision was based on what was good for the whole company, not just AmKor. Disappointed, Lee returned to his office and sent a fax to the president of ABI informing him that, for the good of the company, he wished Bird to remain at AmKor. He noted that he understood the nature of the conflict between Bird and Davenport and that he respected Davenport as an executive. Still, Lee argued, Bird was a valuable resource for the joint venture. Lee closed by asking the ABI president to override Davenport's decision and retain Alan Bird at AmKor.

ABI's Dilemma

Upon receiving both Davenport's letter and Lee's fax, the president of ABI faced a serious dilemma: Whom should he support? What should he do? The president felt there was clearly merit in Davenport's assessment of the situation and that Bird would probably benefit from a reassignment back to San Jose. However, he also felt that Bird (like Davenport) was a valuable employee and did not want to risk losing him. Nor did he wish to alienate the Hangul Group, ABI's partner in the AmKor joint venture.

Before making his decision, the president has called a staff meeting to assess the situation. As a member of his staff, you have been invited to this meeting to offer your own views of the problem. As you prepare for this meeting, consider the following issues:

1. Based on this analysis, how would you describe the nature of the conflict between Bird and Davenport? How would you describe the nature of the conflict between Davenport and Lee? Why have these disputes emerged in the manner they have?
2. Based on your assessment of the situation, what are the potential risks and benefits if the president of ABI supports Davenport's decision? What are the potential risks and benefits if he supports Lee's request?
3. In the initial discussions concerning this problem, Bird's voice was noticeably absent. What accounts for this silence?

4. In your judgment, what is the best course of action from Bird's standpoint? Is he better off remaining in Korea at AmKor, returning to ABI in California, or leaving the company altogether? Why?

5. What recommendations would you make to the president of ABI to resolve this dilemma? Why is this the best possible course of action?

6. Finally, looking back on the experience, what could the company or the key executives involved have done differently to avoid the kinds of conflicts that emerged at AmKor?

NOTES

1. Ihlwan Moon and Chester Dawson, "Building a Camry Fighter," *Business Week,* September 6, 2004, pp. 62–63.

2. Cliff Edwards and Ihlwan Moon, "The Samsung Way," *Business Week,* June 16, 2003, pp. 56–64; David Ricks and Ihlwan Moon, "Samsung Design," *Business Week,* December 6, 2004, pp. 88–90.

3. Randall Schuler, Susan Jackson, and Yadong Luo, *Managing Human Resources in Cross-Border Alliances* (London: Routledge, 2004).

4. Ricky Griffin and Michael Pustay, *International Business* (Upper Saddle River, NJ: Prentice Hall, 2005).

5. Ibid.

6. Jeremy Main, "Making a Global Alliance Work," *Fortune,* December 17, 1990, pp. 121–26.

7. Evan Ramstad, "East Meets West in TV Sets," *Wall Street Journal,* November 26, 2004, p. A7.

8. "The Second Transition: A Survey of Spain," *Economist,* June 24, 2004, pp. 3–16.

9. Helen Wattley-Ames, *Spain Is Different* (Yarmouth, ME: Intercultural, 1999).

10. Edward F. Stanton, *Culture and Customs of Spain* (Westport, CT: Greenwood, 2002).

11. Ibid.

12. "The Second Transition: A Survey of Spain," *Economist,* June 24, 2004, pp. 3–16.

13. Peggy Kenna and Sondra Lacy, *Business Spain: A Practical Guide to Understanding Spanish Business Culture* (Chicago: Passport Books, 1995).

14. Kae Chung, Hak Chong Lee, and Ku Hyun Jung, *Korean Management: Global Strategy and Cultural Transformation* (Berlin: de Gruyter, 1997); Gerardo Ungson, Richard Steers, and Seung-Ho Park, *Korean Enterprise: The Quest for Globalization* (Boston: Harvard Business School Press, 1997).

15. Ungson, Steers, and Park, *Korean Enterprise.*

16. Chris Rowley, Tae-Won Sohn, and Johngseok Bae, eds., *Managing Korean Business: Organization, Culture, Human Resources, and Change* (London: Frank Cass, 2002).

17. Richard Steers, *Made in Korea: Chung Ju Yung and the Rise of Hyundai* (New York: Routledge, 1999).

18. Schuler, Jackson, and Luo, *Managing Human Resources in Cross-Border Alliances*; Oded Shenkar and Yadong Luo, *International Business* (New York: Wiley, 2004).

19. This exercise was adapted from actual events, although the names and some of the circumstances have been changed.

12 Strategies for International Negotiation

GENERAL ELECTRIC MEETS MITSUBISHI

For more than a century, General Electric (GE) dominated the market for electrical goods such as control panels and circuit breakers.[1] But in recent years, increased competition from both Asia and Europe seriously eroded its market share, and the company was determined to reestablish itself in this lucrative global market. GE had a long-standing relationship with Japan's Fuji, but this alliance failed to produce the desired results. Maybe a new partner would help. Jeff Depew, an aspiring young manager, was assigned the task of laying the groundwork to make this happen. Fluent in Japanese, he was sent to Japan with instructions to cultivate a new relationship with Mitsubishi, one of Japan's premier electrical equipment manufacturers and a possible partner for GE's new strategy. It was made clear to him by his boss that success in this assignment would position him well for continued career growth when he returned to the United States.

After he arrived in Tokyo, Depew began to carefully nurture relationships with his counterparts at Mitsubishi and over time won their respect and trust. What he envisioned was a quantum leap of the sort that would catch the attention of GE's CEO, Jack Welch. Welch valued managers who could take control and make deals happen. He wasted little time on the niceties of negotiation and preferred to work with people who thought as big as he did. To Depew, a possible alliance between GE and Mitsubishi was just such a venture. The partnership would catapult them into a position of dominance in the global market with combined annual sales of $3.5 billion. As Depew saw it, the partnership made strategic and economic sense for both partners. The combined company would be the world leader in six of its eight product lines and would allow GE to establish a working relationship with a leading Japanese conglomerate.

After lengthy and promising discussions between the two prospective partners, Depew was finally ready to invite GE's CEO to come to Japan to meet Moriya

249

Shiiki, Welch's counterpart at Mitsubishi. The visit (called an *aisatsu*, or formal ceremonial greeting) would be a brief get-acquainted meeting to demonstrate GE's commitment to the project and to begin to establish a working relationship between the two CEOs. When Welch arrived, Depew briefed him on the progress that had been made, as well as the tasks that remained to be done. While many details of the agreement were yet to be worked out, everything looked good to Depew, and he estimated that a deal could be reached after approximately five months of further cultivation and negotiation. Welch was obviously pleased and excited about the prospects. A meeting was scheduled for the next morning with Mitsubishi.

The scheduled meeting was a standard protocol session—the type of mating dance that precedes all major mergers. Not only did Welch understand this, but he had participated in several such rituals, most recently when he met with the CEO of RCA to consummate its acquisition by GE. The RCA meeting studiously avoided specific discussions about business. Instead, only general issues were discussed, such as the state of the U.S. electronics industry and Japanese competition. It was only later in private meetings that the actual subject of the acquisition arose. The meeting between Welch and Shiiki would proceed along a similar path. The two CEOs would exchange pleasantries, declare their mutual respect for each other, and withdraw. It was too early to discuss details; subordinates would handle those discussions later.

When Jack Welch and his colleagues arrived at the Mitsubishi building for the scheduled meeting, he was both well prepared and enthusiastic. He was ushered into the conference room and formally introduced to Shiiki and his subordinates. To Depew, both executives were impressive. Shiiki was the epitome of the Japanese executive: dignified, elegant, smooth, and very much in control. As they exchanged business cards, both executives began with a profuse exchange of thanks along with the expected expressions of mutual admiration.

But then without notice, Welch quickly ended the pleasantries and launched into a discussion of why a deal was attractive to GE: the product lines were impressive, the cultures could work well together, and everything seemed to be a good fit. The venture would be a powerful concern, one that would allow both Mitsubishi and GE to smash the competition. Shiiki nodded his head quietly while Welch went on to point out that in the past, GE had tried to do deals with other big Japanese companies but had always had troubles. Maybe this time would be different, he observed. He noted that both firms had large bureaucracies, but that this should not get in the way. Then he surprised everyone by suggesting that the two companies should agree to a deal then and there.

Depew was surprised but couldn't betray his emotions in the meeting. He sat quietly but nervously. GE had crossed the protocol line. Perhaps they could have gotten away with this in the United States, but not in Japan, where protocol was religiously observed. It was highly inappropriate to press for an immediate commitment when negotiating with the Japanese—especially when Mitsubishi had already agreed to GE's proposed five-month timetable for closure of the deal. Shiiki looked over at Depew as if to say, "What's going on here?" but Depew didn't have the slightest idea. After a long period of silence, Shiiki reiterated his desire to go ahead with the plan—a subtle yet significant indication of how badly his company wanted to finalize the agreement. However, Shiiki was not about to conclude a final agreement on the spot.

It was well understood by both parties, though not discussed, that Mitsubishi was trying to extricate itself from a long-standing agreement with GE rival Westinghouse. Mitsubishi was aware that Westinghouse was quietly preparing to abandon its business in Japan, and Shiiki needed a new American partner on whom he could depend for the foreseeable future. GE suited his goals perfectly. However, Japanese etiquette required Mitsubishi to inform Westinghouse of its intentions to change partners. But when Shiiki mentioned his obligation to inform Westinghouse before making a formal commitment to GE, Welch questioned why this was necessary. Shiiki tried without success to explain the nature of the relationship, but Welch concluded that his counterpart was trying to play GE against Westinghouse. He reiterated that he didn't want to move forward unless Mitsubishi was unequivocally commited to the partnership. Shiiki assured him that this was the true and that the agreement would be completed in due time.

With that, the meeting broke up amicably and Welch and his colleagues returned to their hotel. Later that evening, Welch observed that he had pressed Shiiki because he concluded that if the agreement was not concluded quickly, it would not be concluded at all. He was convinced that Shiiki's reluctance to quickly agree to the proposal meant that he was not serious about it. The next morning, while Welch made a courtesy call on the Ministry of Trade and Industry, Depew returned to Mitsubishi. This meeting went better than the previous one, and a consensus was soon reached concerning how negotiations should proceed and how the agreement should be structured. The deal was back on track. Welch returned to New York and Depew was assigned the task of moving things forward.

Several weeks later, however, Depew received a call from his boss in New York telling him that Welch was leaning against signing the agreement. Welch felt he had been sandbagged and embarrassed by one of the most prominent leaders of the Japanese business community. The only way to save the deal now, Depew was told, was for Shiiki to write a personal letter of apology to Welch in which he stated unequivocally that he would agree to the proposal. Depew dutifully approached Mitsubishi with his orders. After some negotiation, it appeared that Mitsubishi was on the verge of complying with Welch's demand when Depew received another call from his boss notifying him to break off all negotiations with Mitsubishi. Instead, he was to return to GE's earlier partner, Fuji, and attempt to rebuild relationships so a new joint venture could be developed.

Two months later, Jeff Depew was recalled to New York headquarters. His boss explained that GE had decided to take a different approach to the Asia/Pacific region, focusing more on sales than on business development. As a result of the change, GE was eliminating his position. He now works for General Motors.

What is going on here? How could this happen? And what junior manager would like his or her career cut short by events beyond his or her control? The example of GE and Mitsubishi illustrates just some of the challenges and problems of trying to negotiate contracts across cultures. In this chapter, we will examine several of these issues and consider how global managers can increase their chances of success.

STEPS IN INTERNATIONAL NEGOTIATION

On the surface, the negotiation process is generally the same across most parts of the globe. What varies, however, as evidenced by the above example, is how cultural differences can often affect some of the more subtle aspects of this process. While these differences may often be difficult to detect, a global manager's awareness of them is nonetheless vitally important for a successful negotiation. In international negotiation, culture is both a determinant of negotiation style and scope, as well as a tool to catch your opponent off guard and win concessions. The smart bargainer understands this.

The typical bargaining process passes through six stages: (1) preparation, (2) building a relationship with the other party, (3) exchanging information and making the first offer, (4) persuasion, (5) concessions, and (6) achieving a final agreement (see Exhibit 12.1). Sometimes these stages will flow in a neat, sequential pattern; other times the negotiations will jump back and forth from stage to stage depending on how they are progressing. In either case, each step is characterized by certain focused activities aimed at ultimately reaching an agreement that is viable for both parties.

PREPARATION

The success of an international negotiation often hinges on the preparation and advance planning that go into it. Before meeting with a prospective partner, each side must answer a series of questions that help them understand what they are facing. These questions include:

- *Is it worth negotiating?* Will your negotiation likely lead to a good outcome? Is the other side willing (and able) to negotiate in good faith? Are both sides in the same ballpark so earnest efforts can lead to a compromise?
- *What does your company want from the negotiation?* What does your side hope to achieve? What are the limits beyond which it will not go? Are you being sent by your company to negotiate a settlement or stall for time?
- *What does the other party want?* Can the other party actually deliver on what it promises? Does it need other approvals to proceed (e.g., from its government)? Is it currently negotiating with your competitors? Can you trust it?
- *Is your team prepared to negotiate?* Do you and your team members have the necessary technical skills, negotiation experience, language capabilities, and cultural knowledge to negotiate successfully?
- *Is there an agreed-upon agenda for your negotiation sessions?* Is the agenda as presented consistent with your company goals and objectives?
- *Do you have sufficient time to conclude the negotiations satisfactorily?* Are you being rushed unnecessarily, either by your company or by the other party? Will you know when it's time to leave the negotiating table and call it quits?
- *Do you understand the negotiating environment?* Where will negotiations take place? Will you have secure access to your company headquarters? Will you

Exhibit 12.1

Stages in the International Negotiation Process

Stages of Negotiation	Critical Issues and Questions
1 Preparation	What are the critical issues to be addressed in the negotiation? What do you know about your prospective partner? What are your objectives and limitations in the negotiation? What are your prospective partner's objectives and limitations? What is your plan of action? What are your backup plans?
2 Building the relationship	How important is it to develop a close personal relationship with your prospective partner? If it is important, what is your plan to develop it? How much warm-up is necessary prior to serious negotiations?
3 Exchanging information and first offers	How much information are you willing to share with the other party? How much information do you need from the other party? How will you get this information? What is your first offer? What are your backup offers?
4 Persuasion	How will you convince the other party to make a deal? What persuasion tactics will you use? How will you respond to persuasion tactics by the other party?
5 Concessions	Will you use a sequential or holistic approach to negotiation and concession making? At what point in the negotiations will you make concessions? How far are you willing to go in making concessions?
6 Agreement or dissolution of negotiations	What do you need to make the deal? When do you walk away from the deal? If the negotiations are successful, what steps will be required to make the new partnership work for the long term?

need to adjust for jet lag? Do you require interpreters and, if so, can you trust them?

- *What is your plan?* Finally, do you clearly understand what you are trying to accomplish? What are the principal issues? What are your opening moves?

Experienced negotiators understand the need to be flexible. However, they also understand the importance of knowing exactly how far they or their company are willing to go before it is necessary to pull the plug and return home.

BUILDING THE RELATIONSHIP

In many cultures, business is built on long-standing personal relationships. This is as true in France and Mexico as it is in Japan and Saudi Arabia. People do business with partners they know, people they can trust. As such, many international negotiations begin with both sides trying to establish a personal bond. This does not necessarily mean they plan to become lifelong friends; rather, each side needs to determine whether the other party is sufficiently trustworthy to conclude an agreement and stick with it. In many countries, it is insulting (as well as unproductive) to begin a business discussion until after such relationships have been firmly established. In these cultures, it is often said that business relationships must be "warmed up" before the parties get down to serious negotiations. This is a good principle to remember.

Ironically, the one place where such relationships, while important, are not necessarily critical to a successful negotiation is the United States, where legal contracts are frequently seen as a substitute for personal relationships. Indeed, legal contracts in the United States are typically seen as being far superior to the proverbial handshake among honorable people. (Or, as legendary moviemaker Louis B. Mayer used to say, "A handshake is only as good as the paper it's written on.") As a result, U.S. negotiators are notorious for wanting to get down to business, a practice that frequently leads to frustration and failure. More successful U.S. negotiators understand the critical importance of subtleties and patience, not brashness and drive.

As a result, most successful international managers—regardless of their home country—invest considerable time and effort in getting to know their prospective partners. This frequently includes a variety of social activities (dinners, golf, etc.) where it is often inappropriate to discuss any business whatsoever. The stage is being set.

EXCHANGING INFORMATION AND FIRST OFFERS

When the two parties finally come face-to-face to discuss business, we can again see variations in approach based on cultural differences. Some of these differences are summarized in Exhibits 12.2 and 12.3. Exhibit 12.2 illustrates how cultures can differ in approaching bargaining in general. For example, negotiators in individualistic cultures tend to set high personal goals for bargaining and quickly reject proposals that fall short of their goals, while collectivistic bargainers are more likely to seek mutually beneficial compromises from the beginning of the negotiations (see Chapters 7 and 8). Likewise, high-context negotiators often prefer indirect methods of information sharing (e.g., a quiet discussion over dinner), while low-context negotiators often prefer more direct information sharing (e.g., making formal proposals at the bargaining table). One is not superior to the other; they are just different. However, this difference becomes paramount depending on who is participating in the negotiations.

Similarly, Exhibit 12.3 shows how culture can affect the specific issues of information sharing and first offers. That is, managers in some cultures seek inexhaustible technical details about a product or service being discussed, while managers in other cultures will ignore most of the product details and continue to focus on relationship building. At some point in the process, each side will make its *first offer*, its initial bargaining position. In some cultures (e.g., Russia), first offers are often totally unrealistic, whereas in other cultures (e.g., Japan) they are often close to the

Exhibit 12.2

Cultural Influences on Negotiating Behavior

Cultural Dimensions	Negotiating Behavior
Individualistic	Win-lose; sets high personal goals in bargaining and rejects offers below this as long as possible; focuses on self-interest and personal goal attainment over the interests of other parties
Collectivistic	Win-win; cooperates with group members (often on both sides of the table) in search of a mutually beneficial agreement
Hierarchical	Focuses on using all available power and influence tactics (e.g., authority, status, persuasion) to achieve goals
Egalitarian	Focuses on issues and shares information on priorities and interests, noting similarities and differences
High context	Prefers indirect or subtle information sharing
Low context	Prefers direct or open information sharing

Source: Adapted from J.M. Brett, "Culture and Negotiation," *International Journal of Psychology* 35 (2000): 97–104.

Exhibit 12.3

Information Exchange and First Offers by Culture

Cultures	Information Exchanged	First Offer
Americans	Information provided directly and briefly, often through multimedia presentations; assumption that if agreement can be reached in principle, details can be resolved later	5–10 percent below desired end result
Japanese	Extensive requests for proposal details and technical information; assumption that all details of proposal must be discussed before agreement can be reached	10–20 percent below desired end result
Latin Americans	Focus more on information about the relationship and less on technical details of proposal; preliminary discussions focus on why business should be done together, not on how it should be done	20–40 percent below desired end result
Arabs	Focus more on information about the relationship and less on technical details of proposal; preliminary discussions focus on why business should be done together, not on how it should be done	20–50 percent below desired end result
Russians	Extensive requests for proposal details and technical information; assumption that all details of proposal must be discussed before agreement can be reached	50–60 percent below desired end result

Source: Adapted from Lillian Chaney and Jeannette Martin, *International Business Communication* (Englewood Cliffs, NJ: Prentice Hall, 1995), pp. 183–84.

Exhibit 12.4

Negotiating Tactics in the United States, Japan, and Brazil

Negotiating Tactics	Number of Times Used in Thirty-Minute Bargaining Session		
	Americans	Japanese	Brazilians
Verbal negotiation tactics:			
Offering rewards or incentives	2	1	2
Making promises	8	7	3
Making threats	4	4	2
Making normative appeals to higher goals	1	1	0
Giving orders or commands	6	8	14
Interrupting opponent	10	13	29
Rejections (saying no)	9	6	83
Nonverbal negotiation tactics:			
Silent periods	4	6	0
Facial glazing or staring into space	3	1	5
Touching opponent	0	0	5

Source: Adapted from John Graham, "The Influence of Culture on the Process of Business Negotiations," *Journal of International Business Studies* 14 (1983): 84–88.

final bargaining position. This first offer initiates the negotiating process, which the parties hope will culminate in a final agreement.

PERSUASION

At this point in the negotiations, each party will employ various persuasion techniques to convince the other party that its offer needs improvement—often significant improvement. Persuasion can take one of three forms: verbal negotiation tactics, nonverbal negotiation tactics, and so-called dirty tricks. *Verbal negotiation tactics* include rewards (e.g., we can offer you repeat business if you agree to our terms), promises (e.g., if you do something for us, we will do something for you), threats (e.g., if you don't agree now, we will block your products from local markets), normative appeals (e.g., this is how we do business in this country), commands (e.g., you must accept our offer), interruptions (both parties talking at the same time), and rejections (e.g., refusing the offer).

In the same negotiations, managers may frequently use *nonverbal negotiation tactics*, such as periods of silence, facial glazing (staring into space), and touching. Again, the use of these tactics varies considerably across cultures. In this regard, an interesting study among Japanese, Brazilian, and American managers found significant differences in both verbal and nonverbal bargaining tactics during thirty-minute bargaining sessions (see Exhibit 12.4). Notice, for example, how often negotiators in each country interrupted their opponent, said no, or touched their opponent. What does this say about cultural variations in negotiations?

Finally, *dirty tricks* is the term used by international negotiators to describe unfair, deceitful, or unethical tactics used to win a negotiation. Examples of so-called dirty

Exhibit 12.5

Questionable Tactics in International Negotiations

Questionable Tactics by Negotiators	Possible Responses
Deliberate deception: Deliberately misrepresenting the facts of an offer to make it look better than it is	Point out possible deception to opponent
Stalling: Delaying negotiations and pushing for concessions to close a deal prior to opponent's departure	Do not reveal time of departure
Escalating authority: Agreeing to a deal but then claiming it must be approved by superiors, hoping to extract further concessions	Clarify decision authority prior to negotiations
Good cop–bad cop: One negotiator suggesting an opponent make concessions to win over his or her obstructive partner	Ignore ploy and focus instead on mutual benefits of agreement
Poverty appeal: Appealing to opponent's sense of fairness or equity as the "richer" partner	Ignore ploy and focus instead on mutual benefits of agreement
Appealing to friendship: Pointing to long-standing friendship between parties that should not be jeopardized, thereby pressuring opponent to make concessions to maintain the friendship	Maintain a psychological distance from negotiator that reflects true nature of relationship

Source: Adapted from Michael Kublin, *International Negotiating* (New York: International Business Press, 1995).

tricks that are frequently seen in international negotiations include the following:

- Negotiators may deliberately misrepresent the facts or promise things they know they cannot deliver.
- Negotiators may use stalling tactics to force their opponent's hand; this is frequently seen when negotiators hold up an agreement until they know their opponent is scheduled to depart the country, hoping for a last-minute concession to secure an agreement.
- Negotiators may also tentatively agree to a deal, only to then say that a higher authority must approve the agreement and that another concession will make this approval easier.
- Negotiators may play "good cop–bad cop"; that is, one negotiator may quietly tell his or her opponent that his or her partner is intransigent and needs to be appeased by one more concession.
- Negotiators may claim poverty and point out that their opponent represents a richer company or country and should take pity on them.
- Finally, negotiators may appeal to a long-standing friendship with their opponent or their opponent's firm, even if one doesn't exist.[2]

Exhibit 12.5 summarizes these dirty tricks, along with some suggested responses.

Experts also suggest four general responses to the use of dirty tricks in international bargaining: First, one should avoid using such tricks to set an acceptable standard and encourage one's opponent to be more forthright. Second, one should point out dirty tricks when and where they happen, thereby discouraging their further use. Third, one should be prepared to walk out of a negotiation if the other party fails to negotiate in good faith. Remember, if the other party can't be trusted during negotiations, why should they be trusted after the agreement is signed? Finally, one should keep in mind that ethical systems differ by culture, and that one's opponents may not feel they are doing anything wrong. Remember: Persuasion is an art form and like any art form it has many manifestations. Some of these are principled; some are not. At the end of the day, the question all negotiators must face is whether they wish to do business with the other party. In this decision, the use of dirty tricks by the other party hardly plays an encouraging role.

CONCESSIONS AND AGREEMENT

Obviously, the ultimate goal of a negotiation is to arrive at a mutually agreed upon contract that is legally binding in both countries. To achieve this, concessions must be made. What is interesting here is that culture can at times influence how these concessions are determined. In North America, for example, companies frequently use what is called a *sequential approach to concession making* (see Exhibit 12.6). That is, they prefer to go through a proposed contract sequentially, item by item, and get agreement on each item as they progress.

By contrast, and popular in most of Asia, is the *holistic approach to concession making*. Here, the two parties work their way through the entire proposed agreement but do not agree to anything until they have completed their review. They then discuss the contract in its entirety and make final proposals and counterproposals aimed at reaching a complete agreement. The holistic approach frequently perplexes novice North American negotiators when they learn that a point they thought was already agreed to resurfaces to be discussed later by their Asian counterparts.

A final difference between typical North American and Asian approaches to contract negotiations focuses on the meaning of the contract itself. To most Americans, a contract is a legal document that spells out the obligations of both parties. It represents the culmination of a successful negotiation process. In many parts of Asia (e.g., China, Japan), by contrast, a contract is thought of as a written recognition of a personal relationship between the two parties. As such, it is the beginning, not the end, of the process of mutual benefit as a result of working together. Indeed, many Asian companies prefer to have only very general contracts in the belief that it is impossible to anticipate all future circumstances that may affect the contract. As circumstances change, it is often expected that the contract will be modified to fit the new situation. After all, an honorable person would not take advantage of his or her partner if changes occur that were not caused by the two partners. For example, if an unexpected price change causes one partner to lose money on a transaction, the other partner will often modify his or her payments to accommodate. Honorable people

Exhibit 12.6

Sequential and Holistic Bargaining Strategies

Bargaining Strategy	Negotiation Process
Sequential bargaining	Both parties work through a contract item by item, gaining agreement on each item as the negotiations proceed.
Holistic bargaining	Both parties negotiate the entire contract as a whole, moving back and forth across items until both are satisfied with the entire document.

look after the interests of each other. The American and European legal systems see it somewhat differently.

BASIC NEGOTIATING STRATEGIES

There are two basic strategies for negotiation: competitive negotiation and problem-solving negotiation. The competitive approach views negotiations as a win-lose game, while the problem-solving approach seeks to discover a win-win solution where both sides can benefit if at all possible. Exhibit 12.7 illustrates how these two different strategies are played out during negotiation.

In *competitive negotiations*, each side tries to give as little as possible. Negotiators frequently begin with unrealistically high demands and make concessions only grudgingly. Competitive negotiators will at times use dirty tricks or other tactics that allow them to win. Little thought is given to building a long-term relationship between the parties. And since starting from inflexible positions often leads to outcomes that satisfy neither side, each side often develops negative attitudes toward the other. As a result, losers in the agreement often seek revenge, such as reneging on parts of the contract at a later date or substituting inferior-quality materials in production orders.

By contrast, *problem-solving negotiations* begin with the basic tenet that negotiators must separate positions from interests. Instead of defending a company's position as a major goal in the negotiation process, problem-solving negotiators begin by seeking a mutually satisfactory ground that is beneficial to the interests of both sides. Dirty tricks are avoided because they poison the development of long-term mutually advantageous relationships. Objective information is preferred wherever possible as a basis for discussion and problem-solving efforts, instead of unrealistic sales pitches or hyperbole. Oftentimes, problem-solving negotiation facilitates the identification of creative new ways to provide both parties with what they want to achieve. And even when mutually advantageous solutions are not found, both sides leave the table believing that sincere efforts were made on both sides of the table. This leaves open the possibility of returning to the bargaining table in the future when another opportunity presents itself.

There are three important points to remember regarding the choice between using competitive or problem-solving bargaining strategies: First, it is very easy in cross-cultural negotiations to misread the intentions of the other party. Hence, a detailed understanding of the cultural background of one's opponents becomes

Exhibit 12.7

Competitive and Problem-Solving Bargaining Strategies

Stages in Negotiation	Competitive Strategy	Problem-Solving Strategy
1. Preparation	Identify current economic and other benefits your firm seeks from the deal. Prepare to defend your firm's position.	Define the long-term strategic interests of your firm. Prepare to overcome cross-cultural barriers to defining mutual interests.
2. Relationship building	Look for weaknesses in your opponent's position. Learn about your opponent, but reveal as little as possible.	Adapt to the other side's culture. Separate the people involved in the negotiation from the problems and goals that need to be solved.
3. Information exchange and first offer	Provide as little information as possible to your opponent. Make your position explicit. Make a hard offer that is more favorable to your side than you realistically expect to receive.	Give and demand to receive objective information that clarifies each party's interests. Accept cultural differences in speed of response and type of information needs. Make firm but reasonable first offer.
4. Persuasion	Use dirty tricks and pressure tactics where appropriate to win.	Search for new creative options that benefit the interests of both parties.
5. Concessions	Begin with high initial demands. Make concessions slowly and grudgingly.	Search for mutually acceptable criteria for reaching accord. Accept cultural differences in starting position and in how and when concessions are made.
6. Agreement	Sign only if you win and then ensure that you sign an ironclad contract.	Sign when the interests of your firm are met. Adapt to cultural differences in contracts where necessary.

critical in determining whether he or she is stating a highly inflexible position or offering a genuine opportunity to strike a deal. This is why many successful international negotiators always have advisers at their side who are intimately familiar with the culture and traditions of the other party. Second, culture sometimes predisposes negotiators to select one approach over the other. For example, observers note that some American managers believe there must be a winner and a loser, while many Japanese managers prefer a problem-solving approach. The smart bargainer understands this and adjusts his or her strategy accordingly. Finally, most experts on international negotiation recommend a problem-solving approach, where possible, because it tends to lead to better long-term solutions and relationships.

STRATEGIES FOR SUCCESSFUL INTERNATIONAL NEGOTIATION

Successful international negotiators are comfortable in multicultural environments and are skilled in building and maintaining interpersonal relationships. But a career in this arena is not for the faint of heart; this is a difficult job that requires a number of very specific skills, as well as an ability to handle significant amounts of conflict and stress. Successes come slowly and failures are commonplace. Even so, it is possible to identify a number of personal factors that often differentiate between successful and unsuccessful negotiators: (1) a tolerance for ambiguity; (2) patience, patience, patience; (3) flexibility and creativity; (4) a good sense of humor; (5) solid physical and mental stamina; (6) cultural empathy; (7) curiosity and a willingness to learn new things; and (8) a knowledge of foreign languages.

Beyond these personal qualities, experts suggest several general strategies that have been found to facilitate successful negotiations, including the following:[3]

- Concentrate on building long-term relationships with your partner, not short-term contracts. Long-term partners usually yield greater long-term results for both parties.
- Focus on understanding the organizational and personal interests and goals behind the stated bargaining positions. The Latin phrase *cui bono?* (who benefits?) is certainly appropriate in these situations. What do the various parties to the negotiation hope to gain from an agreement?
- Avoid overreliance on cultural generalizations. While there may be cultural trends within specific countries, no nation is monolithic and people can vary widely in their personal characteristics.
- Be sensitive to timing. Some cultures—and some negotiators—require considerable patience in working toward an agreement, while others demand prompt resolution of all issues or they will go elsewhere.
- Remain flexible throughout the negotiations. Circumstances, available information, and opportunities often change, and success sometimes hinges on both being prepared and being alert.
- Plan carefully. Nowhere is the old adage that knowledge is power more apt than in understanding international negotiations. Solid preparations can make all the difference.
- Learn to listen, not just speak. Develop good listening skills to understand both the content and the context of the message. Use body language and facial expressions to identify informal or subtle cues or intentions.

Based on these strategies, negotiators should be in a better position to pursue productive agreements. With this in mind, we turn from the general to the specific and examine the challenge of negotiating in Japan and Brazil. Where appropriate, comparisons will be made with typical approaches found in the United States.

NEGOTIATING WITH THE JAPANESE: INSIDE THE JAPANESE *KEIRETSU*

Business management in Japan was discussed in some detail in Chapter 9. In this section, we will build on this earlier discussion to examine the specific issue of how typical Japanese firms tend to negotiate with global clients. This will then be compared with typical Brazilian approaches to bargaining and negotiation. Japan and Brazil represent two very different approaches to bargaining and, when compared both against each other and against typical U.S. approaches, they present a complex picture concerning how best to succeed in global negotiations. We begin with the uniquely Japanese concept of *shinyo*.

To understand how international negotiations can vary across cultures, consider what happens when American managers try to negotiate with their Japanese counterparts. As noted above, American and Japanese executives often approach international negotiations very differently. To a large extent, these differences can be attributed to cultural differences that influence interpersonal interactions. For example, a key factor in determining whether to do business with someone in Japan is *shinyo*. *Shinyo* refers to the mutual confidence, trust, and honor that are required on both sides for a business relationship to succeed. Unless you trust your partner implicitly, it is not wise to pursue a business relationship and nothing happens. This concept, while easy to understand, is nonetheless difficult for some foreigners to implement. This is in part because of many Westerners' fervent belief in the power of the legal contract over the importance of a personal relationship.

In addition to *shinyo*, other differences can often be seen between Japanese negotiators and their American counterparts, as shown in Exhibit 12.8. (This exhibit also includes negotiating trends among Brazilian managers, which are discussed below. See Negotiating with Brazilians.)

Adding a touch of humor to this comparison, John Graham and Yoshihiro Sano, in their book entitled *Smart Bargaining*, describe a "typical" American negotiator as someone who resembles John Wayne (or Bruce Willis, Arnold Schwarzenegger, or Sylvester Stallone—take your pick).[4] According to Graham and Sano, the "John Wayne bargaining strategy" is characterized by the following personal beliefs on the part of the highly individualistic negotiator:

- I can do this by myself; I don't need any help.
- I am who I am. If you don't like me, too bad.
- Let's talk on a first-name basis. Formality just gets in my way.
- Of course we'll speak in English. Why would you expect me to speak Japanese?
- I make my own decisions. I don't need to check with anybody.
- Get to the point. Don't waste my time.
- Put your cards on the table.
- Don't just sit there; say something. I don't trust quiet people.
- I don't take no for an answer.
- Let's keep this simple and do one thing at a time.
- A deal is a deal. If you signed it, you own it.

Fortunately, many Americans do not match this stereotype. In fact, many Americans are quite adept at cross-cultural interactions and negotiations. However, some Americans—and a host of others from various countries around the world—are indeed like this, much to the detriment of their companies (and spouses). So, humor aside, it is important to recognize that the rugged individualist seldom achieves his or her goals at the bargaining table. The winners in international negotiation are usually those who make an effort to build solid interpersonal relationships and trust,

Exhibit 12.8

U.S., Japanese, and Brazilian Negotiating Styles

Negotiating Strategy	Americans	Japanese	Brazilians
Ultimate goal	Short-term profitability, often with personal benefit for negotiator	Long-term profitability, usually without personal benefit	Long-term mutually beneficial relationships
Ideal negotiating climate	Straightforward and impersonal	Oblique and at times personal	Impromptu; difficult to generalize
Risk orientation	Risk-oriented	Risk-averse	Risk-averse
Communication style	Low-context; talks directly; frequently blunt; sometimes exaggerates	High context; talks indirectly; seldom blunt; extensive use of technical language	High context; talks indirectly; frequently emotional; frequently exaggerates
Emotional sensitivity	Emotional sensitivity avoided; negotiators often avoid close personal relationships	Emotional sensitivity avoided; strong personal relationships critical for success	Emotional sensitivity highly valued; strong personal relationships critical for success
Basis of decisions	Decisions usually made on a cost-benefit basis for the short term	Decisions usually made on a cost-benefit basis for the long term	Decisions often tied to emotional or family considerations
Importance of face saving	Face saving not critical; embarrassing opponent may lead to an advantage in negotiations	Face saving critical; embarrassing either party to the negotiation should be avoided at all costs	Face saving critical; embarrassing either party to the negotiation should be avoided if possible
Dispute resolution	Preference for contract language and litigation over conciliation for dispute resolution	Preference for conciliation and contract renegotiation over litigation	Preference for conciliation and contract renegotiation over litigation
Conflict	At times argumentative, especially when put on the defensive	Seldom argumentative; uncomfortable with serious conflict	Argumentative, but uncomfortable with serious conflict

and then use this as a foundation to seek mutually advantageous agreements and contracts for the long run.

NEGOTIATING WITH BRAZILIANS: INSIDE THE BRAZILIAN *EMPRESA*

Not surprisingly, Brazil's culture—and its approach to negotiation—differs from that of Japan. In contrast to Japan's position as a long-established industrial power, Brazil is often described as one of the world's most attractive emerging markets. Multinationals from various countries are increasingly establishing subsidiaries or doing business in Brazil in one way or another. In this environment, knowing how to negotiate with Brazilians is crucial for any serious global manager. In other words, international negotiators dealing with Brazil are more likely to succeed if they know a little about the country and understand its culture, its way of doing business, and its negotiation style.

There is an old Brazilian saying: "Brazil is the country of the future—and it always will be." This popular proverb reflects the puzzling reality of a country that has the potential to become a key player in the global economy but has been slow in realizing it. Brazil ranks among the top ten global economies but is seventy-fourth in per capita income. It has a world-class industrial base but a backward agricultural social system that is characteristic of many third world nations.[5] To understand this paradox, it is helpful to know something about Brazil's peoples and cultures.

BRAZILIAN CULTURE AND SOCIAL PATTERNS

Brazil is the world's sixth largest country in landmass and the only Portuguese-speaking country in South America. With a population of 170 million people, it is the world's fifth most populous country and a melting pot of peoples from all over the world.[6] Initially colonized by the Portuguese and later settled by other Europeans, Brazil was a major player in the global slave trade for several centuries, importing more than 3 million slaves between the 1500s and 1800s (compared to about 750,000 in the United States). In contrast to the United States, however, interracial marriage has always been common and has resulted in a largely racially mixed population. Indeed, interracial marriages over the centuries have created an ethnic diversity that makes it difficult to classify people into traditional racial groupings. For this reason, ethnic background has always been less important in Brazil than it is in Europe or North America. The overriding cultural identity of most citizens is that of being Brazilian.

This rich mixture of ethnic backgrounds provided fertile ground for cultural integration. Catholicism blended with African and indigenous religious practices, creating a unique version of Catholicism that is permeated by symbols and rites from other nonwhite religions. This created a culture where Western and non-Western values coexist side by side, even in the world of business. For example, many Brazilian managers follow standard Western business practices but also read the daily horoscopes published in the major business magazines. Superstitious practices are common, even among the well-educated business elite.

However, while racial differences are less important in Brazil, regional differences can be significant and need to be considered when doing business. Different regions of Brazil were settled by peoples from different cultural backgrounds and, as a result, business practices can differ.[7] For example, São Paulo, the business capital of the country, is a cosmopolitan area with a business culture similar to that of other large Western cities. Here, the *paulista* is often portrayed as restless, work-oriented, attached to money and possessions, tenacious, formal, and action-oriented. By contrast, the southern region is largely agricultural and still exhibits the influence of its German and Italian settlers. Here are found the *gauchos,* who are often described as

Exhibit 12.9

Cultural Trends in Brazil and the United States

Brazil	United States
Relationship-focused	Task-focused
Focus on engagement	Focus on solutions
Relationships are diffuse to all situations	Relationships are specific to the situation
Strong personal loyalty to others	Personal loyalty to others varies
Belief in group and family support	Belief in self-help and initiative
Polychronic; belief in the relativity of time	Monochronic; belief in the value of time
Prefers "diplomatic" communication	Prefers direct communication
Nonverbal communication very important	Nonverbal communication less important
Significant displays of emotion	Moderate displays of emotion
Creative problem solving	Analytical problem solving
Focus on improvisation	Focus on planning
Decisions based on emotions	Decisions based on facts
Work as a means to survival	Work as a means of primary satisfaction
Rules as guidelines	Rules are to be followed
Formal working style	Informal working style
Dress style emphasizes fashion and appearance	Dress style emphasizes neatness and comfort

authoritarian, opportunistic, extroverted, individualistic, polite, and explosive. Rio de Janeiro is an important tourist destination given its pleasant warm climate and beautiful beaches. Visitors often describe Rio's local *carioca* as being easygoing, extroverted, friendly, speculative, irreverent, indolent, and favorably disposed to the good life. The central southern part of the country is dotted with gold mines, which have attracted numerous adventurers. As a result, *mineiros* have learned to protect themselves from outsiders and live in protected family circles. They are sometimes described as stern, quiet, introverted, reserved, suspicious, modest, and tolerant. Finally, the northeast of the country has the largest Afro-Brazilian population and a unique culture influenced by African religions, art, and identity. It is also the poorest and most backward part of the country. These regional differences are important to the Brazilian psyche and influence business practices.

Despite these regional differences, it is still possible to identify several important cultural trends shared by most Brazilians. Exhibit 12.9 summarizes these trends, using the United States as a point of reference. Brazilians are known for their relaxed, friendly, informal outlook. Foreigners seldom realize that beneath this layer of informality is a strong sense of pride and face, much like that found in several Asian countries (see Chapter 7). Brazilian informality is perhaps best characterized as "formal informality," as one often needs to balance an informal outlook with cautious, conservative behavior. For example, Brazilians are quick to use first names when meeting new people, but visitors often confuse this with informality when in fact it is only a practical solution for dealing with people's multiple last names. Indeed, in Brazil, alphabetical listings are frequently done based on first names instead of family names.

As in several Asian countries and most Latin American and Latin European countries, Brazilians emphasize relationships. Social relationships are critical and often take precedence over tasks and accomplishments. This focus influences the way businesses are run and deals are made, and cannot be taken lightly. For instance, a business meeting seldom focuses exclusively on business, and discussing family matters, hobbies, and general topics is commonplace. As a general rule Brazilians are not likely to close a deal before they know and trust their partners. They expect businesses to grow as the relationship between the partners grows. As a result, it is not surprising that doing business in Brazil can require a considerable investment of time.

At the same time, Brazilians are polychronic and are not fixated on rigid schedules. They see time as flexible and fluid, and schedules and plans are quickly changed or ignored completely. In addition, meetings seldom begin on time and may be interrupted frequently by other pressing events or unannounced visitors.

An emphasis on pride and personal relationships influences the way Brazilians communicate. The typical communication style is marked by what may be termed "diplomacy." That is, communication is indirect and full of subtleties, exaggerations, and euphemisms. Brazilians tend to avoid conflict and are generally not aggressive. However, the lively way they often express themselves can confuse outsiders. They communicate with their body, use plenty of hand movements, and touch others frequently. Emotions are important to Brazilians, and decisions are often tied closely to emotional issues. Open displays of emotion are commonplace.

ORGANIZATION AND MANAGEMENT IN BRAZIL

The Brazilian *empresa* faces one of the most bureaucratic environments in the world. A World Bank study estimates that Brazil is the second most bureaucratic country in the world, behind only Chad, a landlocked desert republic in north-central Africa.[8] Brazil also has some of the most rigid labor laws of the world, making it prohibitively expensive to dismiss employees. And it requires the largest number of bureaucratic actions to register property or to start or close a business, according to this study. Add to this a slow judiciary system and the situation only gets worse. Taxes are another burden for the Brazilian firm. On average, firms pay about fifty different types of taxes, including city taxes, state taxes, and federal taxes. Still worse, tax laws change quickly and the cost of keeping up with them is high. Just to give one example, there were more than 40,000 changes in Brazil's tax laws in 2003 alone.[9] Doing business in Brazil is not easy.

Brazilians deal with this uncertainty in two principal ways: remaining "under the law" and being flexible and adaptable. The Brazilian competitive scene is complex. On one hand, many small firms cannot afford to operate legally, because of the staggering taxes and bureaucratic costs. As a result, they intentionally remain small enough to go unnoticed by the government; they remain out of sight of the law. This results in one of the largest underground economies in the world (see Chapter 5). Larger firms that play by the rules—including many multinationals—often find it difficult to compete with many smaller firms that can avoid various costs and regulations and sell their products at lower prices. Smaller firms are also more flexible and adaptable during economic swings, which occur regularly in Brazil.

The apparent informality of Brazil's business environment often creates other problems as well. In a country where only 30 percent of the population is classified as middle class or above, selling to the poor is important business. To that end, credit and financing is crucial. However, the poor are likely to work in the underground economy and have a difficult time accounting for their money. Foreign banks are learning this lesson the hard way. Most of the untapped banking market is made up of people that survive the Brazilian way and do not offer the security foreigners require.[10] Brazilians have found ways to deal with this problem, though. For example, Casas Bahia, a prominent Brazilian retailer catering to the poor, finances 87 percent of its sales and has few problems collecting its debts. Its representatives explain that the secret is observing body language and asking questions without hurting the customer. As one manager observes, giving credit is all about "smelling and listening."[11]

On the positive side, Brazilians are considered to be one of the most adaptable people in the world. Indeed, a recent study ranked Brazilian managers as being the most flexible of the managers in the forty-eight countries they studied.[12] The country's permanent economic instability and pressures brought on by a highly bureaucratic government have taught Brazilians to adapt quickly and find innovative ways to deal with problems. Indeed, Brazilians seem eager to find alternative solutions for problems. A popular Brazilian phrase, *"jeitinho brasileiro"* (the Brazilian way), is commonly used to refer to finding creative solutions to seemingly intractable problems. Such creative solutions often include the use of personal influence or relationships to evade official rules.

The result of this unique business environment is a culture of improvisation. On the one hand, Brazilians have an unsettling flexibility and change plans quickly, often to the consternation of foreigners. On the other hand, Brazilians often implement new technologies and work methods more rapidly and with less conflict than many other countries. This innate flexibility makes rules secondary to relationships. Unable to comply with an overwhelming number of impractical rules, Brazilians have a tendency toward particularism; they temper the application of the law with the circumstances in which they find themselves or the people involved in the transaction (see Chapter 7). This characteristic is best expressed in an observation often attributed to Getúlio Vargas, a former Brazilian president: "For our friends, anything; for our enemies, nothing; for everyone else, the law."

Because of Brazil's rigid labor laws and high unemployment, employee mobility is low. As noted above, employers often have a difficult time discharging workers and workers have a difficult time finding other jobs. Therefore, employees tend to remain with the same employer for lengthy periods, developing close friendships with their colleagues and work associates. As a result, managers in Brazil are generally more paternalistic than in North America or Western Europe. Loyalty is usually to the person and members of the immediate group or family, often at the expense of the larger organization.

Typical Brazilian firms concentrate power in the hands of a few people at the top of the organization, and executives often make even insignificant day-to-day decisions. Larger firms create complex control systems and organize hierarchically with

Exhibit 12.10

Percent Who Believe Most People Can Be Trusted

Country	% Agreement	Country	% Agreement
Brazil	7	Russia	37
Turkey	10	Germany	38
Romania	16	Japan	42
Slovenia	17	Switzerland	43
Latvia	18	Iceland	44
Portugal	23	United Kingdom	44
Chile	24	Ireland	44
Nigeria	24	United States	47
Argentina	24	Canada	52
France	24	Netherlands	54
Austria	32	Denmark	58
Mexico	34	China	60
Korea	35	Finland	64
Spain	35	Norway	67
India	35	Sweden	68

Source: Data compiled from World Values Study Group, *World Values Survey* (Ann Arbor: Institute for Social Research, University of Michigan, 2000).

strict controls. But paradoxically, if the circumstances warrant, these controls are quickly disposed of and rules and policies are changed accordingly.

NEGOTIATING STRATEGIES IN BRAZIL

The typical negotiating style of Brazilian managers reflects the country's cultural characteristics and business environment. This style is summarized in Exhibit 12.8 as it compares to typical Japanese and U.S. approaches. At the heart of the Brazilian negotiating style is its emphasis on building, maintaining, and capitalizing on one's personal relationships. Brazilians are often seen as being highly engaged with their opponents or prospective partners during negotiation. They tend to believe that regardless of what happens during and after the negotiation, making friends and enjoying life is important. This focus on relationships leads Brazilians to avoid conflict and attempt to please the other party to the extent possible. There is also a tendency to use indirect language, hide unpleasant information, make false promises, and at times embellish the truth.[13] At the same time, however, Brazilians are more likely to be suspicious of people they do not know, and their trust in strangers is among the lowest in the world, as shown in Exhibit 12.10.

Brazilians' focus on personal relationships has been attributed to a need to deal with what some observers describe as a national inferiority complex.[14] Brazilians tend to be sensitive about their identity. They do not like to be compared with their neighbors and prefer to call themselves South Americans rather than Latin Americans. Brazilians need to feel accepted and become impatient when there is a conflict. When dealing with conflicts, aggressiveness is not a good alternative. Rather, a solution is most likely to emerge through active but friendly engagement.

Brazilians' tendency toward improvisation and flexibility is clear in their negotiation style as well. Many Brazilians do not follow logical steps in a negotiation and instead may jump back and forth between topics. At times, they may not have a clear goal in mind. Risk averse, Brazilians are likely to focus on seemingly irrelevant details, bargaining and negotiating for long periods of time. They enjoy the process of negotiating and are not in a hurry to make a deal. And they seldom make decisions based solely on analysis. Most likely, they consider emotions as well. In a recent article, a prominent Brazilian magazine interviewed successful Brazilian managers about their views on negotiation.[15] Among other things, the managers agreed that successful negotiations are typically conducted informally and with spontaneity. They are guided by intuition and not by reason alone. And finally, real negotiations seldom happen at the negotiation table. Instead, they take place in parallel informal meetings, where the relationship is developed. To be successful in negotiating with Brazilians, foreigners need to be both friendly and patient.

BRAZILIAN VERSUS JAPANESE NEGOTIATING STYLES

Finally, it is interesting to consider the differences between Brazilian and Japanese negotiating styles. The above review suggests that each culture would have few problems negotiating with the other. Both emphasize building strong personal relationships, emotional sensitivity, trust, pride, confidence, and a personal sense of honor. In addition, both communicate indirectly, using context as much as content. And both are uncomfortable with high degrees of conflict.

However, these characteristics are very general and allow for important variations. Brazilians develop relationships by clearly expressing emotions, hugging, and touching the other party, often using exaggerations and euphemisms, and behaving in informal and open ways. By contrast, the Japanese are often hesitant to display emotions, remain silent and physically distant from others, and stress respect and formality when dealing with others. Thus, while the two cultures' values are similar (e.g., strong personal relationships), they are expressed in different ways. Moreover, while both Brazilians and Japanese communicate indirectly and expect the other party to understand innuendos and subtleties, this does not guarantee that the two sides will understand each other. Indirect communication relies on culturally established codes that communicate difficult information without causing embarrassment. However, since these codes are culturally embedded, two indirect communicators from different cultures may have a hard time understanding each other.

Successful (and unsuccessful) negotiators can be found in all cultures. In this chapter, we focused on typical bargaining behavior in Japan and Brazil and compared it to typical American bargaining behavior. Similarities and differences were noted. Even so, it is important to remember that all Japanese do not necessarily fit this pattern; nor do all Brazilians. Differences within cultures, not just differences between cultures, can be found. Successful managers therefore tread cautiously in their international negotiations until they sufficiently understand the particular (and often unique) environment in which they find themselves. Based on this understanding, the global manager is better prepared to succeed.

KEY TERMS

competitive negotiations
dirty tricks
first offer
holistic approach to concession making
nonverbal negotiating tactics
problem-solving negotiations
sequential approach to concession making
verbal negotiating tactics

GLOBAL MANAGER'S WORKBOOK 12.1: NEGOTIATING IN JAPAN

Japanese business and management practices were discussed in Chapter 9. In addition, this chapter focuses on how Japanese firms tend to approach bargaining and negotiation situations. Based on these materials, consider the following questions about international negotiations with Japanese firms:

1. How would you characterize the basic negotiation strategies of a typical Japanese firm?
2. How would managers in a Japanese firm describe typical Western negotiation strategies?
3. If you were advising a small Western company that was about to begin negotiating with a major Japanese *keiretsu*, what advice would you offer to help it succeed?
4. In negotiating a contract with a Japanese firm, what mistakes might you make that could potentially be deal breakers?

GLOBAL MANAGER'S WORKBOOK 12.2: INBEV

In 2004, AmBev and Interbrew negotiated a major partnership to create the largest beer company in the world.[16] The new alliance, called InBev, now produces 15 percent of the beer sold worldwide. The new partnership between the two former rivals received considerable attention in the global business community not just because of its size but also because of its two partners. One is Brazilian; the other is Belgian. Some market analysts questioned whether the new venture could succeed in view of the wide disparity in the cultures of the two partners. Brazil's AmBev corporate culture is characterized by an informal approach to management, an emphasis on spontaneity and innovation, and a constant focus on—some would say an obsession with—the bottom line. In contrast, Belgium's Interbrew is a very traditional firm originally founded in the fourteenth century and still run by a board of directors that includes barons, dukes, and marquises. Its corporate culture is formal, conservative, and some would say aristocratic. Long-term financial stability and security outweigh short-term profit considerations.

How did these two very different companies from two very different cultures come together to form a partnership? With lots of help. Negotiations to create the partnership dragged on for five months and required more than fifty negotiation sessions to close the deal. The efforts of several international banks and legal experts from both countries, as well as from the United States, were also required to consummate the deal. As a result of these lengthy negotiations, the two partners came to understand more about each other's culture, business objectives, and management style. Mistrust evolved into friendship and friendship evolved into partnership. The negotiations were difficult and time-consuming, but in the end they were successful. Today, InBev has become a major player in the worldwide beer industry.

1. How would you characterize the negotiation environment of a typical Brazilian firm?
2. Why did it take so many bankers and lawyers so long to negotiate the InBev partnership?
3. If you were facilitating the early negotiations for a possible partnership between AmBev and Interbrew, what would you do to get the two sides working together? Specifically, what would you do to facilitate intercultural communication? What would you do to help build trust between the two parties?
4. Now that the InBev partnership is established, what should each of the partners do to ensure its long-term success?

NOTES

1. Thomas O'Boyle, *At Any Cost: Jack Welch, General Electric, and the Pursuit of Profit* (New York: Knopf, 1998).

2. Michael Kublin, *International Negotiating* (New York: International Business, 1995).

3. Gary Ferraro, *Cultural Dimensions of International Business* (Upper Saddle River, NJ: Prentice Hall, 2002).

4. John Graham and Yoshihiro Sano, *Smart Bargaining: Doing Business with the Japanese* (New York: Harper and Row, 1989).

5. M. Eakin, *Brazil: The Once and Future Country* (New York: St. Martin's, 1994).

6. "Make or Break: A Survey of Brazil," *Economist,* February 22, 2003, pp. 3–15.

7. T. Lenartowicz and K. Roth, "Does Subculture Within a Country Matter? A Cross-Cultural Study of Motivational Domains and Business Performance in Brazil," *Journal of International Business Studies* 32, no. 2 (2001): 305–25.

8. "Para Enfrentar a Fera" (To Face the Beast), *Exame,* August 25, 2004, http://portalexame.abril.com.br/edicoes/825/economia/conteudo_47434.shtml.

9. Ibid.

10. "O Tropeco dos Estrangeiros" (The Foreigner's Scramble), *Exame,* October 8, 2003, http://portalexame.abril.com.br/financas/conteudo_22366.shtml.

11. "Maestro do Credito" (The Master of Credit), *Exame,* September 24, 2003, http://portalexame.abril.com.br/empresas/conteudo_21191.shtml.

12. "Empresario Brazileiro e o Mais Versatile" (The Brazilian Businessperson Is the Most Versatile), *Gazeta Mercantil,* April 30, 2002, http://www1.folha.uol.com.br/folha/dimenstein/imprescindival/dia/gd300402.htm#1.

13. L. Junqueira, "The Brazilian Way to Deal with the Crisis and Recovery," *Instituto MVC,* October 10, 2004, www.institutomvc.com.br.

14. Leila Magalhaes, "Negociando no Mercosul" (Negotiating in the Mercosur), *Faculdada de Filosofia, Ciencias e Letras de Paranagua,* October 10, 2004, p. 9.

15. "A Arte Do Aperto de Maos" (The Art of the Handshake), *Exame,* April 22, 2003, http://portalexame.abril.com.br/edicoes/790/empresas/conteudo_19844.shtml.

16. "A Formatacao Do Negocio" (Formatting the Deal), *Exame,* March 16, 2004, http://portalexame.abril.com.br/empresas/conteuodo_31657.shtml.

PART III

MANAGING GLOBAL OPERATIONS

13 Staffing Global Operations

UNILEVER GOES TO BRAZIL

Anglo-Dutch consumer products giant Unilever operates numerous divisions and subsidiaries around the world and is well regarded as both a tenacious competitor and a good local citizen. When it purchased Brazilian ice cream maker Kibon, local skeptics assumed that the small company would disappear inside the huge multinational.[1] However, Unilever had other plans. It wanted Kibon to retain its unique Brazilian flavor while at the same time becoming an integral part of Unilever's Latin American business strategy.

To accomplish this, Unilever adopted a gradual strategy of integration, particularly regarding valued local employees. While it replaced Kibon's board of directors, Unilever made a special effort to retain key operating personnel in critical areas, such as production, finance, marketing, and research and development. Local staff members were told of the employees' expanded career opportunities within the larger Unilever family of companies, and generous performance-based bonuses were offered. However, Unilever made it clear that it would implement a new, more aggressive marketing strategy to capture a larger share of the Latin American market.

Local managers were invited to a series of discussions concerning how Kibon might better position itself in a competitive marketplace. Following these discussions, Unilever developed a specific plan of action. Operating efficiencies and some new product development were ordered, and a new identity was designed for the company. Kibon employees who did not support the integration process were offered generous terms to leave the company.

Unilever prides itself on its decentralized approach to global business. It tries to make extensive use of local managerial talent where possible. With its acquisition of Kibon, Unilever worked hard to reduce local employee anxiety and resistance by keeping bureaucratic procedures and outside interference to a minimum. It emphasized that it needed local Brazilian managers to succeed and that these managers, not company headquarters, best understood local markets. The new Kibon was given a simple challenge: Use the global resources of Unilever and local expertise of Kibon to make the venture succeed.

THE INTERNATIONAL STAFFING CHALLENGE

As noted in Chapter 1, being a manager is never easy, but being a global manager can be particularly difficult. In addition to the myriad of often conflicting tasks and responsibilities faced by all managers and supervisors, global managers must also possess a deep understanding of cultural differences and an ability to work with people from highly divergent cultural backgrounds under sometimes very trying circumstances. Not only does failure jeopardize the global manager's career, it also endangers the success or longevity of the entire international business venture. In view of the low success rates of managers tasked for overseas assignments, finding the right individual to fill the global manager role is indeed a critical challenge for any firm in the global economy.

Consider the following problem: As an HR manager for a large multinational mining company, you have been asked to hire the best manager you can find to run your company's operations in Bolivia. The job will require considerable technical expertise as well as managerial competence. Operational success is important, and your reputation (and career) as a manager is riding on your decision. What do you do? Perhaps your first challenge is to decide whether you want to hire a local (i.e., Bolivian) manager to run the facility or someone from another country. There are obvious advantages to hiring local managers in terms of understanding both the language and the local customs. The Bolivian government would probably also be pleased. However, your choice of qualified candidates may be limited. Besides, sending someone from corporate headquarters, perhaps an American or a European, might bring a more international perspective to the Bolivian operations, as well as provide valuable training for one of your company's up-and-coming junior managers. How do you weigh these advantages and disadvantages in a way that will help you make an optimal decision?

As you make your decision, the first thing to understand is that you have three possible options for hiring. In the jargon used by multinational firms, your choices are:

• *Home-country nationals* (also called parent-country nationals)—citizens of the country where the company is headquartered who are assigned to one of its foreign operations. In the example above, if a German multinational selected a German manager to go to Bolivia, he or she would be a home-country national.

• *Host-country nationals*—residents of the host country where the company has its local operations. In the example above, if you hired a Bolivian manager to run the mine, he or she would be a host-country national.

• *Third-country nationals*—employees of a firm who are citizens of neither the country where the firm is headquartered nor the foreign operations where they are assigned. If a German multinational hired a French mining engineer for the assignment in Bolivia, he or she would be a third-country national.

Home-country nationals and third-country nationals are often collectively referred to as *expatriates,* meaning simply employees who come from a different country than the one in which they are working. This is in contrast to *inpatriates,* who are either host-country nationals or third-country nationals who are assigned to work in the company's home country (e.g., assigned to corporate headquarters) to gain critical work experience and advance their career.

INTERNATIONAL STAFFING MODELS

In addition to knowing the variety of managers who are potentially available for overseas assignments, a wise manager also understands the prevailing staffing philosophy of his or her company.[2] Simply put, a staffing philosophy reflects corporate beliefs and policies about how best to staff overseas operations. This philosophy may be written into formal company policy guidelines or may simply reside somewhere informally in the corporate culture. Four basic staffing models, along with their advantages and drawbacks, can be identified (see Exhibit 13.1).

ETHNOCENTRIC STAFFING MODEL

An *ethnocentric staffing model* emphasizes the use of home-country nationals (often sent from company headquarters) to staff most if not all of the senior managerial positions throughout a firm's global operations. This approach is based on the premise that home-office perspectives should override local issues and that expatriate managers will usually be more effective in representing the views of the home office in foreign operations. The ethnocentric staffing model has several advantages. It requires little effort by headquarters to monitor or recruit home-country nationals for higher echelon managerial positions. Likely candidates are often well known at company headquarters. In addition, it provides broad experience for home-country managers in ways that facilitate their long-term career progression within the firm. And it supports highly centralized decision making by headquarters, which some firms prefer.

At the same time, this approach has a number of disadvantages. It can inhibit the development of local management talent since local managers have less upward mobility in the firm. This may lead to a second disadvantage: reduced levels of employee commitment to the organization by local managers who feel trapped under a glass ceiling with few prospect of moving to the top of the firm. Moreover, many home-country nationals, however well intentioned, are poorly prepared for international assignments and often make costly mistakes because they do not understand the local culture in the country to which they are assigned. Finally, in many companies, an overseas assignment can be detrimental to one's long-term career since overseas (home-country) managers are removed from the center of action for several years and top managers may begin to forget about them.

POLYCENTRIC STAFFING MODEL

A *polycentric staffing model* emphasizes the use of host-country nationals in managing overseas operations in the belief that local managers can be more effective in

Exhibit 13.1

International Staffing Models

Advantages	Disadvantages
Ethnocentric:	
Candidates for overseas positions may be better known at headquarters	Inhibits the development of local managers
Allows for relatively rapid employee selection	May reduce local employee commitment to the firm
Provides global experiences for home-country managers	May lead to significant adjustment problems by home-country nationals who cannot adapt to overseas realities
Supports highly centralized decision making from headquarters	May not be conducive to home-country national's career
Polycentric:	
Provides experts on political, legal, and business affairs of each country	May increase coordination and recruitment costs
May reduce training and operating costs	May provide home-country nationals with fewer opportunities to serve overseas
May reduce potential adjustment problems	May make productive host-country nationals too valuable to promote to headquarters
Creates greater local career options for host-country nationals	
Regiocentric:	
Provides experts on political, legal, and business affairs in the region	May increase coordination and recruitment costs
May reduce training and operating costs	Provides home-country nationals fewer opportunities to serve overseas
May reduce potential adjustment problems	May make productive third-country nationals too valuable to promote to headquarters
Creates greater career options in region for third-country nationals	May offend customers if most managers come from a different country in the region
Often provides greater flexibility in regional staffing	
Global:	
Provides experts on political, legal, and business affairs around the world	Increases recruitment and coordination costs
Creates greater career options at home and abroad for all talented employees	May increase employee adjustment problems
Increases applicant pool for valued positions	Often leads to increased training and transportation costs
Creates a diverse and experienced cadre of talented managers for the truly global firm	May cause firms to experience local resistance to bringing in outside managers
Supports the corporate strategy of firms that genuinely want to go global	Requires greater tracking of employees worldwide to facilitate employee development and utilization

negotiating the labyrinth of local customs, laws, traditions, and political intrigues necessary to make the local venture succeed. Using this model, operations in each country are treated separately for HRM purposes, and people and policies are developed to fit local circumstances.

The polycentric staffing model can reduce both training and operating costs by using local host-country nationals. It can also reduce the potential adjustment problems of home-country national managers sent from the home office, since fewer such managers would be taking overseas assignments. It also provides for sound training for host-country nationals, thereby opening greater possibilities for career advancement.

However, this approach can also create significant coordination problems for headquarters based on language, cultural, and loyalty differences. Companies following this path must invest significant resources in ensuring that the overall firm is welcoming of such diversity. At the same time, home-country nationals may lose valuable opportunities to gain overseas experience since host-country nationals fill these positions. And finally, and somewhat ironically, like the ethnocentric model, this approach can limit the career advancement opportunities for host-country nationals because a company may believe that they are needed in their home districts. Successful managers may become too valuable to promote back to the home office.

REGIOCENTRIC STAFFING MODEL

A variation on the polycentric model is called the *regiocentric staffing model,* in which multinational firms organize their HRM policies and staffing criteria by geographic region (e.g., Asia, Europe) instead of by a particular country within that region. For example, many U.S. firms doing business in the European Union will hire a German or French manager to oversee the firm's entire European operations. This is often done to comply with European Union employment guidelines and to develop managers who have a broad-based understanding of doing business across the European Union.

The advantages and drawbacks of the regiocentric staffing model are similar to those of the polycentric model, except that this model provides greater flexibility for multinational firms with strong regional markets and operations. However, when this model is used primarily to save money, it sometimes leads to mixed results. For example, many North American firms use Japanese managers stationed in a regional Tokyo office to cover their entire East Asian markets, a practice that often annoys Chinese and Korean customers, who sometimes feel like second-class customers. A regiocentric model is therefore best used when customers from all regional countries understand and accept managers or representatives from the broader region.

GLOBAL STAFFING MODEL

Finally, the *global staffing model* strives to hire the best person for the job regardless of where he or she comes from. Parent-country nationals, host-country nationals,

Exhibit 13.2

Nationality of Top Managers in Overseas Operations

Parent Companies	% Home-Country Nationals (Ethnocentric)	% Host-Country Nationals (Polycentric)	% Third-Country Nationals (Regiocentric)
Japanese firms	74	26	0
European firms	48	44	8
American firms	32	49	19

Source: Data from Helen Deresky, *International Management: Managing Across Borders and Cultures* (Upper Saddle River, NJ: Prentice Hall, 2003), pp. 394–95.

and third-country nationals are all treated as one group, and the company determines which individual brings the best combination of attributes to a particular job. This approach often leads to a larger applicant pool from which to select prospective managers. It also provides considerable international experience to a large cadre of managers and helps build a truly transnational firm with common core values and aspirations, as managers from various parts of the globe serve together in widely diverse international assignments.

However, the global approach can be costly: the firm may incur additional training and transportation costs, as global managers must be trained and retrained as they are sent to various locations. Moreover, this strategy can be difficult to implement at times because of local restrictions on issuing work permits for foreign nationals and other forms of local resistance. Even so, the global staffing model is probably the best strategy for firms that are trying to become true global companies in every sense of the term.

It is interesting to note that the selection of top executives for overseas operations often varies based on the nationality of the parent company. As shown in Exhibit 13.2, Japanese firms are much more likely to use an ethnocentric staffing model, selecting home-country (i.e., Japanese) executives for their overseas operations, than are their European or American counterparts. At the same time, while U.S. firms prefer to use a polycentric staffing model for executive positions, they are also more likely than Japanese or European firms to use a regiocentric staffing model for other positions, using third-country nationals.

HOST-COUNTRY NATIONALS

As just noted, hiring host-country nationals and hiring home-country nationals bring very different opportunities and challenges to global firms. With this in mind, a critical question facing companies is how to decide between these two staffing strategies. That is, when is it best to hire host-country nationals compared to home-country nationals (or expatriates)? In this and the following section, we compare the relative advantages and disadvantages of each of these staffing strategies for organizing and managing abroad.

PROBLEMS AND PROSPECTS OF HOST-COUNTRY NATIONALS

Hiring host-country nationals yields several advantages for transnational firms, including cost savings, reduced training time, and increased knowledge of local conditions. Moreover, local governments usually like such arrangements, and locals can more easily network with the local business community. Prior to deciding to hire host-country nationals, however, companies must ask a number of key questions:[3]

• *What is the best way to identify local talent?* Nations differ in educational qualifications and formal certifications for job skills. In some countries, nepotism or connections play a significant role in who gets hired. How does the firm find the best people?

• *How can the firm attract the best talent to apply for its jobs?* What recruitment techniques should the firm use to get the word out? Newspaper ads? Personal contacts? Headhunters?

• *How do local laws affect staffing, compensation, and training decisions?* Local legal advice is often helpful to ensure that a company does not run afoul of the law in HRM decisions.

• *Can the firm use parent-country training programs with local employees?* Training methods are not always culturally transferable. Will the company develop its own training materials or buy them from vendors?

• *What is the best way to conduct performance appraisals?* What is customary in the local culture? Are parent-country techniques appropriate?

• *What incentives or rewards should be used to motivate workers?* Cultural factors often lead people to value different incentives (e.g., money, free time, status). Most European countries, for example, emphasize benefits over salaries (largely because of high income taxes), while the United States emphasizes salaries over benefits. How can the firm learn about these differences, and how does the firm make logical choices on compensation packages?

• *How can a company retain its best local managers?* Company loyalty and longevity can vary considerably across nations. What can be done to guarantee that local managers will want to stay with the firm?

These are but a few of the questions that require serious consideration in any decision to hire host-country nationals. Obviously, finding superior local talent from the distance of corporate headquarters can be a real challenge, yet some firms manage to succeed against the odds. Gillette is one of these firms.

DEVELOPING GLOBAL MANAGERS AT GILLETTE

There are many good examples of multinational firms going to great lengths to develop local managerial talent. One such example is Gillette, a U.S.-based company recently acquired by Procter & Gamble specializing in personal grooming products, stationery products, and small electric appliances. Gillette does business in more than two hundred countries. More than 70 percent of its total sales and 75 percent of its employees are outside the United States. Gillette is truly a global company.

To meet the need for managerial talent to run its various operations, Gillette initiated an international management trainee program a number of years ago. Its objective is to hire and develop local talent who want a long-term international career with the company. Applicants to the program must meet several specific requirements. They must be adaptable and have good social skills. Moreover, they must to be younger than thirty years old and single. (Note that this requirement would be illegal in many countries, including the United States.) Finally, applicants must be highly fluent in English, enthusiastic, and mobile.

To train the local managers, Gillette established a structured program that includes the following: Trainees begin work in their home country at one of the company's numerous subsidiaries. This introductory training lasts approximately six months. Next, the trainees are transferred to one of Gillette's three international headquarters, in Boston, London, or Singapore. During the next eighteen months, they study Gillette's global business strategy and network with senior executives. Following this experience, the trainees return to their home countries to assume entry-level management positions. If successful, the new managers are promoted to other assignments, primarily within their own geographic region (e.g., Southeast Asia, Latin America). In the end, the most successful managers return home to their native countries to become senior operating managers.

Gillette has largely taken a regiocentric approach to training. That is, while all trainees gain experience in one of the company's international headquarters, most of their managerial careers will be spent either in their home countries or their home region of the world. In this way, Gillette gains valuable local managerial talent who can provide country-by-country expertise for this highly successful multinational enterprise. Meanwhile, local employees gain opportunities for managerial training and managerial careers that are often unavailable to them in their home countries. Recent graduates of the program have come from such countries as Argentina, Brazil, China, Colombia, Egypt, Guatemala, India, Indonesia, Malaysia, Morocco, New Zealand, Pakistan, Peru, Poland, Russia, South Africa, Turkey, and Venezuela. Gillette hopes its program represents a win-win for everyone involved.

EXPATRIATE MANAGERS

We saw in both the Unilever and Gillette examples that many multinationals prefer to hire local employees to operate overseas branches and subsidiaries. At other times, however, companies find it advantageous to send in talent from the home country, the so-called expatriate. Using expatriate managers for global assignments has at least three advantages for the multinational firm:[4]

• *Enhanced operational control and coordination.* International assignments can help companies coordinate and control operations that are widely dispersed geographically or culturally. With managers traveling back and forth between headquarters and local operations, information flow is increased as expatriate managers come to understand local conditions and challenges and relate these issues back to senior management.

• *Increased information gathering.* International assignments can provide important strategic information for both managers and their companies, especially when the managers spend two or three years in one location and genuinely begin to understand the local culture and customs.

• *Managerial skills development.* International assignments can help managers develop new skills for working with both colleagues and customers around the world. Indeed, many companies (e.g., Procter & Gamble and Colgate-Palmolive) use global assignments as a central part of their management training efforts, especially for potential higher echelon executives.

PROBLEMS AND PROSPECTS OF EXPATRIATE MANAGERS

While such advantages are fairly obvious, finding people who can actually succeed in global assignments can be problematic. Indeed, the first lesson to be learned in international staffing is that while all people may be created equal, their travel skills are not. While traveling abroad (perhaps on a vacation or business trip) is often seen by people as an enjoyable experience, actually living abroad can be frustrating, stressful, and sometimes very unpleasant. For many, staying in a four-star hotel, eating in fine restaurants, seeing new sights, and knowing that soon they will be back in their own bed is far preferable to setting up a household in a strange neighborhood where few people speak their language, finding schools for the kids, shopping in local markets stocked with foods they can't identify, and using public transportation. For others, these same experiences provide a sense of adventure and learning. The challenge for managers—and their companies—is to discover which type of person the potential manager is before getting on the airplane.

By way of summary, Exhibits 13.3 and 13.4 identify several of the potential benefits and possible drawbacks of using either host-country nationals or expatriates. (Note that American, Japanese, and European companies report different problems with their overseas operations.) Selecting the right employees for overseas assignments continues to be a difficult task for most multinational firms throughout the world. So much depends on the quality of employees a firm can attract. Perhaps the best advice here is to first understand a firm's global strategic objectives, as well as its prevailing corporate culture. With this information in mind, managers should be in a better position to determine the appropriate mix of personnel to staff their global operations.

SELECTING EXPATRIATES FOR OVERSEAS ASSIGNMENTS

An important question for all global companies is whom to select for overseas assignments. While many people are interested in such assignments, far fewer are usually qualified. As a result, successful companies approach overseas assignments in a systematic way, beginning with employee selection and progressing to cultural adaptation programs for those finally selected. The first issue to be addressed is what

Exhibit 13.3

Benefits of Hiring Host-Country Nationals and Expatriates

Host-Country Nationals	Expatriates
Critical skills can be developed locally to help improve operational efficiency and effectiveness.	Critical skills can be transferred overseas to help improve local efficiency and effectiveness.
Using host-country nationals is typically (although not always) less expensive than transferring in expatriates.	Providing expatriates with interesting overseas assignments helps retain their services for future assignments.
Host-country nationals have fewer local adjustment problems.	Hiring expatriates provides the firm with opportunities to develop an internationally experienced senior management team.
Host-country nationals have better ties to local government and the local business community.	Expatriates have better ties to the parent company and the global business community.

Exhibit 13.4

Problems with Host-Country Nationals and Expatriates

Problems Reported by Firms	% Firms Reporting Problems		
	Japan	Europe	United States
Host-country Nationals:			
Difficulty in attracting high-quality locals to work for the company	44	26	21
High turnover of locals	32	9	4
Friction between locals and home-country nationals	32	9	13
Complaints about lack of promotional opportunities by locals	21	4	8
Legal challenges to company HR policies by locals	0	10	0
Expatriates:			
Lack of expatriates who have sufficient global management skills	68	39	29
Lack of expatriates who want to work abroad	26	26	13
Reentry problems experienced by returning expatriates	24	39	42

Source: Data from Helen Deresky, *International Management: Managing Across Borders and Cultures* (Upper Saddle River, NJ: Prentice Hall, 2003), pp. 395–97.

qualifications candidates for overseas positions should possess. To ensure that those selected have a reasonable chance of success, companies look for certain characteristics in job applicants.[5] While professional and technical competencies remain prerequisites for most international assignments, other key success factors should also be considered, including the following:

• *Motivation for a foreign assignment.* Is the manager really interested in going abroad or was he or she talked into it? Why does the manager want to go? Is the manager motivated by career concerns, company commitment, or personal goals?

- *Physical and emotional health.* Many overseas assignments can be exhausting, with business meetings during the day and social obligations at night. Such assignments are not for the weak of mind or body. Companies must ensure that managers sent overseas are physically up to the challenge. They should also ensure that managers do not carry with them undue emotional baggage that could degenerate out of control in a stressful foreign environment.
- *Maturity and relational abilities.* Can the manager work independently, accept setbacks gracefully, and adapt to new and strange situations? Does the manager have good interpersonal and cross-cultural skills? Can the manager accept other people as they are or does he or she try to change them to fit a predetermined mold?
- *Family situation.* Will the family be an asset or a liability in an overseas assignment? Are schools available for the children? Does the spouse really want to go? What kind of relational skills do the spouse and children have to help them succeed?
- *Language capabilities.* Learning local languages facilitates learning local cultures. It also helps the manager develop close personal and business relationships abroad. Does the manager speak the local language? Is he or she willing to learn?

These key factors do not guarantee success in an overseas assignment, but they enhance the likelihood of success. What expatriate managers really need to succeed is a combination of these skills, a supportive family, and a supportive company. With these three mutually supportive factors, expatriate managers can focus their energies and talents on running the business for the benefit of all.

MANAGING CULTURAL ADAPTATION

Many people see an international assignment as a great opportunity. It may be an opportunity to advance one's career, to make more money, or to learn new things. It may represent a personal challenge or a way to a more interesting life. Managers who take international assignments report learning new managerial skills, increasing their tolerance for ambiguity, learning new ways of seeing things, and improving their ability to work with others.[6]

However, living and working abroad is not easy. Among U.S. managers, it is estimated that up to 40 percent of overseas assignments end in failure. (Failure is defined as a manager and his or her family returning from an assignment early.) While it is true that U.S. managers have a higher failure rate than their European or Asian counterparts, companies in every region of the world face this problem to some degree. For Americans, the most common reasons for expatriate failure abroad include (in order of frequency): (1) the spouse fails to adapt to the local culture; (2) the manager fails to adapt to the local culture; (3) other family problems; (4) the personality of the manager (e.g., poor fit between manager's personality and local people); (5) excessive demands or responsibilities of the international assignment; (6) the manager's lack of technical proficiency; and (7) the manager's lack of motivation for the international assignment.[7]

Two things should be noted about these findings. First, it is highly likely that in many cases a manager's spouse (regardless of gender) or family may be an excuse for the manager's own desire to return home. It is more socially acceptable for upwardly aspiring managers to blame their spouse or children than to admit personal failure. Second, although it was not examined in this study, lower than expected job performance probably also represents a major reason for expatriate failures.

CULTURE SHOCK

Culture shock is a feeling of distress in response to immersing oneself in a new environment. Culture shock results from information overload and a breakdown in one's capacity to make sense of the environment. People cannot use past experiences to interpret and respond to cues, and their behavior does not produce the expected results, causing heightened anxiety and frustration. In addition, seemingly minor things, such as an inability to find one's favorite food or perform simple tasks such as making a phone call, using public transportation, or mailing a letter often cause confusion and a feeling of loss of control.

Culture shock can take many forms, from a psychological sense of frustration, anxiety, and disappointment to full-fledged chronic depression. Some individuals may experience physiological responses such as insomnia, headaches, or other psychosomatic symptoms. Even so, culture shock is not a disease. Rather, it signifies that an individual is trying to come to terms with his or her new environment, a good starting point for cultural adaptation. The question, therefore, is not how to avoid culture shock, but how to manage it.

STAGES OF CULTURE SHOCK

Even though the experience of being abroad is quite personal and varies widely from person to person, it is possible to identify some important phases in the process of cultural adaptation. As shown in Exhibit 13.5, the process of acculturation can be seen as progressing through four relatively distinct phases: honeymoon, disillusionment, adaptation, and biculturalism.[8]

• *Honeymoon.* Upon first arriving at a foreign location, expatriates frequently experience a great deal of excitement. Things are interesting, sometimes beautiful, and often amusing. The fascination with new things makes the difficulties and differences encountered seem relatively minor, and people often overestimate the ease of adjustment to the foreign culture. This *honeymoon* period can last from only a few days to several months, depending on the person, the nature of the assignment, and the similarity between the home and host countries.

• *Disillusionment.* After the honeymoon period is over and the initial euphoria or excitement fades, the differences in lifestyles, lack of familiar food, and difficulties coping with the uncertainties of the new environment cease to be amusing and become irritating. These difficulties become magnified, and people often feel overwhelmed and psychologically exhausted. The *disillusionment* stage is the most difficult stage in the cultural adaptation process. Many individuals give up at this stage and return home, while others remain in the foreign surroundings but with-

Exhibit 13.5 **Stages in Cultural Adaptation**

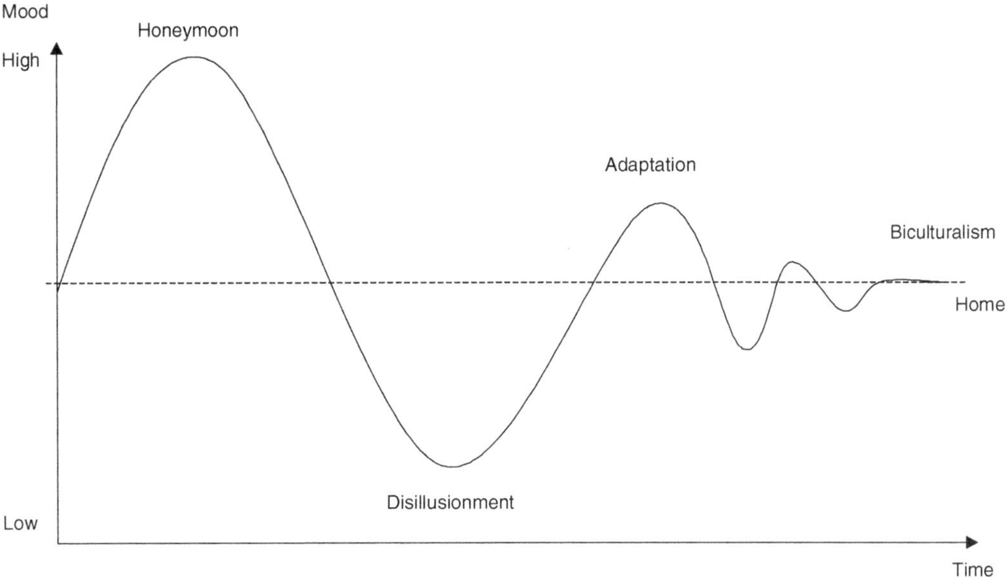

draw emotionally, refusing to speak the local language or interact with locals. Some may even adopt dysfunctional coping behaviors, such as excessive drinking or drug use.

• *Adaptation.* During the *adaptation* stage, people begin to understand the new culture and adjust to everyday living. This stage can still be characterized by mood swings, but their magnitude and intensity are less pronounced than during the disillusionment stage.

• *Biculturalism.* Finally, expatriates begin to gain confidence in their ability to function productively in the new culture and experience a sense of stability. Some people may feel better than they do at home, others may feel worse, but in either case there is a newfound sense of stability, comfort, and competence. During the *biculturalism* stage, they begin believing—sometimes incorrectly—that they now understand local people and customs, and they begin venturing out to learn more about their new home.

COPING WITH CULTURE SHOCK

Culture shock cannot be avoided, but it can be alleviated to some degree through proper advance preparation.[9] This preparation includes understanding both the host country and oneself. The more expatriates understand about the local culture, the easier the transition is likely to be. Learning about local history and geography can help people understand their new environment and facilitate conversations with their new neighbors. When possible, it is often a good idea to visit the host country for a short period prior to moving there. Indeed, many firms send expatriates and their families to the work site for a brief visit prior to the assignment, so they can decide whether the assignment is suitable for themselves and their families.

In addition, learning the local language can facilitate the process of cultural adaptation immensely. Learning the host language can provide the expatriate a sense of being in control and facilitate communication with locals. In addition, locals are often more receptive to foreign visitors if they speak the local language. Interestingly, research has shown that learning new languages facilitates cognitive flexibility, a critical asset for managers who work and move around the globe.[10]

After expatriates get settled in a new country, it is often a good idea to look for mentors, or *cultural translators.* These are individuals who have a good understanding of both cultures and can help the new arrivals make sense out of what they are experiencing. The best cultural translators usually have international experiences of their own, allowing them to recognize and interpret cultural differences as well as the reasons behind them.

MANAGING CULTURAL ADAPTATION AT ROYAL DUTCH/SHELL

To overcome the numerous challenges of working around the globe, many companies have established training and support programs aimed at better preparing both employees and their families for the challenges that lie ahead and thereby reduce the failure rates in overseas assignments. These programs generally begin with an assessment of the employees' flexibility, adaptability, and general abilities and coping skills. They then proceed to provide tailored training that includes such subjects as foreign-language training, cross-cultural training with a particular emphasis on communication, international negotiations skills, working with multicultural teams, sources of local assistance if needed, and safety and security issues. Throughout, the emphasis is on providing expatriates and their families with as much support as the company can reasonably provide.

A good example of such programs can be found at Royal Dutch/Shell.[11] Shell is a global petroleum company with joint headquarters in London and The Hague. The company employs more than 100,000 people, approximately 5,500 of whom live and work abroad at any point in time. Shell's expatriate managers are a highly diverse group, representing more than seventy nationalities and working in more than one hundred countries. The company supports this practice because it realizes that the success of a global company requires the international mobility of its workforce.

By the 1990s, however, Shell was finding it increasingly difficult to recruit key personnel for overseas assignments. To understand the problem, Shell interviewed two hundred expatriate employees and their spouses to uncover their biggest concerns. These data were then used to create a survey that was sent to 17,000 current and former expatriate managers, expatriates' spouses, and employees who had declined international assignments. Surprisingly, the response rate for the survey was 70 percent, clearly suggesting that many employees believed this was an important issue.

According to survey results, five key issues had the greatest influence on the willingness of employees to accept an international assignment. In order of importance, they were: (1) separation from children during their secondary education (the children were often sent to boarding schools in their home countries while their parents were away); (2) harm done to a spouse's career and employment; (3) failure to recognize and involve spouses in the relocation decision; (4) failure to provide adequate information and assistance regarding relocation; and (5) health-related issues, such as access to good hospitals or an ongoing ailment of a family member.

As a result of these findings, Shell implemented a number of programs designed to make it easier for employees to go abroad. To help with the education of children, Shell built elementary schools for employees in locations with heavy expatriate concentrations. For secondary education, they worked with local schools, often providing grants to help upgrade their facilities and educational offerings. They also offered employees an educational supplement for parents wanting to send their children to private schools in the host country.

Helping spouses find suitable employment proved to be a more vexing problem. According to the survey, one-half of the spouses were employed when the international assignment was made, but only 12 percent were able to find suitable work after arriving in their new location. Shell established a spouse employment center to address the problem. The center provides career counseling and support in locating employment opportunities both during and immediately following the overseas assignment. The company also agreed to reimburse up to 80 percent of the costs associated with vocational training or reaccreditation.

Finally, Shell established a global information and advice network, known as the Outpost, to provide support for families contemplating overseas assignments. The Outpost is headquartered in The Hague and now runs forty information centers in more than thirty countries. Staffed by spouses and fully supported by Shell, this global network has helped more than a thousand families prepare for overseas assignments. The center recommends schools and medical facilities and provides housing advice and up-to-date information on employment, overseas study, self-employment, and volunteer work. Clearly, Shell is out in front in providing a supportive work environment for its global employees in a way that also facilities the long-term objectives of the company.

MANAGING REPATRIATION

Repatriation refers to the process of returning expatriates to their home countries. Repatriation may occur because the assignment has been completed, or because of family reasons, failure, or dissatisfaction. Even though repatriation can at times cause as much culture shock as expatriation, organizations and managers alike often overlook the effects. When going home, managers can face *reverse culture shock.*

Reverse culture shock may result from dissatisfaction with the job or the old way of life in the home country. The excitement of foreign travel is gone. Sometimes an expatriate returns to his or her previous job and feels demoted or bored. At other times, the employer may have undergone major changes and the expatriate's skills are no longer useful or valued. In addition, superiors and colleagues may not value the international experience or the skills acquired abroad. Reentry can also be challenging on a personal level. Family and friends may have moved, made new friends, or acquired new interests, and are no longer as available as they were before departure. Finally, sometimes the expatriates themselves have changed. They have incorporated new values, habits, and worldviews that may be at odds with their old friends at home. At the extreme, they can become foreigners in their own land.

Returning expatriates tend to adopt one of three coping strategies:[12]

• *Resocialized returnees. Resocialized returnees* are people who attempt to fit in back in the home culture by ignoring or rejecting what they learned in their foreign assignment. Such returnees typically failed to assimilate into the foreign culture during their overseas assignment, often living in expat communities and minimizing their interactions with the locals. As a result, they tend to find it relatively easy to return psychologically to their home culture.

• *Alienated returnees. Alienated returnees* are at the other end of the spectrum. While abroad, they tend to "go native" and over time begin to reject the values of their home country in favor of the values of their host country. When they return home they feel alienated. They find it difficult to apply their foreign experiences in meaningful ways in their home country. Many simply wish to return to their adopted home.

• *Proactive returnees. Proactive returnees* represent an optimistic breed of traveler. They return home with a conviction that they can succeed in melding the two cultures in positive and productive ways. They realize that they have changed personally as a result of their overseas assignment and want to make use of what they have learned. They often seek out new friends or colleagues with similar experiences or they launch new projects or adventures. Above all, they want to make use of what they have learned abroad.

To reduce the difficulties associated with reentry, many companies create various mechanisms by which expatriates can keep in touch with their colleagues back home at company headquarters. These mechanisms can include special newsletters, regularly scheduled home visits, special Web pages focusing on expatriate concerns, and assigning HR specialists to oversee both overseas assignments and repatriation activities. The key for most major multinational firms (and most expatriates) is to ensure that expatriates do not get lost or forgotten when they are out of their home country. The old adage "out of sight, out of mind" is pertinent in these situations, and responsibility often falls on the expatriates themselves to guarantee that this does not occur.

In summary, staffing international operations presents many challenges to multinational firms. Should they hire local employees, expatriates, or a combination of the two? Regardless of whom they hire, how will they train and develop these people for both the short and long term? How much investment are they willing to make? And what is their overseas management philosophy? Answers to questions such as these largely define the character of the global firm in the eyes of both their overseas employees and their customers. As a result, these issues become critical in helping determine the strategy, structure, and ultimate success or failure of the enterprise.

KEY TERMS

adaptation
alienated returnees
biculturalism
cultural translators
culture shock
disillusionment
ethnocentric staffing model
expatriates
global staffing model
home-country nationals

honeymoon
host-country nationals
inpatriates
polycentric staffing model
proactive returnees
regiocentric staffing model
repatriation
resocialized returnees
reverse culture shock
third-country nationals

GLOBAL MANAGER'S WORKBOOK 13.1: GILLETTE'S INTERNATIONAL TRAINING PROGRAM

An overview of Gillette's International Training Program (ITP) is presented above. This program aims to develop a cadre of well-trained global managers that can help the company succeed in its various international markets. Since 70 percent of Gillette's sales are generated outside the United States, it is important for the company's overall strategy that this training program succeed. Assume that you have been hired by Gillette to provide a review and critique of their program. After reviewing the materials presented above, prepare a report that responds to the following issues:

1. Based on what you understand about the program, what are its principal strengths and weaknesses for Gillette? What are its principal strengths and weaknesses for the employees accepted into the program?
2. Do you agree with Gillette's regiocentric approach to global staffing?
3. All applicants to the ITP must be single, fluent in English, and younger than thirty years of age. What are the pros and cons of each of these three admission criteria? Do you agree or disagree with these criteria? Why?
4. Does Gillette have a special responsibility to ensure that roughly one-half of its ITP trainees are women? These women would then return to fill supervisory and managerial positions throughout the company. What is your recommendation, and why?
5. As an outside consultant, what specific suggestions would you offer to Gillette to make the ITP a better program?

GLOBAL MANAGER'S WORKBOOK 13.2: AMSTEL ENGINEERING

Amstel Engineering is a U.S. firm with 2,300 employees headquartered in San Francisco that does engineering consulting and large-scale construction projects around the world.[13] Regional offices are strategically located in Singapore, Berlin, and Mexico City, in addition to its home office in California. Amstel considers itself to be a true global enterprise. Its principal markets are in North America and the countries of the European Union, although it also does considerable business in the Pacific Rim and considers this to be its strongest emerging market. Company officials also see the Middle East as a strong potential market that has yet to be tapped. Annual revenues have been disappointing over the past two years, except in the Asia-Pacific region.

The company's corporate culture is characterized by innovation and creativity in meeting client needs, a strong commitment to quality and customer service, an inclusive multicultural workplace that values employee diversity, and a heavy emphasis on incentive compensation that rewards high performers and eliminates less productive ones. Amstel values its strong reputation for providing high-quality engineering and construction services around the world.

Amstel recently decided to restructure and revitalize its worldwide marketing efforts to gain a larger share of the global market for both engineering services and construction. To accomplish this, it plans to establish a new position of vice president for international marketing. The person hired will be responsible for introducing fresh ideas and new perspectives into the company and will lead a new initiative to generate additional business. There is currently no suitable internal candidate who is qualified to take on this role, so the company has decided to look outside to fill the position. The job carries a lucrative salary, fringe benefits, and stock options. The person hired will be based in San Francisco but will travel frequently.

After a lengthy search, five finalists have been identified. It is now time to decide whom to hire. Although all five candidates have expressed serious interest in the position, in this highly competitive market the company cannot assume that its first choice will accept an offer, so it is necessary to rank all five candidates in order of preference. In this way, the company is assured of a reasonable likelihood of securing a new vice president to oversee international operations.

The five candidates and their qualifications are as follows:

John Thornton, thirty-six, divorced with one child. John is currently job hunting. His former job as head of marketing for a single-product high-tech firm ended when Bechtel, the engineering giant, bought out the company. John had been with his employer since its inception ten years ago. Having to leave his job was an irony for John since it was largely due to his marketing and product development success that Bechtel was interested in buying the company. You sense that he is a little bitter, and he is clear that the job offered him by Bechtel after the buyout was not worthy of his consideration. He wants a new challenge.

John has an undergraduate degree in engineering and an M.B.A. from Stanford University. He lived in Europe for a time following graduation and has also traveled to Japan and China. He received a Fulbright scholarship five years ago to fund a two-year research project on the marketing of high-tech equipment to Bangladesh.

You have learned through some colleagues at another firm that John has a reputation for being somewhat aggressive and hard driving. He is described as a workaholic who has been known to work eighteen hours a day, six or even seven days a week. He seems to have little time for his personal life. In addition to his native English,

John has a reasonable command of French, although he admits he hasn't used it since his college days.

Peter van de Groot, forty-four, single. Peter is a white South African and the great-grandson of Dutch immigrants to that country. He worked in a key position in the international marketing division of ABB, a Swiss multinational engineering firm, until it withdrew from South Africa eight months ago. While ABB wished to retain him and offered to move him from Cape Town to its European headquarters, Peter decided that it was time to look elsewhere. He had begun to feel somewhat dead-ended in his position and apparently sees the Amstel position as an opportunity to try out new territory.

Like the other candidates for the position, Peter has a long list of accomplishments and is widely recognized as being outstanding in his field. People in your company who have had contacts with him say that Peter is creative, hardworking, and loyal. In addition, you have been told that Peter is a first-rate manager of people who is able to push his people to the highest levels of performance. However, some of his former colleagues describe him as being overly ambitious and sometimes condescending to subordinates.

Peter has a Ph.D. in engineering from Sellenbosch University, a leading South African university, as well as an M.B.A. from Manchester in the United Kingdom. He speaks and reads English, Afrikaans, and Swahili and can converse a bit in Dutch. Peter's male companion, Jan Smuts, would accompany Peter to San Francisco and would like Amstel's assistance in finding suitable employment in the area.

Peter has consistently been a vocal opponent of the old apartheid system in South Africa and remains a social activist. His long-standing support for native African rights has created some political enemies among some leading whites in that country, a principal reason for his interest in emigrating.

Zur Shapira, forty, married with five children. Zur grew up in Israel, the son of Russian immigrants. After receiving his M.B.A. from MIT's Sloan School of Management, he took his first job as a marketing manager for a small French manufacturing firm doing business in Israel. His success with this company led him to be hired away by a British high-tech start-up company in London. Again, he proved to be a successful manager, boosting the company's market share significantly in two years. After five years in England, Zur was offered an opportunity to return to Israel to oversee the international marketing efforts of a new industrial park containing fourteen high-tech firms built around a small research center. He was responsible for coordinating the relationships between the research scientists and the companies, as well as managing the large marketing department. Once again, he showed himself to be a competent manager.

You have learned through your contacts that Zur is highly respected and has extensive networks in the scientific and high-tech world. He is creative in his approach to marketing, often attempting risky strategies that many of his peers dismiss as being too threatening to the well-being of the firm. Zur, however, has generally succeeded in these endeavors.

Zur is a deeply religious man who must leave work by noon on Friday. He will not work on Saturdays nor on any of his religion's major or minor holidays—about eighteen each year. He will, however, work Sundays. In addition to his native Hebrew, he is fluent in English and speaks some French and Arabic.

Jung Chang, fifty, widow with one adult child. Jung is an ethnic Chinese woman who was born and raised in Singapore. Her parents emigrated there from Shanghai in search of a better life. Jung began her teaching career while finishing her Ph.D. in engineering at Columbia University in New York and has published several scientific papers in her area. Her initial research focused on the entrepreneurial skills of small engineering firms like Amstel.

Shortly after graduation, she went to work in the Singapore office of Fuji Heavy Industries and was responsible for securing new construction contracts in Singapore, Indonesia, and Malaysia. However, she continually felt that the company was unwilling to make full use of her skills because of her gender and left after ten years to return to teaching at Singapore's Nanyang Technical University. She has remained there ever since. She continues to write and conduct research on various aspects of marketing in entrepreneurial firms, including engineering firms. In addition, she has maintained an active engineering consulting practice throughout Southeast Asia.

You have learned through your office in Singapore that Jung's only child is twenty-three years old and severely mentally and physically disabled. You sense that part of her interest in the job with Amstel is to provide sufficient income to guarantee his care should anything happen to her. Her son would go to San Francisco with her should she get the job, where he would need to be enrolled in special support programs.

In addition to her fluency in Chinese and English, Jung has some familiarity with Japanese.

Kenji Nakamura, forty-one, married with two children. Kenji is currently a vice president for international marketing for Komatsu, the chief rival of Caterpillar in the heavy equipment manufacturing industry. Kenji lives outside of Osaka in Japan's Kansai region. Some colleagues have told you that he has an excellent reputation as an expert in international marketing and is widely respected in the industry, although he appears to be fairly quiet and shy in dealing with foreigners. The international market share of Komatsu has grown steadily since he joined the firm fifteen years ago.

Kenji started work for Komatsu directly after graduation from Keio University with a degree in engineering and construction, and worked his way up the ranks. He does not have a graduate degree. You sense that Kenji has a keen sense of organizational politics and is skilled in working with people to resolve potential conflicts. Since the Japanese economy has remained relatively flat for the past several years, future prospects for senior Japanese managers are beginning to look bleak. Kenji has told you that he is interested in the long-term growth potential offered by Amstel Engineering.

In addition to speaking Japanese and English, Kenji is able to carry on reasonable conversations in Chinese and has minimal working knowledge of German. His wife is currently a housewife and speaks only Japanese, although his children are fluent in English.

Based on your knowledge of both the company and the five applicants, please do the following:

1. Identify the key criteria that should be used to select among the five applicants for the position of vice president.
2. Based on your criteria, rank each of the five applicants in terms of their qualifications for the job. Provide a rationale for each of your rankings.

Job Candidate	Rank	Justification for Ranking
John Thornton		
Peter van de Groot		
Zur Shapira		
Jung Chang		
Kenji Nakamura		

NOTES

1. Randall Schuler, Susan Jackson, and Yadong Luo, *Managing Human Resources in Cross-Border Alliances* (London: Routledge, 2004).

2. John Cullen and K. Praveen Parboteeah, *Multinational Management: A Strategic Approach* (Cincinnati, OH: Southwestern College Publishing, 2005).

3. Stewart Black, Hal Gregersen, and Mark Mendenhall, *Global Assignments* (San Francisco: Jossey-Bass, 1992).

4. Ibid.

5. Richard Hodgetts and Fred Luthans, *International Management: Culture, Strategy, and Behavior*, 5th ed. (New York: McGraw-Hill/Irwin, 2003).

6. Nancy Adler, *International Dimensions of Organizational Behavior* (Cincinnati, OH: Southwestern College Publishing, 1997).

7. Rosalie Tung, "Expatriate Assignments: Enhancing Success and Minimizing Failure," *Academy of Management Executive* 1, no. 2 (1987): 117–26.

8. L. Chaney and J. Martin, *Intercultural Business Communication* (Upper Saddle River, NJ: Prentice Hall, 1995).

9. Harry Triandis, *Culture and Social Behavior* (New York: McGraw-Hill, 1994).

10. Ibid.

11. E. Smockum, "Don't Forget the Trailing Spouse," *Financial Times,* May 6, 1998, p. 22; Charles Hill, *International Business* (New York: McGraw-Hill/Irwin, 2003).

12. Adler, *International Dimensions of Organizational Behavior.*

13. This exercise was adapted from actual events, although the names and some of the circumstances have been changed.

14 | Managing a Competitive Global Workforce

LINCOLN ELECTRIC'S INCENTIVE SYSTEM

Lincoln Electric Company was founded in Cleveland, Ohio, in 1895 as a small manufacturing company in America's industrial heartland.[1] Today, it primarily manufactures arc-welding equipment and prospers in a highly competitive environment. Forty years ago, there were more than fifty manufacturers in this industry; today there are only six, and Lincoln has 40 percent of this market. By any measure, it is a success story.

Lincoln Electric's business strategy is simple: Sell high-value, high-quality products at competitive prices and provide outstanding customer service. Within the United States, it has a broad-based and well-respected reputation for quality, service, and competitiveness. It has maintained this reputation continuously since the 1930s. Technology has changed little over the years in the industry, and most competitors have access to the latest developments. Price, dependability, and quality represent critical success factors in sales and marketing.

The key to Lincoln Electric's success is its stable, hardworking, and highly skilled workforce. In a country that lavishes sizable executive bonuses on CEOs and other senior managers who can squeeze maximum productivity out of workers, Lincoln was founded—and continues to be run—on the twin principles of self-determination and equal treatment of all workers. And above all, it stresses pay for performance. When James Lincoln assumed control of the company in 1929, he set about clarifying his management philosophy. Lincoln had an abiding respect for the ability of the individual and believed that, correctly motivated, ordinary people could achieve extraordinary results. He felt that his company should be a meritocracy where people were rewarded based on their individual performance. He called his philosophy "intelligent selfishness." He also worked to remove all barriers between workers and managers and created one of the first open-door policies in the United States. All employees—including executives—ate in the same company cafeteria, and there were no reserved parking spaces.

James Lincoln believed firmly that gains in productivity should be shared with consumers in the form of lower prices, with employees in the form of higher pay, and with shareholders in the form of higher dividends. This philosophy was reinforced by the creation of an incentive system that continues unchanged to this day, more than seventy years after its introduction. Following the turn-of-the-century principles of Frederick Taylor and scientific management, all workers at Lincoln are paid on a piece-rate system. That is, they are paid for each unit they produce and do not receive either a salary or an hourly wage. There is no paid vacation, no paid sick leave, and no bonuses or job security for seniority. This principle applies to all employees up to and including the company president with minor adjustments for the nature of managerial work.

In addition to receiving piece-rate pay, workers can earn substantial bonuses based on their individual job performance and company profits. Bonuses are paid twice each year based on performance. Each employee is evaluated on four factors: quantity of work, quality of work, dependability, and cooperation. The first two criteria focus on individual job performance and productivity, while the second two focus on teamwork and cooperation in helping the company attain its corporate objectives.

Under this system, employee bonuses have been paid each year since 1934, and the company claims that its workers are the highest paid blue-collar workers in the world.[2] Indeed, employee bonuses often exceed annual wages, thereby more than doubling workers' incomes. There have been no layoffs in the company's long history, and absenteeism and turnover rates are the lowest in the industry. Indeed, it is said that when a severe snowstorm shuts Cleveland down, Lincoln employees make it to work. And despite its high employee compensation, Lincoln Electric's workers are so productive that the company has a lower cost structure than any of its competitors.

Lincoln Electric runs its operation like a cottage industry. It assumes that its workers are the best in the industry and can work independently. It therefore spends far less than its competitors on supervision; Lincoln Electric has a 100:1 supervisory ratio, compared to the industrial average of 25:1. The money saved is plowed back into company operations or given out in employee bonuses.

It takes a certain kind of employee to survive at Lincoln Electric. Employees must be skilled in their craft, physically strong and healthy, capable of working independently, highly motivated and, above all, mercenary. Money, not job satisfaction, is the principal motivator in this case. People who do not fit this description soon leave or are forced out. Older workers sometimes leave because they find they can't keep up with the fast pace and begin losing income. People who become ill often leave for the same reason. Critics have called it social Darwinism, but for many workers it seemed to fit with America's highly individualistic culture.

CULTURE AND WORK BEHAVIOR

Lester Thurow has suggested that in the new global economy, companies (and countries) will compete based largely on the quality of their human resources.[3]

That is, since most companies and most countries around the world can access the same raw materials, capital, and cheap labor, the ability to access, develop, and maintain human resources that are superior to those of one's competitors will differentiate the winners from the losers in the future. India and China have each proven this in global services and global production, respectively. Countries such as Japan, Germany, the United Kingdom, and the United States learned this a long time ago and chose to invest in higher education, leading-edge research, and the development of new technologies as a means of competing when inexpensive labor is largely unattainable locally. If such countries have a competitive edge, it lies in the technology sector. In all of the above cases from India to China to the United States and Europe, quality employees represent a critical strategic asset in global competition. And the quality, motivation, and work performance of these employees largely rests on cultural foundations.

As noted in Chapter 7, culture represents a potent influence on human behavior in organizations. Remember Fujisawa's observation that while Japanese and American managers may appear on the surface to behave similarly, they in fact often approach similar situations in very different ways. And this variance exists not just in Japan and the United States. Differences in employee behavior can be found around the world. British and Canadian companies motivate their employees primarily through financial incentives, while Germany and the Netherlands focus on providing employment stability and employee benefits. Indonesian and Korean companies prefer rigid and sometimes autocratic organizational hierarchies, where everyone knows their place, while Sweden and Norway stress informality, power sharing, and mutual benefit in the workplace. Some countries such as Germany even combine formality and rigid hierarchies with power sharing and an emphasis on securing mutual benefit for all employees.

Even so, managers involved in international business must recognize that if employee behavior is critical for the success of an organization, and if culture influences such behavior, then culture represents a major influence on the ways companies do business. Knowledge of this fact, as well as an understanding of how culture influences business practices, represents a critical strategic asset for global managers in a highly competitive world. To illustrate this point, we examine cultural differences as they relate to five aspects of management and work behavior: (1) personal work values; (2) incentives and rewards; (3) social loafing and group performance; (4) work and leisure; and (5) executive compensation.

PERSONAL WORK VALUES

Why do people work? How central is work in their lives? Do people live to work or work to live? These questions focus on the topic of personal work values; that is, what is it about work that people genuinely value? What motivates them to go to work? *Personal work values* reflect individual beliefs about desirable end states or modes of conduct for pursuing desirable end states. As such, they serve a useful function by providing individuals with guidelines and standards for determining their own behavior and evaluating the behavior of others. Throughout, the focus is on

understanding how personal values influence employee willingness and prepared-
ness to contribute to the attainment of organizational goals.

From a cross-cultural perspective, questions emerge concerning how variations
across cultures may or may not affect employee behavior in the workplace, as well
as what managers might do to accommodate such variations where they exist. For
example, values concerning the relative importance of individualism versus collectivism can influence the manner in which employees work together. Thus, many
Anglo-Americans tend to assert their individuality and revel in their differences,
while many Japanese tend to emphasize harmonious interdependence with others
and shun the spotlight.[4] Such values can represent an important influence on work-
related behaviors.

Personal work values have been studied systematically from a cross-cultural perspective for many years. One of the earliest studies was conducted by George England.[5] He and his colleagues focused on the impact of such values on employee
behavior and found significant differences across managers in the five countries
they studied. U.S. managers tended to be high in pragmatism, achievement orientation, and demand for competence. They placed a high value on profit maximization,
organizational efficiency, and productivity. Japanese and Korean managers also valued pragmatism, competence, and achievement, but emphasized organizational growth
instead of profit maximization. Indian managers stressed a moralistic orientation, a
desire for stability instead of change, and the importance of status, dignity, prestige,
and compliance with organizational directives. Finally, Australian managers tended
to emphasize a moralistic and humanistic orientation, an emphasis on both growth
and profit maximization, a high value on loyalty and trust, and a low emphasis on
individual achievement, success, competition, and risk.

This initial work by England and his colleagues formed the basis for a subsequent
international study of managerial values called the Meaning of Work Project.[6] This
study sought to identify the underlying meanings that individuals and groups attach
to work in several industrialized nations. In this study, Japan was found to have a
higher number of workers for whom work was their central life interest, compared to
both Americans and Germans, who placed a higher value on leisure and social interaction. A high proportion of Americans saw work as a duty, an obligation that must
be met. Japanese workers showed less interest in individual economic outcomes
from work than their Europeans and American counterparts.

As part of this survey, employees were asked to rank a list of common work goals
in order of importance in their lives. The results for Germany, Japan, and the United
States are shown in Exhibit 14.1. These rankings illustrate that while differences can
obviously be found across cultures, such differences may not be as diverse as is
commonly believed.

A very different example of personal work values can be seen in the African
concept of *ubuntu*. *Ubuntu* is perhaps best described as a clan value that requires
members to serve the needs of other group members even at their own expense.[7] It is
communal in the sense that it requires people to share what they have when someone
else is in need, regardless of who worked to acquire it. It is a manifestation of collectivism, a clan obligation that overrides any sense of ownership or concerns over

Exhibit 14.1

Work Priorities in Germany, Japan, and the United States

Work Goals	Germany	Japan	United States
Interesting work	3	2	1
Good pay	1	5	2
Job security	2	4	3
Job-person fit	5	1	4
Opportunities to learn	9	7	5
Variety in job content	6	9	6
Good interpersonal relations	4	6	7
Job autonomy	8	3	8
Convenient working hours	7	8	9
Opportunities for promotion and growth	10	11	10
Good working conditions	11	10	11

Source: Based on data reported in Meaning of Work International Research Team, *The Meaning of Work: An International View.* (New York: Academic Press, 1987); David Thomas, *International Management: A Cross-Cultural Perspective* (Thousand Oaks, CA: Sage, 2002), pp. 210–12.

inequity in input-output ratios. If your neighbor needs food, for example, it is your responsibility to feed him, even if you are also poor. This concept has no Western equivalent, except possibly compassion. When white Afrikaners began settling in South Africa to operate farms, factories, and mines, they quickly discovered that the incentive systems that they offered the local black population failed to have the desired effect. These systems were based on European values of individual achievement and competition and failed to recognize the communal values inherent in many tribal cultures. Even today, as South Africa emerges from apartheid, the new black government faces the same challenge: how to instill a will to achieve in a country that is rich in natural and human resources but largely lacking in a competitive spirit. This is not modern or traditional; it is simply different.

INCENTIVES AND REWARDS

Work motivation involves questions about how incentives, rewards, and reinforcements influence performance and work behavior.[8] Considerable research has indicated that both national characteristics and cultural characteristics can play significant roles in determining who becomes motivated, as well as who gets rewarded and how. The effects of these characteristics are illustrated in Exhibit 14.2. Culture can influence the effectiveness of incentive systems in at least three ways: (1) what is considered important or valuable by workers; (2) how motivation and performance problems are analyzed; and (3) what possible solutions to motivational problems lie in the feasible set for managers to select from.[9] Thus, while many independent-minded U.S. firms prefer merit-based reward systems as the best way to motivate employees, companies in more collectivistic cultures such as Japan, Korea, and Taiwan frequently reject this approach as being too disruptive of the corporate culture and traditional values. Likewise, firms in environments characterized by long-standing political in-

Exhibit 14.2

National and Cultural Influences on Incentive Systems

National Characteristics	Cultural Characteristics	Effective Incentive Systems
High levels of political or economic instability	Emphasis on team cohesiveness and mutual commitment	Use of group-based incentives and rewards
Long-standing socialist government, policies, or legal system	Preference for egalitarian reward systems	Few individual incentives; emphasis on equal distribution of rewards
Isolated or remote geographic location	Stress on meeting social and community needs	Incentives that reward social interaction and support
Equivocal language or communication patterns	Preference for high-context communication; increased tolerance for ambiguity	Emphasis on either subtlety or symbolism in administration of rewards, depending on the particular culture

Source: Based on Y. Paul Huo and Richard M. Steers, "Cultural Influences on the Design of Incentive Systems: The Case of East Asia," *Asia Pacific Journal of Management* 10, no. 1 (1993): 71–85.

stability, such as Venezuela or Ecuador, often stress group-based incentives to reinforce high team spirit and commitment to the organization.

In addition, the specific rewards that employees themselves seek from the job can vary across cultures. Some cultures emphasize security, while others emphasize harmony and congenial interpersonal relationships, and still others emphasize individual status and respect. For example, a study examined employees of a large multinational electrical equipment manufacturer operating in forty countries around the world and found important similarities as well as differences in what rewards employees wanted in exchange for good performance.[10] Interestingly, in all countries, the most important rewards that were sought involved recognition and achievement. Second in importance were improvements in the immediate work environment and employment conditions such as pay and work hours. Beyond this, however, a number of differences emerged in terms of preferred rewards. Some countries, such as England and the United States, placed a low value on job security compared to workers in many nations, while French and Italian workers placed a high value on security and good fringe benefits and a low value on challenging work. Scandinavian workers de-emphasized getting ahead and instead stressed greater concern for others on the job and for personal freedom and autonomy. Germans placed high on security, fringe benefits, and getting ahead, while Japanese ranked low on personal advancement and high on having good working conditions and a congenial work environment.

Many merit pay systems in the United States attempt to link compensation directly to corporate financial performance, thereby stressing equity. Other cultures believe compensation should be based on group membership or group effort, thereby stressing equality. This issue requires an assessment of distributive justice across cultures, especially as it relates to individualism or collectivism. One example of this can be seen in an effort by a U.S. multinational corporation to institute an individually based bonus system for its sales representatives in a Danish subsidiary. The sales force rejected the proposal because it favored one group over another. The Danish employees felt that all employees should receive the same amount of bonus instead of a given percent of one's salary, reflecting a strong sense of egalitarianism (see Chapter 7).[11]

Similarly, a study of Indonesian oil workers found that individually based incentive systems created more controversy than results. As one manager commented, "Indonesians manage their culture by a group process, and everybody is linked together as a team. Distributing money differently amongst the team did not go over that well; so, we've come to the conclusion that pay for performance is not suitable for Indonesia."[12] Similar results were reported in studies comparing Americans with Chinese, Russians, and Indians. In all three cases, Americans expressed greater preference than their counterparts for rewards to be based on performance instead of equality or need.[13]

It is interesting to note that the basis for some incentive systems has evolved over time in response to political and economic changes. China is frequently cited as an example of a country that is attempting to blend quasi-capitalistic economic reforms with a reasonably static socialist political state. On the economic front, China's economy has demonstrated considerable growth, as entrepreneurs are increasingly allowed to initiate their own enterprises largely free from government control. And within existing and former state-owned enterprises, some movement can be seen toward what is called a reform model of incentives and motivation (see Chapter 7). In this regard, a distinction can be made between the traditional Chinese incentive model, in which egalitarianism is stressed and rewards tend to be based on age, loyalty, and gender, and the new reform model, in which merit and achievement receive greater emphasis and rewards tend to be based on qualifications, training, level of responsibility, and performance. However, some researchers have suggested that the rhetoric in support of the reform model far surpasses actual implementation to date.

In Japan, meanwhile, efforts to introduce Western-style merit pay systems frequently led to an increase in overall labor costs. Since the companies that adopted the merit-based reward system could not simultaneously reduce the pay of less productive workers for fear of causing them to lose face and disturbing group harmony (*wa*), everyone's salary tended to increase.

Similar results concerning the manner in which culture can influence reward systems as well as other personnel practices emerged from a study among banking employees in Korea.[14] Two Korean banks were owned and operated as joint ventures with banks in other countries, one from Japan and one from the United States. In the American joint venture, U.S. personnel policies dominated management practice in the Korean bank, while in the Japanese joint venture, a blend of Japanese and Korean HRM policies prevailed. Employees in the joint venture with the Japanese bank were significantly more committed to the organization than employees in the U.S. joint venture. Moreover, the Japanese-affiliated bank also demonstrated significantly higher financial performance.

Cultural differences concerning uncertainty, risk, and control can also affect employee preferences for fixed versus variable compensation. More risk-oriented American managers are frequently prepared to convert 100 percent of their pay to variable compensation, while more risk-averse European managers would seldom commit to more than 10 percent.[15] Similarly, cultural variations can influence employee preferences for financial or nonfinancial incentives. Thus, Swedes will typically prefer additional time off for superior performance instead of additional income (due in part to their high tax rates), while if given a choice Japanese workers would prefer financial incentives (with a distinct preference for group-based incentives). Japanese workers tend to take only about half of their sixteen-day holiday entitlement (compared to thirty-five days in France and Germany) because taking all the time available may show a lack of commitment to the group. Japanese workers who take their full vacations or refuse to work overtime are frequently labeled *wagamama* (selfish). As a result, *karoshi* (death by overwork) is a serious concern in Japan, while Swedes see taking time off as part of an inherent right to a healthy and happy life.[16]

SOCIAL LOAFING AND GROUP PERFORMANCE

A key concern of high-performance work teams is maximizing the collective contribution of group members toward the attainment of important goals. In a competitive global economy, collective action becomes a strategic advantage that can differentiate winners from losers. Therefore, any tendencies by group members to restrict output in the belief that others will take up the slack represents a serious impediment to organizational effectiveness. This behavior is generally referred to as *social loafing* or the *free rider effect*.

Social loafing as a group phenomenon has been scrutinized in a small but important number of studies. Individuals may loaf in a group setting because they assume that others will ensure the attainment of the collective good, thereby freeing them up to redirect their individual efforts towards the attainment of additional personal gains. However, social loafing can be successful only when individual behavior can be hidden behind group behavior.

To accomplish this, group norms must support, or at least tolerate, a high level of individualism. It is therefore not surprising that loafing behavior tends to be more prevalent in more individualistic countries such as the United States and those of Western Europe than in more collectivistic countries such as those in East Asia. For example, in a study of Chinese and U.S. managers, it was found that the individualistic American groups engaged in significantly more social loafing than the more collectivist Chinese groups.[17] The implications for management are clear. Building cross-cultural teams must recognize how culture may affect both team dynamics and team results. (This issue is discussed in greater detail in Chapter 16.)

WORK AND LEISURE

It is often said that people in some societies work to live, while others live to work. We hear that Americans work harder than Europeans but that many Asians work

Exhibit 14.3

Vacation Policies in Selected Countries

Country	Typical Annual Vacation Policy
France	Two and a half days paid leave for each full month of service during the year
Germany	Eighteen working days paid leave following six months of service
Hong Kong	Seven days paid leave following twelve months of continuous service with same employer
Indonesia	Twelve days paid leave after twelve months of full service
Italy	Varies according to length of service, but usually between four and six weeks paid leave
Japan	Ten days paid leave following twelve months of continuous service, providing employee has worked at least 80 percent of this time
Malaysia	Varies according to length of service but usually between eight and sixteen days paid leave
Mexico	Six days paid leave
Philippines	Five days paid leave
Saudi Arabia	Fifteen days of paid leave upon completion of twelve months of continuous service with the same employer
Singapore	Seven days paid leave following twelve months of continuous employment
United Kingdom	No statutory requirement; most salaried staff receive about five weeks of paid leave; paid leave for workers based on individual labor contracts
United States	No statutory requirement; typically varies based on length of service and job function, usually between five and fifteen days paid leave annually

Source: Adapted from V. Frazee, "Vacation Policies Around the World," *Personnel Journal* 75 (1997): 9; and A. Phatak, R. Bhagat, and R. Kashlak, *International Management* (New York: McGraw-Hill/Irwin, 2004), p. 125.

harder than Americans. Several EU countries now have a standard thirty-five-hour workweek, while the norm in the United States is closer to forty-five. Many Europeans can retire at fifty-five, while most Americans must work until sixty or sixty-five. We see newspaper articles seeking to identify the hardest-working people in the world, as well as the laziest. We see wide variations in vacation time taken across countries, ranging from one or two weeks in much of Asia to four or five weeks in much of Europe (see Exhibit 14.3 for examples). The unanswered question throughout this debate is whether working harder than anyone else is a badge of honor or a sign of necessity or, worse still, some deep psychological malfunction.

In the never-ending search for competitive advantage, a key variable is labor cost and productivity. Consider: Not only does Europe have higher labor costs than the

United States does, but the average European worker is significantly less productive than his or her American counterpart on an annual basis. A recent study by the Paris-based Organization for Economic Cooperation and Development (OECD) found that the average U.S. worker produced $35,500 in goods and services annually, while the average European worker produced only $25,200, or 69 percent of the productivity of their U.S. counterparts.[18] This suggests that European companies are at a significant competitive disadvantage in the global marketplace. Among other things, their goods and services will likely cost more. However, a second study found that the vacation-loving French and Belgians outproduce Americans on a per-hour basis.[19] They work fewer hours but make each hour count more. At a certain point, the study concluded, there is a negative rate of return on productivity resulting from working too long. So, how do we calculate productivity—annually or hourly? Which is better for employees? Which is better for companies? And which is better for national economic development?

Now consider vacations. A recent *Business Week* survey found that Americans now take less vacation time than even the Japanese or the Koreans.[20] Specifically, the study found that on average employees took the following vacation times (including public holidays): forty-two days in Italy, thirty-seven days in France, thirty-five days in Germany, thirty-four days in Brazil, twenty-eight days in Britain, twenty-six days in Canada, twenty-five days in South Korea, twenty-five days in Japan, and thirteen days in the United States. Obviously these are averages, and considerable variations can be found across the workforce. Even so, consider the effects of such long hours on home life, personal relationships, and even health. In the United States, the average employee gives back 1.8 unused vacations days annually, worth $20 billion to employers. Some companies, such as SAS Institute, the world's largest privately held software company, are bringing the world to the workplace. Employees can consult nutritionists and doctors in their on-site medical facilities and bring their kids to on-site day camps, day care centers, and kindergartens. Again the question arises: Are such long hours necessary to get or stay ahead—either as an individual or as a corporation—or are they a sign of something else?

Finally, consider health and job satisfaction. It might be suggested that while Europeans load up on vacation time, Americans load up on consumer products. As the work pace quickens, health-related problems are rising, most notably heart problems resulting from job-related stress. So is employee dissatisfaction. A recent poll among U.S. workers found that, given a choice between two weeks of extra pay and two weeks of vacation, employees preferred the extra vacation by a 2:1 margin. However, the pressure to succeed and concern about the economy and job security frequently lead American workers in the opposite direction, toward more work and less play.

While perhaps overly simplistic, the work versus leisure conundrum provides an easy conceptual entry into cultural differences, especially as they relate to the world of work. It indicates how central work is in some people's lives. However, this debate is only part of a larger debate over the social and economic consequences of increasing globalization. As noted in Chapter 2, many people believe—correctly or incorrectly—that the quickening pace of globalization and the competitive intensity of the new

Exhibit 14.4

Average CEO Compensation Compared to Worker Income

Country	Pay Ratio	Country	Pay Ratio	Country	Pay Ratio
United States	475	United Kingdom	24	Netherlands	16
Venezuela	50	Thailand	24	France	14
Brazil	49	Australia	23	New Zealand	13
Mexico	47	South Africa	22	Sweden	12
Singapore	44	Canada	20	Germany	12
Argentina	44	Italy	20	Switzerland	11
Malaysia	42	Belgium	18	Japan	11
Hong Kong	41	Spain	16	South Korea	8

Source: Based on data from *The Economist,* September 30, 2000, p. 110. Numbers express the ratios between the average CEO compensation and the average compensation received by the average factory worker in each country.

global economy are changing how people live in ways not imagined earlier. The open question is whether these changes are for the better or for the worse.

EXECUTIVE COMPENSATION

Finally, consider the issue of executive compensation across cultures. Much has been written about excessive executive compensation, particularly in the United States. From a motivational standpoint, compensation is seen as the key to hiring and retaining the best executive leadership available. While it is true that incentive systems work, the question that many people are asking is, How much money is necessary to hire and motivate the right CEO? In the United States, we hear increasing concerns about the "imperial CEO," referring to what many consider to be excessive rewards that in many cases are not even tied to executive or corporate performance. In many cases, they are tied to the manipulation of stock prices, often by illegal or certainly unethical means. Issues of fairness abound.

What has many people upset is that while executives are making increasing amounts of money, rank-and-file workers are often making less, especially in the United States. Consider the following fact: Twenty years ago, the average American CEO made forty times the salary of the average factory worker in his or her company. Now this figure is well over four hundred times! Worse still, the United States seems to be way out in front of other nations in terms of this imbalance between workers' and executives' pay. Another way to understand this is to look at average CEO compensation compared to the average factory worker on a country-by-country basis, as shown in Exhibit 14.4. While aggregate data always contain some systematic errors—for example, the data for Korea do not include owner-CEOs, who can become incredibly wealthy even if they are officially paid very little—it is difficult to believe that the magnitude of these results is far from accurate. Recent laws passed in the United States and elsewhere, as well as stockholder suits and prosecutions for illegal activities, may begin to redress some of the more brazen inequities.

MOTIVATION ACROSS CULTURES

Work motivation can be defined as that which energizes, directs, and sustains human behavior in the workplace.[21] Without a highly motivated workforce that uses its brains, not just its backs, competitive advantage becomes highly problematic. This is particularly true as we move further into an era where technology and knowledge often determine winners and losers. Simply put, competitive organizations need all of their employees striving on behalf of the organization's goals and objectives, not just the people at the top. The challenge for the global manager is to accomplish this within a work context where behavior is often determined by cultural variance. As noted above, culture influences a wide variety of attitudes and behaviors. The question for managers, then, is how to use this knowledge to further the organization's competitive edge.

CULTURE, MOTIVATION, AND PERFORMANCE

How can we make sense out of these various findings concerning the role of culture in work motivation? What implications can be identified for global managers? To answer these questions, it may be useful to consider a process model of culture, motivation, and work behavior, as shown in Exhibit 14.5. As a point of departure, we must recognize that cultural differences represent a fundamental influence on both individual and environmental characteristics. Culture provides the stage upon which life events transpire. Individual characteristics that can be influenced by cultural variations include the development of one's self-concept, personal values and beliefs, and individual needs, traits, and aspirations. Environmental characteristics that can be influenced by culture include family and community structures, values and norms, education and socialization experiences, occupational and organizational cultures, the status of economic development, and the political and legal system. Some cultures emphasize hard work and sacrifice, while others emphasize social relationships and enjoyment. Some stress individual achievement, while others stress group achievement. Some stress communal rewards, while others stress individual rewards. Culture also influences the beliefs and values of one's family and friends; younger members of a society learn what to believe in and what to strive for at least in part from older generations. Educational institutions are significantly influenced by culture, as are organizational and occupational values.

As a result of these individual and environmental characteristics, people enter the workplace already imbued with a set of culturally derived work norms and values about what constitutes acceptable or fair working conditions, what they wish to gain in exchange for their labor, how hard they intend to work, and how they view their career. Included in this group of work norms and values are the general strength and quality of the employee work ethic, individual versus group achievement norms, proclivity toward egalitarianism, tolerance for ambiguity, social loafing or free rider effect, and norms concerning conformity and deviance from group wishes.

However, culturally based influences on work norms and values are not universal. Even in the most collectivistic societies, individual differences exist, although the magnitude of variation may differ by culture. Professionals tend to expect more from

Exhibit 14.5   **Culture, Motivation, and Work Behavior**

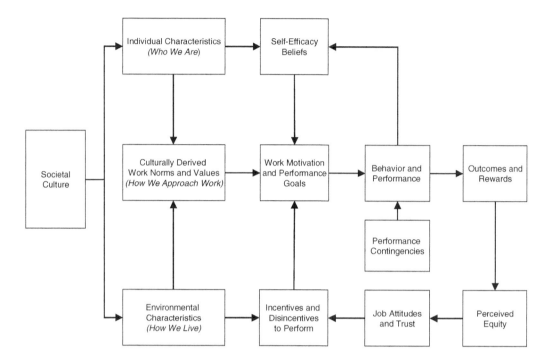

the workplace in terms of status, rewards, and freedom of action than do most blue-collar workers in both Japan and the United States, for example. Moreover, some cultures attempt to minimize status and reward differences between occupational groupings (e.g., Sweden), while others tend to enhance them (e.g., Korea). Individual and group assessments of equity, or what is deemed to be fair and just, seem to underlie this process across cultures.

In addition, culture influences one's self-efficacy beliefs through education and socialization experiences, as well as the level of incentives and disincentives that are offered to employees in exchange for their labor. As we might expect, incentives and disincentives are frequently influenced by such factors as education level, occupation, corporate personnel practices, level of economic prosperity, group norms, and the political and legal system in which people work.

As shown in Exhibit 14.5, work motivation and employee performance goals are largely influenced by three factors: (1) culturally derived work norms and values, (2) self-efficacy beliefs, and (3) rewards, incentives, and disincentives that result from performance. Work norms and values are important because they help determine the nature and quality of work effort, whether effort is to be based on the individual or on the group, beliefs about the equity and equality of incentives, and levels of work-related uncertainty that can be tolerated on the job. Self-efficacy is important because it determines one's confidence to put forth effort on the job. Finally, intrinsic and extrinsic rewards of various types are important because they provide both the incentives and the disincentives to perform. Expectations concerning possible rewards represent a powerful force for employee motivation, although the magnitude and type of such incentives may vary across cultures. For example, considerable research indicates that in many Western societies pay-for-performance compensation systems can significantly help to raise productivity. In other cultures, however, merit-based systems frequently fail due to egalitarian norms.

Company-based incentives can also have the effect of creating disincentives to perform, largely through the intervention of group norms. Social phenomena, such as social loafing, and sanctions governing levels of output frequently serve to restrict the impact of incentives on performance. In some cases, employees are pressured by colleagues not to break group-determined production quotas, despite incentives to do so. In other cases, employees are legitimately concerned about working themselves out of a job if they perform at high levels.

We would expect work motivation and an employee's performance goals to influence actual performance. However, this motivation alone is insufficient to guarantee high performance. In addition, employees must possess several performance contingencies, including having relevant personal abilities and job skills, a clear understanding of the requirements of the task, and the appropriate tools and technology to complete task assignments efficiently. To a large extent, available educational opportunities, on-the-job training, supervisory competence, and the company's or country's ability to secure relevant job technology to support employee efforts determine these factors. Obviously, the acquisition of some of these performance contingencies is also influenced by cultural factors.

As a result of subsequent job performance, employees receive a variety of outcomes and rewards. These can be extrinsic or intrinsic in nature. The manner in which employees interpret these consequences will largely influence their perceived equity, as well as the nature and quality of their resulting job attitudes. To the extent that employees believe that the rewards they receive are fair and just, we would expect them to develop more positive work attitudes, as well as increased confidence and trust in management to be fair. To the extent that employees see the rewards and outcomes as unfair or inequitable, we would expect them to develop more negative attitudes, as well as increased distrust of the future actions of management. The nature and quality of both job attitudes and employee trust then feed back to influence how employees view future incentives offered by their employer, thereby influencing subsequent work motivation and performance goals. Moreover, when employee performance levels are high, we would also expect self-efficacy beliefs to be reinforced, thereby increasing or at least preserving subsequent motivational levels. We would expect the opposite impact on self-efficacy and subsequent motivation when employee performance levels are low.

MOTIVATIONAL STRATEGIES

Based on this model, what lessons can be drawn concerning how to motivate employees in different cultures? To answer this question, we can combine the motivational model just described with the "big five" cultural dimensions discussed in

Chapter 8. As shown in Exhibit 14.6, finding the most appropriate motivational techniques depends on what culture managers are working in, and differences in techniques across cultures can be substantial.

Consider two examples: First, successful incentives programs in individualistic cultures would likely emphasize individual performance and rely heavily on financial rewards, while such incentives in more collectivistic cultures would likely rely more heavily on group-based incentives and seniority-based rewards. As Akio Morita, the late founder of Sony Corporation frequently observed, "To motivate employees, you must bring them into the family and treat them like respected members of it."[22] While this assertion may make sense in Japan, it probably makes less sense in several other cultures. Second, successful supervision in more hierarchical cultures would tend to be more directive, while supervision in more egalitarian cultures would tend to be more consultative. In both examples, it can be seen that the successful global manager bases his or her motivation and reward strategies on a clear understanding of these cultural differences.

With all these differences in motivational practices, it is interesting to ask where employees report the greatest levels of satisfaction. As shown in Exhibit 14.7, the results are not unpredictable. The most satisfied employees are not found in richer countries or the countries of a particular continent. They are not found in countries that claim certain religious affiliations, nor are they found exclusively in either large or small countries. Instead, the most satisfied employees tend to be found in those countries where the prevailing management systems and motivational programs are compatible with and supportive of local cultures. These findings caution against a presumed "best practices" approach to management and motivation across diverse cultures. Ignoring cultural influences on employee work behavior is clearly done at a manager's—and an organization's—peril.

LEADERSHIP ACROSS CULTURES

If leadership styles can vary widely across companies in a single country (e.g., Google and General Motors in the United States; Deutsche Bank and SAP in Germany; NTT DoCoMo and Komatsu in Japan), imagine how difficult it is to generalize about leadership differences across countries. While several serious attempts have been made to do just this (e.g., the GLOBE study discussed in Chapter 7), results are tentative at best. In fact, it is difficult to gauge with any degree of certainty how management or leadership styles vary across cultures, let alone which leadership style might be most successful in a particular culture.

CULTURAL DIFFERENCES AND THE MANAGERIAL ROLE

One of the more interesting attempts to study culture as it relates to leader behavior was conducted by INSEAD professor Andre Laurent.[23] He focused his attention on understanding the normative managerial role (that is, what is expected of managers) and discovered significant differences across cultures. He asked managers from different cultures a series of questions dealing with effective management. His results

Exhibit 14.6

Culture and Work Motivation Strategies

Cultural Dimensions	Motivational Strategies

Relationship with the Environment:

Mastery
: Create a competitive environment within the organization to stimulate best efforts
Emphasize performance-based incentives using monetary rewards
Showcase high performers
Encourage thinking big; conquer the environment
View employees as a gene pool; encourage turnover among poor performers
Provide assertiveness training programs

Harmony
: Emphasize harmony and team effort for collective results
Emphasize seniority or membership-based incentives
Showcase team efforts and organization-wide accomplishments
Encourage respect for traditions and the environment
Encourage continued membership for entire work force

Social Organization:

Individualism
: Emphasize extrinsic rewards (e.g., pay) tied to personal achievement
Emphasize individually based incentives
Stress personal responsibility for accomplishment
View employees as performers
Provide employees with autonomy and opportunities for advancement

Collectivism
: Emphasize intrinsic rewards (e.g., meaningful work) tied to commitment and loyalty
Emphasize group-based incentives
Stress group norms and moral persuasion
View employees as family members
Build teams and networks focused on task performance

Power Distribution:

Hierarchical
: Emphasize extrinsic rewards and sizable salary differentials
Provide clear directives to subordinates
Support decisive and powerful leaders
Reward subordinate compliance with management directives

Egalitarian
: Emphasize intrinsic rewards and minimal salary differentials
Encourage participative or consultative decision making
Support flexible and collaborative leaders
Reward constructive feedback and creativity

Rule Orientation:

Rule-based
: State rules, regulations, and policies clearly and publicly
Enforce rules and regulations uniformly
Tie rewards to rule compliance
Where possible, provide employees with security and certainty
Where possible, make decisions based on objective criteria

Relationship-based
: Create opportunities for employees to develop social relationships at work
Invest time meeting with employees individually and in groups; build relationships and informal networks
Use influential people to help motivate
Account for extenuating circumstances in rule enforcement
Where possible, show patience with first-time rule breakers
Keep your word; build trust with employees

Time Orientation:

Monochronic
: Provide simple and straightforward directions, one task at a time
Provide strict time limits for each project; require intermittent written progress reports
Focus on the job; keep personal relations to a minimum

Polychronic
: Identify task requirements but let employees choose how best to accomplish them
Provide flexible time limits for various tasks; check progress through personal discussions
Focus on personal relations as a means of succeeding on the job

Exhibit 14.7

Job Satisfaction Across Cultures

Country	% Employees Reporting High Job Satisfaction	Country	% Employees Reporting High Job Satisfaction
Denmark	61	Argentina	38
India (middle class)	55	Austria	36
Norway	54	Israel	33
United States	50	Brazil	28
Ireland	49	France	24
Canada	48	Japan	16
Germany	48	South Korea	14
Australia	46	China	11
Mexico	44	Czech Republic	11
Slovenia	40	Ukraine	10
United Kingdom	38	Hungary	9

Source: Adapted from M. Boyle, "Nothing Is Rotten in Denmark," *Fortune,* February 19, 2001, pp. 242–43.

demonstrate wide variations in responses across cultures, as shown in Exhibit 14.8. For each set of responses, note how far apart typical managers are in responding to rather simple statements about appropriate managerial behavior. For each of the three questions, the percentage of managers in agreement ranges from 10 to 78 percent, 17 to 83 percent, and 26 to 74 percent, respectively. These percentages aren't even close. If managers from different countries differ so much in their descriptions of the correct managerial role, it is no wonder that significant differences can be found in actual management style across national boundaries.

A similar study by Hampden-Turner and Trompenaars also found significant differences across managers based on culture, as shown in Exhibit 14.9. For example, leaders in the United States, Sweden, Japan, Finland, and Korea showed more overall drive and initiative than leaders in Portugal, Norway, Greece, and the United Kingdom. Likewise, leaders in Sweden, Japan, Norway, and the United States tended to be more willing to delegate authority than leaders in Greece, Portugal, Spain, and Italy. Findings such as these suggest that leadership is culturally sensitive and that effective leadership strategies can at times vary across cultures.

Other studies confirm this conclusion. For example, one study found that British managers were more participative than their French and German counterparts.[24] Two possible reasons were suggested for this. First, England is more egalitarian than France and the political environment supports this approach. Second, top British managers tend not to be involved in the day-to-day affairs of the business and delegate many key decisions to middle- and lower-level managers. The French and Germans, by contrast, tend to prefer a more work-centered, authoritarian approach. While it is true that German codetermination leads to power sharing with employees throughout the organization, some have argued that this has resulted not from German culture but rather from German laws. By contrast, Scandinavian countries make

Exhibit 14.8

Cultural Differences in the Managerial Role

	% Managers Who Agree with Each Statement		
Country	"Managers must have the answers to most questions asked by subordinates."	"The main reason for a chain of command is so people know who has authority."	"It is okay to bypass the chain of command to get something done efficiently."
China	74	70	59
France	53	43	43
Germany	46	26	45
Indonesia	73	83	51
Italy	66	—	56
Japan	78	50	—
Netherlands	17	31	44
Spain	—	34	74
Sweden	10	30	26
United States	18	17	32
United Kingdom	27	34	35

Source: Data from Andre Laurent's study of managerial behavior, reported in John Saee, *Managing Organizations in a Global Economy* (Mason, OH: Thompson/Southwestern, 2005), pp. 39–42.

wide use of participative leadership approaches, again following from their somewhat more egalitarian culture.

On the other side of the world, Japanese managers tend to be somewhat authoritarian but at the same time listen to the opinions of their subordinates. One study found that Japanese managers place greater confidence in the skills and capabilities of their subordinates than do their counterparts in other cultures.[25] Another feature of Japanese leadership is an inclination to give subordinates ambiguous instead of highly specific goals. That is, many Japanese managers tell their workers what they want in a general way but leave it to the workers to determine the details and the work plan. This practice contrasts sharply with that of typical U.S. managers, who like to take a hands-on management-by-objectives approach to project management.

A good example of this can be seen in the leadership style of Konosuke Matsushita, founder of the Matsushita Business Group (Panasonic, Quasar, and National).[26] Matsushita encouraged his employees at all levels to visualize the results of any projects, not just to ask how to build something. His management style stressed what he called the seven spiritual values of his company: (1) national service through industry, (2) fairness in all things, (3) harmony and cooperation in social relations, (4) struggle for betterment, (5) courtesy and humility, (6) adjustment and assimilation, and (7) gratitude. To develop these spiritual values, Matsushita established a management training school for his employees based on Buddhist principles, something not often seen in the West. In doing so, he placed his personal reputation behind his company's determination to achieve greatness on behalf of both company and country.

Exhibit 14.9

Cultural Differences in Leader Behavior

Country	Leader's Sense of Drive and Initiative	Country	Leader's Willingness to Delegate Authority
United States	74	Sweden	76
Sweden	72	Japan	69
Japan	72	Norway	69
Finland	70	United States	66
Korea	68	Singapore	65
Netherlands	67	Denmark	65
Singapore	66	Canada	64
Switzerland	66	Finland	63
Belgium	65	Switzerland	62
Ireland	65	Netherlands	61
France	65	Australia	61
Austria	63	Germany	61
Denmark	63	New Zealand	61
Italy	62	Ireland	60
Australia	62	United Kingdom	59
Canada	62	Belgium	55
Spain	62	Austria	54
New Zealand	59	France	54
Greece	59	Italy	47
United Kingdom	58	Spain	44
Norway	55	Portugal	43
Portugal	49	Greece	38

Source: Adapted from C. Hampden-Turner and F. Trompenaars, *The Seven Cultures of Capitalism* (New York: Doubleday, 1993). Findings are expressed in percentage of agreement by managers.

LEADERSHIP STRATEGIES

Based on this discussion, consider how managers from various countries can adapt their approach to leadership based on cultural differences (see Exhibit 14.10). For example, leaders in mastery-oriented cultures such as those found in North America and parts of Western Europe can demand excellence from their employees and establish a competitive work environment to encourage greater effort. However, such efforts will likely fail in more harmony-oriented cultures such as Mexico or China. In these countries, leaders are advised to build a mutually supportive work environment and stress a balance between accomplishing key business goals and maintaining social harmony. Likewise, leaders in monochronic cultures, again such as those found in North America, need to establish clear task-directed goals and specific deadlines for task accomplishment. By contrast, leaders in more polychronic cultures such as

Exhibit 14.10

Culture and Leadership Strategies

Cultural Dimensions	Leadership Strategies

Relationship with the Environment:

Mastery	Demand excellence; encourage or cajole employees to try harder Set challenging goals Provide employees with opportunities for achievement and advancement Create a competitive work environment Focus attention on current activities and goals Tie rewards to performance
Harmony	Encourage employees to strive for a balance between corporate goals and societal good Create a mutually supportive work environment Encourage all employees to build relations with the external community Focus attention on long-term activities and goals Tie rewards to personal integrity and commitment to organization

Social Organization:

Individualism	Focus on individual assignments and accountability Tie rewards to individual performance Establish written policies or agreements governing work goals and rewards Appeal to employees' need for achievement
Collectivism	Focus on group assignments and accountability Tie rewards to group performance Establish and nurture personal relationships with employees Appeal to employees' sense of duty and commitment

Power Distribution:

Hierarchical	Use directive, autocratic leadership style Focus on top-down decision making Rebuff challenges to one's authority
Egalitarian	Use consultative, participative leadership style Focus on participative decision making Accept questions or reasoned challenges from subordinates

Rule Orientation:

Rule-based	Make sure everyone understands your priorities and objectives Demonstrate clearly who is in charge Reward those who follow stipulated policies and punish those who don't Make clear and public decisions on matters that affect employees Build confidence and a sense of security in followers
Relationship-based	Where possible, lead through informal contacts and relationships Make maximum use of social networks to accomplish critical tasks Show subordinates that they can achieve desired rewards by supporting you Where possible, show patience and flexibility in leading others Recognize that there are many ways to attain success

Time Orientation:

Monochronic	Provide clear job assignments with specific and realistic deadlines Expect punctuality in meetings and work assignments Don't overload employees with too many diverse assignments Focus on specific short-term assignments where possible
Polychronic	Provide clear job assignments, but set deadlines prior to when work is actually required Expect delays in meetings and work assignments Recognize that employees can manage multiple and conflicting job assignments Be tolerant of personal issues commingling with work activities

France or Italy should expect delays in meeting goals and must accommodate greater interactions between work goals and nonwork activities. In both cases, successful managers develop an awareness of such differences and adapt their leadership style to the extent possible to match the local culture.

KEYS TO SUCCESSFUL GLOBAL LEADERSHIP

Finally, as noted above, successful global managers adapt both their approach to employee motivation and their leadership style to fit local cultures. A critical question in this regard is how managers can accomplish this. Research has shown that while all managers are capable of adjusting their management style to some degree, some are better at it than others. The key question thus becomes, Which managers are more likely to succeed in adapting to various cultures and becoming successful global managers? The answer lies in a series of personal traits that successful global managers seem to have in abundance. These are as follows:[27]

- *Cosmopolitan outlook.* Be sufficiently flexible to operate comfortably in different cultural environments.
- *Intercultural communication skills.* Know at least one foreign language and understand and appreciate the complexities of interacting with people from other cultures.
- *Cultural sensitivity.* Appreciate cultural differences and use experiences in different national, regional, and organizational cultures to build relationships with culturally diverse people.
- *Rapid acculturation.* Have an ability to adjust quickly to strange and different surroundings.
- *Knowledge of cultural and institutional influences on management.* Understand how national cultures and social institutions affect the management process.
- *Facilitator of subordinates' intercultural development.* Have an ability to use one's experiences to help subordinates prepare for overseas assignments.
- *Ability to create cultural synergy.* Understand how to build cross-cultural teams and capitalize on cultural diversity for the benefit of the organization.
- *Global learning.* Understand and use international media, transportation, and travel in ways that support the global enterprise.

Many of these global leadership traits can be developed through personal initiative and hard work; others probably cannot. Even so, this list nicely summarizes what companies want to see in global managers in order to succeed abroad. It seems clear that as the world of business draws closer together, companies in all countries will require managers who can work in a truly global environment. In this environment, successful managers bring a depth and breadth of understanding of how to capitalize on cultural differences in ways that enhance both corporate goals and employee welfare. In large measure, this is what distinguishes managers who can succeed in their local surroundings from managers who can succeed in the international business arena.

KEY TERMS

free rider effect
karoshi
personal work values
social loafing
ubuntu

GLOBAL MANAGER'S WORKBOOK 14.1: PERSONAL WORK VALUES

Rank the following ten work-related values from 1 to 10 in order of their importance to you in your future job and career. While all of these traits may be important to you, the emphasis here is on the relative importance of each dimension. When you have finished, compare your results with those of others. Where are the differences most significant? What are the managerial implications of these differences?

_____	Challenging work
_____	Good pay and fringe benefits
_____	Good social relationships at work
_____	Group accomplishment
_____	Job security
_____	Opportunities to learn and develop on the job
_____	Personal control over my work
_____	Personal recognition
_____	Respect from others
_____	Variety in my work activities

GLOBAL MANAGER'S WORKBOOK 14.2: LINCOLN ELECTRIC GOES INTERNATIONAL

In the early 1990s, Lincoln Electric decided to expand its operations internationally and become a bigger player in the emerging global economy.[28] It first set its sights on Germany, buying a small German arc-welding equipment manufacturer called Messer Griesheim. None of the American executives involved in the acquisition decision had any international experience, but they believed that because they had been so successful in the United States, success would likewise follow elsewhere. John Gonzales, vice president of engineering, was assigned to be managing director of the new acquisition. Like the other executives, Gonzales also lacked international experience and, in addition, decided to run the venture from Lincoln Electric's home office in Cleveland, Ohio.

One of his first decisions was to retain the local German managers, since they best understood local customs and work practices. It was assumed that the Lincoln Electric compensation system would be adapted to fit local conditions, leading to increased productivity through heightened individual motivation. As Lincoln Electric's CEO observed several years later, "Our managers didn't know how to run foreign operations, nor did they understand foreign cultures. Consequently, we had to rely on the people in our foreign companies—people we didn't know and who didn't us."[29]

Once the purchase had been completed, it quickly became apparent that the local German managers were either unable or unwilling to introduce Lincoln Electric's individualistic incentive plan among workers, who were used to a somewhat more collectivistic work culture. Finally, out of exasperation, U.S. headquarters ordered it done.

The response of the employees was quick and decisive. Employee grievances and even lawsuits arose challenging the newly imposed system, which was seen by many as being exploitative and even inhumane. Workers were being asked to work ever harder with little consideration to the quality of living. Many workers rejected the piece-rate concept on principle, while others preferred extra leisure time over higher wages and were not prepared to work as hard as their U.S. counterparts.

After a visit to the German facility to see firsthand what was happening, Lincoln Electric's president observed, "Even though German factory workers are highly skilled and, in general solid workers, they do not work nearly as hard or as long as the people in our Cleveland factory. In Germany, the average factory workweek is thirty-five hours. In contrast, the average workweek in Lincoln's U.S. plants is between forty-three and fifty-eight hours, and the company can ask people to work longer hours on short notice—a flexibility that is essential for our system to work. The lack of such flexibility was one of the reasons why our approach would not work in Europe."[30]

At the same time, a major recession was hitting Europe and sales declined sharply. Between the "poor work attitude" of the German workers and the decline in sales, Lincoln Electric had to make a decision that would satisfy the shareholders and employees back home who were subsidizing the German venture. In 1993, it closed the Messer factory and decided to export U.S.-made products to Germany instead.

Looking back over their German misadventure, Lincoln Electric executives drew what for them was a surprising conclusion: "We had long boasted that our unique culture and incentive system—along with the dedicated, skilled workforce that the company had built over the decades—were the main sources of Lincoln's competitive advantage. We had assumed that the incentive system and culture could be transferred abroad and that the workforce could be quickly replicated."[31]

Lincoln Electric's disappointment in Germany was soon replaced with optimism following its experience with a Mexican subsidiary that occurred about the same time. The company had purchased a unionized manufacturing plant in Mexico City. Despite the fact the piece-rate systems are generally rejected by Mexican workers (like their German counterparts), Lincoln introduced the system gradually and only following discussions with workers in the plant. Initially, when employees expressed reservations about the Lincoln plan, executives asked for two Mexican volunteers to test-drive the system. They were guaranteed that they would not lose money under the system during the trial period, but could keep any additional income they earned. Two employees reluctantly agreed to try the system.

Soon, as the two workers began making more than their colleagues did, other employees asked to join the plan. Over the next two years, everyone in the plant gradually asked to join. Today, the Mexican facility continues to prosper under the Lincoln incentive system.

Comparing the two experiences, Lincoln Electric concluded that moving across borders must be done slowly and only after a thorough understanding of local cultures. Moreover, it learned that transplanting ideas—whether they relate to incentive systems, management practices, or anything else—can succeed only after a thorough dialogue with the workers who are directly involved.

QUESTIONS FOR DISCUSSION

1. First, using the materials from this chapter and Chapter 8, complete the cultural profiles for the United States, Germany, and Mexico in the space below. What are the principal differences across the three countries? What are the principal similarities?

Cultural Dimensions	United States	Germany	Mexico
Relationship with the environment			
Social organization			
Power distribution			
Rule orientation			
Time orientation			

2. Based on your assessment, is the Lincoln Electric incentive system as applied in Cleveland, Ohio, compatible with the general culture of the United States?
3. Would you like to work at Lincoln Electric–USA? Why or why not?
4. From what you have discovered, what motivates employees in Germany? What makes a good leader in Germany?
5. Based on your answer to question 4, why did Lincoln Electric encounter so much difficulty transferring its incentive program to Germany? What, if anything, could the U.S. executives have done better to make this approach succeed?
6. From what you have learned, what motivates employees in Mexico? What makes a good leader in Mexico?
7. Why do you think the Mexican venture succeeded while the German venture failed?

8. In view of the rush toward globalization, do you believe that more countries in the future will adopt incentive systems similar to Lincoln Electric's as a means of increasing job performance? If not, how can companies from cultures that do not support Lincoln-like systems compete and survive as the global economy becomes less and less forgiving?

Notes

1. J. O'Connell, "Lincoln Electric: Venturing Abroad," *Harvard Business School Case* 9—398-095, April 1998; Charles Hill, *International Business* (New York: McGraw-Hill/Irwin, 2003); Donald Hastings, "Lincoln Electric's Harsh Lessons from International Expansion," *Harvard Business Review,* May–June 1999, pp. 163–178; Randall Schuler, Susan Jackson, and Yadong Luo, *Managing Human Resources in Cross-Border Alliances* (London: Routledge, 2004).

2. Hastings, "Lincoln Electric's Harsh Lessons."

3. Lester Thurow, *Head-to-Head: The Coming Economic Battle Among Japan, Europe, and America* (New York: Warner, 1993).

4. H.R. Markus and S. Kitayama, "Culture and the Self: Implications for Cognition, Emotion, and Motivation," *Psychological Review* 98, no. 2 (1991): 224–53.

5. George England, *The Manager and His Values* (Cambridge, MA: Ballinger, 1975).

6. Meaning of Work International Research Team, *The Meaning of Work: An International View* (New York: Academic Press, 1987); David Thomas, *International Management: A Cross-Cultural Perspective* (Thousand Oaks, CA: Sage, 2002), pp. 210–12.

7. Mzamo Mangaliso, "Building Competitive Advantage from Ubuntu," *Academy of Management Executive* 15, no. 3 (2001): 23–35.

8. Lyman Porter, Greg Bigley, and Richard Steers, *Motivation and Work Behavior,* 7th ed. (New York: McGraw-Hill/Irwin, 2003); Richard Steers, Richard Mowday, and Debra Shapiro, "The Future of Work Motivation," *Academy of Management Review* 29, no. 3 (2004): 379–85.

9. Paul Huo and Richard Steers, "Cultural Influences on the Design of Incentive Systems: The Case of East Asia," *Asia Pacific Journal of Management* 10, no. 1 (1993): 71–85.

10. Richard M. Steers and Carlos Sanchez-Runde, "Culture, Motivation, and Work Behavior," in *Handbook of Cross-Cultural Management,* ed. Martin J. Gannon and Karen L. Newman (Oxford: Blackwell, 2002), pp. 190–216.

11. Ibid.

12. Ibid., p. 205.

13. Ibid.

14. Sang Nam, "Culture, Control, and Commitment in an International Joint Venture," *International Journal of Human Resource Management* 6 (1995): 553–67.

15. Steers and Sanchez-Runde, "Culture, Motivation, and Work Behavior."

16. Ibid.

17. Christopher Earley, *Face, Harmony, and Social Structure* (New York: Oxford University Press, 1997).

18. Gregory Viscusi, "U.S. Production Still Tops Europe's," *Register Guard,* August 27, 2002, p. B-1.

19. Diane Brady, "Rethinking the Rat Race," *Business Week,* August 26, 2002, p. 143.

20. Ibid.

21. Porter, Bigley, and Steers, *Motivation and Work Behavior.*

22. Akio Morita, *Made in Japan: Akio Morita and Sony* (New York: Dutton, 1986), p. 130.

23. Andre Laurent, "The Cultural Diversity of Western Conceptions of Management," *International Studies of Management and Organization* 13, nos. 1–2 (Spring-Summer 1983): 75–96.

24. Richard Hodgetts and Fred Luthans, *International Management: Culture, Strategy, and Behavior*, 5th ed. (New York: McGraw-Hill/Irwin, 2003).

25. James Abbeglen and George Stalk, *Kaisha: The Japanese Corporation* (New York: Harper and Row, 1985).

26. John Kotter, *Matsushita Leadership: Lessons from the 20th Century's Most Remarkable Entrepreneur* (New York: Free Press, 1997).

27. Phillip Harris, Robert Moran, and Sarah Moran, *Managing Cultural Differences,* 6th ed. (Amsterdam: Elsevier, 2004).

28. O'Connell, "Lincoln Electric"; Hastings, "Lincoln Electric's Harsh Lessons."

29. Hastings, "Lincoln Electric's Harsh Lessons," p. 166.

30. Ibid., p. 174.

31. Ibid., p. 178.

Managing Total Quality and Employee Involvement

Is Siemens Still German?

In early 2002, industrial workers at the Siemens power generator factory in Erfurt, Germany, made then-CEO Heinrich von Peirer an honorary member of their works council. His membership was a gesture of gratitude for the company's efforts to keep the inefficient factory open. By 2004, however, von Peirer was no long welcome on the council. Instead, he delivered a stern message to Siemens workers: Only those employees who were innovative and flexible could be sure of keeping their jobs. Increasingly, von Peirer warned, the company would grow by building facilities outside of Germany's expensive borders. Indeed, today, many observers are asking whether with so many overseas employees Siemens is still a German company.[1]

To be fair, Siemens's remains Germany's fourth largest private employer, and its top management is predominantly German. However, looks can be deceiving. In 1994, Siemens had 218,00 German employees out of a worldwide workforce of 376,000. Today, it has 167,000 German employees out of a total worldwide workforce of 415,000. What is happening here? Simply put, two things are occurring simultaneously. For starters, Siemans's global markets are expanding more rapidly than its German markets. The German economy remains sluggish. At the same time, Germany's generous pay and fringe benefits package makes Germany one of the most expensive places in the world to manufacture. Siemens recently projected a 44 percent decline in its German workforce over the next decade. As a result, Siemens has opened new manufacturing facilities in such diverse locations as Eastern Europe, Latin America, North America, and Asia. First, manufacturing jobs were exported, then software development.

Still, some German labor leaders do not appear to sense a need for change. As one union official leader observed, "I don't think the machines will run optimally [overseas]." Siemens managers seem to disagree. Von Peirer noted that such talk was "sharply divorced from reality."[2] Skilled workers can be found all over the world, he noted. Indeed, in late 2004, Siemens's new incoming CEO, Klaus Kleinfeld, immediately announced plans to further streamline both the firm's antiquated organization structure and its worldwide manufacturing operations.[3] More German job cuts are planned.

As a result, pressure has increased on German labor unions to improve productivity and hold back wage increases. There is even talk in some circles of rolling back some of Germany's famed employee benefits. Meanwhile, the German government talks endlessly about the need to remain (or perhaps become) competitive, but it does little. German goods are the envy of the world, and German workers enjoy benefits and freedom not seen in most of the rest of the world. The question is whether this can continue in the face of increased global competition.

QUALITY AND COMPETITIVE ADVANTAGE

As Siemens is discovering, there are many ways to compete in the global marketplace. Most approaches focus on either low cost or high quality, or a combination of the two. That is, most firms try to compete by undercutting the competition on the price, by offering products that may be more expensive but have added value in some way, or by offering the best value for the money. Because of their very high labor costs, most German firms can't compete based on cost, so they emphasize quality. As a result, when consumers purchase a German product—especially automobiles— they realize that they will pay a premium but anticipate that they are getting a superior product.

To accomplish this, German firms must routinely turn out products that consumers around the world prize above all others. Germany's pursuit of this goal is rooted in the concept of *total quality management* (TQM). TQM drives their product development, manufacturing, marketing, and management style. It is a way of thinking, and it represents the central theme underlying most German companies as competitive entities. This is not to suggest that Germany has a monopoly on quality; many firms in various countries can equal and sometimes surpass Germany in making quality products. Still, German engineering prowess remains a global standard that many companies envy. Therefore, we will use German firms in this chapter as an example of how companies can compete based on the quality of their products or services.

Quality is important for companies for at least three reasons. First, quality can represent a competitive advantage to those firms who can convince customers that their products are genuinely superior. For example, many Korean firms initially had difficulty selling their products in quality-conscious Europe until they could upgrade the quality of their products so European consumers saw value in purchasing them. Second, quality is often directly related to productivity. Higher product quality means fewer defects, which means rework time and expense and fewer costly recalls and warranty repairs. Making it right the first time is usually a safe way to reduce overall operating costs. Finally, quality helps firms develop and maintain customer loyalty and secure repeat business. When consumers have had a good experience with a particular brand, they are likely to become repeat customers.

Quality can be measured along several dimensions, including performance characteristics (i.e., does the product outperform the competition?), special features (i.e., does the product have features not found in competitors?), reliability, durability, serviceability, and aesthetics.[4] We can also distinguish between actual quality and perceived quality. Some products (e.g., Sony, Audi) carry a reputation for superior craftsmanship that allows them to command premium prices, even though the products may be no better than those of the competition.

In an effort to standardize quality measures, the International Organization for Standardization (ISO in French) has developed an internationally acceptable set of quality standards for a host of products. These guidelines, collectively called *ISO 9000*, provide a commonly acceptable basis for quality certification that has become increasingly important in international business. For instance, when Korean companies began striving to produce world-class products for global markets, ISO 9000 certification became critical. It told potential customers that these products were made to an international standard and were therefore worthy of purchase.

EMPLOYEE INVOLVEMENT AND QUALITY

High-quality products depend heavily on high-quality employees. And high-quality employees are usually those who are not just well trained but also well informed. They are contributing members of the organization. The extent to which companies share information, knowledge, power, and rewards throughout the organization in an effort to maximize their return on human capital is generally referred to as *employee involvement*. (It also referred to as participative management.) The assumption underlying most employee involvement programs is that rank-and-file workers are often best able to understand work processes—and how to improve these processes—and that involving all employees is the surest way to get everyone on board for any organizational effort to improve quality or productivity. Employee involvement reduces resistance to change and often sparks creativity among those people best able to facilitate such change. To be truly effective, however, these efforts must go well beyond allowing workers to have control over their own jobs and include attempts by firms to allow employees to influence decisions affecting work groups and sometimes the entire organization. To succeed, rank-and-file employees need information, support, and power to become genuine partners with managers in running the organization.

Research on employee involvement consistently suggests that it leads to several desirable organizational outcomes, including improved decision quality, increased commitment to implementing the chosen decision, enhanced employee development as a result of being allowed to participate in key decisions affecting their jobs, and increased job satisfaction and self-efficacy.[5]

Employee involvement takes many different forms both within and between cultures. In Japan, for example, culture and traditions dictate that managers consult with their workers on many aspects of individual and departmental performance. Individual employees are encouraged to step forward with ideas to improve operations or product development. As a result, employee suggestion systems abound in Japanese companies. However, organization-wide issues are typically left to senior managers. By contrast, Germany long ago enacted a series of federal laws that mandate employee participation in virtually all key decisions an organization makes. This form of participation normally takes place through elected representatives to management boards, rather than having individual employees step forward with ideas or suggestions. Finally, the situation in the United States is somewhat difficult to describe since it is characterized by wide variations in the amount of allowed participation. Some U.S. companies support broad-based employee participation, while others shy away from it. No cultural or legal mandates require participation, so prevailing organizational norms are set by either corporate culture or senior management. Thus, while we hear about employee involvement and participative management in all three countries, their meaning and implementation strategies can vary considerably.

Employee involvement efforts frequently include the use of *self-managing teams*. Self-managing teams exist when managers designate a whole project or work process to a team of employees and then allow the team to determine how best to design and implement the assigned task. This is job enrichment in action. These groups require both autonomy and managerial support. They also frequently require considerable information pertaining to the background of the task and how it fits into the larger organizational purpose (something senior managers are often reluctant to provide in some cultures), as well as training in managing group processes.

STRATEGIES FOR TOTAL QUALITY MANAGEMENT

Successful total quality management programs typically integrate TQM efforts with employee involvement programs on the assumption that the people closest to the products or services targeted for improvement must be included in any change efforts. TQM represents a systematic integrated effort to continuously improve the quality of a product or service. Although wide variations can be found across various TQM programs, most efforts exhibit similar characteristics. Such programs begin with a strategic commitment to quality. Top managers must be willing to commit the necessary resources to achieve genuine continuous improvement. Without strong executive support—including a willingness to invest resources—few long-term results will emerge. Based on this support, TQM programs typically focus on four interrelated ingredients to succeed (see Exhibit 15.1):

• *Quality employees.* Employees at all levels must be involved in the effort. This is particularly true for shop-floor workers, who actually make the products. Without employee involvement and commitment to results, little will be gained. German firms use an employee involvement model called codetermination to achieve this, as described below.

• *Quality materials.* Materials used in manufacture must be of the highest quality. This often requires firms to work closely with their suppliers to help them make parts according to company standards. For example, Japanese companies have proven to be masters at developing such partnerships with their suppliers.

Exhibit 15.1

Components of a Total Quality Management Program

Critical Components	Required Actions
Quality employees	Hire, retain, and motivate highly skilled, involved, and committed employees at all levels of the organization.
Quality materials	Select only the best available materials, working in close partnership with suppliers.
Quality equipment	Use state-of-the-art equipment and technologies to facilitate efficiencies and overall quality control.
Continuous improvement	Benchmark all results on a regular basis and set specific quantitative and qualitative improvement goals.

• *Quality equipment.* Investments must be made in state-of-the-art equipment and manufacturing technologies to facilitate efficiency and overall manufacturing quality control. Many U.S. firms excel in this category by investing in the latest manufacturing technologies.

• *Continuous improvement.* Successful firms are always on the lookout for new or improved methods for getting the work done. As noted above, Japanese companies do this by stressing employee suggestion plans. Many Japanese factories have bulletin boards publicly listing the number of suggestions made by each small production unit over the past month. As a result, and not surprisingly, employees in Japanese firms make fifty times the number of suggestions that their American counterparts make. Indeed, many Japanese employees complain of undue pressures to continually offer suggestions.

STATISTICAL PROCESS CONTROL

Companies using TQM methods have a variety of tools and techniques available to them to facilitate their goals. These include statistical process controls and benchmarking. *Statistical process control* is the application of mathematics to quality control where targeted numeric levels of quality are established and then factory managers monitor production to ensure that these targets are met. Oftentimes, these controls involve establishing acceptable ranges for measures. For instance, Perrier targets filling its bottles of water with 23 fluid ounces but allows for deviations between 22.8 and 23.2 ounces. Over time, bottles are selected from the production line for testing. As long as 99.9 percent of the bottles tested fall within the established parameters, production continues. When the percentage falls below this level, production is stopped and the process is readjusted.

BENCHMARKING

A second key TQM approach is benchmarking. *Benchmarking* is the process of studying how other firms do something and then imitating or improving on this process. It establishes a standard against which to compare one's own company's products or services. For example, when Xerox began losing significant market share in the copier market to its Japanese rivals (notably Canon), it began trying to understand how the competitor's products were made. It purchased a number of Canon copiers and dismantled them. To Xerox's surprise, the Canon copiers were superior in both design and manufacture and less expensive to produce. Xerox used these findings to improve their own copiers to make them more competitive in both price and quality. As a result, sales increased.

AUTOMATION

Competing with advanced technologies is commonplace in many companies around the world, and no single country has a monopoly on such techniques. Technologically advanced products are highly sought after by customers in markets ranging from automobiles to electronics. Even so, notable trends can be identified across countries that serve to differentiate companies in a very general way in their approaches to using technology as a strategic asset in manufacturing. In the United States, for example, manufacturing is often characterized by extensive use of *automation* techniques. The principal aim of automation is to replace work done by employees with work done by machines. The challenge is how best to use automation to manufacture good products at competitive prices. Indeed, American companies frequently use automation as a substitute for workers, instead of as a complement to them. In doing so, they often try to compete based on cheap labor, often with mixed results.

PROCESS SIMPLIFICATION

By contrast, many Japanese companies emphasize process simplification to achieve a competitive edge. *Process simplification* involves finding easier, more efficient ways to manufacture something. This might include reducing *cycle times* in the manufacturing process (i.e., reducing the time it takes an employee to complete a work cycle or make one part) or using fewer parts in design and manufacture. For example, when the 1997 Toyota Camry was introduced, it contained 20 percent fewer parts than its predecessor had. As a result, its selling price was actually reduced over the previous year, making it more competitive. Camry sales soon reached number one in the U.S. market. In 2002, an even newer Camry was introduced, again with 20 percent fewer parts than its 1997 predecessor had and again at a lower price. In this way, Toyota continued to raise the bar for its competitors, who had to struggle to keep up.

TECHNOLOGICAL COMPLEXITY

German manufacturers seldom use product simplification methods. Instead, they stress *technological complexity* and product superiority. That is, many German firms try to develop the most sophisticated products they can using the latest technologies, even if this leads to higher production costs and higher prices. Technological complexity makes for superior products, it is believed. For example, the new BMW 7 Series has more than 120 electric motors, including 38 motors just to adjust the seats, plus dozens of microprocessors to control everything from the humidity inside the car to the angle at which the wipers rest on the windshield.[6] And at Volkswagen, engineers built a fully integrated electrical system. That is, the starter, horn, lights, stereo system, and security system are all tied to a single wire, instead of separate wires for each system, as found in American and Japanese cars. It is an engineering masterpiece. However, while German cars may be more technologically sophisticated than their Japanese or American rivals, they can also be more error-prone. When something goes wrong, everything can be adversely affected. If the lighting system goes out, the security system also goes out. In Japanese cars, by contrast, where process simplification is stressed, there are actually five wiring systems, each somewhat autonomous from the others. As a result, product assembly is easier and cheaper because it is less complex. Moreover, if the car's lighting system fails, for example, this has less impact on other electrical systems, such as the stereo and the security system. This is not to say that one system is superior, only that each is based on a different assumption about the best approach to production technologies. Even so, in 2004, German cars—including luxury brands—were rated behind both Japanese and American cars in overall reliability, demonstrating that there is often a cost for technological complexity.[7]

Finally, it is interesting to note that when U.S. companies sought advice on how to improve the quality of their products or the production technologies used in manufacture, they asked the Japanese, not the Germans. As a result, American manufacturing techniques tend to stress a combination of process simplification and extensive use of automation.

TQM AND CODETERMINATION: INSIDE THE GERMAN KONZERN

Nowhere is the issue of quality in manufacturing more important than in the various large and small companies that comprise Germany's industrial base.[8] We therefore focus in this section on Germany and its approach to quality management. As will be seen, a major ingredient in Germany's approach to TQM is its unique methods of involving employees at all levels of the organization in efforts to manufacture the best products possible. These methods include a nationwide public-private partnership that sponsors intensive worker apprenticeship programs and a state-mandated codetermination system that provides a significant voice in the management of firms to employees at all levels in the organizational hierarchy. As a starting point in this analysis, consider the culture and social customs that characterize Germany and its business institutions.

GERMAN CULTURE AND SOCIAL PATTERNS

A number of social scientists have attempted to describe German culture in general terms. Geert Hofstede, for example, has described the typical German as relatively individualistic (although not so extreme as Americans), high on uncertainty avoidance and masculinity, and relatively low on power distance.[9] Hall and Hall add that Germans tend to be very punctual about time, follow schedules closely, demand order, value their personal space, respect power and position, and seek detailed information prior to decision making. Indeed, Hall and Hall quote a French executive as saying that "Germans are too busy managing to think creatively."[10]

To foreign observers, Germans tend to be conservative, formal, and polite.[11] Formal titles are important in conversations, and privacy and protocol are valued. In business, Germans tend to be assertive but not aggressive. Although firms are often characterized by strict departmentalization, decisions tend to be made based on broad-based discussion and consensus building among key stakeholders. Negotiations are based on extensive assessments of data and plans and, since Germany is a low-context culture, communication is explicit and easily understood by foreigners.

ORGANIZATION OF GERMAN BUSINESS FIRMS

As with companies in any country, it is difficult to generalize about the nature or structure of the typical German firm (*Konzern* in German). Like the United States, German firms generally take one of two legal forms: a limited partnership, designated by a *GmbH* (*Gesellschaft mit beschraenkter Haftung*) following the company name, or a public stock company, designated by an *AG* (*Aktiengesellschaft*) following the name. So the company Volkswagen AG is a public company with publicly traded stock. In German conglomerates, the parent company is often referred to as the *Muttergesellschaft* (literally, "mother company").

German firms are typically led from the top by two boards. At the very top is the *supervisory board* (or *Aufsichtsrat*), as shown in Exhibit 15.2. This board, much like a board of directors in U.S. firms, is responsible for ensuring that the principal corporate objectives are met over the long term. Its members are typically elected for five years and can be changed only by a vote of 75 percent of the voting shares. A key function of the supervisory board is to oversee the activities of the *management board* (or *Vorstand*), which consists of the top management team of the firm and is responsible for its actual strategic and operational management. These two boards are jointly responsible for the success or failure of the German enterprise.

COMPETITIVE STRATEGIES OF *MITTELSTAND* FIRMS

Most people are familiar with the names of a number of large and successful German companies, including Siemens, BMW, Volkswagen, DaimlerChrysler, Beyer, and BASF. What many people fail to realize, however, is that the real strength of the German economy actually relies less on these large companies and more on its 2.5 million small and medium-sized firms. These so-called *Mittelstand* (medium-sized) firms account for more than two-thirds of the nation's economy and more than 80 percent of its private-sector employment. Examples of *Mittelstand* firms include Rational (restaurant ovens), Trumpf (machine tools), and Playmobil (toys).

Germany's *Mittelstand* firms compete in the global marketplace through a strat-

Exhibit 15.2   **Organization of a Typical German *Konzern***

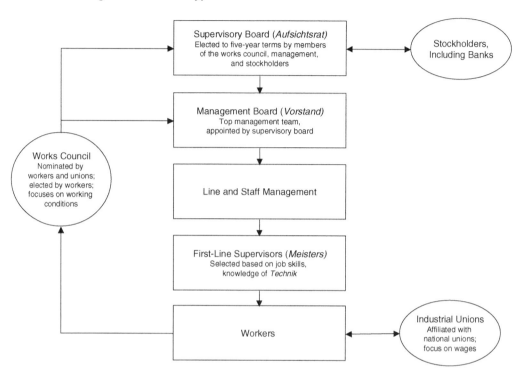

egy that has served them well for several decades (see Exhibit 15.3). This strategy can be summarized as follows: First, because of their high cost structure, most *Mittelstand* firms ignore markets characterized by low prices and prefer instead to focus on markets where quality or other product uniqueness can command a high price. Within these markets, they focus on making superior products using advanced technologies or superior craftsmanship, or both. They then compete based on customer satisfaction, not profit maximization. To supplement this effort, German firms hire and train the best workers they can find, not the cheapest. They make extensive use of apprenticeship programs and *Technik* (see Basis of German Engineering below) as competitive weapons. All employees, regardless of level in the organization, are empowered to an extent seldom seen elsewhere to help achieve the firm's mission. This is done largely through codetermination (see Labor Relations and Codetermination below). Finally, German firms prefer to take a long-term perspective to market development and can be patient when necessary. This is possible largely because most companies have close ties with major German banks and other financial institutions that are patient about getting a return on their investment, unlike those in North America, where investors often require a shorter payback period.

Unfortunately, as noted above, recent increases in the cost of labor and production have increasingly threatened the competitiveness of many of these *Mittelstand* firms. As a result, some firms are beginning to curtail many of their German-based opera-

Exhibit 15.3

Competitive Strategies of German *Mittelstand* Firms

Business Strategies	Competitive Advantage
Focus on a specific up-scale market niche	Customers in up-scale markets tend to focus on quality and service over cost, precisely where *Mittelstand* firms, with their higher operating costs, are best able to compete.
Produce only high quality products	German products are recognized for high quality, advanced engineering, and superior craftsmanship, making it easier for new German entrants to capitalize on this reputation.
Ensure complete customer satisfaction	Local representatives of *Mittelstand* firms tend to be highly skilled in both sales and service, providing customers with ready access to after-sale support when needed.
Emphasize employee selection and training	Employees are hired for their skills and long-term potential, not their cost, and receive ongoing training and skills upgrades throughout their careers.
Maintain strong employee commitment and involvement	Employees at all levels tend to remain with *Mittelstand* firms for long periods and are encouraged to take an active role in manufacturing, quality control, and service.
Take a long-term approach to market development	Private ownership and close relations with lenders allow managers to make sizable up-front investments in technology and new products and recoup investment over the long term.

tions in favor of manufacturing facilities in other lower-cost countries (notably in southern and Eastern Europe). Increasing emphasis is being placed on using technology to increase productivity. Whether these moves will threaten the competitive basis of *Mittelstand* firms (e.g., German craftsmanship) over the long term remains to be seen.

BASIS OF GERMAN ENGINEERING

A hallmark of German firms is the technical competence they bring to the manufacture of so many diverse products. German engineering is world famous. A major reason for this fame lies in the training of managers and workers. Line managers in German firms are typically better trained technically than their European or American counterparts, with closer relations between them and technical experts in the firm. In contrast to American managers, most German managers are trained as engineers and have completed some form of craft apprenticeship training program. The typical German organization is distinguished by its tightly knit technical staff superstructure, closely linked to supervisory and managerial tasks which, when combined, produce high levels of performance. Compared to French or British industry, German firms have a lower center of gravity; that is, they have less proliferation of administrative and support staff and more hands-on shop-floor managers.

From the first-line supervisor (a position usually held by a *Meister*, or master technician) on up, managers are respected for what they know rather than who they are. They tend to be far less controlling than many of their U.S. counterparts. Instead, it is assumed that workers and supervisors will meet deadlines, will guarantee quality and service, and do not require close supervision. Independence within agreed-upon parameters characterizes the working relationship between managers and the workers they oversee.

Behind the organizational facade of German firms is a particular notion of technical competence commonly referred to as *Technik*. This term describes the knowledge and skills required for work.[12] It is the science and art of manufacturing high-quality and technologically advanced products. The success of *Technik* in German manufacturing is evidenced by the fact that more than 40 percent of Germany's GDP is derived from manufacturing. Indeed, Germany is responsible for more than half of all EU-manufactured exports. It is for this reason that knowledge of *Technik* represents a principal determinant in the selection of supervisors and managers.

A principal method for developing this technical competence in workers begins with widespread and intensive *apprenticeship training* programs.[13] It is estimated that more than 65 percent of fifteen- and sixteen-year-old Germans enter some form of vocational training program. Apprenticeship programs exist not only for manual occupations but also for many technical, commercial, and managerial occupations.

There are two principal forms of vocational training in Germany. The first consists of general and specialized training programs offered by vocational schools and technical colleges. The second, referred to as the *dual system*, combines in-house apprenticeship training with part-time vocational training, leading to a skilled-worker certificate. There are more than four hundred nationally recognized vocational certificates. Qualifications for each certificate are standardized throughout the country, leading to a well-trained workforce with skills that are not company-specific. This certificate training can be followed by attendance at one of the many *Fachschule*, or advanced vocational colleges. Graduation from a *Fachschule* facilitates the achievement of a *Meister*, or master technician, certification (see Exhibit 15.4).

The dual system of apprenticeship training represents a partnership of employers, unions, and the government. Costs are typically shared between companies and the government on a two-thirds/one-third basis. Employers are legally required to release young workers for vocational training. German companies are also widely known for their enthusiastic support of company-sponsored training programs. The Mercedes-Benz division of DaimlerChrysler, for example, regularly offers 180 vocational courses to its employees. Each year, the company has more than 600 employees studying in vocational or modular management development courses, as well as more than 4,000 employees who participate in some form of formal training at the company's training center.

It should be noted that in recent years some people have criticized the complexity

Exhibit 15.4

Germany's Dual System of Vocational Training

Stages	Type of Training	Skills Developed
1	Dual-system apprenticeship training	Part-time attendance at vocational school (*Berufsschule*) combined with part-time in-plant apprenticeship training
2	Skilled-worker certificate (*Facharbeiterbrief*)	Certification that worker has achieved minimum requirements to be employed in a specific craft
3	Work experience as a skilled worker	Worker applies his or her knowledge during multiyear work experience
4	Advanced vocational school training (*Fachschule*)	Highly rated and experienced workers apply for selective admission to one of Germany's many schools for advanced skills training
5	Certification as a *Meister*	Upon completion of advanced training, worker is certified as knowledgeable in *Technik* and therefore qualified for position of *Meister*

of German apprenticeship programs, as well as the length of time required for certification.[14] It has been argued that this lengthy certification procedure hinders entrepreneurship and Germany's competitive position in the world by limiting access to many professions, inhibiting change in those professions, and stifling creativity and innovation. However, German unions—and many companies—have resisted change.

LABOR RELATIONS AND CODETERMINATION

The German industrial relations system is highly standardized, extensively organized through state regulation, and characterized by formal recognition of employee rights at all levels of the firm.[15] This concept of fostering strong employee participation in corporate decision making is generally referred to (especially in Europe) as industrial democracy. *Industrial democracy* refers to a consensus among a country's national leaders and citizens that employees at all levels of organizations have a right to be involved in decisions affecting their long-term welfare. Nowhere is the concept of industrial democracy better illustrated than in Germany, where strong industrial unions, codetermination, and works councils characterize the workplace environment.

On a national level, the German constitution guarantees all citizens the right to join unions and engage in collective bargaining. It also indirectly guarantees the right of companies to join employer associations. At present, 42 percent of German industrial workers (and 30 percent of all German employees) are members of unions; 80 percent of these are members of a branch of Germany's largest trade union, the Deutsche Gewerkschaftsbund. Moreover, the national government plays a strong role in industrial relations. All political parties have strong factions representing workers' interests, although the Social Democratic Party has the closest links to

Exhibit 15.5

Labor Relations in the United States and Germany

Characteristics	United States	Germany
Percentage of workers unionized	14	30
Common form of union	Multi-industry	Industrywide
Contract coverage	Parties to contract	Industrywide
Largest national union*	AFL-CIO	DGB
Character of union-management relations	Often highly adversarial	Typically consultative
Focus of collective bargaining and contract negotiations	Wages, hours, working conditions, and employee benefits	Wages, hours, working conditions, employee benefits, and quality of work life
Bargaining strategy	Often decentralized	Highly centralized
Grievance resolution procedure	Strike or voluntary arbitration	Appeal to labor courts
Employee participation rights in management codetermination and works councils	Little or none	Mandated
Degree of involvement in national political parties	Moderate	Strong

*AFL-CIO: American Federation of Labor–Congress of Industrial Organizations; DGB: Deutscher Gewerkschaftsbund (German Trade Union Federation).

unions. Extensive legislation covers labor standards, benefits, discrimination, plant closures, and employee rights.

Collective bargaining agreements are negotiated on an industrywide basis, either nationally or regionally (see Exhibit 15.5). Little direct bargaining takes place between unions and employers at the plant level. As a result, wage differentials across companies in similar industries are small. Employment disputes are usually settled through labor courts, consisting of three persons: a professional judge who is a specialist in labor law, a union representative, and a representative of the employer's association. These courts have jurisdiction over both individual employment contracts and collective contracts involving industrial disputes.

On a company level, a legally binding *codetermination* system (*Mitbestimmung* in German) supports worker rights. This system is based on the belief that both shareholders and employees have a right to influence company policies, and that profit maximization must be tempered with concern for social welfare. Under codetermination, workers may exercise their influence on corporate affairs through representatives on the supervisory board. Typically, one-half to one-third of the members of this board are elected by the workers—normally through their works

Exhibit 15.6

Codetermination and Participation Rights in Germany

Codetermination Rights	Participation Rights
Working hours	Human resource planning
Payment methods	Employee dismissals
Hiring and transfers	Work procedures
Social amenities	Operational changes
Training programs	Job description changes
Regulations governing vacations	Work design changes
Safety regulations	
Performance appraisal methods	

council—while stockholders elect the remainder. German workers can in this way have a significant influence on strategic decision making. Moreover, many serious labor problems are discussed and resolved at this executive level before they grow into major conflicts.

On a plant level, workers exercise their influence through *works councils*. Works councils typically have no rights in the economic management of the firm but have considerable influence in HRM policies and practices. Their principal task is to ensure that companies follow regulations that exist for the benefit of their employees. Works councils therefore have the right to access considerable company information concerning the running of the firm, including economic performance. Rights granted to works councils are divided into *codetermination rights* (the right to approve or reject management decisions) and *participation rights* (the right to be consulted on management decisions). Examples of each of these rights are shown in Exhibit 15.6.

CODETERMINATION AT VOLKSWAGEN AG

Over the years, Volkswagen AG has had its ups and downs in the global marketplace. The largely state-owned German conglomerate not only manufactures and sells cars around the world but is also involved in banking, leasing, insurance, real estate, and transportation. Its automobile companies include British-based Bentley, Italian-based Bugatti, Spanish-based Seat, Czech-based Skoda, and, of course, German-based Audi and Volkswagen. From its German manufacturing center in Wolfsburg, VW has attempted to accomplish two seemingly contradictory goals: remain a sales leader in the global auto industry while building and maintaining a workers' paradise for its employees. The contradiction results from the company's need to remain cost-competitive in the highly cost-sensitive car market while its labor costs continue to escalate.

The success—or failure—of Volkswagen's efforts over time is emblematic of the challenges of Germany's codetermination system. Consider the following: Back in 1992, the company's principal car-manufacturing facilities in Germany faced a bleak future as car sales plummeted.[16] The European automobile industry was in crisis, with economic recession and flat consumer purchasing power. Automobile plant capacity far outstripped demand, and Japanese companies were increasingly successful in capturing a greater share of the relatively stagnant market. Sales at Volkswagen dropped 20 percent in just one year, requiring a massive reduction in working hours by company employees. Indeed, the company had 30,000 more workers than it needed. Its supervisory board concluded that poor economic conditions would remain for several years and that in order to survive it had to find a way to reduce its operating costs by 20 percent (approximately $1 billion) as soon as possible to match the decline in sales.

As Volkswagen faced this challenge, the business and social environments in which key decisions would be made differed sharply from those the company would have faced in the United States. For starters, 20 percent of Volkswagen's stock was owned by the state of Lower Saxony, where the company's principle manufacturing facilities were located. In addition, 90 percent of all employees at Volkswagen were unionized. Since the company's constitutional contract required approval of more than 80 percent of the shareholders on all important decisions, any cost-cutting plan that involved large layoffs was highly problematic. Lower Saxony and the IG-Metall union also had strong representation on Volkswagen's supervisory board, where cost-reduction strategies would be openly discussed. Major layoffs were not a viable option.

In addition to its governance structure, Volkswagen had spent decades developing a culture of cooperation and inclusion among all its employees. Key features of this culture include:

- Widespread dissemination of detailed information on the state of the company to employees, IG-Metall union, and works councils
- A receptive climate for unions
- Informal codetermination in advance of formal decisions
- An emphasis on consensus in decision making
- A norm of implementing decisions once they are made

In creating and supporting this culture, Volkswagen was by no means abandoning its objectives of profitability and shareholder value. Instead, it believed (as did many German companies) that all the principal stakeholders of the company—including employees—should be protected when major corporate decisions were made. In other words, capital and labor were seen as joint responsibilities of the company. From the standpoint of top management, VW had to find a solution that was acceptable to both sides. On the one hand, a reduction in labor costs was required to enhance operating efficiency and competitiveness, particularly in the face of reduced demand for its product. On the other hand, the method of achieving this cost reduction had to be acceptable to rank-and-file employees.

As the management and supervisory boards examined the problem, several traditional solutions, such as early retirement, temporary reductions in working hours, and consensual termination agreements, were eliminated due primarily to excessive costs associated with their implementation. The only viable solution from management's standpoint was to reduce the workweek of all employees without compensatory payments. The question then was how to gain the support of labor to this course of action.

Volkswagen opened negotiations with IG-Metall in 1993. At first, union representatives rejected even the basic idea of reducing the workweek without compensation. Over time, however, they became convinced of the necessity of change. From then on, the question was how to achieve the company's goal with the minimum amount pain for employees. Union leaders and works council members held focus groups with employees to discuss various options and seek suggestions and ideas. These proposals were summarized and fed back to management.

After thorough negotiations, IG-Metall and the management board agreed on a compromise plan that shortened working hours without compensation while simultaneously increasing worker productivity. Management did not receive the magnitude of working-hour reductions it had sought, but the increased productivity agreements were designed to compensate for this loss. The three-part plan was as follows: First, Volkswagen converted its workforce to a four-day workweek, reducing working hours from thirty-six hours to twenty-eight hours and reducing labor costs by 20 percent. However, at the same time, the company and union agreed to eliminate several bonuses, holidays, and other perquisites that historically had been salary add-ons and use this money to continue paying workers for a full thirty-six-hour week. As a result, workers could receive their full regular pay but could no longer count on as many add-ons during lean times. Second, workers were encouraged to take more time off without pay for holidays or to pursue educational opportunities. Employees could even take blocks of up to three months off at one time without pay, a feature that proved to be particularly popular with younger employees. Finally, it was agreed that the company would increase the working hours of trainees while decreasing the hours for older workers, with obvious implications for reduced costs.

Efforts to increase productivity were also agreed upon. This was accomplished by: (1) scheduling manufacturing based more closely on actual customer demand instead of building costly inventories in anticipation of demand; (2) enhancing continuous improvement efforts focusing on reducing the costs and time associated with manufacture; and (3) emphasizing employee training at all levels to improve employee skills and effectiveness.

The plan was implemented with mixed reactions from employees. Suspicion was high in some areas, but with the strong backing (and buy-in) of the union, most workers complied with the plan. Over time, however, most workers finally came to accept the plan. Three years after implementation, in a 1996 employee survey, 50 percent of the workforce said they were satisfied with the plan (especially the four-day workweek), while 15 percent said they were dissatisfied. The remaining workers (35 percent) claimed to be indifferent about the new plan. In interviews with workers, the union found that the most positive outcomes of the new plan were the four-day workweek, which allowed more free time with friends and family, and the continuous improvement plan, which asked workers for their suggestions, opinions, expectations, and ideas. But above all, Volkswagen work-ers—a full 75 percent—stressed the importance of protecting the jobs of their fel-low workers. In the end, workers kept their jobs (although at reduced income levels), the company reduced its costs sufficiently to meet the realities of the marketplace, and society at large did not experience massive unemployment with its associated social welfare costs.

By 1999, as the market for cars improved, Volkswagen began shifting back toward increased working hours with increased paychecks. However, it succeeded in retaining many of the features first agreed to and implemented in 1993. Fore-most among these were the four-day workweek, reduced hours for senior work-ers, continuous improvement efforts, available time off without pay, and comprehensive employee training. It also succeeded in retaining agreement by the union that working hours could again be reduced should economic condi-tions require it.

By 2004, serious problems again emerged as Volkswagen's cost of production proved to be uncompetitive and it lost significant market share to its Japanese and European rivals.[17] Management asserted that producing cars in Germany increased the cost of each vehicle by almost $3,000 compared to producing the same cars in Eastern Europe. (Several VW models are already produced there.) Management went further to say that unless German labor unions agreed to a multiyear wage and ben-efit freeze, it would be necessary to move close to 30,000 jobs out of the country. Union leaders at IG-Metall disagreed and threatened to strike if their workers did not receive significant wage increases plus job security guarantees. In the end, a com-promise was again reached, but the questions remain: With a high and inflexible cost structure, how long can German industry remain viable in an increasingly competi-tive global economy? And how long can German workers enjoy job benefits that far outstrip those received by comparable workers in other countries, even in the Euro-pean Union?

KEY TERMS

apprenticeship training	*Meister*
automation	*Mittelstand* firms
benchmarking	participation rights
codetermination	process simplification
codetermination rights	self-managing teams
cycle times	statistical process control
dual system	supervisory board
employee involvement	*Technik*
industrial democracy	technological complexity
ISO 9000	total quality management (TQM)
Konzern	works councils
management board	

GLOBAL MANAGER'S WORKBOOK 15.1:
SKODA-VOLKSWAGEN ALLIANCE

Skoda has a century-long history of building automobiles.[18] Located in the small town of Mlada Boleslav, nearly forty miles from Prague in the Czech Republic, Skoda survived—and even prospered—until the latter years of Communist domination. When the Czech Republic began converting to a market economy in the late 1980s, Skoda was determined to seek Western assistance to reinvent itself. It turned to Volkswagen AG, which purchased a 30 percent equity share of the company in 1991 and subsequently raised its stake to 70 percent. The new joint venture was managed by a five-member board, consisting of two Czechs (Skoda's chairman and vice president for human resources) and three Germans appointed by Volkswagen.

By 1996, the joint venture had already produced results. Product quality had risen to international standards and new models had been introduced. Local suppliers were now supplying quality parts and components at competitive prices. With factory modernization, production, sales, and wages had all risen, while the number of factory workers had been reduced. The remaining workers received better training in advanced manufacturing methods. That same year, Skoda won its country's Best Company of the Year Award. The question on everyone's mind was whether Skoda was indeed still a Czech company or whether it had become a Volkswagen or German clone.

From the beginning of the joint venture, the goal was to transfer knowledge and expertise to the Czech firm. German technicians were temporarily transferred to Skoda to facilitate this goal. German and Czech managers were paired as part of a tandem system for purposes of local employee development. As one German manager noted, integration of the locals, not domination, was the goal. During the initial stages of the partnership, the tandem system helped train the Czech managers and provided the requisite confidence to succeed. As time went on, most German managers returned to Germany and shop-floor operations were increasingly assumed by Czech managers. However, VW retained control over strategic decision making in view of its equity position in the company.

In the initial stages of the venture, Czech managers felt they had a great deal to offer in view of their long history in automobile manufacturing. However, the Germans rarely asked their opinions. As one Czech manager noted, if the Germans come and change everything, it's like saying the local workers did everything poorly and the Germans will do it correctly. It was also noted that the Germans on the scene showed little interest in the Czech legal system, history, or culture.

A major stumbling block in the beginning was the difficulty each side had understanding the other. Indeed, language was always a problem. The German visitors felt that the local Skoda workers should work hard to learn German—the language of the parent company. Many Czech workers, on the other hand, preferred to speak English as a common (or perhaps neutral) language. This issue was never resolved. To get ahead in the company, Czech managers had to speak either English or German. The absence of Czech-language skills on the part of the German managers troubled many Czechs, especially the line workers.

There was also the issue of expectations. One Czech manager noted that in the Czech national culture, people are more action-oriented and less theoretical, while the Germans are more concept-oriented and prepare things systematically. The initial challenge was to ensure that everyone understood that there were different ways to reach the same target.

Throughout, the Germans emphasized efficiency and organization. They also stressed training, appropriate work clothes, equipment, discipline on the shop floor, and cleanliness and orderliness in the factory. At the same time, some Czech managers and workers complained about the materialism of their German counterparts. They also complained that Czech workers had lost their innate sense of loyalty to Skoda.

Both sides agreed that the joint venture had been a success and had brought a change in the mind-set of the Czechs. They now saw the company in strategic and competitive terms. Even so, many remained reluctant to accept responsibility. An experienced German manager observed that what was missing at Skoda was self-confidence. The Czechs needed to be given a chance to grow and develop in their own way. Soon, they should be capable of running a highly efficient firm. The question seemed to be whether their German partners would let them do it.

QUESTIONS FOR DISCUSSION

1. What did each side hope to gain from the Skoda-Volkswagen alliance? Did each side get what it wanted?
2. Why did the Skoda-Volkswagen alliance develop so smoothly? What did each side do to facilitate its success?
3. What problems remain for the Skoda-Volkswagen alliance? What can be done now to prepare for these problems?
4. If Germany's approach to employee participation works so well, why isn't it used more widely in other parts of the industrialized world?
5. What problems will German industry face as they attempt to retain their traditional management methods yet remain competitive in an increasingly challenging global environment?

GLOBAL MANAGER'S WORKBOOK 15.2: TQM AROUND THE WORLD

Successful TQM and employee involvement programs can be found in many different geographic regions of the world, but not all. With this in mind, consider the following questions:

1. TQM as a philosophy of management seems to flourish in highly industrialized nations (e.g., Germany, Japan) but experiences widespread problems in less developed ones. Why do you think this is?
2. Both German and Japanese companies make extensive use of TQM and employee participation methods to enhance their global competitiveness. Are there similarities across the two cultures that support these efforts?

3. Are there differences between Germany and Japan in the reasons they support TQM and employee participation?
4. Do you agree or disagree with the following proposition? Why?

North American companies (in both the United States and Canada) have highly divergent attitudes toward the value of TQM and employee involvement as a tool for global competitiveness. Some companies strongly support these efforts, while many others prefer to rely on automation and technology-driven quality control instead of person-driven quality control. Moreover, many companies seem content to manufacture products of reasonably good but not outstanding quality for the marketplace. As a result, the value of employees as a basic instrument in building total quality into products varies significantly across North American companies.

NOTES

1. Jack Ewing, "Is Siemens Still German?" *Business Week*, May 17, 2004, pp. 50–52; Matthew Karnitschnig, "Siemens Names Kleinfeld as CEO: May Herald Cuts," *Wall Street Journal*, July 8, 2004, p. A3.

2. Matthew Karnitschnig, "For Siemens, Move to U.S. Causes Waves Back Home," *Wall Street Journal*, September 8, 2003, p. A1.

3. Karnitschnig, "Siemens Names Kleinfeld as CEO."

4. David Garvin, "Competing on the Eight Dimensions of Quality," *Harvard Business Review*, November–December 1987, pp. 101–9.

5. Steven Shane and Mary Ann von Glinow, *Organizational Behavior* (New York: McGraw-Hill, 2003).

6. Neal Boudette, "A Bad Report Card for European Cars," *Wall Street Journal*, November 9, 2004, p. D1.

7. Ibid.

8. Jack Ewing, "An Uncertain Giant: A Survey of Germany," *Economist*, December 7, 2002, pp. 3–20; Jack Ewing, "The Decline of Germany," *Business Week*, February 17, 2003, pp. 42–53.

9. Geert Hofstede, *Culture's Consequence: International Differences in Work Related Values*, rev. ed. (Thousand Oaks, CA: Sage, 2001).

10. Edward T. Hall and Mildred Hall, *Understanding Cultural Differences: Germans, French, and Americans* (Yarmouth, ME: Intercultural, 1990).

11. Richard Hill, *We Europeans* (Brussels: Europublications, 1997).

12. Ingrid Brunstein, ed., *Human Resource Management in Western Europe* (Berlin: de Gruyter, 1995).

13. John Cullen and K. Praveen Parboteeah, *Multinational Management: A Strategic Approach* (Cincinnati, OH: Southwestern College Publishing, 2005).

14. John Miller, "Employment Rules Hinder EU," *Wall Street Journal*, August 16, 2004, p. A11.

15. "German Industrial Relations: Slowly Losing Their Chains," *Economist*, February 21, 2004, p. 49; Almut Schoenfeld, "Germany Rethinks Generous Perks for Civil Servants," *Wall Street Journal*, April 5, 2004, p. A17.

16. Cornelia Kothen, William McKinley, and Andreas Georg Scherer, "Alternatives to Organizational Downsizing: A German Case Study," *M@n@gement* 2, no. 3 (1999): 263–86.

17. Mark Landler, "At VW, Threat of Job Losses Hits Nerves," *International Herald Tribune*, September 16, 2004, pp. 1, 8.

18. Diane Cyr, "Organizational Transformation at Skoda in the Czech Republic: An HRM Perspective," in *Readings and Cases in International Human Resource Management*, ed. Mark Mendenhall and Gary Oddou (Cincinnati, OH: Southwestern, 1997), pp. 379–91; Landler, "At VW, Threat of Job Losses Hits Nerves."

16 Managing Multicultural Teams

TEAMWORK AT REAL MADRID

In many parts of the world, few things ignite more passion and patriotism than a World Cup football match (soccer to Americans). France's victory in the 1998 World Cup championship led to the largest popular celebration in that country since the liberation of Paris in 1944. Postwar Germany used its World Cup victory in 1954 to help heal the wounds from World War II and reestablish pride in its country. But perhaps the most enthusiastic fans come from Britain. While the British people are often described as being among the most polite in the Western world, the same cannot be said about their football fans. British fans are notorious for their lack of civility toward foreign opponents, and street fights are common wherever UK teams play. This unruly behavior has even led some European cities to ban UK fans during match days. It is somewhat ironic that in an increasingly integrated European Union that officially and actively opposes rampant nationalism, football is the lone exception. Hurling insults at foreign opponents is widely accepted as a legitimate, if awkward, demonstration of national pride and patriotism.[1]

While the World Cup is the most famous competition in football, professional footballers make a living playing for clubs around the world. Like elsewhere, football clubs comprise a multimillion-dollar industry and need to pay high salaries to hire and retain the best players. In this highly competitive environment, only a few elite European clubs have the financial power to hire the best football players in the world. Among these teams is Spanish-based Real Madrid.

Real Madrid counts on high-profile superstars from such countries as France, Portugal, Argentina, Brazil, Great Britain, and of course Spain. During normal times, these players from all over the world comprise an elite team that takes part in Spanish, European, and other club-based championships. However, during the World Cup and other country-based championships, the players return to their home countries and join national teams, and former teammates from clubs such as Real Madrid are likely to play against each other. Clubs dislike releasing their expensive players to play on these national teams but have no choice: this is how the game is played and this is what the fans want. As noted above, football is more than a sport or a business; it is also a symbol of national pride.

Football experts say that football teams symbolize national character. Each nation has a style and a football temperament, which is what makes the World Cup so interesting. As one observer notes, the Brazilians play like they dance; the Germans play like they make cars, with lots of technical efficiency and not much left to the imagination; the English run hard all the time, maybe because of the weather; the Spanish are a mosaic of regional styles, which has yet to find a national pattern. And the Italians are a paradox. In every other area they export style and flair to the world; but in football they've allowed the ideal of collective organization to crush individual talent.

Now consider the challenges of managing such a multicultural team. On one hand, Real Madrid counts on superb talent—nothing less than the world's best football players. On the other hand, each of these players brings to the field a unique national style, which in itself is a cause of national pride. Furthermore, the various players represent their home countries, not Real Madrid, during the highly volatile World Cup matches. How can Real Madrid respect and preserve the individual styles and uniqueness of its players, while at the same time creating a well-synchronized winning team? Real Madrid fans are asking the same question, as recent successes have eluded them. The challenge facing Real Madrid is not unique to football teams.

Companies around the world are increasingly relying on multicultural and multinational teams to build and run new production facilities, create new products, develop new marketing strategies, and so forth. The question for global managers is both simple and challenging: How can companies create, nurture, and capitalize on multicultural teams to become or to remain competitive in today's hostile business environment?

ROLE OF MULTICULTURAL TEAMS

A *multicultural team* is a group of employees selected from two or more countries who are brought together to coordinate, develop, or manage some aspect of a firm's global operations.[2] Multicultural teams are most commonly used in marketing, operations, and R&D, although they can be found throughout the organization. Companies usually turn to such teams either when they need specific cross-cultural expertise on some aspect of the business (e.g., developing a new product marketing strategy for a particular geographic region) or when they partner with a foreign firm (e.g., form a strategic alliance or international joint venture). Many firms prefer using such teams because they can often do a better job than teams consisting exclusively of either home-country nationals or host-country nationals. Multicultural teams provide an opportunity to integrate widely differing social, cultural, and business perspectives into key decisions affecting the success of international operations.

Multicultural teams come in a variety of shapes, forms, and sizes. As shown in Exhibit 16.1, at least five principal types can be identified. Some companies use multicultural development teams or product launch teams to help develop or refine products that are aimed at multiple international markets. Gaining local insight on

Exhibit 16.1

Types of Multicultural Business Teams

Types of Teams	Purpose of Teams
Business development/product launch team	Team members selected from multiple nationalities to develop or launch a product that has global or regional sales potential
Functional business team	Team members selected from multiple nationalities to oversee a specific functional area (e.g., R & D, international marketing)
International joint-venture business team	Team members selected from two or more global firms to oversee or manage an international joint venture
Regional headquarters business team	Team members selected from across a particular region (e.g., Latin America) to oversee regional strategy and operations
Corporate headquarters business team	Team members at company headquarters selected globally to oversee international strategy and/or global operations

product preferences can make for a single product that can be sold in many divergent nations—but only if various local representatives are present at the inception of product development. Other firms use multicultural functional business teams in such areas as international marketing or R&D, again to bring cultural diversity to help solve specific challenges. Multicultural teams exist naturally in both regional and global headquarters of many transnational firms, where representatives from the various regions come together to jointly chart overall corporate strategy. And multicultural teams can be found in various international strategic alliances and joint ventures.[3] In each case, multicultural teams bring international expertise to decision making and managerial actions that are otherwise missing in less diverse teams.

PROMISES AND PITFALLS OF MULTICULTURAL TEAMS

Managers frequently ask whether they are better off working exclusively with people from their own culture or whether there is value added from working with people from diverse cultures. Indeed, managers in every country have asked this question. While the politically correct answer favors cultural diversity, the reality is considerably more complex. As Percy Barnevik, the former CEO of Swiss-based ABB observed, "When we sit together as Germans, Swiss, Americans, and Swedes, with many of us living, working, and traveling in different places, the insights can be remarkable. But you have to force people into these situations. Mixing nationalities doesn't just happen."[4] Consider: If it is difficult to get Germans, Swiss, Swedes, and Americans to sit down and work together, how much more difficult would it be for Germans, Chinese, Mexicans, and Saudis to do it? Or French, Nigerians, Afghanis, and Filipinos? The larger the cultural gap, the greater the difficulty in building multicultural teams. Despite this fact,

Exhibit 16.2

Impact of Multicultural Teams on Managerial Behavior

Managerial Behavior	Impact of Multicultural Teams
Creativity and problem solving	Frequently more creative in developing ideas and solutions
Group cohesiveness	Often more difficult to develop closely knit groups
Understanding foreign markets	Often increases understanding of global markets
International marketing	Often more effective in working with international customers
Decision-making effectiveness	Frequently takes longer to make decisions or reach consensus, but resulting decisions are often more realistic and comprehensive
Time to implementation	Action plans can take longer to implement
Work habits	Different work habits can lead to conflicts and misunderstandings
Managing employees	Often better understanding of multinational employees

however, success in the global marketplace increasingly requires people from very different cultures to work together to make global enterprises succeed. If there is a challenge for global managers, this is surely it.

The use of multicultural teams can often add value to an organization's efforts. At the same time, however, it can also create problems. Some advantages and disadvantages of using global business teams are summarized in Exhibit 16.2. On the positive side, multicultural teams can frequently facilitate greater creativity and problem solving due to the diverse views at the table. Such teams can also increase both understanding of local markets and the development of productive relationships with local customers. Finally, such teams can at times enhance employee relations in view of the breadth of various managers' cultural backgrounds.

At the same time, however, multicultural teams are not without their problems. It is often more difficult and requires more time to develop group cohesiveness when team members' backgrounds are highly diverse. Moreover, if often takes more time to both reach decisions and implement them, again due to differences in how decision-making processes are viewed. Finally, people's work habits—the way they approach even simple tasks at work—not only can differ significantly across cultures but can lead to considerable misunderstandings, conflict, and mistrust.

Consider, for example, what happened when three electronics giants—IBM, Siemens, and Toshiba—tried to form a strategic alliance to develop a new computer chip. Scientists from all three companies were brought to a state-of-the-art research facility in upstate New York to design the next-generation semiconductor. The idea was to pool their knowledge to beat the competition. Unfortunately, each group of scientists quickly identified problems with the joint venture. German scientists from Siemens were shocked to find their Toshiba colleagues closing their eyes and appearing to sleep during meetings. They failed to understand that such behavior is a common practice in Japan for concentrating on what is being said. At the same time, the Japanese scientists from Toshiba, who were used to working in groups, found it uncomfortable to sit in small individual offices all day and speak English. And American IBM managers complained that the Germans planned too much and that the Japanese wouldn't make clear and decisive decisions. Intergroup trust evaporated as suspicions began to circulate that some researchers were withholding information from the group. Finally, the alliance melted away.[5]

Nancy Adler argues that cultural diversity in work teams provides the biggest asset for teams when team members are engaged in difficult discretionary tasks requiring innovation.[6] Under such circumstances, the differing perspectives provided by having people from different cultures around the table frequently lead to greater insights and a wider array of possible solutions. However, according to Adler, when teams are working on simple tasks or are working on implementation problems as opposed to creative or strategic problems, multicultural teams may be of less value. Indeed, they may slow the process. Thus, a multicultural team's greatest asset appears to be during the planning and development (or analysis) stage, not the implementation (or action) stage.

CREATING SUCCESSFUL MULTICULTURAL TEAMS

Successful multicultural teams exhibit a high degree of mutual trust and self-confidence. This can be difficult to achieve at times in view of the fact that team members from different cultures may be accustomed to working in different ways. For example, Americans, Germans, and Swiss typically spend little time getting acquainted with one another and prefer to get started on the tasks facing the group, while many Latin Americans, Southern Europeans, and Arabs prefer to spend considerable time initially getting to know one another before setting to work on concrete issues. This contrast between task orientation and relationship orientation can at times present difficulties in creating cohesion and trust.

While generalizations are always difficult, it is possible to identify several guidelines to consider when choosing members for multicultural teams to ensure that the appropriate mix of talents is achieved.[7] These include the following:

• *Diversity.* Team members should not be selected based exclusively on their cultural diversity. While diversity is important to represent various points of view, team members must also have clear and solid task-related abilities to get the job done. In one way or another, all team members must bring management skills to the table.

• *Flexibility.* Team members must recognize and be prepared to deal with their differences. A key goal here should be to facilitate a better understanding of cross-cultural differences and generate a higher level of both rapport and job performance. The question members want to ask is how the team can learn from or capitalize on their diversity. This suggests that it would be useful in many cases for team members to discuss their various conceptions of what a team culture should be like, including appropriate norms governing acceptable behavior. For example, is it acceptable to interrupt speakers? Is English the only acceptable language at the table? How blunt or frank can team members be in expressing their opinions?

• *Team leader.* Since teams consisting of diverse members typically have greater difficulty agreeing on things, the team leader must redouble his or her efforts to help the group clearly define both its goals and the means for achieving its goals. Goals are most helpful when they require members to cooperate and develop mutual respect in carrying out their tasks.

• *Power orientation.* All members of the team must feel comfortable with the power distribution of the committee. This is not to suggest that all members must necessarily feel that they have equal power or can participate as equals. Such a situation conflicts with social norms in many cultures. Rather, all team members must clearly understand and accept the manner in which decisions will be made.

• *Mutual respect.* It is important that all members of the team have mutual respect for one another. Every team member must be heard. However, this does not mean that team leaders should assume that all members are comfortable discussing problems or issues in a large group setting. Responsible team leaders will understand when people are comfortable talking in public and when it is useful to break off and have smaller one-on-one conversations.

• *Feedback.* As the team develops, it is important that the team leader provide useful feedback on team progress to reassure team members that they are on the right track and are succeeding in making multiculturalism work.

STRATEGIES FOR MANAGING MULTICULTURAL TEAMS

Recruiting and staffing multicultural teams is only the first challenge faced by global firms. Beyond this, strategies and mechanisms must be developed to create truly effective work teams—to get members of divergent cultures to actually work together as a team. Susan Schneider and Jean-Louis Barsoux have suggested several ways to accomplish this.[8] They begin by noting that multicultural teams face two fundamental challenges in order to accomplish their mission. First, they must identify their areas of responsibilities and organize their members, and, second, they must develop productive group processes to facilitate collective efforts toward goal attainment. These activities are summarized in Exhibit 16.3.

Managing tasks involves making sure that all team members understand why the group was formed. This includes clarifying the mission and goals of the team, setting a clear agenda and operating rules for team management, clarifying individual roles and responsibilities, clarifying how decisions will be made, and identifying who is responsible for task accomplishment. By contrast, managing group processes includes developing and completing team-building activities, understanding communication flows and patterns among group members, facilitating participation across team members, specifying methods of conflict resolution, and clarifying how and when performance will be assessed.

Multicultural teams that make use of such techniques to manage both tasks and processes typically have an easier time completing their assigned responsibilities in

Exhibit 16.3

Strategies for Managing Multicultural Teams

Team Management Issues	Challenges to Team Effectiveness
Managing tasks:	
Mission and goal setting	Identifying team mission, goals, and objectives; identifying performance expectations
Task structuring	Agenda setting; creating operating rules and procedures; establishing time management procedures
Roles and responsibilities	Division of labor; responsibility charting; team interdependencies; role of leader
Decision making	Delegation of authority; selection and role of a leader; determination of how decisions should be made
Accountability	Identifying who is responsible for task accomplishment
Managing group processes:	
Team building	Team-building activities; trust building; opportunities for social interaction
Communication patterns	Selection of a working language; challenges of language fluency; appropriate use of information technologies
Participation	Guaranteeing everyone a voice; balancing quiet and more vocal members; getting the best from everyone
Conflict resolution	Accommodating legitimate differences of opinion; managing constructive conflict; eliminating destructive conflict; strategies for compromise
Performance evaluation	How and when to evaluate performance; one-way versus two-way evaluations; role of feedback; who evaluates performance

Source: Based on Susan Schneider and Jean-Louis Barsoux, *Managing Across Cultures*, 2nd ed. (London: Prentice Hall, 2003).

a creative and productive manner. Group objectives, specific responsibilities, and ground rules are clearly understood by all members. By contrast, groups that fail to manage these activities tend to do less well because they spend needless time assessing and reassessing goals and objectives and reinventing solutions to recurring problems that could have been dealt with more easily had a structure and process been squarely in place to guide behavior.

MANAGING MULTICULTURAL TEAMS: INSIDE THE FRENCH *SOCIÉTÉ*

To understand how culture can play a decisive role in the success or failure of multicultural teams, we examine the challenges of creating partnerships in two very different cultures: France and Malaysia. Each of these cultures brings its own energies, uniqueness, and challenges. We begin in France.

Exhibit 16.4

Trends in U.S. and French Cultures

United States	France
Optimistic	Fatalistic
Uncomfortable with conflict	Comfortable with conflict
Quick to make superficial friends	Slow to make deep friends
Trust based on past accomplishments	Trust based on firsthand knowledge
Considerable upward social mobility	Little upward social mobility
Monochronic, linear	Polychronic, multitasking

Source: Adapted from Edward T. Hall and Mildred Hall, *Understanding Cultural Differences: Germans, French, and Americans* (Yarmouth, ME: Intercultural Press, 1990).

FRENCH CULTURE AND SOCIAL PATTERNS

When a senior executive from one of Japan's largest companies was asked where he would consider locating a manufacturing facility in Europe, he responded, "Anywhere but France. The French are different and just too hard to get along with."[9] What is the basis for such a comment? To say that the French are "different" tells us very little. The question we must answer is how and why they are different. To understand this, we briefly consider the essence of French culture, as well as the nature of French work organizations. As with any culture, it is difficult to capture the essence of a people in a few phrases. People tend to vary considerably within particular cultures, not just between cultures. Perhaps nowhere is this truer than with respect to the French. Even the French will point to sizable differences between Parisians and provincials and between the peoples of the various provinces.[10] Even so, it is possible on a general level to identify some cultural trends, as shown in Exhibit 16.4.

According to noted anthropologists Edward and Mildred Hall, the French tend to be friendly, humorous, and frequently sarcastic.[11] The French admire people who have strong opinions and openly disagree with them, in contrast with many Americans, who often prefer people that agree with them. As a result, the French are accustomed to conflict and will frequently assume in negotiations that many issues simply cannot be reconciled. (*"C'est la vie!"* or "Such is life!") Americans, by contrast, tend to believe that most conflicts can be resolved if both parties make the effort and are willing to compromise. Perhaps Americans are more optimistic, while French are more fatalistic.

In addition, personal relationships are very important to the French and can take considerable time to develop. The French tend to evaluate a person's trustworthiness based on firsthand experience, while Americans tend to base such assessments on past achievements, reputation, or evaluation by others.

In France, one's social class—aristocracy, upper bourgeoisie, upper-middle bourgeoisie, middle class, lower-middle class, or lower class—is important, and social interactions are frequently influenced by stereotypes. Moreover, most French can

Exhibit 16.5

Characteristics of U.S. and French Firms

U.S. Companies	French Companies
Wide variations in degree of power centralization	Power typically highly centralized at the top of the organization
Less distinction within organizations between managers and workers	Clear distinctions between managers (*cadre*) and workers
Goal-directed management	Aristocratic management
Top managers come from a wide variety of schools	Top managers mostly trained in a small set of elite engineering schools (*grandes écoles*)
Management by encouragement or incentive	Management by criticism
Live to work	Work to live
Forty or more hours per week; ten to fifteen days vacation per year	Thirty-five hours per week; thirty days vacation per year

expect little change in their social class, regardless of their accomplishments. It is difficult, if not impossible, to climb the social ladder. To make matters worse for some Americans, the French tend to be very status-conscious and sometimes enjoy showing off their status and culture to friends and strangers alike. As one French student replied when asked about the primary difference between the French and Americans, "The French have more culture."[12] While many Americans may reject this assertion, or even question what it means (i.e., what does it mean to have "more" culture?), they too are often seen bragging about their own cultural superiority.

ORGANIZATION AND MANAGEMENT IN FRANCE

A French company is typically referred to as a *société,* or association. Incorporated firms are referred to as *société anonyme,* or simply S.A. Compared to typical U.S. firms, most French organizations tend to be highly centralized with rigid structures and reporting channels (see Exhibit 16.5). As a result, decisions frequently take considerable time both to make and to implement. Foreigners frequently complain about encountering excessive red tape when dealing with French companies.[13] In addition, many French managers are seen as highly autocratic and often more interested in protecting their personal turf than in working with others in the organization to achieve significant results. French managers seldom share information with subordinates, in the belief that knowledge is power.

Reflecting a tradition of class-consciousness, there is often a large class distinction made at work between managers (or *cadre*) and workers.[14] Most senior executives of France's leading companies (as well as most of France's top political leaders) graduate from a small set of elite polytechnic universities called *grandes écoles.* The program of study at these schools historically emphasized engineering and mathematics over business in the belief that anyone who can master mathematics can accomplish almost anything. However, this focus is now changing, and these institutions are globalizing at a rapid pace. School ties are routinely maintained and exploited throughout one's career.

On the job, French leaders are often formal, impersonal, and authoritarian. In interpersonal relations, they can be critical of individuals and institutions alike. A French schoolteacher observed that "the operating principle of French education is negative reinforcement."[15] This tendency carries over to the workplace, where subordinates are routinely criticized. By contrast, Americans tend to believe a bit more in the value of positive reinforcement and incentives over punishment.

Rules and regulations proliferate in French organizations, much as they do in German firms. However, their use and implementation can be quite different. While many Germans use policies and procedures to improve the efficiency of operations, the French prefer *savoir faire* (a certain way of doing something with style) as a substitute for following structured procedures. Cultural expectations require German managers to remain on schedule, maintain commitments, and deal with problems as they arise. By contrast, the more individualistic French are more likely to be concerned with following proper professional protocol. Even so, unlike the Germans, they will often ignore rules when they interfere with the attainment of a key goal.[16]

In the workplace (and in contrast to the corporate cultures in many U.S. firms), many French employees are not motivated by competition or the desire to emulate their colleagues. Outsiders frequently claim that they don't have the same work ethic that many Americans and Asians have. French workers avoid overtime work, work an average (and legally mandated) thirty-five-hour workweek, and receive one of the longest vacations in the world. While the French admire the industriousness of Americans and Asians, they believe that quality of life is often more important than success at work and attach great importance to their leisure time. However, few would argue that they work hard during regularly scheduled hours and have a reputation for high productivity. This reputation results in part from a French tradition of craftsmanship and in part from the fact that a high percentage of French workers are employed in small, independent businesses where quality is respected.

Many American managers believe that it is more difficult to get along with the French than with citizens of any other European country. Not surprisingly, many French managers feel the same about Americans. Consider the following examples. According to Hall and Hall, many American managers criticize their French counterparts because they:[17]

- Don't delegate
- Don't keep their subordinates informed
- Don't feel a sense of responsibility toward their subordinates
- Refuse to accept responsibility of things
- Are not team players
- Are overly sensitive to hierarchy and status
- Are highly authoritarian

- Are not interested in improving their job skills or knowledge
- Are primarily concerned with their own self-interest
- Are less mobile than Americans

At the same time, Hall and Hall quote several French managers who hold similarly negative opinions about their American counterparts:[18]

- American managers in Europe are not creative; they are too tied to their check-lists. Success is not achieved by logic and procedure alone.
- American executives are reliable and hardworking, and often charming and innocent. But they are too narrow in their focus; they are not well rounded. They have no time for cultural interests and lack appreciation for art, music, and philosophy.
- Too many American executives are preoccupied with financial reporting. This syndrome produces people who avoid decisions.
- Americans don't know how to present themselves. They sprawl and slouch and have no finesse.

Who is right here? Maybe perceptions by both sides are correct to some extent. Clearly one factor that may help explain these differing perceptions is the fundamental difference between French and American cultures in terms of their time orientation. As noted in Chapter 8, most American are decidedly *monochronic,* meaning that they tend to stress a high degree of scheduling in their lives, concentration of effort on one activity at a time, and elaborate codes of behavior built around promptness in meeting obligations and appointments. Put more simply, many Americans tend to be a bit linear in their thinking and behavior, always focusing on the ultimate goal. By contrast, most French are *polychronic,* stressing human relationships and social interaction over arbitrary schedules and appointments and engaging in several activities simultaneously with frequent interruptions. To the French, the journey is probably more important than the ultimate destination.

MANAGING MULTICULTURAL TEAMS: INSIDE THE MALAYSIAN BUMIPUTRA FIRM

Malaysia represents an interesting example of a multicultural society and, as such, illustrates the potential difficulties of managing multicultural teams. While the above example of working with the French illustrates the challenges of cross-cultural management, imagine the challenges when Westerners work in a culture that is itself multiethnic, consisting of native Malays, Indians, and Chinese.

MALAYSIAN CULTURE AND SOCIAL PATTERNS

Malaysia is a nation of 21 million people situated in Southeast Asia. Fifty-nine percent of the population is native Malay, often called *bumiputras* (or "sons of the soil"). Another 32 percent of the population is ethnic Chinese, and 9 percent are of Indian origin. Islam is the official religion of Malaysia, and nearly all Malays are Muslim. Non-Malays are free to choose other religions. The Chinese are largely Buddhist, with some Taoists, Christians, and Confucianists. In fact, many Chinese practice multiple religions. Indians tend to be Hindu or Sikh, but some are Christian.

A person's ancestral background is often important in determining social status and future opportunities.[19] Wealth is highly admired, and many *bumiputra* Malaysians believe that success or failure is the result of fate or the will of God. Others, like the Chinese, have a somewhat greater tendency to believe that people control their own destiny. Malaysians from all three cultural backgrounds value the family above all else and often use family connections to gain employment and other advantages. Families, in turn, place a high value on personal loyalty and education as a means to get ahead. While all people identify with being Malaysian, they will often identify more strongly with their ethnic background than with their national citizenship.

From a culinary standpoint, Muslims do not eat pork, Hindus do not eat beef, and the Chinese eat everything. Everyone eats rice.

For many years, the government has supported an affirmative action program in hiring and promotion that favors the majority *bumiputra*s over ethnic Chinese and Indians, arguing that such a program is necessary to overcome traditional Chinese dominance in business. *Bumiputra* employees are generally thought to be less aggressive and less experienced in business, and can be both humble and shy with strangers compared to the Chinese and Indians. *Bumiputra* firms often enjoy special access to government funding and government contracts.

ORGANIZATION AND MANAGEMENT IN MALAYSIA

Bumiputra firms tend to be run based on principles that are consistent with the Malaysian culture. Organizations tend to be somewhat flat, with power centered at the top. Many businesses are family-owned and family-run. Communication both within an organization and between organizations and their customers is often subtle and generally transmitted in an indirect style. Maintaining one's humility and modesty is crucial. Strong emotions are seldom exhibited, work activities tend to be polychronic, and work goals are modest. Managers are often hired based on family connections, although competence is also important. Status is important at all levels of the hierarchy.

While differences can obviously be found across different Malaysian *bumiputra* firms, common characteristics include the following:

- Managers place a high value on protocol, rank, and status.
- Self-confidence and ability to be sensitive to the needs of others are valued managerial qualities.
- Managerial legitimacy is based on education and family background.
- Social relationships are based on collectivist principles.
- Business is largely based on long-term mutual trust.
- High-context communication is important.
- Employee selection is based on a combination of family connections, cultural grouping, and skills and abilities.

- Managers must show concern for subordinates' welfare.
- It is acceptable to terminate employees for poor performance.
- Firms are reluctant to lay off employees during difficult economic times.

Working with Malaysians can require a considerable degree of cultural sensitivity. Not only are one's status and position in the organizational hierarchy important, but also power distances tend to be very high. In business transactions, this means sending business representatives who are of at least an equivalent rank to one's prospective customers. Sending someone of lower rank can be deemed insulting. In the workplace, respect for older workers is important, even by managers who have greater authority. As in many Asian countries, age is highly respected and conveys a sense of both wisdom and authority over others.

Maintaining politeness and harmony are also important, and open conflict is avoided at any cost. Above all, visitors must not cause others in any of the three ethnic groups to lose face. Preserving respect and dignity, even in the face of disagreement, is fundamental to understanding all Malaysians.

Family relationships are important, as families form the basis of this highly collectivistic society among all ethnic groups—Malays, Chinese, and Indians. Participative decision making is commonplace, so long as group elders allow it. In negotiations, compromise and collaboration are preferred over confrontation, competition, or a winner-takes-all approach.[20] This emphasis on moderation reflects both Chinese and Malay teachings. Therefore, listening carefully to one's partners and watching for body language become critical in this high-context culture.

Among ethnic Chinese in particular, this collectivism often extends beyond the family into something called a *pok chow*.[21] *Pok chow* translates roughly as "gang contracting"; it exists when groups of workers band together to seek and conduct work as a team. (Indeed, it represents an ancient Chinese version of the contemporary self-managing team.) Members join together by mutual consent and determine their own work rules, division of labor, and procedures for dividing up their compensation. They frequently even elect their own leaders. They then sell their services to firms or to other employers looking for work to be done. *Pok chow* crews are especially popular in the construction industry in Malaysia, where employers have to deal only with crew leaders and can dispense with other complicated organizational procedures or requirements.

In summary, significant cultural differences can be found between the French and the Malaysians. Each culture has developed work and business relationships that serve their unique cultures, and foreign visitors are best advised to first understand and then adapt to these circumstances.

This book has covered a lot of ground in a relatively short space. For purposes of discussion, it has been divided into three interrelated parts: the emerging global economy; culture, organization, and strategy; and managing global operations. For each part, the implications for managing in an increasingly complex and challenging international business environment were highlighted. Applications from both countries and companies were included throughout to illustrate the materials discussed. Each chapter concluded with two opportunities to apply what has been learned in various cases and exercises.

Throughout, our aim has been to present materials that could prove useful and timely for global managers and their firms. In this endeavor, a specific effort was made to integrate issues of culture with those of management in the belief that success in the global economy requires a detailed understanding of both. Successful global managers move with ease across international borders and adapt readily to changing circumstances. They look for a competitive edge wherever they can find it. But most important of all, they continually learn from their surroundings and apply what they have learned to their work and career. In this regard, we close with two lessons from history that can teach us a great deal about managerial success in today's competitive world. The lessons come from Europe and Asia and focus on Christopher Columbus and Mahatma Gandhi.

Christopher Columbus is widely credited with being the first European explorer to "discover" America. (Some scholars disagree with this assertion and argue instead that the Vikings landed and colonized the northeastern tip of Canada five centuries earlier, but this is another story.) Columbus is also widely, if incorrectly, credited with proving that the world was round instead of flat. The controversies surrounding Columbus aside, what many scholars have overlooked in this story is that Columbus succeeded in his quest of discovery because he was wrong, not because he was right. Consider: Ancient Greek mathematicians demonstrated long before Columbus that the world was round. They even estimated with amazing accuracy that the earth was approximately twenty-five thousand miles in circumference. Columbus and his maritime contemporaries understood this, if many peasants did not. Most explorers of the time reasoned with some accuracy that India and the Spice Islands—their targeted objective—was roughly eight thousand miles to the west of Spain. They also reasoned that in view of this distance, such a voyage was impossible. Given prevailing technology of the time, no ship could travel so far without running out of supplies. Columbus studied available maps and charts of the time and concluded, incorrectly, that his contemporaries were wrong and that India was only about three thousand miles away, a journey he considered risky but possible. So off he sailed in 1492. After seventy-one days at sea and, ironically, just over three thousand miles west of Spain, Columbus sailed into the Caribbean and concluded that he had reached India. And as they say, the rest is history.

The lesson of this story is simple. If Columbus had had accurate information, he never would have attempted the voyage. But he believed he was right and he initiated action based on this belief. As he continued his journey as an explorer, he adapted his strategies and tried to learn from his mistakes. Likewise, many contemporary managers often discover that some of their greatest successes result from accident, hunch, or simple luck. All managers make mistakes and miscalculate—some more than others. Managerial success is seldom linear; there are many bumps and detours along the way. What differentiates winners from losers, however, is both their steadfastness and determination of purpose and their ability to learn, adapt and, where possible, capitalize on their mistakes.

The second lesson is more direct and takes us back to a quotation from the Preface of this book by Mahatma Gandhi: "We must be the change we wish to see in others." That is, the real challenge for global managers is leadership, not followership. The challenge is how to build both a more prosperous company and a more prosperous world. To accomplish this, successful global managers must bring people together in symbiotic ways that create value for the firm and its surroundings. In this endeavor, an understanding of how cultures differ and how they influence both organizational and managerial processes emerges as an essential ingredient in a successful global manager's toolkit.

KEY TERMS

bumiputra	multicultural team
cadre	*pok chow*
grandes écoles	polychronic
monochronic	*société*

GLOBAL MANAGER'S WORKBOOK 16.1: MANAGING TEAMS IN FRANCE AND MALAYSIA

Based on what you have read about the cultures and business practices in France and Malaysia, consider the following questions about building and managing multicultural teams:

1. In your view, what are the principal differences between France and Malaysia as they relate to management and business practices?
2. Based on these differences, how would you approach managing a multicultural team that includes several French members?
3. Based on these differences, how would you approach managing a multicultural team that includes several Malaysian members?
4. Going beyond France and Malaysia to the larger global economy, what general advice would you offer to young managers being sent overseas for the first time to work in a team consisting of people from several nationalities?

GLOBAL MANAGER'S WORKBOOK 16.2: PHARMACIA'S EXECUTIVE TEAM

When the two pharmaceutical companies Upjohn and Pharmacia decided to merge in 2000, a central question was where to locate their new corporate headquarters.[22] Upjohn had long been headquartered in Kalamazoo, Michigan, and suggested that the new venture be run from there. Nor surprisingly, Pharmacia, headquartered in Stockholm, had a different idea and suggested Sweden as its preferred location. After considerable negotiation, neither side would yield, so it was decided to move the new headquarters and its hundred-member executive staff to London, England, instead. The new venture would be known as Pharmacia Corporation. Principal manufacturing centers for the new 30,000-employee company would remain in Kalamazoo, Stockholm, and Milan, Italy, and division managers from these operations would fly back and forth to London as needed. It was an inauspicious beginning.

Clashes between the parties began almost immediately. The hard-driving, mission-oriented Americans from Upjohn routinely clashed with the more consensus-oriented Swedes from Pharmacia. The Americans wanted more cost cutting and accountability, while the Swedes wanted to keep their employees informed and sought feedback on how to move the company forward. American managers scheduled meetings throughout the month of August, a common holiday time for the Swedes. At the same time, the more internationally experienced Swedes were surprised by the parochial manner and lack of sophistication of their American counterparts. Swedish managers had long worked with people from across Europe and tended to be more adaptable and flexible than their American counterparts. Upjohn's culture had banned smoking and required drug and alcohol testing of its employees, while Pharmacia's culture served liquor in the company cafeteria and provided ashtrays in each conference room. Finally, the Upjohn-based CEO kept his managers on a tight leash and required frequent reports, budgets, and staffing updates. Swedish members of the executive team considered this detail of reporting to be a waste of time and soon simply stopped complying until the CEO finally resigned. Meanwhile, the Italians concluded that the Americans were trying to take over the "partnership" and began resisting calls for cooperation. No one was happy.

To put the conflict into perspective, a Swedish executive observed, "I see in America a more can-do approach to things. They try to overcome problems as they arise. A Swede may be slower on the start-up. He sits down thinks over all the problems, and once he is reasonably convinced he can tackle them, only then will he start running."[23] Another Swedish executive added, "The Swedish approach is more the engineering approach: 'Tell me why and how this thing works.' The American approach is much more direct. Their attitude is: 'Don't teach me to be an expert, just tell me what I need to know to do my job.'"[24]

The original impetus behind the merger was the compatibility of product lines of the two companies. The new company was well placed in the global marketplace, with a broad range of highly competitive pharmaceutical products. However, the ongoing cultural conflicts between members of the executive team led to lost opportunities and less than anticipated sales and profits.

In 2002, New York–based Pfizer acquired Pharmacia for $60 billion, closed its London headquarters, and fired most of its former executives. As a result of the acquisition, Pfizer was able to significantly expand its product line of successful drugs and is now the largest pharmaceutical company in the industry, with 122,000 employees and annual sales of $45 billion. As Pfizer CEO Hank McKinnell observed, "We are an evolving company in a changing world. We've grown, in our 155 years, from a small family-owned business to a specialty chemical company to a diversified manufacturing firm to a research-based pharmaceutical company that is now the world's largest and most valuable company devoted to healthcare."[25]

QUESTIONS FOR DISCUSSION

1. How would you characterize the nature of the conflict between the Americans and Swedes at Pharmacia? What caused this conflict?

2. Did locating the new corporate headquarters in London help or hurt attempts to bridge the cultural divide between the two parties? Why?
3. If you were brought in as an outside consultant, what would you suggest to help resolve the conflicts on the executive team?
4. What can other companies learn from the Pharmacia example to avoid making similar mistakes in the future?

NOTES

1. "Citizens of the World," *Economist,* June 1, 2002, p. 6.
2. Anil Gupta and Vijay Govindarajan, *Global Strategy and Organization* (New York: Wiley, 2004).
3. Charles Snow, "Types of Transnational Teams," *Transnational Teams Resources Guide,* Transnational Teams Project, ICEDR (Lexington MA: International Consortium for Executive Development Research, 1993).
4. David Thomas, *Essentials of International Management: A Cross-Cultural Perspective* (Thousand Oaks, CA: Sage, 2002), p. 167.
5. E.S. Browning, "Computer Chip Project Brings Rivals Together, but the Cultures Clash," *Wall Street Journal,* May 3, 1994, p. A1.
6. Nancy Adler, *International Dimensions of Organizational Behavior* (Cincinnati, OH: Southwestern, 1997).
7. Richard Hodgetts and Fred Luthans, *International Management: Culture, Strategy, and Behavior,* 5th ed. (New York: McGraw-Hill/Irwin, 2003).
8. Susan Schneider and Jean-Louis Barsoux, *Managing Across Cultures,* 2nd ed. (London: Prentice Hall, 2003).
9. Senior executive, Japanese multinational corporation, personal communication with the author.
10. Richard Hill, *We Europeans* (Brussels: Europublications, 1997).
11. Edward T. Hall and Mildred Hall, *Understanding Cultural Differences: Germans, French, and Americans* (Yarmouth, ME: Intercultural, 1990).
12. Cited in John Hooker, *Working Across Cultures* (Stanford, CA: Stanford Business Books, 2003), p. 234.
13. David Hickson, ed., *Management in Western Europe* (Berlin: de Gruyter, 1993).
14. Jean-Louis Barsoux and Peter Lawrence, "The Making of a French Manager," *Harvard Business Review,* July–August 1991, pp. 1–8.
15. Hall and Hall, *Understanding Cultural Differences*, p. 99.
16. Ingrid Brunstein, ed., *Human Resource Management in Western Europe* (Berlin: de Gruyter, 1995).
17. Hall and Hall, *Understanding Cultural Differences*.
18. Ibid.
19. Joseph Putti, *Management: Asian Context* (New York: McGraw-Hill, 1991); Richard Lewis, *When Cultures Collide* (London: Nicholas Brealey, 1999); Martin Gannon, *Understanding Global Cultures,* 2nd ed. (Thousand Oaks, CA: Sage, 2001); Derek Torrington and Chwee Huat Tan, *Human Resources Management for Southeast Asia* (New York: Prentice Hall, 1994).
20. R. Frank and P. Cook, *The Winner-Take-All Society* (New York, Free Press, 1995).
21. Martin Gannon, *Understanding Global Cultures,* 2nd ed. (Thousand Oaks, CA: Sage, 2001).
22. Based on Randall Schuler, Susan Jackson, and Yadong Lou, *Managing Human Resources in Cross-Border Alliances* (London: Routledge, 2004), pp. 92–93.
23. Ibid., p. 93.
24. Ibid., p. 93.
25. Pfizer.com, http://www.pfizer.com/are/mn_about_message.html.

APPENDIX

Managing in the Global Economy: A Field Project

This project is designed to provide an opportunity to apply what has been learned throughout this book. It involves the completion of a major research project focusing on identifying a suitable new plant location for a company (in Part 1) and then considering how you would prepare yourself to run this new plant (in Part 2). Completing this project will require research and analysis, as well as reflection and introspection. That is, it will require you to look outside at the environment where you plan to do business, as well as inside at the kind of global manager you plan to become. The end result of this project is a written paper that applies what has been learned to a real company doing business globally.

PART 1. NEW FACILITY LOCATION DECISION

To begin the exercise, select a well-known manufacturing company that does business across a variety of national boundaries. This could be a computer company such as Dell Computer or Hewlett-Packard, a consumer products company such as Procter and Gamble or Unilever, and so forth. Now, assume that this company is in the planning stages to build a new manufacturing facility overseas. You have been asked to take the lead in identifying two possible locations for the facility in two different regions of the world and then prepare an analysis of the pros and cons of locating the facility in each of the two sites. The new venture will require skilled, dependable local workers. Product quality, operating costs, long-term operational stability, and ease of delivery to targeted markets will be the principal determinants of success in this new venture. With this information in mind, begin your analysis here.

1. *The company.* What company did you select for your study? Briefly describe the company, including its current scope of operations, its product lines, and where it currently does business.
2. *Global business strategy.* Briefly summarize your company's long-term glo-

bal business strategy, as you understand it. What are the company's principal critical assets to help it achieve this strategy?

3. *Initial location strategy.* With this strategy in mind, select two possible countries for a suitable location for your new overseas facility. (These countries must be located on two different continents; you may not select your home country.) Why did you select these two countries as possible sites for your company's future expansion?

4. *Economic profiles.* Develop a brief economic profile for each country, including principal industries and products, population bases, GNPs, transportation and other infrastructure, and forms of government. From an economic standpoint, what are the principal advantages and disadvantages of each country as a possible location?

5. *Political risk.* In your judgment, what are the principal political risks associated with establishing your new facility in each of the two countries? What is your assessment of the pros and cons of investing in each location?

6. *Legal issues.* Identify any laws or legal issues that may adversely affect your company's operation in each country. How can your company work to keep its employees (both home country and host country) out of trouble with the local authorities?

7. *Cultural profiles.* Describe the principal cultural differences between the two countries as they may affect the success or failure of the new venture. This assessment can be based on the big five classification as a starting point, but should go well beyond this to highlight principal cultural differences as they affect business practices in the two countries.

8. *HRM/labor relations.* What can we learn about prevailing HRM and labor relations practices in each country that may affect either the company's selection of a country or its success in operating there?

9. *Mode of entry.* Should your company initiate this new venture by itself or as part of a joint venture or strategic alliance with a local firm? Why?

10. *Site recommendation.* Finally, based on your analysis, which of the two possible sites would you recommend to your company for its new facility? Why?

PART 2. PREPARING FOR THE OVERSEAS ASSIGNMENT

In Part 2, assume that your company has agreed with your site recommendation. Construction will begin shortly, and you have been asked to move to the new location to oversee the construction. Once the new facility is complete, you will take over as its first managing director. You should plan to be there for about three years. You will begin your new assignment immediately and must be prepared to leave for the new site in ninety days. Upon arrival, you will need to hire a competent workforce—both workers and local area managers—to staff the facility. Moreover, as managing director, you will be responsible both for a successful start-up and for subsequent operations of the entire facility. Indeed, this will be a good career move for you, so long as you succeed. As you approach this new assignment, however, it is important that you be fully prepared. Your supervisor has therefore asked you to prepare a report outlining how you intend to accomplish the following items in a timely fashion:

1. *Strengths and weaknesses.* As of today, how would you characterize your own principal strengths and weakness as a manager prepared for an overseas assignment? What do you think you will be particularly good at? In what areas do you feel you need additional training or development?
2. *First actions.* What is the first thing you are going to do—right now, today— to begin preparing for your new assignment?
3. *Advance preparation.* During the coming three months, while you are still in your home country, how will you prepare yourself personally and professionally for this new assignment? What exactly is your plan of action?
4. *Continuing development.* When you arrive at your new location, how will you continue to develop your expertise in cross-cultural management?
5. *Staffing plan.* What is your staffing plan? That is, considering what you have learned about the country, how do you plan to recruit and hire the workers and managers needed to start the plant? (We estimate that you will require about thirty low- and midlevel managers and perhaps one hundred employees for the start-up.)
6. *Compensation strategy.* Based on your understanding of local customs, what approach will you take to compensation, incentives, and rewards for both managers and workers? What is your compensation philosophy or strategy?
7. *Employee relations.* How will you establish rapport with the local workers? Is this strategy different than what you would use in your home country? If so, why?
8. *Community relations.* What will you do after your arrival to build good relations with the local community?
9. *Management philosophy.* What approach do you intend to take in managing the facility? Describe what you consider to be the optimal management style for facilitating productivity, employee retention, and employee satisfaction. How does this strategy fit with the culture and challenges you may encounter abroad? How do you plan to implement this management style, both for yourself and among your newly hired local managers?
10. *Employee participation.* Is it a good idea to try to incorporate some form of employee participation and involvement in your new workforce? If so, what are the most appropriate ways of doing so in a culturally consistent manner?
11. *Teams.* Is there anyplace in your management model for the use of teams? If so, how will you implement this aspect of your organization and management in a manner that is consistent with the local culture?
12. *Protection against exploitation.* What can you do at the beginning of this operation to ensure that employees at all levels are not exploited, by the company, by managers, or by fellow workers?
13. *Performance assessment.* Finally, how will you know when you succeed? How should corporate headquarters evaluate your performance on this assignment? As part of this question, please draft a performance evaluation form that can be used to judge your job performance.

Name and Company Index

Subject Index

Page numbers in **bold** indicate exhibits.

Page numbers in **bold** indicate exhibits.

Page numbers in **bold** indicate exhibits.

Page numbers in **bold** indicate exhibits.

Richard M. Steers is the Kazumitsu Shiomi Professor of Management at the Lundquist College of Business, University of Oregon. He holds a B.A. from Whittier College, an M.B.A. from the University of Southern California, and a Ph.D. from the University of California, Irvine. He is a past president and fellow of the Academy of Management and the author or co-author of twenty-two books on subjects ranging from organizational behavior and work motivation to international management.

Luciara Nardon is a Visiting Assistant Professor of Management at the Lundquist College of Business, University of Oregon. She holds a B.A. from the Universidade Federal do Rio Grande do Sul (Brazil), a Master's Degree from Universidad de Ciencias Empresariales y Sociales (Argentina), an M.B.A. from Claremont Graduate University, and a Ph.D. from the University of Oregon. She has extensive management experience in control systems and strategic planning in both the U.S. and Brazilian retail industry.

For Product Safety Concerns and Information please contact our EU representative GPSR@taylorandfrancis.com Taylor & Francis Verlag GmbH, Kaufingerstraße 24, 80331 München, Germany

T - #0102 - 230425 - C0 - 254/178/22 - PB - 9780765615510 - Gloss Lamination